Paolo Ciancarini Michael J. Wooldridge (Eds.)

Agent-Oriented Software Engineering

First International Workshop, AOSE 2000
Limerick, Ireland, June 10, 2000
Revised Papers

Series Editors

Gerhard Goos, Karlsruhe University, Germany
Juris Hartmanis, Cornell University, NY, USA
Jan van Leeuwen, Utrecht University, The Netherlands

Volume Editors

Paolo Ciancarini
University of Bologna, Department of Information Science
Mura Anteo Zamboni 7, 40127 Bologna, Italy
E-mail: ciancarini@cs.unibo.it

Michael J. Wooldridge
The University of Liverpool, Department of Computer Science
Chadwick Building, Peach Street, Liverpool L69 7ZF, UK
E-mail: M.J.Wooldridge@csc.liv.ac.uk

Cataloging-in-Publication Data applied for

Die Deutsche Bibliothek - CIP-Einheitsaufnahme

Agent oriented software engineering : first international workshop ; revised papers / AOSE 2000, Limerick, Ireland, June 10, 2000. Paolo Ciancarini ; Michael Wooldridge (ed.). - Berlin ; Heidelberg ; New York ; Barcelona ; Hong Kong ; London ; Milan ; Paris ; Singapore ; Tokyo : Springer, 2001
(Lecture notes in computer science ; Vol. 1957)
ISBN 3-540-41594-7

CR Subject Classification (1998): D.2, I.2.11, F.3, D.1, C.2.4

ISSN 0302-9743
ISBN 3-540-41594-7 Springer-Verlag Berlin Heidelberg New York

Springer-Verlag Berlin Heidelberg New York
a member of BertelsmannSpringer Science+Business Media GmbH

Printed in Germany

Typesetting: Camera-ready by author
Printed on acid-free paper SPIN: 10780995 06/3142 5 4 3 2 1 0

Preface

Software engineers have derived a progressively better understanding of the characteristics of complexity in software. It is now widely recognised that *interaction* is probably the most important single characteristic of complex software. Software architectures that contain many dynamically interacting components, each with their own thread of control and engaging in complex coordination protocols, are typically orders of magnitude more complex to correctly and efficiently engineer than those that simply compute a function of some input through a single thread of control.

Unfortunately, it turns out that many (if not most) real-world applications have precisely these characteristics. As a consequence, a major research topic in computer science over at least the past two decades has been the development of tools and techniques to model, understand, and implement systems in which interaction is the norm. Indeed, many researchers now believe that in the future, computation itself will be understood chiefly as a process of interaction.

Since the 1980s, software agents and multi-agent systems have grown into what is now one of the most active areas of research and development activity in computing in general. There are many reasons for the current intensity of interest, but certainly one of the most important is that the concept of an agent as an autonomous system, capable of interacting with other agents in order to satisy its design objectives, is a natural one for software designers. Just as we can understand many systems as being composed of essentially passive objects, which have a state and upon which we can perform operations, so we can understand many others as being made up of interacting, semi-autonomous agents.

This recognition has led to the growth of interest in agents as a new paradigm for software engineering. The aim of the AOSE-2000 workshop, held at the ICSE 2000 conference in Limerick, Ireland, in June 2000, was to investigate the credentials of agent-oriented software engineering, and to gain an understanding of what agent-oriented software engineering might look like.

Some 32 papers were submitted to the workshop, and after refereeing, about half were accepted for presentation. After the workshop, these papers were revised in light of the discussions at the workshop and, together with a selection of invited papers (by Bussmann, Petrie, Rana, and Shehory), these revised papers make up the volume you are now reading.

We are convinced that agents have a significant role to play in the future of software engineering. This book offers insights into the issues that will shape that future.

September 2000

Paolo Ciancarini
Michael Wooldridge

Organising Committee

Paolo Ciancarini	(CHAIR)	University of Bologna, Italy email ciancarini@cs.unibo.it
Michael Wooldridge	(CO-CHAIR)	University of Liverpool, UK email M.J.Wooldridge@csc.liv.ac.uk

Programme Committee

Carlos Angel Iglesias Fernandez	Spain
Dennis Heimbinger	Germany
Michael Huhns	USA
Nicholas Jennings	UK
Liz Kendall	Australia
Yannis Labrou	USA
Jaeho Lee	Korea
James Odell	USA
Andrea Omicini	Italy
Jan Treur	The Netherlands
Jeffrey Tsai	USA
Robert Tolksdorf	Germany
Franco Zambonelli	Italy

Topics of Interest

The workshop invited the submission of papers covering all aspects of agent-oriented software engineering, but particularly the following:

- Methodologies for agent-oriented analysis and design
- Relationship of agent-oriented software to other paradigms (e.g., OO)
- UML and agent systems
- Agent-oriented requirements analysis and specification
- Refinement and synthesis techniques for agent-based specifications
- Verification and validation techniques for agent-based systems
- Software development environments and CASE tools for AOSE
- Standard APIs for agent programming
- Formal methods for agent-oriented systems, including specification and verification logics
- Engineering large-scale agent systems
- Experiences with field-tested agent systems
- Best practice in agent-oriented development
- Market and other economic models in agent systems engineering
- Practical coordination and cooperation frameworks for agent systems

We were particularly interested in papers that addressed the following questions:

1. The "OO mindset" contains about half a dozen key concepts – class, instance, encapsulation, inheritance, polymorphism, and so on. In your view, what are the key concepts in the "agent-oriented" mindset? If you had to identify just one, then what would it be and why? How do we identify what should and should not be modelled/implemented as an agent? What are the key features you look for in a problem that suggests an agent-based solution?
2. Over the past few years, there has been an increasing trend in the object-oriented community towards the development of "agent-like" features. Examples include distributed objects (CORBA, RMI), applets, mobile object systems, and coordination mechanisms and languages. This trend is likely to continue at least in the short term. Given this, how does an agent-oriented software engineering view sit in relation to other software paradigms, in particular, object-oriented development? What are the key attributes of agent-oriented development that make it unique and distinctive?
3. What is the impact of agent-oriented languages and tools on the software development process? How can legacy software architectures be integrated with agent- or multi-agent-oriented applications? Which specification, design, implementation, maintenance, or documentation systems and strategies have to be adopted in order to deal with agent-oriented issues?
4. Agent-based solutions are not appropriate to all applications. One of the keys to the success of agent-oriented software engineering is therefore to identify the application requirements that indicate an agent-based solution. What are the key properties that indicate an agent-based approach is appropriate?

Contents

Part I: Conceptual Foundations

Agent-Oriented Software Engineering: The State of the Art 1
Michael Wooldridge and Paolo Ciancarini

Interaction-Oriented Programming 29
Michael N. Huhns

Issues in Agent-Oriented Software Engineering 45
Jürgen Lind

Agent-Based Software Engineering 59
Charles Petrie

Software Architecture Attributes of Multi-agent Systems 77
Onn Shehory

Part II: UML for AOSE

Agent UML: A Formalism for Specifying Multiagent Software Systems 91
Bernhard Bauer, Jörg P. Müller, and James Odell

Agent-Oriented Modeling with Graph Transformation 105
Ralph Depke, Reiko Heckel, and Jochen Malte Küster

Representing Agent Interaction Protocols in UML 121
James Odell, H. Van Dyke Parunak, and Bernhard Bauer

Part III: Methodologies for AO Analysis and Design

On the Identification of Agents in the Design of Production Control Systems 141
Stefan Bussmann, Nicholas R. Jennings, and Michael Wooldridge

Agent Software Engineering with Role Modelling 163
Elizabeth A. Kendall

Designing Agent-Oriented Systems by Analysing Agent Interactions 171
Simon Miles, Mike Joy, and Michael Luck

SODA: *Societies and Infrastructures in the Analysis and Design of Agent-Based Systems* 185
Andrea Omicini

A Modelling Approach for Agent Based Systems Design 195
Omer F. Rana

An Overview of the Multiagent Systems Engineering Methodology 207
Mark F. Wood and Scott A. DeLoach

Security for Mobile Agents 223
Nobukazu Yoshioka, Yasuyuki Tahara, Akihiko Ohsuga, and Shinichi Honiden

Organizational Abstractions for the Analysis and Design of Multi-agent Systems 235
Franco Zambonelli, Nicholas R. Jennings, and Michael Wooldridge

Part IV: Reuse

Reuse and Abstraction in Verification: Agents Acting in Dynamic Environments 253
Catholijn M. Jonker, Jan Treur, and Wieke de Vries

Part V: Applications and Experiences

Strategy Selection-Based Meta-level Reasoning for Multi-agent Problem-Solving 269
K. Suzanne Barber, David C. Han, and Tse-Hsin Liu

Introducing the Adaptive Agent Oriented Software Architecture and Its Application in Natural Language User Interfaces 285
Babak Hodjat and Makoto Amamiya

Adding Extensible Synchronization Capabilities to the Agent Model of a FIPA-Compliant Agent Platform 307
Agostino Poggi and Giovanni Rimassa

Author Index 323

Agent-Oriented Software Engineering: The State of the Art

Michael Wooldridge[†] and **Paolo Ciancarini**[*]

[†] Department of Computer Science
University of Liverpool
Liverpool L69 7ZF, UK
M.J.Wooldridge@csc.liv.ac.uk

[*] Dipartimento di Scienze dell'Informazione
University of Bologna
Mura Anteo Zamboni 7, 47127 Bologna, Italy
ciancarini@cs.unibo.it

Abstract. Software engineers continually strive to develop tools and techniques to manage the complexity that is inherent in software systems. In this article, we argue that *intelligent agents* and *multi-agent systems* are just such tools. We begin by reviewing what is meant by the term "agent", and contrast agents with objects. We then go on to examine a number of prototype techniques proposed for engineering agent systems, including methodologies for agent-oriented analysis and design, formal specification and verification methods for agent systems, and techniques for implementing agent specifications.

1 Introduction

Over the past three decades, software engineers have derived a progressively better understanding of the characteristics of complexity in software. It is now widely recognised that *interaction* is probably the most important single characteristic of complex software. Software architectures that contain many dynamically interacting components, each with their own thread of control, and engaging in complex coordination protocols, are typically orders of magnitude more complex to correctly and efficiently engineer than those that simply compute a function of some input through a single thread of control.

Unfortunately, it turns out that many (if not most) real-world applications have precisely these characteristics. As a consequence, a major research topic in computer science over at least the past two decades has been the development of tools and techniques to model, understand, and implement systems in which interaction is the norm.

Many researchers now believe that in future, computation itself will be understood as chiefly as a process of interaction. This has in turn led to the search for new computational abstractions, models, and tools with which to conceptualise and implement interacting systems.

Since the 1980s, software agents and multi-agent systems have grown into what is now one of the most active areas of research and development activity in computing generally. There are many reasons for the current intensity of interest, but certainly one of the most important is that the concept of an agent as an autonomous system, capable of interacting with other agents in order to satisfy its design objectives, is a natural one for software designers. Just as we can understand many systems as being composed of essentially passive objects, which have state, and upon which we can perform operations, so we can understand many others as being made up of interacting, semi-autonomous agents.

Our aim in this article is to survey the state of the art in agent-oriented software engineering. The article is structured as follows:

- in the sub-sections that follows, we provide brief introductions to agents and multi-agent systems, and comment on the relationship between agents and objects (in the sense of object-oriented programming);
- in section 2, we survey some preliminary *methodologies* for engineering multi-agent systems — these methodologies provide structured but non-mathematical approaches to the analysis and design of agent systems, and for the most part take inspiration either from object-oriented analysis and design methodologies or from knowledge-engineering approaches; and finally,
- in section 3, we comment on the use of *formal* methods for engineering multi-agent systems.

We conclude the main text of the article with a brief discussion of open problems, challenges, and issues that must be addressed if agents are to achieve their potential as a software engineering paradigm. In an appendix, we provide pointers to further information about agents.

1.1 What are Agent-Based Systems?

Before proceeding any further, it is important to gain an understanding of exactly what we mean by an agent-based system. By an *agent-based system*, we mean one in which the key abstraction used is that of an *agent*. Agent-based systems may contain a single agent, (as in the case of user interface agents or software secretaries [50]), but arguably the greatest potential lies in the application of *multi*-agent systems [5]. By an *agent*, we mean a system that enjoys the following properties [75, pp.116–118]:

- *autonomy*: agents encapsulate some state (that is not accessible to other agents), and make decisions about what to do based on this state, without the direct intervention of humans or others;
- *reactivity*: agents are *situated* in an environment, (which may be the physical world, a user via a graphical user interface, a collection of other agents, the INTERNET, or perhaps many of these combined), are able to *perceive* this environment (through the use of potentially imperfect sensors), and are able to respond in a timely fashion to changes that occur in it;
- *pro-activeness*: agents do not simply act in response to their environment, they are able to exhibit goal-directed behaviour by *taking the initiative*;

- *social ability*: agents interact with other agents (and possibly humans) via some kind of *agent communication language* [28], and typically have the ability to engage in social activities (such as cooperative problem solving or negotiation) in order to achieve their goals.

These properties are more demanding than they might at first appear. To see why, let us consider them in turn. First, consider *pro-activeness*: goal directed behavior. It is not hard to build a system that exhibits goal directed behavior — we do it every time we write a procedure in Pascal, a function in C, or a method in Java. When we write such a procedure, we describe it in terms of the *assumptions* on which it relies (formally, its *pre-condition*) and the *effect* it has if the assumptions are valid (its *post-condition*). The effects of the procedure are its *goal*: what the author of the software intends the procedure to achieve. If the pre-condition holds when the procedure is invoked, then we expect that the procedure will execute *correctly*: that it will terminate, and that upon termination, the post-condition will be true, i.e., the goal will be achieved. This is goal directed behavior: the procedure is simply a plan or recipe for achieving the goal. This programming model is fine for many environments. For example, its works well when we consider *functional systems* — those that simply take some input x, and produce as output some some function $f(x)$ of this input. Compilers are a classic example of functional systems.

But for non-functional systems, this simple model of goal directed programming is not acceptable, as it makes an important limiting assumption. It assumes that the environment *does not change* while the procedure is executing. If the environment does change, and in particular, if the assumptions (pre-condition) underlying the procedure become false while the procedure is executing, then the behavior of the procedure may not be defined — often, it will simply crash. Similarly, it is assumed that the goal, that is, the reason for executing the procedure, remains valid at least until the procedure terminates. If the goal does *not* remain valid, then there is simply no reason to continue executing the procedure.

In many environments, neither of these assumptions are valid. In particular, in domains that are *too complex* for an agent to observe completely, that are *multi-agent* (i.e., they are populated with more than one agent that can change the environment), or where there is *uncertainty* in the environment, these assumptions are not reasonable. In such environments, blindly executing a procedure without regard to whether the assumptions underpinning the procedure are valid is a poor strategy. In such dynamic environments, an agent must be *reactive*, in just the way that we described above. That is, it must be responsive to events that occur in its environment, where these events affect either the agent's goals or the assumptions which underpin the procedures that the agent is executing in order to achieve its goals.

As we have seen, building purely goal directed systems is not hard. Similarly, building *purely reactive* systems — ones that *continually* respond to their environment — is also not difficult; we can implement them as lookup tables that simply match environmental stimuli to action responses. However, what turns out to be very hard is building a system that achieves an effective *balance* between goal-directed and reactive behavior. We want agents that will attempt to achieve their goals systematically, perhaps by making use of complex procedure-like recipes for action. But we don't want our agents to continue blindly executing these procedures in an attempt to achieve a goal either when it is clear that the procedure will not work, or when the goal is for some reason no longer valid. In such circumstances, we want our agent to be able to react to the new situation, in time for the reaction to be of some use. However, we do not want our agent to be *continually* reacting, and hence never focussing on a goal long enough to actually achieve it.

On reflection, it should come as little surprise that achieving a good balance between goal directed and reactive behavior is hard. After all, it is comparatively rare to find humans that do this very well. How many of us have had a manager who stayed blindly focussed on some project long after the relevance of the project was passed, or it was clear that the project plan was doomed to failure? Similarly, how many have encountered managers who seem unable to stay focussed at all, who flit from one project to another without ever managing to pursue a goal long enough to achieve *anything*? This problem — of effectively integrating goal-directed and reactive behavior — is one of the key problems facing the agent designer. As we shall see, a great many proposals have been made for how to build agents that can do this — but the problem is essentially still open.

Finally, let us say something about *social ability*, the final component of flexible autonomous action as defined here. In one sense, social ability is trivial: every day, millions of computers across the world routinely exchange information with both humans and other computers. But the ability to exchange bit streams is not really social ability. Consider that in the human world, comparatively few of our meaningful goals can be achieved without the *cooperation* of other people, who cannot be assumed to *share* our goals — in other words, they are themselves autonomous, with their own agenda to pursue. This type of social ability — involving the ability to dynamically negotiate and coordinate — is much more complex, and much less well understood, than simply the ability to exchange bitstreams.

An obvious question to ask is why agents and multi-agent systems are seen as an important new direction in software engineering. There are several reasons [40, pp.6–10]:

- *Natural metaphor.*
  Just as the many domains can be conceived of consisting of a number of interacting but essentially passive *objects*, so many others can be conceived as interacting, active, purposeful *agents*. For example, a scenario currently driving much R&D activity in the agents field is that of software agents that buy and sell goods via the Internet on behalf of some users. It is natural to view the software participants in such transactions as (semi-)autonomous agents.
- *Distribution of data or control.*
  For many software systems, it is not possible to identify a single locus of control: instead, overall control of the systems is distributed across a number computing nodes, which are frequently geographically distributed. In order to make such systems work effectively, these nodes must be capable of autonomously interacting with each other — they must agents.

- *Legacy systems.*
  A natural way of incorporating legacy systems into modern distributed information systems is to *agentify* them: to "wrap" them with an agent layer, that will enable them to interact with other agents.
- *Open systems.*
  Many systems are *open* in the sense that it is impossible to know at design time exactly what components the system will be comprised of, and how these components will be used to interact with one-another. To operate effectively in such systems, the ability to engage in flexible autonomous decision-making is critical.

1.2 On the Relationship between Agents and Objects

Programmers familiar with object-oriented approaches often fail to see anything novel or new in the idea of agents. When one stops to consider the relative properties of agents and objects, this is perhaps not surprising. Objects are defined as computational entities that *encapsulate* some state, are able to perform actions, or *methods* on this state, and communicate by message passing. There are clearly close links between agents and objects, which are made stronger by our tendency to anthropomorphisize objects. For example, the following is from a textbook on object-oriented programming:

> There is a tendency [...] to think of objects as "actors" and endow them with human-like intentions and abilities. It's tempting to think about objects "deciding" what to do about a situation, [and] "asking" other objects for information. [...] Objects are not passive containers for state and behaviour, but are said to be the agents of a program's activity. [37, p.7]

While there are obvious similarities, there are also significant differences between agents and objects. The first is in the degree to which agents and objects are autonomous. Recall that the defining characteristic of object-oriented programming is the principle of encapsulation — the idea that objects can have control over their own internal state. In programming languages like Java, we can declare instance variables (and methods) to be `private`, meaning they are only accessible from within the object. (We can of course also declare them `public`, meaning that they can be accessed from anywhere, and indeed we must do this for methods so that they can be used by other objects. But the use of `public` instance variables is usually considered poor programming style.) In this way, an object can be thought of as exhibiting autonomy over its state: it has control over it. But an object does not exhibit control over it's *behavior*. That is, if an object has a public method `m`, then other objects can invoke `m` whenever they wish — once an object has made a method `public`, then it subsequently has no control over whether or not that method is executed.

Of course, an object *must* make methods available to other objects, or else we would be unable to build a system out of them. This is not normally an issue, because if we build a system, then we design the objects that go in it, and they can thus be assumed to share a "common goal". But in many types of multi-agent system, (in particular, those that contain agents built by different organisations or individuals), no such common goal can be assumed. It cannot be for granted that an agent i will execute an action (method) a just because another agent j wants it to — a may not be in the best interests of i. We thus do not think of agents as invoking methods upon one-another, but rather as *requesting* actions to be performed. If j requests i to perform a, then i may perform the action or it may not. The locus of control with respect to the decision about whether to execute an action is thus different in agent and object systems. In the object-oriented case, the decision lies with the object that invokes the method. In the agent case, the decision lies with the agent that receives the request. This distinction between objects and agents has been nicely summarized in the following slogan: *Objects do it for free; agents do it because they want to.*

The second important distinction between object and agent systems is with respect to the notion of flexible (reactive, pro-active, social) autonomous behavior. The standard object model has nothing whatsoever to say about how to build systems that integrate these types of behavior. One could point out that we can build object-oriented programs that *do* integrate these types of behavior. And indeed we can, but this argument misses the point, which is that the standard object-oriented programming model has nothing to do with these types of behavior.

The third important distinction between the standard object model and our view of agent systems is that agents are each considered to have their own thread of control. Agents are assumed to be continually active, and typically are engaged in an infinite loop of observing their environment, updating their internal state, and selecting and executing an action to perform. In contrast, objects are assumed to be quiescent for most of the time, becoming active only when another object requires their services by dint of method invocation.

Of course, a lot of work has recently been devoted to *concurrency* in object-oriented programming. For example, the Java language provides built-in constructs for multi-threaded programming. There are also many programming languages available (most of them admittedly prototypes) that were specifically designed to allow concurrent object-based programming. But such languages do not capture the idea we have of agents as *autonomous* entities. Perhaps the closest that the object-oriented community comes is in the idea of *active objects*:

> An active object is one that encompasses its own thread of control [...]. Active objects are generally autonomous, meaning that they can exhibit some behavior without being operated upon by another object. Passive objects, on the other hand, can only undergo a state change when explicitly acted upon. [6, p.91]

Thus active objects are essentially agents that do not necessarily have the ability to exhibit flexible autonomous behavior.

To summarize, the traditional view of an object and our view of an agent have at least three distinctions:

- agents embody stronger notion of autonomy than objects, and in particular, they decide for themselves whether or not to perform an action on request from another agent;
- agents are capable of flexible (reactive, pro-active, social) behavior, and the standard object model has nothing to say about such types of behavior;
- a multi-agent system is inherently multi-threaded, in that each agent is assumed to have at least one thread of control.

2 Agent-Oriented Analysis and Design

The first main strand of work we consider on approaches to developing agent systems involves principled but *informal* development methodologies for the analysis and design of agent-based system. These can be broadly divided into two groups:

- those that take their inspiration from object-oriented development, and either extend existing OO methodologies or adapt OO methodologies to the purposes of AOSE [10, 45, 77, 54, 18, 3, 44, 56, 70];
- those that adapt knowledge engineering or other techniques [8, 49, 36, 16].

In the remainder of this section, we review some representative samples of this work. As representatives of the first category, we survey the AAII methodology of Kinny et al [45], the Gaia methodology of Wooldridge et al [77], and summarise work on adapting UML [54, 18, 3]. As representatives of the second category, we survey the Cassiopeia methodology of Collinot et al [16], the DESIRE framework of Treur et al [8], and the use of Z for specifying agent systems [49].

Kinny et al: The AAII Methodology The Australian AI Institute (AAII) has been developing agent-based systems for a decade. The primary development environment in which this work has been carried out is the belief-desire-intention technology [74] of the Procedural Reasoning System (PRS) and its successor, the Distributed Multi-Agent Reasoning System (DMARS) [62]. The PRS, originally developed at Stanford Research Institute, was the first agent architecture to explicitly embody the belief-desire-intention paradigm, and has proved to be the most durable agent architecture developed to date. It has been applied in several of the most significant multi-agent applications so far built, including an air-traffic control system called OASIS that is currently undergoing field trials at Sydney airport, a simulation system for the Royal Australian Air Force called SWARMM, and a business process management system called SPOC (Single Point of Contact), that is currently being marketed by Agentis Solutions [29]. The AAII methodology for agent-oriented analysis and design was developed as a result of experience gained with these major applications. It draws primarily upon object-oriented methodologies, and enhances them with some agent-based concepts. The methodology itself is aimed at the construction of a set of models which, when fully elaborated, define an agent system specification.

The AAII methodology provides both *internal* and *external* models. The external model presents a system-level view: the main components visible in this model are agents themselves. The external model is thus primarily concerned with agents and the relationships between them. It is not concerned with the internals of agents: how they are constructed or what they do. In contrast, the internal model is entirely concerned with the internals of agents: their beliefs, desires, and intentions.

The external model is intended to define inheritance relationships between agent classes, and to identify the instances of these classes that will appear at run-time. It is itself composed of two further models: the *agent model* and the *interaction model*. The agent model is then further divided into an *agent class model* and an *agent instance model*. These two models define the agents and agent classes that can appear, and relate these classes to one-another via inheritance, aggregation, and instantiation relations. Each agent class is assumed to have at least three attributes, for beliefs, desires, and intentions. The analyst is able to define how these attributes are overridden during inheritance. For example, it is assumed that by default, inherited intentions have less priority than those in sub-classes. The analyst may tailor these properties as desired.

Details of the internal model are not given, but it seems clear that developing an internal model corresponds fairly closely to implementing a PRS agent, i.e., designing the agent's belief, desire, and intention structures.

The AAII methodology is aimed at elaborating the models described above. It may be summarised as follows:

1. Identify the relevant *roles* in the application domain, and on the basis of these, develop an *agent class hierarchy*. An example role might be weather monitor, whereby agent i is required to make agent j aware of the prevailing weather conditions every hour.
2. Identify the responsibilities associated with each role, the services required by and provided by the role, and then determine the *goals* associated with each service. With respect to the above example, the goals would be to find out the current weather, and to make agent j aware of this information.
3. For each goal, determine the plans that may be used to achieve it, and the context conditions under which each plan is appropriate. With respect to the above example, a plan for the goal of making agent j aware of the weather conditions might involve sending a message to j.
4. Determine the belief structure of the system — the information requirements for each plan and goal. With respect to the above example, we might propose a unary predicate $windspeed(x)$ to represent the fact that the current wind speed is x. A plan to determine the current weather conditions would need to be able to represent this information.

Note that the analysis process will be iterative, as in more traditional methodologies. The outcome will be a model that closely corresponds to the PRS agent architecture. As a result, the move from end-design to implementation using PRS is relatively simple.

Wooldridge et al: Gaia The Gaia[1] methodology is intended to allow an analyst to go systematically from a statement of requirements to a design that is sufficiently detailed that it can be implemented directly. Note that we view the requirements capture phase as being independent of the paradigm used for analysis and design. In applying Gaia, the analyst moves from abstract to increasingly concrete concepts. Each successive move introduces greater implementation bias, and shrinks the space of possible systems that could be implemented to satisfy the original requirements statement. (See [42, pp.216-222] for a discussion of implementation bias.) Analysis and design can be thought of as a process of developing increasingly detailed *models* of the system to be constructed.

[1] The name comes from the Gaia hypothesis put forward by James Lovelock, to the effect that all the organisms in the earth's biosphere can be viewed as acting together to regulate the earth's environment.

Abstract Concepts	Concrete Concepts
Roles	Agent Types
Permissions	Services
Responsibilities	Acquaintances
Protocols	
Activities	
Liveness properties	
Safety properties	

Table 1. Abstract and concrete concepts in Gaia

Gaia borrows some terminology and notation from object-oriented analysis and design, (specifically, FUSION [15]). However, it is not simply a naive attempt to apply such methods to agent-oriented development. Rather, it provides an agent-specific set of concepts through which a software engineer can understand and model a complex system. In particular, Gaia encourages a developer to think of building agent-based systems as a process of *organisational design*.

The main Gaian concepts can be divided into two categories: *abstract* and *concrete*; abstract and concrete concepts are summarised in Table 1. Abstract entities are those used during analysis to conceptualise the system, but which do not necessarily have any *direct* realisation within the system. Concrete entities, in contrast, are used within the design process, and will typically have direct counterparts in the run-time system.

The objective of the analysis stage is to develop an understanding of the system and its structure (without reference to any implementation detail). In the Gaia case, this understanding is captured in the system's *organisation*. An organisation is viewed as a collection of roles, that stand in certain relationships to one another, and that take part in systematic, institutionalised patterns of interactions with other roles.

The idea of a system as a society is useful when thinking about the next level in the concept hierarchy: *roles*. It may seem strange to think of a computer system as being defined by a set of roles, but the idea is quite natural when adopting an organisational view of the world. Consider a human organisation such as a typical company. The company has roles such as "president", "vice president", and so on. Note that in a concrete *realisation* of a company, these roles will be *instantiated* with actual individuals: there will be an individual who takes on the role of president, an individual who takes on the role of vice president, and so on. However, the instantiation is not necessarily static. Throughout the company's lifetime, many individuals may take on the role of company president, for example. Also, there is not necessarily a one-to-one mapping between roles and individuals. It is not unusual (particularly in small or informally defined organisations) for one individual to take on many roles. For example, a single individual might take on the role of "tea maker", "mail fetcher", and so on. Conversely, there may be many individuals that take on a single role, e.g., "salesman".

A role is defined by four attributes: *responsibilities*, *permissions*, *activities*, and *protocols*. *Responsibilities* determine functionality and, as such, are perhaps the key attribute associated with a role. An example responsibility associated with the role of company president might be calling the shareholders meeting every year. Responsibilities are divided into two types: *liveness properties* and *safety properties* [57]. Liveness properties intuitively state that "something good happens". They describe those states of affairs that an agent must bring about, given certain environmental conditions. In contrast, safety properties are *invariants*. Intuitively, a safety property states that "nothing bad happens" (i.e., that an acceptable state of affairs is maintained across all states of execution). An example might be "ensure the reactor temperature always remains in the range 0-100".

In order to realise responsibilities, a role has a set of *permissions*. Permissions are the "rights" associated with a role. The permissions of a role thus identify the resources that are available to that role in order to realise its responsibilities. Permissions tend to be *information resources*. For example, a role might have associated with it the ability to read a particular item of information, or to modify another piece of information. A role can also have the ability to *generate* information.

The *activities* of a role are computations associated with the role that may be carried out by the agent without interacting with other agents. Activities are thus "private" actions, in the sense of [65].

Finally, a role is also identified with a number of *protocols*, which define the way that it can interact with other roles. For example, a "seller" role might have the protocols "Dutch auction" and "English auction" associated with it; the Contract Net Protocol is associated with the roles "manager" and "contractor" [66].

Odell et al: Agent UML Over the past two decades, many different notations and associated methodologies have been developed within the object-oriented development community (see, e.g., [6, 64, 15]). Despite many similarities between these notations and methods, there were nevertheless many fundamental inconsistencies and differences. The Unified Modelling Language — UML — is an attempt by three of the main figures behind object-oriented analysis and design (Grady Booch, James Rumbaugh, and Ivar Jacobson) to develop a single notation for modelling object-oriented systems [7]. It is important to note that UML is *not* a methodology; it is, as its name suggests, a language for documenting models of systems; associated with UML is a methodology known as the Rational Unified Process [7, pp.449–456].

The fact that UML is a de facto standard for object-oriented modelling promoted its rapid takeup. When looking for agent-oriented modelling languages and tools, many researchers felt that UML was the obvious place to start [54, 18, 3]. The result has been a number of attempts to adapt the UML notation for modelling agent systems. Odell and colleagues have discussed several ways in which the UML notation might usefully be extended to enable the modelling of agent systems [54, 3]. The proposed modifications include:

- support for expressing concurrent threads of interaction (e.g., broadcast messages), thus enabling UML to model such well-known agent protocols as the Contract Net [66];
- a notion of "role" that extends that provided in UML, and in particular, allows the modelling of an agent playing many roles.

Both the Object Management Group (OMG) [55], and the Foundation for Intelligent Physical Agents (FIPA) [27] are currently supporting the development of UML-based notations for modelling agent systems, and there is therefore likely to be considerable work in this area.

Treur et al: DESIRE In an extensive series of papers (see, e.g., [8, 19]), Treur and colleagues have described the DESIRE framework. DESIRE is a framework for the design and formal specification of compositional systems. As well as providing a graphical notation for specifying such compositional systems, DESIRE has associated with it a graphical editor and other tools to support the development of agent systems.

Collinot et al: Cassiopeia In contrast to Gaia and the AAII methodology, the Cassiopeia method proposed by Collinot et al is essentially *bottom up* in nature [16]. Essentially, with the Cassiopeia method, one starts from the *behaviours* required to carry out some task; this is rather similar to the behavioural view of agents put forward by Brooks and colleagues [9]. Essentially, the methodology proposes three steps:

1. identify the *elementary behaviours* that are implied by the overall system task;
2. identify the *relationships* between elementary behaviours;
3. identify the *organisational behaviours* of the system, for example, the way in which agents form themselves into groups.

Collinot et al illustrate the methodology by way of the design of a RoboCup soccer team (see [38]).

Luck and d'Inverno: Agents in Z Luck and d'Inverno have developed an agent specification framework in the Z language [68], although the types of agents considered in this framework are somewhat different from those discussed above [48, 49]. They define a four-tiered hierarchy of the entities that can exist in an agent-based system. They start with *entities*, which are inanimate objects — they have attributes (colour, weight, position), but nothing else. They then define *objects* to be entities that have capabilities (e.g., tables are entities that are capable of supporting things). *Agents* are then defined to be objects that have goals, and are thus in some sense active; finally, *autonomous agents* are defined to be agents with motivations. The idea is that a chair could be viewed as taking on my goal of supporting me when I am using it, and can hence be viewed as an agent for me. But we would not view a chair as an *autonomous* agent, since it has no motivations (and cannot easily be attributed them). Starting from this basic framework, Luck and d'Inverno go on to examine the various relationships that might exist between agents of different types. In [49], they examine how an agent-based system specified in their framework might be implemented. They found that there was a natural relationship between their hierarchical agent specification framework and object-oriented systems:

> The formal definitions of agents and autonomous agents rely on inheriting the properties of lower-level components. In the Z notation, this is achieved through schema inclusion [...]. This is easily modelled in C++ by deriving one class from another. [...] Thus we move from a principled but abstract theoretical framework through a more detailed, yet still formal, model of the system, down to an object-oriented implementation, preserving the hierarchical structure at each stage. [49]

The Luck-d'Inverno formalism is attractive, particularly in the way that it captures the relationships that can exist between agents. The emphasis is placed on the notion of agents acting for another, rather than on agents as rational systems, as we discussed above. The types of agents that the approach allows us to develop are thus inherently different from the "rational" agents discussed above. So, for example, the approach does not help us to construct agents that can interleave pro-active and reactive behaviour. This is largely a result of the chosen specification language: Z. This language is inherently geared towards the specification of operation-based, functional systems. The basic language has no mechanisms that allow us to easily specify the ongoing behaviour of an agent-based system[2].

2.1 Discussion

The predominant approach to developing methodologies for multi-agent systems is to adapt those developed for object-oriented analysis and design: hence the AAII methodology takes inspiration from Rumbaugh's work, Gaia takes inspiration from FUSION, and so on. There are obvious advantages to such an approach, the most obvious being that the concepts, notations, and methods associated with object-oriented analysis and design (and UML in particular) are increasingly familiar to a mass audience of software engineers. However, there are several disadvantages. First, the kinds of *decomposition* that object-oriented methods encourage is at odds with the kind of decomposition that *agent oriented* design encourages. Put crudely, agents are more coarse-grained computational objects than are agents; they are typically assumed to have the computational resources of a UNIX process, or at least a Java thread. Agent systems implemented using object-oriented programming languages will typically contain many objects (perhaps millions), but will contain far fewer agents. A good agent oriented design methodology would encourage developers to achieve the correct decomposition of entities into either agents or objects.

Note that an alternative would be to model every entity in a system as an agent. However, while this may be in some sense conceptually clean, does not lead to efficient systems (see the discussion in [76]). The situation reflects the treatment of integer data types in object-oriented programming languages; in "pure" OO languages, all data types, including integers, are objects. However, viewing such primitive data types as objects, while ensuring a consistent treatment of data, is not terribly efficient, and for this reason, more pragmatic OO languages (such as Java) do not treat integers, booleans, and the like as objects.

Another problem is that object-oriented methodologies simply do not allow us to capture many aspects of agent systems; for example, it is hard to capture in object models such notions as an agent pro-actively generating actions or dynamically reacting to changes in their environment, still less how to effectively cooperate and negotiate with other self-interested agents. The extensions to UML proposed by Odell et al [54, 18, 3] address some, but by no means all of these deficiencies. At the heart of the problem is the problem of the relationship between agents and objects, which has not yet been satisfactorily resolved.

[2] There are of course extensions to Z designed for this purpose.

Note that a valuable survey of methodologies for agent-oriented software engineering can be found in [35].

3 Formal Methods for AOSE

One of the most active areas of work in agent-oriented software engineering has been on the use of *formal methods* (see, e.g., [75] for a survey). Broadly speaking, formal methods play three roles in software engineering:

- in the *specification* of systems;
- for *directly programming* systems; and
- in the *verification* of systems.

In the subsections that follow, we consider each of these roles in turn. Note that these subsections pre-suppose some familiarity with formal methods, and logic in particular.

3.1 Formal Methods in Specification

In this section, we consider the problem of *specifying* an agent system. What are the requirements for an agent specification framework? What sort of properties must it be capable of representing? Taking the view of agents as practical reasoning systems that we discussed above, the predominant approach to specifying agents has involved treating them as *intentional systems* that may be understood by attributing to them *mental states* such as beliefs, desires, and intentions [17, 75, 74]. Following this idea, a number of approaches for formally specifying agents have been developed, which are capable of representing the following aspects of an agent-based system:

- the *beliefs* that agents have — the information they have about their environment, which may be incomplete or incorrect;
- the *goals* that agents will try to achieve;
- the *actions* that agents perform and the effects of these actions;
- the *ongoing interaction* that agents have — how agents interact with each other and their environment over time.

We refer to a theory which explains how these aspects of agency interact to generate the behaviour of an agent as an *agent theory*. The most successful approach to (formal) agent theory appears to be the use of a *temporal modal logic* (space restrictions prevent a detailed technical discussion on such logics — see, e.g., [75] for extensive references). Two of the best known such logical frameworks are the Cohen-Levesque theory of intention [14], and the Rao-Georgeff belief-desire-intention model [60, 74]. The Cohen-Levesque model takes as primitive just two attitudes: beliefs and goals. Other attitudes (in particular, the notion of *intention*) are built up from these. In contrast, Rao-Georgeff take intentions as primitives, in addition to beliefs and goals. The key technical problem faced by agent theorists is developing a formal model that gives a good account of the interrelationships between the various attitudes that together comprise an agents internal state [75]. Comparatively few serious attempts have been made to specify real agent systems using such logics — see, e.g., [26] for one such attempt.

A specification expressed in such a logic would be a formula φ. The idea is that such a specification would express the desirable behavior of a system. To see how this might work, consider the following, intended to form part of a specification of a process control system.

if
  i believes valve 32 is open
then
  i should intend that j should believe valve 32 is open

Expressed in the BDI logic developed in [74], this statement becomes the formula:

$$(\mathsf{Bel}\ i\ Open(valve32)) \Rightarrow (\mathsf{Int}\ i\ (\mathsf{Bel}\ j\ Open(valve32)))$$

It should be intuitively clear how a system specification might be constructed using such formulae, to define the intended behavior of a system.

One of the main desirable features of a software specification language is that it should not dictate *how* a specification will be satisfied by an implementation. The specification above has exactly this property: it does not dictate how agent i should go about making j aware that valve 32 is open. We simply expect i to behave as a rational agent given such an intention [74].

There are a number of problems with the use of languages such as for specification. The most worrying of these is with respect to their semantics. The semantics for the modal connectives (for beliefs, desires, and intentions) are given in the normal modal logic tradition of possible worlds [11]. So, for example, an agent's beliefs in some state are characterized by a set of different states, each of which represents one possibility for how the world could actually be, given the information available to the agent. In much the same way, an agent's desires in some state are characterized by a set of states that are consistent with the agent's desires. Intentions are represented similarly. There are several advantages to the possible worlds model: it is well studied and well understood, and the associated mathematics of correspondence theory is extremely elegant. These attractive features make possible worlds the semantics of choice for almost every researcher in formal agent theory. However, there are also a number of serious drawbacks to possible worlds semantics. First, possible worlds semantics imply that agents are logically perfect reasoners, (in that their deductive capabilities are sound and complete), and they have infinite resources available for reasoning. No real agent, artificial or otherwise, has these properties.

Second, possible worlds semantics are generally *ungrounded*. That is, there is usually no precise relationship between the abstract accessibility relations that are used to characterize an agent's state, and any concrete computational model. As we shall see in later sections, this makes it difficult to go from a formal specification of a system in terms of beliefs, desires, and so on, to a concrete computational system. Similarly, given a concrete computational system, there is generally no way to determine what the beliefs, desires, and intentions of that system are. If temporal modal logics such as are to be taken seriously as *specification* languages, then this is a significant problem.

3.2 Formal Methods in Implementation

Specification is not (usually!) the end of the story in software development. Once given a specification, we must implement a system that is correct with respect to this specification. The next issue we consider is this move from abstract specification to concrete computational model. There are at least three possibilities for achieving this transformation:

1. manually refine the specification into an executable form via some principled but informal refinement process (as is the norm in most current software development);
2. directly execute or animate the abstract specification; or
3. translate or compile the specification into a concrete computational form using an automatic translation technique.

In the subsections that follow, we shall investigate each of these possibilities in turn.

Refinement. At the time of writing, most software developers use structured but informal techniques to transform specifications into concrete implementations. Probably the most common techniques in widespread use are based on the idea of top-down refinement. In this approach, an abstract system specification is *refined* into a number of smaller, less abstract subsystem specifications, which together satisfy the original specification. If these subsystems are still too abstract to be implemented directly, then they are also refined. The process recurses until the derived subsystems are simple enough to be directly implemented. Throughout, we are obliged to demonstrate that each step represents a true refinement of the more abstract specification that preceded it. This demonstration may take the form of a formal proof, if our specification is presented in, say, Z [68] or VDM [42]. More usually, justification is by informal argument. Object-oriented analysis and design techniques, which also tend to be structured but informal, are also increasingly playing a role in the development of systems (see, e.g., [6]).

For *functional* systems, which simply compute a function of some input and then terminate, the refinement process is well understood, and comparatively straightforward. Such systems can be specified in terms of pre- and post-conditions (e.g., using Hoare logic [32]). Refinement calculi exist, which enable the system developer to take a pre- and post-condition specification, and from it systematically derive an implementation through the use of proof rules [53]. Part of the reason for this comparative simplicity is that there is often an easily understandable relationship between the pre- and post-conditions that characterize an operation and the program structures required to implement it.

For agent systems, which fall into the category of Pnuelian reactive systems (see the discussion in chapter 1), refinement is not so straightforward. This is because such systems must be specified in terms of their *ongoing* behavior — they cannot be specified simply in terms of pre- and post-conditions. In contrast to pre- and post-condition formalisms, it is not so easy to determine what program structures are required to realize such specifications. As a consequence, researchers have only just begun to investigate refinement and design technique for agent-based systems.

Directly Executing Agent Specifications. One major disadvantage with manual refinement methods is that they introduce the possibility of error. If no proofs are provided, to demonstrate that each refinement step is indeed a true refinement, then the correctness of the implementation process depends upon little more than the intuitions of the developer. This is clearly an undesirable state of affairs for applications in which correctness is a major issue. One possible way of circumventing this problem, which has been widely investigated in mainstream computer science, is to get rid of the refinement process altogether, and *directly execute* the specification.

It might seem that suggesting the direct execution of complex agent specification languages is naive — it is exactly the kind of suggestion that detractors of logic-based AI hate. One should therefore be very careful about what claims or proposals one makes. However, in certain circumstances, the direct execution of agent specification languages *is* possible.

What does it mean, to execute a formula φ of logic L? It means generating a logical model, M, for φ, such that $M \models \varphi$ [24]. If this could be done without interference from the environment — if the agent had complete control over its environment — then execution would reduce to constructive theorem-proving, where we show that φ is satisfiable by building a model for φ. In reality, of course, agents are *not* interference-free: they must iteratively construct a model in the presence of input from the environment. Execution can then be seen as a two-way iterative process:

- environment makes something true;
- agent responds by doing something, i.e., making something else true in the model;
- environment responds, making something else true;
- ...

Execution of logical languages and theorem-proving are thus closely related. This tells us that the execution of sufficiently rich (quantified) languages is not possible (since any language equal in expressive power to first-order logic is undecidable).

A useful way to think about execution is as if the agent is *playing a game* against the environment. The specification represents the goal of the game: the agent must keep the goal satisfied, while the environment tries to prevent the agent from doing so. The game is played by agent and environment taking turns to build a little more of the model. If the specification ever becomes false in the (partial) model, then the agent loses. In real reactive systems, the game is never over: the agent must continue to play forever. Of course, some specifications (logically inconsistent ones) cannot ever be satisfied. A *winning strategy* for building models from (satisfiable) agent specifications in the presence of arbitrary input from the environment is an execution algorithm for the logic.

Concurrent METATEM is a programming language for multiagent systems, that is based on the idea of directly executing linear time temporal logic agent specifications [25, 23]. A Concurrent METATEM system contains a number of concurrently executing agents, each of which is programmed by giving it a temporal logic specification of the behavior it is intended the agent should exhibit. An agent specification has the form $\bigwedge_i P_i \Rightarrow F_i$, where P_i is a temporal logic formula referring only to the present or past, and F_i is a temporal logic formula referring to the present or future. The $P_i \Rightarrow F_i$

formulae are known as *rules*. The basic idea for executing such a specification may be summed up in the following slogan:

on the basis of the past *do* the future.

Thus each rule is continually matched against an internal, recorded *history*, and if a match is found, then the rule *fires*. If a rule fires, then any variables in the future time part are instantiated, and the future time part then becomes a *commitment* that the agent will subsequently attempt to satisfy. Satisfying a commitment typically means making some predicate true within the agent. Here is a simple example of a Concurrent METATEM agent definition:

$$
\begin{array}{l}
\bullet ask(x) \Rightarrow \Diamond give(x) \\
(\neg ask(x)\ \mathcal{Z}\ (give(x) \wedge \neg ask(x))) \Rightarrow \neg give(x) \\
give(x) \wedge give(y) \Rightarrow (x = y)
\end{array}
$$

The agent in this example is a controller for a resource that is infinitely renewable, but which may only be possessed by one agent at any given time. The controller must therefore enforce mutual exclusion. The predicate $ask(x)$ means that agent x has asked for the resource. The predicate $give(x)$ means that the resource controller has given the resource to agent x. The resource controller is assumed to be the only agent able to "give" the resource. However, many agents may ask for the resource simultaneously. The three rules that define this agent's behavior may be summarized as follows:

- Rule 1: if someone asks, then eventually give;
- Rule 2: don't give unless someone has asked since you last gave; and
- Rule 3: if you give to two people, then they must be the same person (i.e., don't give to more than one person at a time).

Concurrent METATEM agents can communicate by asynchronous broadcast message passing, though the details are not important here.

Compiling Agent Specifications. An alternative to direct execution is *compilation*. In this scheme, we take our abstract specification, and transform it into a concrete computational model via some automatic synthesis process. The main perceived advantages of compilation over direct execution are in run-time efficiency. Direct execution of an agent specification, as in Concurrent METATEM, above, typically involves manipulating a symbolic representation of the specification at run time. This manipulation generally corresponds to reasoning of some form, which is computationally costly (and in many cases, simply impracticable for systems that must operate in anything like real time). In contrast, compilation approaches aim to reduce abstract symbolic specifications to a much simpler computational model, which requires no symbolic representation. The "reasoning" work is thus done off-line, at compile-time; execution of the compiled system can then be done with little or no run-time symbolic reasoning. As a result, execution is much faster. The advantages of compilation over direct execution are thus those of compilation over interpretation in mainstream programming.

Compilation approaches usually depend upon the close relationship between models for temporal/modal logic (which are typically labeled graphs of some kind), and automata-like finite state machines. Crudely, the idea is to take a specification φ, and do a *constructive proof* of the implementability of φ, wherein we show that the specification is satisfiable by systematically attempting to build a model for it. If the construction process succeeds, then the specification is satisfiable, and we have a model to prove it. Otherwise, the specification is unsatisfiable. If we have a model, then we "read off" the automaton that implements φ from its corresponding model. The most common approach to constructive proof is the *semantic tableaux* method of Smullyan [67].

In mainstream computer science, the compilation approach to automatic program synthesis has been investigated by a number of researchers. Perhaps the closest to our view is the work of Pnueli and Rosner [58] on the automatic synthesis of reactive systems from branching time temporal logic specifications. The goal of their work is to generate reactive systems, which share many of the properties of our agents (the main difference being that reactive systems are not generally required to be capable of rational decision making in the way we described above). To do this, they specify a reactive system in terms of a first-order branching time temporal logic formula $\forall x \; \exists y \; A\varphi(x, y)$: the predicate φ characterizes the relationship between inputs to the system (x) and outputs (y). Inputs may be thought of as sequences of environment states, and outputs as corresponding sequences of actions. The A is the universal path quantifier. The specification is intended to express the fact that in all possible futures, the desired relationship φ holds between the inputs to the system, x, and its outputs, y. The synthesis process itself is rather complex: it involves generating a Rabin tree automaton, and then checking this automaton for emptiness. Pnueli and Rosner show that the time complexity of the synthesis process is double exponential in the size of the specification, i.e., $O(2^{2^{c.n}})$, where c is a constant and $n = |\varphi|$ is the size of the specification φ. The size of the synthesized program (the number of states it contains) is of the same complexity.

Similar automatic synthesis techniques have also been deployed to develop concurrent system skeletons from temporal logic specifications. Manna and Wolper present an algorithm that takes as input a linear time temporal logic specification of the *synchronization* part of a concurrent system, and generates as output a program skeleton (based upon Hoare's CSP formalism [33]) that realizes the specification [52]. The idea is that the functionality of a concurrent system can generally be divided into two parts: a functional part, which actually performs the required computation in the program, and a synchronization part, which ensures that the system components cooperate in the correct way. For example, the synchronization part will be responsible for any mutual exclusion that is required.

Perhaps the best-known example of this approach to agent development is the *situated automata* paradigm of Rosenschein and Kaelbling [63]. In this approach, an agent has two main components:

- a *perception* part, which is responsible for observing the environment and updating the internal state of the agent; and
- an *action* part, which is responsible for deciding what action to perform, based on the internal state of the agent.

Rosenschein and Kaelbling developed two programs to support the development of the perception and action components of an agent respectively. The RULER program takes a declarative perception specification and compiles it down to a finite state machine. The specification is given in terms of a theory of knowledge. The semantics of knowledge in the declarative specification language are given in terms of possible worlds, in the way described above. Crucially, however, the possible worlds underlying this logic are given a precise computational interpretation, in terms of the states of a finite state machine. It is this precise relationship that permits the synthesis process to take place.

The action part of an agent in Rosenschein and Kaelbling's framework is specified in terms of *goal reduction rules*, which encode information about how to achieve goals. The GAPPS program takes as input a goal specification, and a set of goal reduction rules, and generates as output a set of *situation action rules*, which may be thought of as a lookup table, defining what the agent should do under various circumstances, in order to achieve the goal. The process of deciding what to do is then very simple in computational terms, involving no reasoning at all.

3.3 Formal Verification

Once we have developed a concrete system, we need to show that this system is correct with respect to our original specification. This process is known as *verification*, and it is particularly important if we have introduced any informality into the development process. For example, any manual refinement, done without a formal proof of refinement correctness, creates the possibility of a faulty transformation from specification to implementation. Verification is the process of convincing ourselves that the transformation was sound. We can divide approaches to the verification of systems into two broad classes: (1) *axiomatic*; and (2) *semantic* (model checking). In the subsections that follow, we shall look at the way in which these two approaches have evidenced themselves in agent-based systems.

Axiomatic Approaches: Deductive Verification. Axiomatic approaches to program verification were the first to enter the mainstream of computer science, with the work of Hoare in the late 1960s [32]. Axiomatic verification requires that we can take our concrete program, and from this program systematically derive a logical theory that represents the behavior of the program. Call this the program theory. If the program theory is expressed in the same logical language as the original specification, then verification reduces to a proof problem: show that the specification is a theorem of (equivalently, is a logical consequence of) the program theory.

The development of a program theory is made feasible by *axiomatizing* the programming language in which the system is implemented. For example, Hoare logic gives us more or less an axiom for every statement type in a simple Pascal-like language. Once given the axiomatization, the program theory can be derived from the program text in a systematic way.

Perhaps the most relevant work from mainstream computer science is the specification and verification of reactive systems using temporal logic, in the way pioneered by Pnueli, Manna, and colleagues [51]. The idea is that the computations of reactive systems are infinite sequences, which correspond to models for linear temporal logic. Temporal logic can be used both to develop a system specification, and to axiomatize a programming language. This axiomatization can then be used to systematically derive the theory of a program from the program text. Both the specification and the program theory will then be encoded in temporal logic, and verification hence becomes a proof problem in temporal logic.

Comparatively little work has been carried out within the agent-based systems community on axiomatizing multiagent environments. I shall review just one approach.

In [71], an axiomatic approach to the verification of multiagent systems was proposed. Essentially, the idea was to use a temporal belief logic to axiomatize the properties of two multiagent programming languages. Given such an axiomatization, a program theory representing the properties of the system could be systematically derived in the way indicated above.

A temporal belief logic was used for two reasons. First, a temporal component was required because, as we observed above, we need to capture the ongoing behavior of a multiagent system. A belief component was used because the agents we wish to verify are each symbolic AI systems in their own right. That is, each agent is a symbolic reasoning system, which includes a representation of its environment and desired behavior. A belief component in the logic allows us to capture the symbolic representations present within each agent.

The two multiagent programming languages that were axiomatized in the temporal belief logic were Shoham's AGENT0 [65], and Fisher's Concurrent METATEM (see above). The basic approach was as follows:

1. First, a simple abstract model was developed of symbolic AI agents. This model captures the fact that agents are symbolic reasoning systems, capable of communication. The model gives an account of how agents might change state, and what a computation of such a system might look like.
2. The histories traced out in the execution of such a system were used as the semantic basis for a temporal belief logic. This logic allows us to express properties of agents modeled at stage (1).
3. The temporal belief logic was used to axiomatize the properties of a multiagent programming language. This axiomatization was then used to develop the program theory of a multiagent system.
4. The proof theory of the temporal belief logic was used to verify properties of the system (cf. [20]).

Note that this approach relies on the operation of agents being sufficiently simple that their properties can be axiomatized in the logic. It works for Shoham's AGENT0 and Fisher's Concurrent METATEM largely because these languages have a simple semantics, closely related to rule-based systems, which in turn have a simple logical semantics. For more complex agents, an axiomatization is not so straightforward. Also, capturing the semantics of concurrent execution of agents is not easy (it is, of course, an area of ongoing research in computer science generally).

Semantic Approaches: Model Checking. Ultimately, axiomatic verification reduces to a proof problem. Axiomatic approaches to verification are thus inherently limited by the difficulty of this proof problem. Proofs are hard enough, even in classical logic; the addition of temporal and modal connectives to a logic makes the problem considerably harder. For this reason, more efficient approaches to verification have been sought. One particularly successful approach is that of *model checking* [13]. As the name suggests, whereas axiomatic approaches generally rely on syntactic proof, model-checking approaches are based on the semantics of the specification language.

The model-checking problem, in abstract, is quite simple: given a formula φ of language L, and a model M for L, determine whether or not φ is valid in M, i.e., whether or not $M \models_L \varphi$. Verification by model checking has been studied in connection with temporal logic [13]. The technique once again relies upon the close relationship between models for temporal logic and finite-state machines. Suppose that φ is the specification for some system, and π is a program that claims to implement φ. Then, to determine whether or not π truly implements φ, we proceed as follows:

- take π, and from it generate a model M_π that corresponds to π, in the sense that M_π encodes all the possible computations of π;
- determine whether or not $M_\pi \models \varphi$, i.e., whether the specification formula φ is valid in M_π; the program π satisfies the specification φ just in case the answer is "yes."

The main advantage of model checking over axiomatic verification is in complexity: model checking using the branching time temporal logic CTL [12] can be done in time $O(|\varphi| \times |M|)$, where $|\varphi|$ is the size of the formula to be checked, and $|M|$ is the size of the model against which φ is to be checked — the number of states it contains.

In [61], Rao and Georgeff present an algorithm for model checking BDI systems. More precisely, they give an algorithm for taking a logical model for their (propositional) BDI logic, and a formula of the language, and determining whether the formula is valid in the model. The technique is closely based on model-checking algorithms for normal modal logics [13]. They show that despite the inclusion of three extra modalities (for beliefs, desires, and intentions) into the CTL branching time framework, the algorithm is still quite efficient, running in polynomial time. So the second step of the two-stage model-checking process described above can still be done efficiently. Similar algorithms have been reported for BDI-like logics in [4].

The main problem with model-checking approaches for BDI is that it is not clear how the first step might be realized for BDI logics. Where does the logical model characterizing an agent actually come from? Can it be derived from an arbitrary program π, as in mainstream computer science? To do this, we would need to take a program implemented in, say, PASCAL, and from it derive the belief-, desire-, and intention-accessibility relations that are used to give a semantics to the BDI component of the logic. Because, as we noted earlier, there is no clear relationship between the BDI logic and the concrete computational models used to implement agents, it is not clear how such a model could be derived.

3.4 Discussion

This section is an updated and modified version of [73], which examined the possibility of using logic to engineer agent-based systems. Since this article was published, several other authors have proposed the use of agents in software engineering (see, e.g., [39]).

Structured but informal refinement techniques are the mainstay of real-world software engineering. If agent-oriented techniques are ever to become widely used outside the academic community, then informal, structured methods for agent-based development will be essential. One possibility for such techniques, followed by Luck and d'Inverno, is to use a standard specification technique (in their case, Z), and use traditional refinement methods (in their case, object-oriented development) to transform the specification into an implementation [49]. This approach has the advantage of being familiar to a much larger user-base than entirely new techniques, but suffers from the disadvantage of presenting the user with no features that make it particularly well-suited to agent specification. It seems certain that there will be much more work on manual refinement techniques for agent-based systems in the immediate future, but exactly what form these techniques will take is not clear.

With respect to the possibility of directly executing agent specifications, a number of problems suggest themselves. The first is that of finding a concrete computational interpretation for the agent specification language in question. To see what we mean by this, consider models for the agent specification language in Concurrent METATEM. These are very simple: essentially just linear discrete sequences of states. Temporal logic is (among other things) simply a language for expressing *constraints* that must hold between successive states. Execution in Concurrent METATEM is thus a process of generating constraints as past-time antecedents are satisfied, and then trying to build a next state that satisfies these constraints. Constraints are expressed in temporal logic, which implies that they may only be in certain, regular forms. Because of this, it is possible to devise an algorithm that is guaranteed to build a next state if it is possible to do so. Such an algorithm is described in [1].

The agent specification language upon which Concurrent METATEM is based thus has a concrete computational model, and a comparatively simple execution algorithm. Contrast this state of affairs with languages like , where we have not only a temporal dimension to the logic, but also modalities for referring to beliefs, desires, and so on. In general, models for these logics have *ungrounded* semantics. That is, the semantic structures that underpin these logics (typically accessibility relations for each of the modal operators) have no concrete computational interpretation. As a result, it is not clear how such agent specification languages might be executed.

Another obvious problem is that execution techniques based on theorem-proving are inherently limited when applied to sufficiently expressive (first-order) languages, as first-order logic is undecidable. However, complexity is a problem even in the propositional case. For "vanilla" propositional logic, the decision problem for satisfiability is NP-complete [20, p.72]; richer logics, or course have more complex decision problems.

Despite these problems, the undoubted attractions of direct execution have led to a number of attempts to devise executable logic-based agent languages. Rao proposed an executable subset of BDI logic in his AGENTSPEAK(L) language [59]. Building on this work, Hindriks and colleagues developed the 3APL agent programming language [30, 31]. Lespérance, Reiter, Levesque, and colleagues developed the GOLOG language throughout the latter half of the 1990s as an executable subset of the situation calculus [46, 47]. Fagin and colleagues have proposed *knowledge-based programs* as a paradigm for executing logical formulae which contain epistemic modalities [20, 21]. Although considerable work has been carried out on the properties of knowledge-based programs, comparatively little research to date has addressed the problem of how such programs might be actually executed.

Turning to automatic synthesis, we find that the techniques described above have been developed primarily for propositional specification languages. If we attempt to extend these techniques to more expressive, first-order specification languages, then we again find ourselves coming up against the undecidability of quantified logic. Even in the propositional case, the theoretical complexity of theorem-proving for modal and temporal logics is likely to limit the effectiveness of compilation techniques: given an agent specification of size 1,000, a synthesis algorithm that runs in exponential time when used off-line is no more useful than an execution algorithm that runs in exponential time on-line.

Another problem with respect to synthesis techniques is that they typically result in finite-state, automata-like machines, which are less powerful than Turing machines. In particular, the systems generated by the processes outlined above cannot modify their behavior at run-time. In short, they cannot learn. While for many applications, this is acceptable — even desirable — for equally many others, it is not. In expert assistant agents, of the type described in [50], learning is pretty much the *raison d'etre*. Attempts to address this issue are described in [43].

Turning to verification, axiomatic approaches suffer from two main problems. First, the temporal verification of reactive systems relies upon a simple model of concurrency, where the actions that programs perform are assumed to be atomic. We cannot make this assumption when we move from programs to agents. The actions we think of agents as performing will generally be much more coarse-grained. As a result, we need a more realistic model of concurrency. One possibility, investigated in [72], is to model agent execution cycles as intervals over the real numbers, in the style of the temporal logic of reals [2]. The second problem is the difficulty of the proof problem for agent specification languages. The theoretical complexity of proof for many of these logics is quite daunting.

Hindriks and colleagues have used Plotkin's structured operational semantics to axiomatize their 3APL language [30, 31].

With respect to model-checking approaches, the main problem, as we indicated above, is again the issue of ungrounded semantics for agent specification languages. If we cannot take an arbitrary program and say, for this program, what its beliefs, desires, and intentions are, then it is not clear how we might verify that this program satisfied a specification expressed in terms of such constructs.

4 Conclusions

Agent-oriented software engineering is at an early stage of evolution. While there are many good paper arguments to support the view that agents represent an important direction for software engineering, there is as yet a dearth of actual experience to underpin these arguments. Preliminary methodologies and software tools to support the deployment of agent systems are beginning to appear, but slowly. In this final section, we point to some of what we believe are the key obstacles that must be overcome in order for AOSE to become "mainstream":

- *Sorting out the relationship of agents to other software paradigms — objects in particular.*
  It is not yet clear how the development of agent systems will coexist with other software paradigms, such as object-oriented development.
- *Agent-oriented methodologies.*
  Although, as we have seen in this article, a number of preliminary agent-oriented analysis and design methodologies have been proposed, there is comparatively little consensus between these. In most cases, there is not even agreement on the kinds of concepts the methodology should support. The waters are muddied by the presence of UML as the predominant modelling language for object-oriented systems [7]: we suggested earlier that the kinds of concepts and notations supported by UML are not necessarily those best-suited to the development of agent systems.
- *Engineering for open systems.*
  We argued that agents are suitable for *open* systems. In such systems, we believe it is essential to be capable of reacting to unforeseen events, exploiting opportunities where these arise, and dynamically reaching agreements with system components whose presence could not be predicted at design time. However, it is difficult to know how to *specify* such systems; still less how to implement them. In short, we need a better understanding of how to engineer open systems.
- *Engineering for scalability.*
  Finally, we need a better understanding of how to safely and predictably engineer systems comprised of massive numbers of agents dynamically interacting with one-another in order to achieve their goals. Such systems seem prone to problems such as unstable/chaotic behaviours, feedback, and so on, and may fall prey to malicious behaviour such as viruses.

Appendix: How to Find Out More About Agents

There are now many introductions to intelligent agents and multiagent systems. Ferber [22] is an undergraduate textbook, although as its name suggests, this volume focussed on multiagent aspects rather than on the theory and practice of individual agents. A first-rate collection of articles introducing agent and multiagent systems is Weiß [69]. Two collections of research articles provide a comprehensive introduction to the field of autonomous rational agents and multiagent systems: Bond and Gasser's 1988 collection, *Readings in Distributed Artificial Intelligence*, introduces almost all the basic problems in the multiagent systems field, and although some of the papers it contains are now rather dated, it remains essential reading [5]; Huhns and Singh's more recent collection sets itself the ambitious goal of providing a survey of the whole of the agent field, and succeeds in this respect very well [34]. For a general introduction to the theory and practice of intelligent agents, see Wooldridge and Jennings [75], which focuses primarily on the theory of agents, but also contains an extensive review of agent architectures and programming languages. For a collection of articles on the applications of agent technology, see [41]. A comprehensive roadmap of agent technology was published as [40].

References

1. H. Barringer, M. Fisher, D. Gabbay, G. Gough, and R. Owens. METATEM: A framework for programming in temporal logic. In *REX Workshop on Stepwise Refinement of Distributed Systems: Models, Formalisms, Correctness (LNCS Volume 430)*, pages 94–129. Springer-Verlag: Berlin, Germany, June 1989.
2. H. Barringer, R. Kuiper, and A. Pnueli. A really abstract concurrent model and its temporal logic. In *Proceedings of the Thirteenth ACM Symposium on the Principles of Programming Languages*, pages 173–183, 1986.
3. Bernhard Bauer, Jörg P. Müller, and James Odell. Agent UML: A formalism for specifying multiagent software systems. In P. Ciancarini and M. Wooldridge, editors, *Agent-Oriented Software Engineering — Proceedings of the First International Workshop (AOSE-2000)*. Springer-Verlag: Berlin, Germany, 2000.
4. M. Benerecetti, F. Giunchiglia, and L. Serafini. A model checking algorithm for multiagent systems. In J. P. Müller, M. P. Singh, and A. S. Rao, editors, *Intelligent Agents V (LNAI Volume 1555)*. Springer-Verlag: Berlin, Germany, 1999.
5. A. H. Bond and L. Gasser, editors. *Readings in Distributed Artificial Intelligence*. Morgan Kaufmann Publishers: San Mateo, CA, 1988.
6. G. Booch. *Object-Oriented Analysis and Design (second edition)*. Addison-Wesley: Reading, MA, 1994.
7. G. Booch, J. Rumbaugh, and I. Jacobson. *The Unified Modeling Language User Guide*. Addison-Wesley: Reading, MA, 1999.
8. F. Brazier, B. Dunin-Keplicz, N. R. Jennings, and J. Treur. Formal specification of multiagent systems: a real-world case. In *Proceedings of the First International Conference on Multi-Agent Systems (ICMAS-95)*, pages 25–32, San Francisco, CA, June 1995.
9. R. A. Brooks. *Cambrian Intelligence*. The MIT Press: Cambridge, MA, 1999.
10. Birgit Burmeister. Models and methodologies for agent-oriented analysis and design. In Klaus Fischer, editor, *Working Notes of the KI'96 Workshop on Agent-Oriented Programming and Distributed Systems*. 1996. DFKI Document D-96-06.
11. B. Chellas. *Modal Logic: An Introduction*. Cambridge University Press: Cambridge, England, 1980.
12. E. M. Clarke and E. A. Emerson. Design and synthesis of synchronization skeletons using branching time temporal logic. In D. Kozen, editor, *Logics of Programs — Proceedings 1981 (LNCS Volume 131)*, pages 52–71. Springer-Verlag: Berlin, Germany, 1981.
13. E. M. Clarke, O. Grumberg, and D. A. Peled. *Model Checking*. The MIT Press: Cambridge, MA, 2000.
14. P. R. Cohen and H. J. Levesque. Intention is choice with commitment. *Artificial Intelligence*, 42:213–261, 1990.
15. D. Coleman, P. Arnold, S. Bodoff, C. Dollin, H. Gilchrist, F. Hayes, and P. Jeremaes. *Object-Oriented Development: The* FUSION *Method*. Prentice Hall International: Hemel Hempstead, England, 1994.
16. Anne Collinot, Alexis Drogoul, and Philippe Benhamou. Agent oriented design of a soccer robot team. In *Proceedings of the Second International Conference on Multi-Agent Systems (ICMAS-96)*, pages 41–47, Kyoto, Japan, 1996.

17. D. C. Dennett. *The Intentional Stance*. The MIT Press: Cambridge, MA, 1987.
18. Ralph Depke, Reiko Heckel, and Jochen Malte Kuester. Requirement specification and design of agent-based systems with graph transformation, roles, and uml. In P. Ciancarini and M. Wooldridge, editors, *Agent-Oriented Software Engineering — Proceedings of the First International Workshop (AOSE-2000)*. Springer-Verlag: Berlin, Germany, 2000.
19. B. Dunin-Keplicz and J. Treur. Compositional formal specification of multi-agent systems. In M. Wooldridge and N. R. Jennings, editors, *Intelligent Agents: Theories, Architectures, and Languages (LNAI Volume 890)*, pages 102–117. Springer-Verlag: Berlin, Germany, January 1995.
20. R. Fagin, J. Y. Halpern, Y. Moses, and M. Y. Vardi. *Reasoning About Knowledge*. The MIT Press: Cambridge, MA, 1995.
21. R. Fagin, J. Y. Halpern, Y. Moses, and M. Y. Vardi. Knowledge-based programs. *Distributed Computing*, 10(4):199–225, 1997.
22. J. Ferber. *Multi-Agent Systems*. Addison-Wesley: Reading, MA, 1999.
23. M. Fisher. A survey of Concurrent METATEM — the language and its applications. In D. M. Gabbay and H. J. Ohlbach, editors, *Temporal Logic — Proceedings of the First International Conference (LNAI Volume 827)*, pages 480–505. Springer-Verlag: Berlin, Germany, July 1994.
24. M. Fisher. An introduction to executable temporal logic. *The Knowledge Engineering Review*, 11(1):43–56, 1996.
25. M. Fisher and M. Wooldridge. Executable temporal logic for distributed A.I. In *Proceedings of the Twelfth International Workshop on Distributed Artificial Intelligence (IWDAI-93)*, pages 131–142, Hidden Valley, PA, May 1993.
26. M. Fisher and M. Wooldridge. On the formal specification and verification of multi-agent systems. *International Journal of Cooperative Information Systems*, 6(1):37–65, 1997.
27. The Foundation for Intelligent Physical Agents. See `http://www.fipa.org/`.
28. M. R. Genesereth and S. P. Ketchpel. Software agents. *Communications of the ACM*, 37(7):48–53, July 1994.
29. M. P. Georgeff and A. S. Rao. A profile of the Australian AI Institute. *IEEE Expert*, 11(6):89–92, December 1996.
30. K. V. Hindriks, F. S. de Boer, W. van der Hoek, and J.-J. Ch. Meyer. Formal semantics for an abstract agent programming language. In M. P. Singh, A. Rao, and M. J. Wooldridge, editors, *Intelligent Agents IV (LNAI Volume 1365)*, pages 215–230. Springer-Verlag: Berlin, Germany, 1998.
31. K. V. Hindriks, F. S. de Boer, W. van der Hoek, and J.-J. Ch. Meyer. Control structures of rule-based agent languages. In J. P. Müller, M. P. Singh, and A. S. Rao, editors, *Intelligent Agents V (LNAI Volume 1555)*. Springer-Verlag: Berlin, Germany, 1999.
32. C. A. R. Hoare. An axiomatic basis for computer programming. *Communications of the ACM*, 12(10):576–583, 1969.
33. C. A. R. Hoare. Communicating sequential processes. *Communications of the ACM*, 21:666–677, 1978.
34. M. Huhns and M. P. Singh, editors. *Readings in Agents*. Morgan Kaufmann Publishers: San Mateo, CA, 1998.
35. C. A. Iglesias, M. Garijo, and J. C. Gonzalez. A survey of agent-oriented methodologies. In J. P. Müller, M. P. Singh, and A. S. Rao, editors, *Intelligent Agents V (LNAI Volume 1555)*. Springer-Verlag: Berlin, Germany, 1999.
36. Carlos Iglesias, Mercedes Garijo, José C. González, and Juan R. Velasco. Analysis and design of multiagent systems using MAS-CommonKADS. In M. P. Singh, A. Rao, and M. J. Wooldridge, editors, *Intelligent Agents IV (LNAI Volume 1365)*, pages 313–326. Springer-Verlag: Berlin, Germany, 1998.

37. NeXT Computer Inc. *Object-Oriented Programming and the Objective C Language*. Addison-Wesley: Reading, MA, 1993.
38. The Robot World Cup Initiative. See `http://www.RoboCup.org/`.
39. N. R. Jennings. Agent-based computing: Promise and perils. In *Proceedings of the Sixteenth International Joint Conference on Artificial Intelligence (IJCAI-99)*, pages 1429–1436, Stockholm, Sweden, 1999.
40. N. R. Jennings, K. Sycara, and M. Wooldridge. A roadmap of agent research and development. *Autonomous Agents and Multi-Agent Systems*, 1(1):7–38, 1998.
41. N. R. Jennings and M. Wooldridge, editors. *Agent Technology: Foundations, Applications and Markets*. Springer-Verlag: Berlin, Germany, 1998.
42. C. B. Jones. *Systematic Software Development using VDM (second edition)*. Prentice Hall, 1990.
43. L. P. Kaelbling. *Learning in Embedded Systems*. The MIT Press: Cambridge, MA, 1993.
44. Elizabeth A. Kendall. Agent software engineering with role modelling. In P. Ciancarini and M. Wooldridge, editors, *Agent-Oriented Software Engineering — Proceedings of the First International Workshop (AOSE-2000)*. Springer-Verlag: Berlin, Germany, 2000.
45. D. Kinny, M. Georgeff, and A. Rao. A methodology and modelling technique for systems of BDI agents. In W. Van de Velde and J. W. Perram, editors, *Agents Breaking Away: Proceedings of the Seventh European Workshop on Modelling Autonomous Agents in a Multi-Agent World, (LNAI Volume 1038)*, pages 56–71. Springer-Verlag: Berlin, Germany, 1996.
46. Y. Lésperance, H. J. Levesque, F. Lin, D. Marcu, R. Reiter, and R. B. Scherl. Foundations of a logical approach to agent programming. In M. Wooldridge, J. P. Müller, and M. Tambe, editors, *Intelligent Agents II (LNAI Volume 1037)*, pages 331–346. Springer-Verlag: Berlin, Germany, 1996.
47. H. Levesque, R. Reiter, Y. Lespérance, F. Lin, and R. Scherl. Golog: A logic programming language for dynamic domains. *Journal of Logic Programming*, 31:59–84, 1996.
48. M. Luck and M. d'Inverno. A formal framework for agency and autonomy. In *Proceedings of the First International Conference on Multi-Agent Systems (ICMAS-95)*, pages 254–260, San Francisco, CA, June 1995.
49. M. Luck, N. Griffiths, and M. d'Inverno. From agent theory to agent construction: A case study. In J. P. Müller, M. Wooldridge, and N. R. Jennings, editors, *Intelligent Agents III (LNAI Volume 1193)*, pages 49–64. Springer-Verlag: Berlin, Germany, 1997.
50. P. Maes. Agents that reduce work and information overload. *Communications of the ACM*, 37(7):31–40, July 1994.
51. Z. Manna and A. Pnueli. *Temporal Verification of Reactive Systems — Safety*. Springer-Verlag: Berlin, Germany, 1995.
52. Z. Manna and P. Wolper. Synthesis of communicating processes from temporal logic specifications. *ACM Transactions on Programming Languages and Systems*, 6(1):68–93, January 1984.
53. C. Morgan. *Programming from Specifications (second edition)*. Prentice Hall International: Hemel Hempstead, England, 1994.
54. James Odell, H. Van Dyke Parunak, and Bernhard Bauer. Representing agent interaction protocols in UML. In P. Ciancarini and M. Wooldridge, editors, *Agent-Oriented Software Engineering — Proceedings of the First International Workshop (AOSE-2000)*. Springer-Verlag: Berlin, Germany, 2000.
55. The Object Management Group (OMG). See `http://www.omg.org/`.
56. Andrea Omicini. Soda: Societies and infrastructures in the analysis and design of agent-based systems. In P. Ciancarini and M. Wooldridge, editors, *Agent-Oriented Software Engineering — Proceedings of the First International Workshop (AOSE-2000)*. Springer-Verlag: Berlin, Germany, 2000.

57. A. Pnueli. Specification and development of reactive systems. In *Information Processing 86*. Elsevier Science Publishers B.V.: Amsterdam, The Netherlands, 1986.
58. A. Pnueli and R. Rosner. On the synthesis of a reactive module. In *Proceedings of the Sixteenth ACM Symposium on the Principles of Programming Languages (POPL)*, pages 179–190, January 1989.
59. A. S. Rao. AgentSpeak(L): BDI agents speak out in a logical computable language. In W. Van de Velde and J. W. Perram, editors, *Agents Breaking Away: Proceedings of the Seventh European Workshop on Modelling Autonomous Agents in a Multi-Agent World, (LNAI Volume 1038)*, pages 42–55. Springer-Verlag: Berlin, Germany, 1996.
60. A. S. Rao and M. Georgeff. BDI Agents: from theory to practice. In *Proceedings of the First International Conference on Multi-Agent Systems (ICMAS-95)*, pages 312–319, San Francisco, CA, June 1995.
61. A. S. Rao and M. P. Georgeff. A model-theoretic approach to the verification of situated reasoning systems. In *Proceedings of the Thirteenth International Joint Conference on Artificial Intelligence (IJCAI-93)*, pages 318–324, Chambéry, France, 1993.
62. A. S. Rao and M. P. Georgeff. Formal models and decision procedures for multi-agent systems. Technical Note 61, Australian AI Institute, Level 6, 171 La Trobe Street, Melbourne, Australia, June 1995.
63. S. J. Rosenschein and L. P. Kaelbling. A situated view of representation and control. In P. E. Agre and S. J. Rosenschein, editors, *Computational Theories of Interaction and Agency*, pages 515–540. The MIT Press: Cambridge, MA, 1996.
64. J. Rumbaugh, M. Blaha, W. Premerlani, F. Eddy, and W. Lorensen. *Object-Oriented Modeling and Design*. Prentice Hall, Englewood Cliifs, NJ, 1991.
65. Y. Shoham. Agent-oriented programming. *Artificial Intelligence*, 60(1):51–92, 1993.
66. R. G. Smith. *A Framework for Distributed Problem Solving*. UMI Research Press, 1980.
67. R. M. Smullyan. *First-Order Logic*. Springer-Verlag: Berlin, Germany, 1968.
68. M. Spivey. *The Z Notation (second edition)*. Prentice Hall International: Hemel Hempstead, England, 1992.
69. G. Weiß, editor. *Multi-Agent Systems*. The MIT Press: Cambridge, MA, 1999.
70. Mark Wood and Scott A. DeLoach. An overview of the multiagent systems engineering methodology. In P. Ciancarini and M. Wooldridge, editors, *Agent-Oriented Software Engineering — Proceedings of the First International Workshop (AOSE-2000)*. Springer-Verlag: Berlin, Germany, 2000.
71. M. Wooldridge. *The Logical Modelling of Computational Multi-Agent Systems*. PhD thesis, Department of Computation, UMIST, Manchester, UK, October 1992.
72. M. Wooldridge. This is MYWORLD: The logic of an agent-oriented testbed for DAI. In M. Wooldridge and N. R. Jennings, editors, *Intelligent Agents: Theories, Architectures, and Languages (LNAI Volume 890)*, pages 160–178. Springer-Verlag: Berlin, Germany, January 1995.
73. M. Wooldridge. Agent-based software engineering. *IEE Proceedings on Software Engineering*, 144(1):26–37, February 1997.
74. M. Wooldridge. *Reasoning about Rational Agents*. The MIT Press: Cambridge, MA, 2000.
75. M. Wooldridge and N. R. Jennings. Intelligent agents: Theory and practice. *The Knowledge Engineering Review*, 10(2):115–152, 1995.
76. M. Wooldridge and N. R. Jennings. Pitfalls of agent-oriented development. In *Proceedings of the Second International Conference on Autonomous Agents (Agents 98)*, pages 385–391, Minneapolis/St Paul, MN, May 1998.
77. M. Wooldridge, N. R. Jennings, and D. Kinny. A methodology for agent-oriented analysis and design. In *Proceedings of the Third International Conference on Autonomous Agents (Agents 99)*, pages 69–76, Seattle, WA, May 1999.

Interaction-Oriented Programming

Michael N. Huhns

Department of Computer Science and Engineering, University of South Carolina
Columbia, SC 29208 USA

huhns@sc.edu

Abstract. This paper describes a new approach to the production of robust software. We first motivate the approach by explaining why the two major goals of software engineering—*correct* software and *reusable* software—are not being addressed well by the current state of software practice. We then describe a methodology based on active, cooperative, and persistent software components, i.e., *agents*, and show how the methodology produces robust and reusable software. We derive requirements for the structure and behavior of the agents, and report on preliminary experiments on applications based on the methodology. We conclude with a roadmap for development of the methodology and ruminations about uses for the new computational paradigm.

1 Introduction

Computing is in the midst of a paradigm shift. After decades of progress on representations and algorithms geared toward individual computations, the emphasis is shifting toward *interactions* among computations. The motivation is practical, but there are major theoretical implications. Current techniques are inadequate for applications such as ubiquitous information access, electronic commerce, and digital libraries, which involve a number of independently designed and operated subsystems. The metaphor of interaction emphasizes the autonomy of computations and their ability to interface with each other and their environment. Therefore, it can be a powerful conceptual basis for designing solutions for the above applications.

Unfortunately, the field of software engineering has been progressing slowly. This should not be surprising, for three reasons:

1. Software systems are the most complicated artifacts people have ever attempted to construct
2. Software systems are (supposedly) guaranteed to work correctly only when *all* errors have been detected and removed, which is infeasible in light of the above complexity
3. The effect of an error is unrelated to its size, i.e., a single misplaced character out of millions can render a system useless or, worse, harmful.

1.1 Progress in Software Engineering

Software engineering concerns both the process of producing software and the software that is produced. The major goal for the software is that it be correct, and the major goal for the process is that it be conducted efficiently. One fundamental approach to meeting these goals is to exploit modularity and reuse of code. The expectations are that small modules are easier to debug and verify, and therefore more likely to be correct, that small modules will be more likely to be reused, and that reusing debugged modules is more efficient than coding them afresh. A few examples of software engineering practice based on this approach are the following [5]:

- Parameterized subroutines provide code reuse within an application
- Libraries of subroutines encourage code sharing across applications
- Object-oriented methods allow tailoring of library routines via inheritance and polymorphism
- Client/server paradigms, such as the world-wide web, ODBC, OLAP, and SQL databases, permit sharing of data across platforms
- Remote procedure calls, such as Sun's Java RMI and Microsoft's COM, enable code to be shared across platforms
- Transaction processors, such as Tuxedo and Encina++, enable transactions to be shared
- Distributed object technologies, such as OMG CORBA and Microsoft DCOM, allow sharing of tailorable code across platforms.

Programming paradigms have evolved from machine language in the 1950's, procedural programming in the 1960's, structured programming in the 1970's, and object-based and declarative programming in the 1980's. In the 1990's, methods for structuring collections of objects are being developed, including frameworks, design patterns, scenarios, and protocols.

However, software has not kept pace with the increased rate of performance for processors, communication infrastructure, and the computing industry in general [30]. Whereas processor performance has been increasing at a 48% annual rate and network capacity at a 78% annual rate, software productivity has been growing at a 4.6% annual rate and the power of programming languages and tools has been growing at an 11% annual rate. CASE tools, meant to formalize and promote software reuse, have not been widely adopted [19]. By a different metric, the industry standard for good commercial software is approximately six defects per KLOC (thousand lines of code), and this rate has held constant for decades [13].

Table 1. Features of Programming Languages and Paradigms (from [30])

Concept	Procedural Language	Object Language	Multiagent Language
Abstraction	Type	Class	Society
Building Block	Instance, Data	Object	Agent
Computation Model	Procedure/Call	Method/Message	Perceive/Reason/Act
Design Paradigm	Tree of Procedures	Interaction Patterns	Cooperative Interaction
Architecture	Functional Decomposition	Inheritance and Polymorphism	Managers, Assistants, and Peers
Modes of Behavior	Coding	Designing and Using	Enabling and Enacting
Terminology	Implement	Engineer	Activate

The procedural and declarative approaches to programming suffer from being primarily line-at-a-time techniques, with a basis in functional decomposition. Object technology improves these by replacing decomposition with inheritance hierarchies and polymorphisms. It enables design reuse of larger patterns and components. However, inheritance and polymorphism are just as complex and error prone as decomposition, and the great complexity of interactions among objects limits their production and use to a small community of software engineers. By focusing on encapsulating data structures into objects and the relationships among objects, it supports a data-centric view that makes it difficult to think about sequences of activity and dataflow. Scenarios overcome this difficulty by depicting message sequences and threads of control, but they are not well supported by current object languages. Table 1 summarizes the major features of existing software paradigms, and the features promised by the multiagent-based approach described below.

1.2 A New Software Paradigm

We believe it is time to consider a completely different approach to software systems. We propose one based on the (intentionally provocative) recognition that

- errors will *always* be a part of complex systems
- error-free code can at times be a *disadvantage*
- where systems interact with the complexities of the physical world, there is a concomitant *power* that can be exploited.

We suggest an open architecture consisting of redundant, agent-based modules. The appropriate analogy is that of a large, robust, natural system. We motivate our approach by means of the following four examples.

Example 1: Avoiding Deadlocks and Livelocks. Sometimes, when two people approach each other on a narrow sidewalk, they move from side-to-side in unison a few times until they find a way to pass. Now, imagine two robots in a similar situation: if they are each programmed identically and accurately, then they might move in unison and be deadlocked forever. If, however, one had a small flaw in its programming, then it would eventually act differently and break the deadlock.

This example illustrates a key concept: *errors can sometimes make a system more robust*. Individual components do not have to be perfect, if there are a sufficient number of them, if their capabilities are basically sound, and if their responsibilities overlap.

Such deadlock behavior is actually quite common—it can occur anytime two processes access a common resource, e.g., when two applications attempt to update a database, bid at an auction, or communicate over a channel at the same time. When the possibility of the deadlock is known in advance, a solution is to deliberately introduce uncertainty into one or both of the processes; this is the basis for conflict resolution in the CSMA/CD Ethernet protocol.

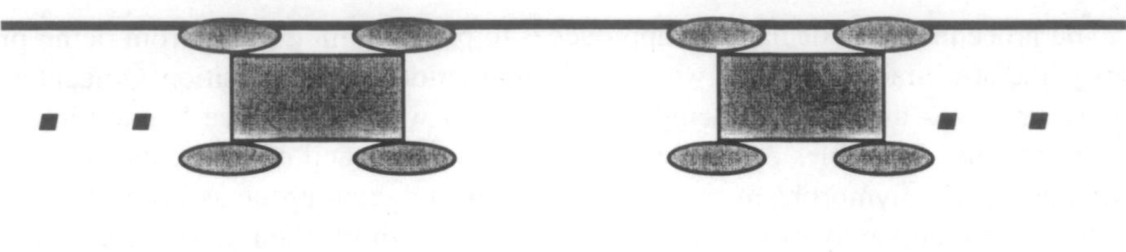

Fig. 1. Robots meeting in a hallway might move in unison and "livelock", unless one operates differently than the other

Example 2: Forming a Circle. Consider asking a group of children to form a circle. This they will be able to do, relatively independent of the number of children, their sizes, and their ages, without requiring any further directions as to who should stand where. The formation of the circle will be robust with respect to the removal or addition of children. It will even accommodate a few children who do not understand the request. This "circle algorithm" succeeds because each element of the solution is intelligent and autonomous, and possesses basic knowledge of the problem domain. Each element is not, however, required to be perfect.

Contrast this with a conventional approach to developing software for arranging items in a circle. A programmer would first define classes for the items, with attributes describing their size and shape. The programmer would then construct a central control module that, using trigonometry, would compute the precise locations for each of the items. The control module would have to be written to accommodate an arbitrary number of items having a variety of sizes and shapes. Changing any one of the parameters would require the control module to recompute the locations of all items. More significantly, changing the way in which the shape or size of an item is defined would require the control module to be rewritten. (For example, if the control module expected items to be defined in terms of their length and width, then it would have to be modified to handle items defined in terms of their radius.)

Example 3: Navigating on Mars. Consider an autonomous vehicle roaming on Mars. There is a very simple algorithm that enables the vehicle to maneuver around obstacles: when an obstacle is encountered, the vehicle

1. Backs up 1 meter
2. Turns clockwise 90 degrees
3. Moves forward 1 meter
4. Turns counterclockwise 90 degrees
5. Goes forward on its original course.

Although in theory it appears that the vehicle can easily become trapped, in practice the vehicle is able to wriggle through any configuration of obstacles that it can physically fit between, *because it cannot move exactly 1 meter or turn exactly 90 degrees*. Its errors in these motions give it the variability it needs to move eventually in just the right

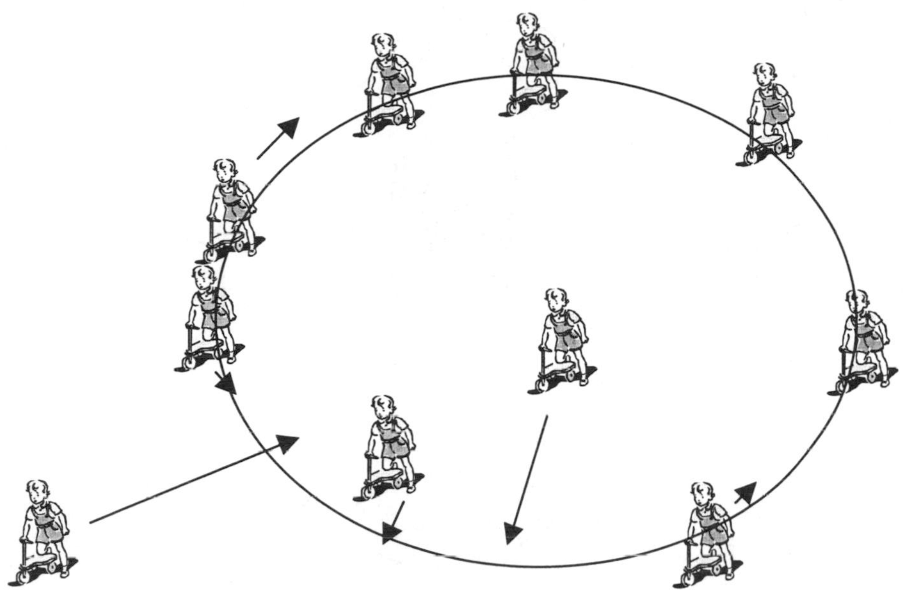

Fig. 2. Children (and autonomous agents) can be a robust circle-forming algorithm

way to go around an obstacle. Surprisingly, attempts to increase its precision not only increase its complexity, but also make it more likely to become trapped. In essence, *reducing errors can make the system less robust.*

Example 4: Business Software Objects—Avoiding a Pay Cut. As a more general and fundamental example, most business software components are intended to be models of some real object within the business, such as an employee. A problem is that, unlike the entities they represent, conventionally implemented components are passive. Why is this a problem? If someone accidentally reduced the salary of an employee by 50%, a conventional software component would not protest. Like real employees, agents implemented as components with the extra ability to take action would not allow such accidents. As we describe next, agents can also do a lot more.

2 Interaction-Based Software Development

The behavior of any system depends on its construction and the environment in which it operates. When the system contains a number of components that interact with each other and a complex environment, the behavior can be difficult to predict and control. Traditional software interfaces are rigid. Often the slightest error in the implementation of a component can have far-reaching repercussions on the behavior of the entire system. However, the output of a component may be erroneous because of its malfunctioning, its environment being out of its design range, or an erroneous input from

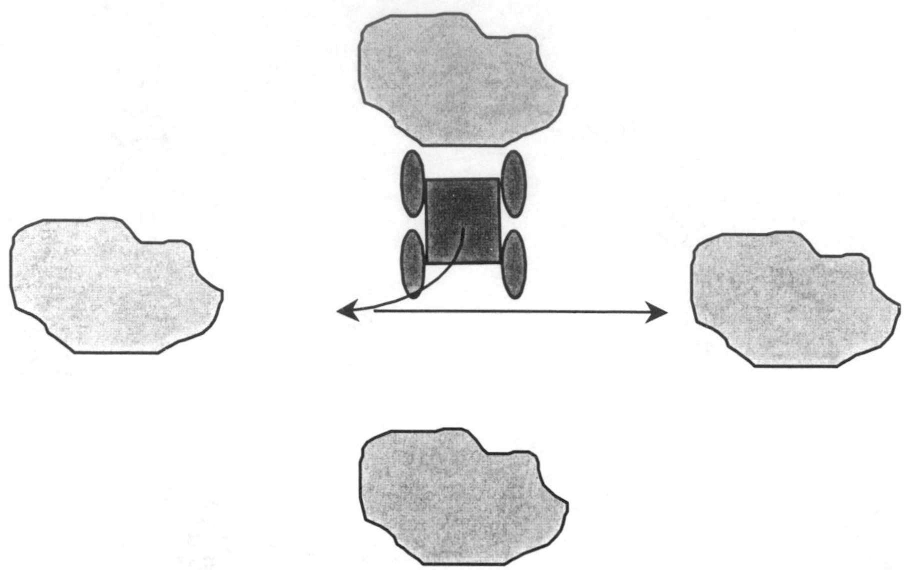

Fig. 3. A robot navigating on Mars can wriggle between obstacles via a very simple algorithm that takes advantage of errors in its movement through the environment

another component. Traditional approaches for software or hardware fault tolerance are rigid in that they use fixed means, e.g., averaging or voting, to correct errors.

By contrast, we are developing an approach in which the interactions among components are defined in a more robust manner using higher-level abstractions such as social commitments and team intentions. These abstractions enable us to design the components to be more flexible toward their inputs and outputs. Moreover, in real-life situations, a component may be forced to release results that are almost certainly erroneous—it may lack the time and resources to await definite inputs and process them properly. Our approach can handle these situations naturally, whereas traditional approaches are incapable of even representing such situations.

Our approach presupposes that the components are able to enter into social commitments to collaborate with others, to change their mind about their results, and to negotiate with others. They must be long-lived (to even detect errors that manifest later in the execution) and persistent (to resolve them). In other words, the components are interacting agents functioning in teams. The agents can detect not only errors, but also opportunities in general. They can volunteer to take advantage of those opportunities, to form teams, negotiate solutions, and enact them in a persistent manner. One risk with such systems is that their persistence may get them into livelocks where interactions prevent progress. It is essential that the agents be able to explore their way out of livelocks. Interestingly, "errorful" behavior by some members of the team can facilitate this exploration, especially in complex environments where the concurrently executing mix of agents is determined dynamically.

Our approach is based a number of important tenets:

Interaction	Persistent action
Teamwork founded on social commitments	Negotiation
Exploration	Error tolerance and exploitation

Although some of these tenets are shared with some recent approaches, e.g., aspect-oriented and agent-oriented programming, no existing approach captures all of them. It appears desirable to try to exploit their synergistic mix.

2.1 Requirements for a New Class of Applications

Thanks to ongoing advances in computer systems, new classes of applications are evolving. These applications require a number of important properties beyond traditional approaches:

Disintermediation (the direct association between users and their software [40]). Providing a user with seamless access to and interaction with remote information, application, and human resources requires a distributed active-object architecture [51].

Dynamic composability and execution. A system should execute as a set of distributed parts, but the resources required will be mostly unknown until run-time: this requires an infrastructure to enable their discovery and composition as needed.

Interaction. There might be subtle and critical patterns of interaction among the components, but the specific interactions may be unknown until run-time, and may vary: this requires that the patterns of interaction be explicitly represented and reasoned with.

Error tolerance and exploitation. As the deployed systems become increasingly complex, they should not only tolerate, but where possible exploit, errors in their components.

Two major convergences now give us the means to address the above requirements. First, large information environments dealing not only with information, but also with the physical world are available to provide crucial computing and communication resources, as well as ready contact with reality. Second, technical advances in computer science provide a foundation for agent architecture and languages. These advances go hand-in-hand, because the existence of the expanding infrastructure changes the trade-offs in carrying out the dictates of the science.

A recent computing paradigm is based on Java, and the ability it provides for users and applications to download the specific functionality they want at the moment they request it. In particular, Java Beans possess two interfaces: one that governs the interaction of a bean with its environment at run-time, and a second that describes the behavior of the bean to developers at program-creation or compile time. DCOM provides a similar capability for COM objects. Such capability is leading to the rise of a software-component industry, which will produce and then distribute on demand the components that have a users' desired functionality [Yourdon 1996]. Each user can be presented with a unique customized environment. However, because of this uniqueness, how can component providers be confident that their components will behave properly?

This is a problem that can be solved by agent-based components that actively cooperate with other components to realize the user's goals and that express their behavior in terms of their intentions and commitments.

2.2 Agent-Based Software

Programming based on teams of agents will build on results generated by a large number of researchers. In particular, efforts under the DARPA Intelligent Integration of Information program for developing mediators, wrappers, and agent communications form one of the foundations for our work. We extend the efforts into a complete programming paradigm with a formal semantics. Our extensions and formal semantics are based on the work on agent-oriented programming by [41], [53], and [21].

A wide variety of software programs have been developed recently that are characterized as software agents [17]. One category of such agents focuses on the interaction between a user and a computing environment. A second category of agent-based software is focused on the interaction among computing agents. The basic issues addressed concern interoperability among geographically distributed agents executing on heterogeneous platforms. There are two different approaches for communication among the agents. The procedural scripting approach causes execution of a remote task by sending a procedural script for interpreted execution at the remote site. Examples of this approach are Telescript and Tcl [20]. The declarative approach takes the view that only a declarative description of the task should be sent to the remote site. An example of this approach is ACL [11].

What we are proposing differs from current work in software agents in that

- We are not researching new agent capabilities per se
- We are not developing an agent-based system for some new application domain
- We are investigating how agents can be the fundamental building blocks for the construction of general-purpose software systems, with the anticipated benefits of robustness and reuse
- We are characterizing agents in terms of *mental abstractions*, and multiple agents in terms of their *interactions*, as follows.

Mental abstractions for agents are beliefs, knowledge, desires, goals, and intentions, whereas multiagent abstractions are

- Social: about collections of agents
- Organizational: about teams and groups
- Ethical: about right and wrong actions
- Legal: about contracts and compliance

These abstractions matter because modern applications go beyond traditional metaphors and models in terms of their dynamism, openness, and trustworthiness. They involve virtual enterprises and electronic commerce, such as in manufacturing supply chains and autonomous logistics, community-ware and social interfaces, and problem solving by collaborative groups. The architecture of future information systems will be agent-oriented, as shown in Figure 4.

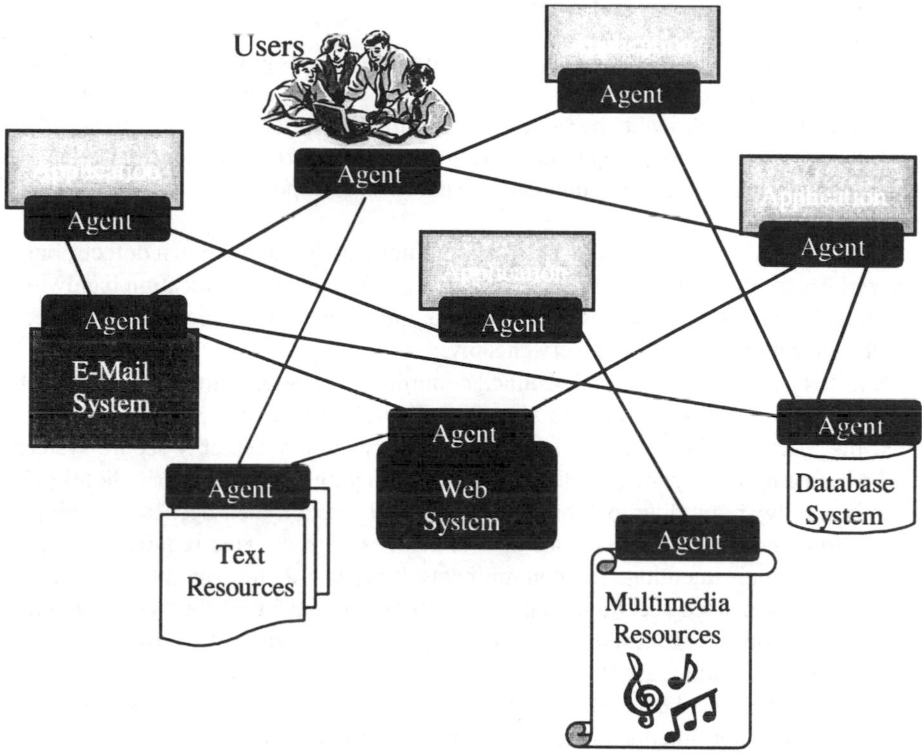

Fig. 4. Architecture for an agent-oriented information system, indicating collaborations among users, applications, and resources

Techniques for creating and maintaining societies of autonomous active objects (agents) will be useful not only for large open information environments, but also for large open physical environments. For example, new efficiencies in logistics could result from considering each supply item being deployed to be intelligent (implemented via a "smart card") with a local goal to reach a destination and an ability to take advantage of a global distribution system.

Such information environments are too complex to be centrally developed or controlled. The only alternative is for intelligence to be embedded at many places to provide distributed management. Each locus of intelligence is an autonomous *agent* that must be *long-lived* (to execute unattended for long periods), *adaptive* (to explore and learn about its environment), and *social* (to interact with others to leverage knowledge and capabilities, so as to achieve individual as well as collective goals). Composed as they are of active social entities, *multiagent systems* are ideally suited to the challenges of software development described above. *Teams*, with different members playing specific roles and cooperating to achieve some higher end, emphasize the social and organizational aspects of multiagent systems.

2.3 System Redundancy and Adaptation

In some circumstances, robustness in the presence of errors is governed by redundancy. That is, if each software module is deemed to be behaving either correctly or incorrectly, then two modules with the same intended functionality are sufficient to detect an error in one of them, and three modules are sufficient to correct the incorrect behavior. Fundamentally, the amount of redundancy required is well specified by information and coding theory.

HP Labs has built a massively parallel computer with 220,000 known defects, but it still yields correct results [8]. As long as there is sufficient communication bandwidth to find and use healthy resources, it can tolerate the defects. Allowing so many defects enables the computer to be built very cheaply.

Similarly, a National Research Council committee last year, in addressing the problem of software security, published a report called *Trust in Cyberspace*, which advocated the "Theory of Insecurity." The theory suggests that acceptably secure systems can be built out of components that have known vulnerabilities and security holes [25].

When software modules exhibit more complex behavior, then deeper reasoning is needed to determine whether or not the behavior is correct. This requires agents to communicate their intentions and commitments. They can then be monitored to determine if they have acted according to their intentions and have kept their commitments. Activating a group of agents then becomes a type of nondeterministic programming.

Self-adaptive software [29] evaluates its own behavior and changes the behavior when the evaluation indicates that it is not accomplishing what the software is intended to do, or when better functionality or performance is possible. This implies that the software has alternative ways of accomplishing its purpose, along with enough knowledge of its construction and awareness of its current operation to enable effective changes to be made at runtime. Self-adaptive software requires components to maintain models of themselves and the other components with which they might interact [23]. In a control-system metaphor, runtime software is treated like a factory, with inputs and outputs and a monitoring and control facility that manages the factory to improve its performance [27].

Intentional programming attempts to coordinate the cooperation of independently developed abstraction objects, termed intentions. Intentions are not executed at runtime, but are called at programming time [42].

2.4 Agent Capabilities

Figure 4 illustrates how agents might represent, i.e., act on behalf of, various kinds of passive or non-agent like components and entities in an environment, and how they might interact to provide next-generation services to users and applications. Success in this requires that

- Agents stay aware of their own roles, capabilities, and weaknesses by maintaining a model of themselves
- Agents stay aware of their team by maintaining models of its members and their roles

- Agents maintain models of other teams in which they might play a role
- Agents learn from interactions about the goals, capabilities, and intentions of other agents
- Agents rely on commitments from other agents, and maintain commitments to other agents.

2.5 Ontologies: Modeling Objects, Resources, and Agents

A key to enabling agents to interact productively is for them to construct and maintain models of each other, as well as the passive components in their environment. Unfortunately, the agents' models will be mutually incompatible in syntax and semantics, not only due to the different things being modeled, but also due to mismatches in underlying hardware and operating systems, in data structures, and in usage. In attempting to model some portion of the real world, information models necessarily introduce simplifications that result in semantic incompatibilities.

Ontologies appear to be well suited for reconciling heterogeneous semantics. We have been developing mediating mechanisms based on domain-specific ontologies to yield the appearance and effect of semantic homogeneity among agents at the knowledge level [34]. However, if there are n entities in the environment, then each would need a model of each of the other entities, resulting in $n(n-1)/2$ models that must be maintained. This is infeasible for large domains. We solve this via two means. First, agents maintain and advertise models of themselves, resulting in a total of n models. Second, we consider the source of the models. How should one agent represent another, and how should it acquire the information it needs to construct a model in that representation?

This has, we believe, a simple and elegant answer: *the agent should presume that unknown agents are like itself, and it should choose to represent them as it does itself.* Thus, as an agent learns more about other agents, it only has to encode any differences that it discovers. The resultant representation can be concise and efficient, and has the following advantages:

- An agent has a head start in constructing a model for a just-encountered agent.
- An agent has to manage only one kind of model and one kind of representation.
- The same inference mechanisms it uses to reason about its own behavior can reason about the behaviors of other agents; an agent trying to predict what another will do has only to imagine what it itself would do in a similar situation.
- As information about other agents is acquired through observations and interactions, models of them can be updated, and will diverge from the default.

We portray an agent as a rational decision-maker that perceives and interacts with its environment. Agents are rational in the context of all other agents, because they are aware of the other agents' constraints, preferences, intentions, and commitments and act accordingly.

3 Semantics

If agents are constructed modularly, the challenge is in specifying and generating the right interactions. We term our approach interaction-oriented programming (IOP), and include in it high-level abstractions and techniques that capture the structure of the desired interactions. We identify three layers of IOP, from lower to upper:

- *Coordination*, which enables the agents to operate in a shared environment
- *Commitment*, which reflects the agents' obligations to one another, capturing their social structure and the norms governing their behavior
- *Collaboration*, which supports reaching agreement, forming and maintaining teams, and performing complex joint activities.

Informal concepts, such as competition, often have variants that may be classified into different layers. For example, bidding in an auction requires no more than coordination, whereas commerce involves commitments, and negotiation involves protocols for collaboration.

Pieces of the above layers have been studied in distributed computing, databases, and distributed artificial intelligence (DAI), but usually not from a programming perspective. The distributed computing and database work focuses on narrower problems of synchronization, and eschews high-level concepts such as social commitments. Thus it is less flexible, but more robust, than the DAI work. Our contribution will be in enhancing and synthesizing ideas into a framework that is *rigorous* yet flexible.

4 Preliminary Results and Discussion

In preliminary experiments, we have constructed a large group of agents, each implemented as a concurrently executing Java thread and interacting through a base class environment. The agents each have an understanding of what a circle is, what it means to be part of a circle, where the nearest agents are located, and an estimate of how close the group is to being in a circle. The agents have the ability to reason about where they should be on a circle and the direction they should move to get there. They also have the ability to help move nearby agents that do not seem to be located or moving properly. Into this environment, we have introduced a few agents that do not have the ability to move properly or are stationary. The group overcomes this and produces an acceptable circle. We have anecdotal evidence, via one comparison, that such an implementation can be constructed more rapidly and robustly than a conventional object-oriented implementation in C++.

The Team-Oriented Paradigm

We propose an open architecture consisting of multiple, redundant, agent-based components interacting via a verified kernel. To program and activate a team will require a resolution of who (role) will do what (subtask), when (coordination), how (capabilities), where (resources or location), and why (team plan and external requirements). In addition, there are the aggregate matters of how many agents per role and how much resources are needed. The main steps are agent *creation* (compilation), team *configuration* (linkage), and team *activation* (execution).

The above matters presuppose an agent factory with rich protocols for discovery and software configuration that inherently accommodate flexibility through negotiation. In a general setting, the agents could join and activate teams with minimal programmer intervention. Their negotiated commitments to one another would lead to coordinated and coherent action by the entire team even as the membership of the team evolves and some members behave imperfectly.

We believe that implementing software as a large number of intelligent, but not perfect agents will be successful. Our approach imposes requirements on the structure and behavior of the agents, and facilitates a formal semantics. We will supply the meta-model, architecture, and formal semantics to realize this approach. Prototypes are being developed using an iterative process called User-Centered Software Engineering.

5 Conclusion

We have proposed and begun investigation of a new software development paradigm—a *cooperative paradigm*—based on interacting agents, active objects, and active wrappers of legacy components. The resultant methodology and language, *interaction-oriented programming*, represent a fundamental extension of the earlier paradigms, with greater expressive power, different conceptual foundations, such as the beliefs held by the components, and new modeling techniques.

Techniques for creating and maintaining societies of autonomous active objects (agents) will be useful not only for large open information environments, but also for large open physical environments. For example, such techniques would yield new efficiencies in logistics: by considering each item of material to be an intelligent entity residing on a "smart card" whose goal is to reach a destination, a distribution system could manage more complicated schedules and surmount unforeseen difficulties. Languages are required for creating and maintaining such environments—an interaction-oriented programming language satisfies this requirement.

Just as today almost anyone can create a web page and contribute information to the Web, so the proposed paradigm will enable anyone to create and contribute customized components to software applications. We are in the midst of a trend toward *disintermediation*—the direct association between users and their software—that enables people to be responsible for their own computing, often without formal training or the support of professional intermediaries. This is healthy, but an infrastructure such as we propose is needed that can

- Analyze component interoperability and then cope with incompatibility
- Support the dynamic reconfiguration of loosely confederated processes and agents
- Monitor and manage persistent autonomous processes (extending the notion of daemons).

It is claimed that the major impediment to the realization of component-based development is *quality* of the components [32]. The proposed paradigm mitigates this through massive redundancy, leading to increased robustness. (A system that is stuck and making no progress can try one of its less popular alternatives.)

References

1. Jean-Marc Andreoli, Paolo Ciancarini, and Remo Pareschi, "Interaction Abstract Machines," in Gul Agha, Peter Wegner, and Akinori Yonezawa, eds., *Research Directions in Concurrent Object-Oriented Programming*, MIT Press, Cambridge, MA, 1993, pp. 257–280.
2. Antoine Beugnard, Jean-Marc Jezequel, Noel Plouzeau, and Damien Watkins, "Making Components Contract Aware," *IEEE Computer*, Vol. 32, No. 7, July 1999, pp. 38–45.
3. Fred P. Brooks, *The Mythical Man-Month*, Anniversary Edition, Addison-Wesley, Reading, MA, 1995.
4. F-C. Cheong, "OASIS: An Agent-Oriented Programming Language for Heterogeneous Distributed Environments," Ph.D. Thesis, University of Michigan, 1992.
5. Adam Cheyer, "Agent-Based Interoperation," CSLI Seminar Series on Intelligent Agents, Stanford University, April 27, 1995.
6. Cynthia Della Torre Cicalese and Shmuel Rotenstreich, "Behavioral Specification of Distributed Software Component Interfaces," *IEEE Computer*, Vol. 32, No. 7, July 1999, pp. 46–53.
7. Helder Coelho, Luis Antunes, and Luis Moniz, "On Agent Design Rationale," in *Proceedings of the XI Simposio Brasileiro de Inteligencia Artificial (SBIA)*, Fortaleza (Brasil), October 17–21, 1994, pp. 43–58.
8. Peter Coffee, "Perfect Computers Cost Too Much," *PC Week*, July 6, 1998, p. 54.
9. Philip R. Cohen and Hector J. Levesque, "Persistence, Intention, and Commitment," in *Intentions in Communication*, Philip R. Cohen, Jerry Morgan, and Martha E. Pollack, eds., MIT Press, 1990.
10. Les Gasser, "Social conceptions of knowledge and action: DAI foundations and open systems semantics," *Artificial Intelligence*, Vol. 47, 1991, pp. 107–138.
11. Michael Genesereth and Stephen Ketchpel, "Software Agents," *Communications of the ACM*, Vol. 37, No. 7, 1994, pp. 48–53.
12. R. Goodwin, "Formalizing Properties of Agents," Technical Report CMU-CS-93-159, Department of Computer Science, Carnegie-Mellon University, 1993.
13. Les Hatton, "Does OO Sync with How We Think?" *IEEE Software*, May 1998, pp. 46–54.
14. Michael N. Huhns, "Agent Teams: Building and Implementing Software," *IEEE Internet Computing*, Vol. 4, No. 1, January/February 2000, pp. 90–92.
15. Michael N. Huhns, "Multiagent-Oriented Programming," *Intelligent Agents and Their Potential for Future Design and Synthesis Environments*, Ahmed K. Noor and John B. Malone, editors, NASA Langley Research Center, Hampton, VA, February 1999, pp. 215–238.
16. Michael N. Huhns and Munindar P. Singh, "A Multiagent Treatment of Agenthood," *Applied Artificial Intelligence: An International Journal*, Vol. 13, No. 1–2, January–March 1999, pp. 3–10.
17. Michael N. Huhns and Munindar P. Singh, eds., *Readings in Agents*, Morgan Kaufmann Publishers, Inc., San Francisco, CA, 1997.
18. Michael N. Huhns, editor, *Distributed Artificial Intelligence*, Pitman/Morgan Kaufmann, 1987.
19. Juhani Iivari, "Why Are CASE Tools Not Used?" *Communications of the ACM*, Vol. 39, No. 10, October 1996, pp. 94–103.
20. K. Indermaur, "Baby Steps," *Byte*, March 1995, pp. 97–104.
21. Nicholas R. Jennings, "On Agent-Oriented Software Engineering," *IEEE Internet Computing*, Vol. 3, No. 4, 1999, pp. XXX.
22. Nicholas R. Jennings, "Commitments and conventions: The foundation of coordination in multi-agent systems," *The Knowledge Engineering Review*, Vol. 2, No. 3, 1993, pp. 223–250.

23. Gabor Karsai and Janos Sztipanovits, "A Model-Based Approach to Self-Adaptive Software," *IEEE Intelligent Systems*, Vol. 14, No. 3, May/June 1999, pp. 46–53.
24. Elizabeth A. Kendall, Margaret T. Malkoun, and Chong Jiang, "Multiagent System Design Based on Object-Oriented Patterns," *Journal of Object-Oriented Programming*, June 1997, pp. 41–47.
25. Stephen Kent, "An Interview with Stephen Kent," *IEEE Spectrum*, Vol. 37, No. 1, January 2000, p. 37.
26. David Kinny and Michael Georgeff, "Modelling and Design of Multi-Agent Systems," in J.P. Muller, M.J. Wooldridge, and N.R. Jennings, eds., *Intelligent Agents III — Proceedings of the Third International Workshop on Agent Theories, Architectures, and Languages*, Springer-Verlag, Berlin, 1997, pp. 1–20.
27. Mieczyslaw M. Kokar, Kenneth Baclawski, and Yonet A. Eracar, "Control Theory-Based Foundations of Self-Controlling Software," *IEEE Intelligent Systems*, Vol. 14, No. 3, May/June 1999, pp. 37–45.
28. David Krieger and Richard M. Adler, "The Emergence of Distributed Component Platforms," *IEEE Computer*, Vol. 31, No. 3, March 1998, pp. 43–53.
29. Robert Laddaga, "Creating Robust Software through Self-Adaptation," *IEEE Intelligent Systems*, Vol. 14, No. 3, May/June 1999, pp. 26–29.
30. Ted Lewis, "The Next 10,0002 Years: Part II," *IEEE Computer*, May 1996, pp. 78–86.
31. David L. Martin, Adam J. Cheyer, and Douglas B. Moran, "The Open Agent Architecture: A framework for building distributed software systems," *Applied Artificial Intelligence*, Vol. 13, No. 1–2, 1999, pp. 92–128.
32. Bertrand Meyer and Christine Mingins, "Component-Based Development: From Buzz to Spark," *IEEE Computer*, Vol. 32, No. 7, July 1999, pp. 35–37.
33. Robin Milner, "Elements of Interaction," *Communications of the ACM*, Vol. 36, No. 1, January 1993, pp. 78–89.
34. Allen Newell, "The knowledge level," *Artificial Intelligence*, Vol. 18, No. 1, 1982, pp. 87–127.
35. Cherri M. Pancake, "The Promise and the Cost of Object Technology: A Five-Year Forecast," *Communications of the ACM*, Vol. 38, No. 10, October 1995, pp. 33–49.
36. M. J. Pont and E. Moreale, "Towards a Practical Methodology for Agent-Oriented Software Engineering with C++ and Java," Leicester University Technical Report 96-33, December 1996.
37. C.V. Ramomoorthy and Wei-tek Tsai, "Advances in Software Engineering," *IEEE Computer*, Vol. 29, No. 10, October 1996, pp. 47–58.
38. Anand S. Rao and Michael P. Georgeff, "Modeling rational agents within a BDI-architecture," in *Proceedings of the International Conference on Principles of Knowledge Representation and Reasoning*, 1991, pp. 473–484.
39. D. Riecken, "Introduction to the Special Issue on Intelligent Agents," *Communications of the ACM*, Vol. 37, No. 7, 1994, pp. 18–21.
40. Mary Shaw, "Outlook on Software System Design," *IEEE Computer*, Vol. 31, No. 1, January 1998, p. 32.
41. Yoav Shoham, "Agent-Oriented Programming," *Artificial Intelligence*, Vol. 60, No. 2, June 1993, pp. 51–92.
42. Charles Simonyi, "The Future is Intentional," *IEEE Computer*, Vol. 32, No. 5, May 1999, pp. 56–57.
43. Munindar P. Singh and Michael N. Huhns, "Social Abstractions for Information Agents," in *Intelligent Information Agents*, Matthias Klusch, ed., Kluwer Academic Publishers, Boston, MA, 1999.
44. Clement Szyperski, *Component Software: Beyond Object-Oriented Programming*, Addison Wesley Longman, 1998.

45. Milind Tambe, David V. Pynadath, and Nicolas Chauvat, "Building Dynamic Agent Organizations in Cyberspace," *IEEE Internet Computing*, Vol. 4, No. 2, March/April 2000.
46. Jose M. Vidal and Edmund H. Durfee, "Learning Nested Agent Models in an Information Economy," *Journal of Experimental and Theoretical Artificial Intelligence (special issue on learning in distributed artificial intelligence systems)*, 1998.
47. Guijun Wang, Liz Ungar, and Dan Klawitter, "Component Assembly for OO Distributed Systems," *IEEE Computer*, Vol. 32, No. 7, July 1999, pp. 71–78.
48. Peter Wegner, "Why Interaction is More Powerful Than Algorithms," *Communications of the ACM*, Vol. 40, No. 5, May 1997, pp. 80–91.
49. Peter Wegner, "Interactive Software Technology," *CRC Handbook of Computer Science and Engineering*, May 1996, pp. 1–24.
50. Peter Wegner, "Interactive Foundations of Object-Based Programming," *IEEE Computer*, October 1995, pp. 70–72.
51. Darrell Woelk, Michael Huhns, and Christine Tomlinson, "Uncovering the Next Generation of Active Objects," *Object Magazine*, July–August 1995, pp. 33–40.
52. Michael J. Wooldridge, "Agents and Software Engineering," *Proceedings AIIA*, 1998.
53. Michael J. Wooldridge, "Agent-Based Software Engineering," *IEE Proceedings on Software Engineering*, Vol. 144, No. 1, February 1997, pp. 26–37.
54. Michael J. Wooldridge and Nicholas R. Jennings, "Software Engineering with Agents: Pitfalls and Pratfalls," *IEEE Internet Computing*, Vol. 3, No. 3, May/June 1999.
55. Michael J. Wooldridge, Nicholas R. Jennings, and David Kinny, "A Methodology for Agent-Oriented Analysis and Design," in Oren Etzioni, Jean-Pierre Muller, and Jeffrey Bradshaw, eds., *Agents'99: Proceedings of the third International Conference on Autonomous Agents*, Seattle, WA, May 1999.
56. Edward Yourdon, "Java, the Web, and Software Development," *IEEE Computer*, August 1996, pp. 25–30.

Issues in Agent-Oriented Software Engineering

Jürgen Lind

German Research Center for AI (DFKI)
Im Stadtwald B36
D-66123 Saarbrücken, Germany

lind@dfki.de

Abstract. In this paper, I will discuss the conceptual foundation of agent-oriented software development by relating the fundamental elements of the agent-oriented view to those of other, well established programming paradigms, especially the object-oriented approach. Furthermore, I will motivate the concept of autonomy as the basic property of the agent-oriented school and discuss the development history of programming paradigms that lead to this perspective on software systems. The paper will be concluded by an outlook on how the new paradigm can change the way we think about software systems.

1 Introduction

Agents and multi-agent systems are currently one of the most interesting research fields in the computer science community; especially the natural way of capturing the structure and the behavior of complex systems has stimulated this huge interest. But is this enough to make agent-oriented software engineering (AOSE) a new software paradigm? What makes the idea distinctive from other approaches? How does it fit in a more general picture of software engineering?

In this paper, I will present my personal viewpoint on agent-oriented software engineering firstly by discussing the interrelationships of AOSE concepts (agent, agent architecture, role, etc.) and secondly by relating AOSE to other programming paradigms. Especially the relation between object-oriented and agent-oriented methods is particularly interesting because they seem to be closely related. In order to clarify their relationship, I will describe the levels of abstraction that are involved in a certain programming paradigm in general and of object-orientation and agent-orientation in particular. I will then identify aspects they have in common as well as their main differences. Furthermore, I will point out what could be the major contributions of the agent oriented paradigm to software engineering and provide an outlook on how the new paradigm can change the way we think about software systems.

2 Aspects of programming paradigms

The term "programming paradigm" is extremely fuzzy because it is often used to capture a set of different software-related aspects under a particular catch-phrase. These

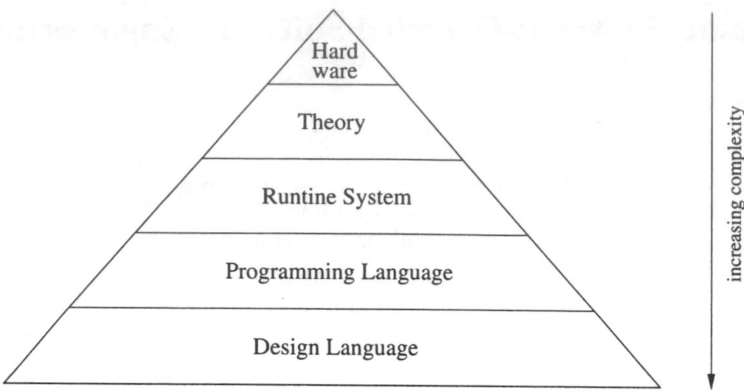

Fig. 1. Levels of Abstraction

different aspects are often located on different levels of abstraction and their interrelationships are seldom explicitly formulated. In this paper, I will use the triangle shown in Figure 1 to describe the different levels of abstraction that in my view make up a programming paradigm. The form a triangle was chosen to express the fact that the number of concepts (and therewith the complexity) on a particular level of abstraction increases on higher levels. Furthermore, a layered approach is quite common in computer science theories to clearly separate the concepts on different levels of abstraction. The main advantage of a layered approach is that no knowledge of lower levels is necessary to understand and to work with higher level concepts because ideally, each level of abstraction represents a conceptually closed framework. In reality, unfortunately, the higher level theories are not only much more complex then lower level ones, but they are often incomplete [22]. Therefore, it is often necessary to combine several higher level theories to obtain a full coverage of the part of the world that should be modeled.

Note furthermore, that the distinctions between the different levels are not too sharp. Because of the fact that most programming models are assumed to be essentially equal in their computational power (Church's thesis), any programming model can be implemented in terms of any other model. Thus, it is possible to write object-oriented software in a purely imperative programming language or to implement a deductive database in an object-oriented framework. In the following sections, I have therefore tried to produce a break-down of concepts that clearly separates intra-model aspects and that allows for an inter-model comparison of these concepts. I am well aware that some concepts can be shifted along the abstraction hierarchy, but I think that the current assignment to a particular level is adequate.

2.1 Hardware

The first level of abstraction encapsulates the architecture that is implemented in the computer hardware. Today, most computers still have the von Neumann architecture that was introduced in the late 1940s [12]. The architecture consists of a *processor* that is subdivided into units for computation and control and a *memory* store that holds the instructions and the data of the program.

This architecture is still common in modern computers although it has been greatly optimized by using techniques such as pipelining, caching or parallelism to speed up computation. A recent trend in the hardware community is to turn away from integrated, large-scale systems and towards networks of normal personal computers that jointly work on a computationally demanding task. These virtual supercomputers combine the advantage of lower costs through the use of standard hardware with an extreme scalability that allows to add more computational resources whenever this is necessary. In one vision on the future of the Internet [23], the entire net becomes a virtual supercomputer that makes individual computational power obsolete.

However, whether sequential, parallel or distributed, from the point of view of a programming paradigm, all hardware looks the same. There have been attempts to build hardware architectures that implement a particular programming paradigm directly into the hardware device, but none of these attempts has been successful. Therefore, we can safely assume that all programming paradigms share the same ground.

2.2 Theories

On the next higher level of abstraction, however, things are different. Theories are conceptualizations of a particular computational model that abstracts away from the characteristics of the hardware. The first theories were aimed at capturing the in-principle capability of a computational device in order to allow for general statements about what can be automatically computed and what cannot [41]. Turing's theory, for example, is a radical mathematical conceptualization of the von Neumann architecture that enables us to formally analyze all possible programs that can be executed on such an architecture. Other computational theories are intended as tools to help the programmer to express the ideas of what a program is supposed to do more naturally. An early computational theory that was meant as the foundation of a "natural" way of programming is declarative programming [17] but it has been demonstrated by empirical investigations in cognitive psychology that this claim does not necessarily hold true [32].

Let's start the comparison of the object-oriented and agent-oriented issues with the entities that are handled on this level of abstraction. In the object-oriented world, these entities are the *objects*. An object can be anything ranging from a concrete entity from the real world to a conceptual entity that only exists in the designers head. Each object within the system is associated with a particular *class* that determines the objects basic properties. Classes can be linked with each other in several ways. Probably the best known relation between two classes is *inheritance* that models a conceptual extension of a common base specification. During their lifetime, objects communicate by sending *messages* to each other. These messages can be used to request services from the receiving object such as to provide internal information or to change the current state. Although there are several additional concepts in the object-oriented paradigm I will restrict myself to this brief introduction and refer the reader unfamiliar with object-oriented concepts to the available literature, eg. [4]. In summary, the collection of object-oriented concepts is clear and manageable in size and does not vary greatly in different object-oriented approaches.

In the agent-oriented universe, on the other hand, we are faced with the first serious problem as there is no single agreed definition of the entities that are dealt with. The existing *agent theories* are more or less built upon one out of two widely accepted notions of agency [44]. In the *strong notion* of agency, an agent is modeled in terms of mentalistic notions such as beliefs, desires and intentions. Furthermore, the strong notion requires that these mental concepts have an explicit representation within the implementation of the agent. Thus, this notion forces a *white-box* on the agent. The *weak notion* of agency, on the other hand, requires only a *black-box* view on the agent in that it defines an agent only in terms of its observable properties. According to this definition, an agent is anything that exhibits autonomy, reactivity, pro-activity, social ability [44].

In my opinion, these two notions of agency are both too strict. I would argue for a more pragmatic definition of agency that allows the designer to decide what should be an agent regardless of a particular implementation or a minimal degree of external properties. I call this the *very weak notion* of agency. To explain why this absence of formal aspects still makes sense, I have to fall back upon a famous article from the early days of Artificial Intelligence.

In [22], the author argues that it is useful to ascribe mental qualities such as beliefs, goals, desires, wishes etc. to machines (or computer programs) whenever it helps us to understand the structure of a machine or a program or to explain or predict the behavior of the machine or the program. McCarthy does not impose any constraints such as a minimal required complexity onto the entities that we want to ascribe mental categories or onto the mental categories that we would like to use. In his view, ascribing mental qualities is a means of understanding and of communication between humans, ie. it is a purely conceptual tool that serves the purpose of expressing existing knowledge about a particular program or its current state.

> "All the [...] reasons for ascribing belief's are epistemological; i.e. ascribing beliefs is needed to adapt to limitations on our ability to acquire knowledge, use it for prediction, and establish generalizations in terms of the elementary structure of the program. Perhaps this is the general reason for ascribing higher levels of organization to systems."

To illustrate why this point of view is reasonable, McCarthy uses the example of a program that is given in source code form. It is possible to completely determine the programs behavior by simulating the given code, ie. no mental categories are necessary to describe this behavior. Why would we still want to use mental categories to talk and reason about the program? In the original paper, McCarthy discusses several reasons for this. In the following list, I have selected those reasons that seem to be most relevant to me:

1. The programs state at a particular point in time is usually not directly observable. Therefore, the observable information is better expressed in mental categories.
2. A complete simulation may be too slow, but a prediction about the behavior on the basis of the ascribed mental qualities may be feasible.
3. Ascribing mental qualities can lead to more general hypothesis about the programs behavior then a finite number of simulations.

4. The mental categories (eg. goals) that are ascribed are likely to correspond to the programmers intentions when designing the program. Thus, the program can be understood and changed more easily.
5. The structure of the program is more easily accessible then in the source code form.

Especially the fourth point in the above enumeration is extremely important for AOSE because the task of understanding existing software becomes increasingly important in the software industry and is likely to outrange the development of new software [1]. Thus, if it becomes easier to access the original developers idea (that is eventually manifested in the design) it becomes easier to understand the design and this leads to higher cost efficiency in software maintenance.

A more general conclusion from McCarthy's approach is the idea that *anything can be an agent*. This view has been discussed from controversial points of view [44] and it has been argued that it does not buy us anything whenever the system is so simple that it can be perfectly understood. I do not agree with this. In my view, the conceptual integrity that is achieved by viewing every intentional entity – be it a simple as it may – in the system as an agent leads to a much clearer system design and it circumvents the problem to decide whether a particular entity is an agent or not. In my personal experience, this problem can be quite annoying during the design phase whenever two software designers have different views.

In the above paragraphs, I have identified the basic structural elements of object-orientation and agent-orientation, respectively. Now I will outline some of the basic concepts of describing and arranging these elements and point out some fundamental similarities that can be identified.

As I have already said above, the basic descriptional element is object-oriented programming is the class. A class definition specifies the class variables of an object and the methods the object accepts. Classes can be linked with each other via several forms: one class inherit from another class such that the new class is an extension of the existing class, instances of two classes can collaborate with each other by exchanging messages, and finally they can have a structural connection in that one instance of a class contains an instance of the class.

These concepts correspond to the agent-oriented world by replacing class with *role*, state variable with *belief/knowledge* and method with *message*. Thus a role definition describes the agent's capabilities, the data that is needed to produce the desired results and the requests that trigger a particular service. Besides this fundamental relation, there are many other conceptual similarities between object-orientation and agent-orientation that can be mapped onto each other. Due to the limited space, however, these are briefly summarized in Table 1.

Turning away from the conceptual issues and similarities of the two programming approaches, we will now come to more technical aspects of the runtime environment and discuss the general structure for object-oriented and agent-oriented systems, respectively.

2.3 Runtime System

The runtime system of a particular programming paradigm provides the environment for the program interpretation and these environments can be radically different. In

	OOP	AOP
Structural Elements		
	abstract class	generic role
	class	domain specific role
	class variables	knowledge, belief
	methods	capabilities
Relations		
	collaboration (`uses`)	negotiation
	composition (`has`)	holonic agents
	inheritance (`is`)	role multiplicity
	instantiation	domain-specific role + individual knowledge
	polymorphism	service matchmaking

Table 1. Mapping OOP to AOP

the more simple forms, they are restricted to administrative tasks such as managing the heap or they provide slightly more elaborate services such as garbage collection. However, there also exist very complex runtime environment that provide complete reasoning engines for logic programming [17] that are for example used in declarative programming languages such as Prolog [5].

Objects and agents and the various relationships that exist between them within their respective programming model are conceptual abstractions that require an implementation such that they can be used by higher levels of abstraction. In the following paragraphs, I will divide the implementation of the theoretical concepts into the implementation of the entities themselves and an implementation of a meta-level that manipulates the basic entities.

In an object-oriented runtime system, the objects are statically represented by the *object architecture*. This architecture is usually quite simple as it only contains the current state of the object and the relation to the objects class (which determines the operations that can be performed on the object). An object is usually represented as arbitrary collection of data elements with associated functions and the granularity of objects is potentially not limited. However, efficiency issues dictate that not every entity is modeled as an object and so in reality this conceptual benefit is slightly weakened. The *object management system* is responsible for representing the relations such as inheritance between the defined classes and object manipulation such as creating or destroying objects. Furthermore, the object management system is also responsible for dynamic aspects such as method selection of polymorphous objects, exception handling or garbage collection.

In an agent-oriented runtime system, things are distinctly more complicated although similar in their general structure. The basic entities are the agents that are implemented by their *agent architecture*. Agent architectures are often built upon a particular theory such as BDI [35] and establish the link between the abstract concepts "agent" and "role" in that they provide the runtime environment for the role descriptions that make up the agent. Thus, we have the fundamental relation [21]

$$agent = roles + architecture$$

However, agent architectures are far more complex then the object architecture, especially because of the dynamic aspects that must be dealt with. Because of the richness of the agent-oriented world, there exists a large number of different agent architectures [27, 28, 15]. Due to the vast number of approaches, it is impossible to identify *the* best or most general architecture. However, the smallest common denominator seems to be the basic *perceive – reason – act* cycle that is oriented at the minimal agent model of [36]: in each iteration, the agent perceives the state of its environment, integrates the perception in its knowledge base that is used to derive the next action which is then executed. This generic cycle is a useful abstraction as it provides a black-box view on the agent architecture and encapsulates specific aspects.

The task of the *agent management system* as the meta-level of an agent based runtime environment is to provide a "life-space" for the agents, ie. a collection of mechanisms that enables the agents to get in contact with each other. To enable agents of different designers to interact with each other, it is necessary to standardize the basic services that are provided by agent management system. One such standard is defined in [10].

2.4 Programming Language

On this level of abstraction, the syntactical framework for the manipulation of the entities on the runtime level is defined. The programs that are written in a particular programming language are either directly interpreted by the runtime system or they are compiled into an intermediate format that is understood by the runtime system or directly to assembler code.

The syntactical constructs that are provided by the programming language should allow the programmer to use the underlying semantic concepts efficiently and to express the intended functionality of the program elegantly. For example, it is generally possible to implement a particular conceptual model with any general purpose language, e.g. it is possible to write object-oriented programs in C, but in general, it is much easier and more comfortable for the programmer if the terms of the conceptual framework can be used directly. Even an integration of several conceptual models into a single high level programming language can be problematic as is often difficult to find a good combination of concepts that is not overwhelming for the average user and then to find a concise syntactical representation for these different concepts.

I think that object-orientation as well as agent-orientation are such general concepts that can be attached to almost any other programming language. In the case of object orientation, this approached work for languages such C, leading to C++ [38], Cobol (ObjectCobol [9]), perl [42] and numerous other languages. But not only imperative languages have been enhanced with objects. The Mozart programming system [34], for example, provides a very elegant combination of constraint-logic programming with object-oriented concepts.

In the context of agent-oriented software engineering, these trends are not so clear until now. Currently, there is no – at least to my knowledge – widely accepted agent-oriented programming language that goes beyond the experimental state. However, some approaches are designed as an extension of established languages, eg. JAM Agents [14] that combine agent-oriented concepts with Java [39].

2.5 Design Language

Design languages are further abstractions from a particular programming language that aim at the conceptual modeling of a system at a more coarse grained level. Design languages often use graphical notations that make it easier fro the designer to access the overall system structure. Probably the currently best known design language is the *Unified Modeling Language (UML)* [3] that tries to integrate several, until then separated design notations, under a common hat. The UML provides a variety of structural elements with well defined semantics that can be flexibly combined into diagrams that capture different aspects of a software system. The core UML language can thus be used to describe a software system from the requirements specification to the final design. An example for using the UML within the context of agent-based systems is discussed in [7]. Due to the general nature of the core UML, however, it is not always suited for all problem areas, and therefore, extensions that cover special aspect have already been proposed [11]. One way is to extend the UML by providing new structural elements and diagrams that enhance the expressive power of the base language. This way is favored by the OMG/FIPA in the development of AGENTUML [31] which proposes an extension of the UML with respect to agent-oriented concepts. As part of the AGENTUML in the FIPA standard [2], [30] suggests an extension of the UML by a completely new diagram type called *protocol diagrams*. These diagrams combine elements of UML interaction diagrams and state diagrams to model the roles that can be played by an agent in the course of interacting with other agents. The new diagram type allows for the specification of multiple threads within an interaction protocol and supports protocol nesting and protocol templates based on generic protocol descriptions.

In a more general sense, however, design languages should not necessarily be constraint to modeling aspects of the system. In my personal view, I would count general software architecture frameworks or frameworks for a particular application area to design languages as well. The reason for this view is that these frameworks provide their own set of structural abstractions that represent a "language" on this particular level of abstraction.

In the object-oriented community, examples for such frameworks include Java Beans [40] as a means to provide off-the-shelf components together with flexible interconnection mechanisms between the basic structural elements, or software development environments such as Visual C++ [25] that focus on a support for the development of graphical user interfaces. In the latter case, the structural elements of the design language are graphical elements that are combined according to a given grammar that regulates how different elements can be put together.

In the agent-based world – although a relatively new area –, a large number of different frameworks already exists. This may be due to the fact, that the increasing

	Machine Language	Structured Programming	Object-Oriented Programming	Agent-Oriented Programming
Structural Unit	Program	Subroutine	Object	Agent
Relation to Previous level		Bounded unit of Program	Subroutine + persistent local state	Object + independent thread of execution + Initiative

Table 2. Historic development of programming paradigms [33]

complexity can only be dealt with by using adequate tool support. Examples for agent-based design languages range from source-level frameworks such as SIF [37] up to complex and powerful tools such as the ZEUS toolkit [29] from British Telecom that provides drag-and-drop mechanisms for putting together multi-agent applications.

3 A Historic Perspective

In this section, I will discuss a few historic aspects in the development of programming paradigms that can be helpful in understanding why the agent-oriented approach is a natural successor to the prior development.

In [33], Table 3 is used to capture the historic development from machine language to agent-oriented programming. In the early days of programming, a program was thus seem as a monolithic block without any inherent structure. This view was subsequently changed in that it was recognized that a program is made up from several smaller structural units, ie. subroutines. However, the concept of subroutines alone was not powerful enough as it emphasized the control flow aspect of programming and neglects the data that is involved. Consequently, the view changed a second time, this time grouping data and computation together in a single structural unit called an "object". Currently, we are faced with the third change of perspective, leading away from merely passive objects and facing towards active structural units which we call "agents".

I like the above presentation of the historic development because I think that it captures the main ideas in a concise form. However, I am not completely satisfied with the characterization of agents in the above table. While the requirement of an independent thread of execution sounds very technical, the term "initiative" is to fuzzy to be operationalized. To draw on the basic ideas of [33] but to develop a more coherent structure, I suggest the three-step characterization shown in Figure 2.

In the first step, programs are seen as a collection of *functions* that establish a well-defined goal. These functions can be described as an imperative sequence of statements (*imperative programming*), as a collection of mathematical expressions that are linked together (*functional programming*) or as a set of goals without imposing a particular way of achieving the goal onto the interpreter (*declarative programming*).

In the next development step, a program is interpreted in terms of the *data* that is manipulated and the *functions* that operate on that data. This leads to structured programming where semantically related aspects of the program are spatially related. An

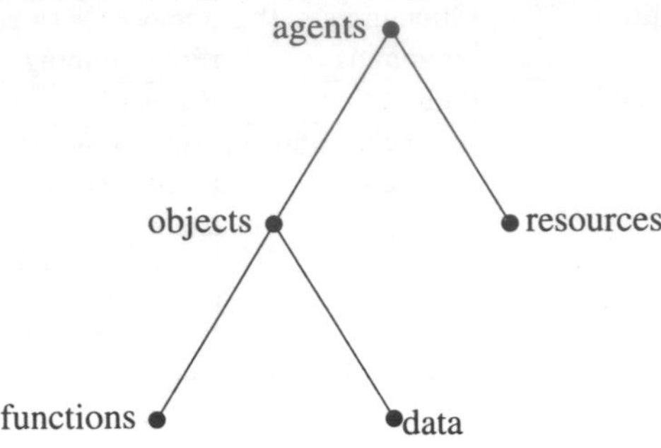

Fig. 2. Historic development

even stronger and explicit relation between data and functions is introduced by abstract data types, eventually leading to object-oriented programming.

In the final step of the characterization, the objects are augmented with *resources* such as computation time, that can be freely used. This freedom in the (internal) resource allocation process lead to the concept that I find most fundamental for agent-oriented programming: *autonomy*. Although the weak notion of agency has identified autonomy as a central concept of the agent-oriented viewpoint, it was only credited as one among others. I would argue, on the other hand, that autonomy is more fundamental then the other aspects of the the weak notion and that it is even a prerequisite for the others. For example, pro-activeness can only be achieved when the agent is free to decide when to become active; the same argument holds for reactivity.

The idea of agents as autonomous agents is so striking and revolutionary because it leads to a new way of thinking about software systems. Such a system is no longer a collection of passive objects. Rather, these objects have a "life of their own", ie. they are perceived and modeled by the designer as active entities. This view on complex systems is completely different from traditional approaches in that it explicitly accepts the fact the system designer is not responsible for specifying the systems dynamics down to the least bit. Instead, the designer sets out the initial state and specifies the initial goals of the autonomous agents and then the system takes over. In such a system, there is no such thing as the "central scrutinizer" [46] that controls everything. Rather, the ongoing interactions determine the overall system behavior [13].

Another major advantage of the agent-oriented view is that it supports the principle of locality even better then the object-oriented view does. In object-oriented systems, the control-flow specification is spread all over the entire program code. The agent-oriented view introduces a further tool for conceptual grouping that comes with the agents well defined bounds [19]. All elements that make up the control-flow of a particular agent are grouped under the common concept, making it easier to identify larger units of the program that belong together semantically.

4 The bottom line

After the sobering remarks about the basic similarities of the agent- and object-oriented approaches one may be tempted to conclude that agent-orientation are just the emperor's new clothes. But that is not what I was trying to say. Even if the technical contributions or agent-oriented software engineering are not really revolutionary the conceptual contribution is nonetheless huge. Agent-oriented software engineering provides an epistemological framework for effective communication and reasoning about complex software system on the basis of mental qualities. It provides a consistent new set of terms and relations that adequately capture complex systems and that support easier and more natural development of these systems.

As an example for the importance of a clear terminological framework, consider abstract data types (ADTs) and objects. It is argued in [43], that objects are essentially the same thing then ADTs that were introduced years earlier. But: why do programmers prefer objects over ADTs? I think because the terminological framework provided by object-oriented approaches allows the programmer a more natural way of modeling because it allows for thinking in terms of the real world that should be modeled by a software system. Furthermore, I think that it will be a major reason for the success of the agent-oriented view that programmers already use some sort of mentalistic notion to develop their object-oriented systems that is subsequently translated into object-oriented terms. This additional transformation can be dropped as soon as the adequate tools for expressing the ideas directly in the already used terminology become available.

As a second point that I have explained above, I think that adding autonomy as an accepted property of formerly passive objects is the main contribution of the agent-oriented view. It leads to a completely different modeling approach that stimulates a system design built upon the desirable properties [6] of loose coupling between system components with a high cohesion of these components.

I shall now return to the initial question of the paper that was whether agent-oriented software engineering is really a new programming paradigm or not. To answer this question, consider the following quote from the Webster On-line Dictionary [24]

> Main Entry: par·a·digm
> Pronunciation: `'par-&-"dIm` also `-"dim`
> Function: *noun*
> Etymology: Late Latin *paradigma*, from Greek *paradeigma*, from *paradeiknynai* to show side by side
> Date: 15th century
> **1 : example, pattern**; *especially*: an outstandingly clear or typical example or archetype
> **2 :** an example of a conjugation or declension showing a word in all its inflectional forms
> **3 :** a philosophical and theoretical framework of a scientific school or discipline within which theories, laws, and generalizations and the experiments performed in support of them are formulated

According to this definition, the answer to the above question is clearly "yes" because agent-oriented software engineering provides us with the required new framework, built upon the basic property of autonomy, that allows for the modeling and understanding of agent-based applications. Furthermore, I think that the agent-oriented view is a necessary prerequisite for accepting artificial intelligence at all because I think that we must get used to ascribing basic qualities such as goal, beliefs, desires before we can ascribe "intelligence" to a machine.

5 Where next?

It must be the goal for the agent community to broaden the acceptance of the new paradigm among the people who really develop software, ie. software engineers. But just as it was the case with object-oriented technology, I do not believe that this acceptance will develop quickly. Object-oriented technology was around for about 10-15 years before it became a widely accepted and naturally used software engineering discipline. So the question one may ask in this respect is why it takes so long for a new paradigm to become state of the art? An interesting answer to this question is provided in Kuhn's theory about the *Structure of Scientific Revolutions* [18]. According to Kuhn's theory, scientific development is not a continuous flow, but rather a sequence of disjoint revolutions. Every such a revolution is preceded by a phase of normal scientific activities in which the researches use the current state of the art (the current paradigm) as the general background of their daily work and the research questions are draw from yet unsolved problems of the current paradigm and can in principle be solved within the existing framework. From time to time, however, a question is raised or a phenomenon is observed that cannot be answered or explained within the current paradigm. These anomalies require a radical change of perspective, ie. a new general research paradigm that can deal with the newly observed phenomena. This is then called a revolution. Ideally, the new paradigm should also capture the past experiences although this is not always possible. As an example for this sort of scientific development, consider Newton's theory on mechanics. Newton's mechanics was the research framework for several hundred years until several observations on the atomic level could not be explained in Newton's theory. This lead to the development of quantum mechanics that were able explain the observations on the atomic level.

The major point in Kuhn's theory is, that the new research paradigm is not introduced into the research by established researchers that "convert" to the new paradigm. Rather, it is introduced by the upcoming generation of young researchers that grow up in the spirit of the new paradigm and that they naturally accept as the general framework. Scientific history is full of examples for this process. The above mentioned theory of quantum mechanics is such an examples, as is Darwin's theory on the origin of species [8]. On a much more specific level, this observation is also true for object-oriented software development. While some established researches neglected the novelty in the concepts [43], it was readily accepted by the younger generation and it is now a widely accepted programming paradigm.

In the near future of agent-oriented software engineering, however, it is necessary to make the main contributions accessible to the people that should use it. Therefore, we need conceptual frameworks to such as described in [16,20,26,45] that support the development of agent-oriented applications.

References

1. Helmut Balzert. *Lehrbuch der Software-Technik*, volume II. Spekrum Akademischer Verlag, 1998.
2. Bernhard Bauer, Jörg P. Müller, and James Odell. Agent UML: A Formalism for Specifying Multiagent Software Systems. In *Proceeedings of the First International Workshop on Agent-Oriented Software Engineering (AOSE-2000) held at the 22nd International Conference on Software Engineering*, Limerick, Ireland, 2000.
3. G. Booch, J. Rumbaugh, and I. Jacobson. *The Unified Modeling Language User Guide*. Addison Wesley, 1999.
4. Grady Booch. *Object-Oriented Analysis and Design With Applications*. Addison-Wesley, 1994.
5. W. F. Clocksin and C. S. Mellish. *Programming in Prolog*. Springer Verlag, 1994.
6. S. D. Conte, H. E. Dunsmore, and V. Y. Chen. *Software Engineering Metrics and Models*. The Benjamin/Cummings Publishing Company, 1996.
7. Ralph Depke, Reiko Heckel, and Jochen Malte Küster. Requirement Specification and Design of Agent-Based Systems with Graph Transformation, Roles, and UML. In *Proceeedings of the First International Workshop on Agent-Oriented Software Engineering (AOSE-2000) held at the 22nd International Conference on Software Engineering*, Limerick, Ireland, 2000.
8. Adrian Desmond and James Moore. *Darwin*. Rowolt, 1994.
9. E. Reed Doke and Bill C. Hardgrave. *An Introduction to Object Cobol*. John Wiley & Sons, 1998.
10. FIPA. Fipa '98 specification parts 1–13, version 1.0, 1998. The Foundation for Intelligent Physical Agents.
11. R. France and B. Rumpe, editors. *UML99 - The Unified Modelling Language - Beyond The Standard*, number 1723 in LNCS. Springer, 1999.
12. J. L. Hennessy and D. A. Patterson. *Computer Architecture: A Quantitative Approach*. Morgan Kaufmann Publishers Inc., 1990.
13. Michael N. Huhns. Interaction-oriented programming. In *Proceeedings of the First International Workshop on Agent-Oriented Software Engineering (AOSE-2000) held at the 22nd International Conference on Software Engineering*, Limerick, Ireland, 2000.
14. Intelligent Reasoning Systems. Jam agent architecture, 2000. http://members.home.net/marcush/IRS/.
15. C. G. Jung. *Theory and Pratice of Hybrid Agents*. PhD thesis, Universität des Saarlandes, 1999.
16. Elizabeth A. Kendall. Agent software engineering with role modelling. In *Proceeedings of the First International Workshop on Agent-Oriented Software Engineering (AOSE-2000) held at the 22nd International Conference on Software Engineering*, Limerick, Ireland, 2000.
17. Robert Kowalski. *Logic for Problem Solving*. North Holland, Amsterdam, 1979.
18. Thomas S Kuhn. *The structure of scientific revolutions*. Univ. of Chicago Press, 2nd edition, 1975.
19. Susan E. Lander. Issues in Multiagent Design Systems. *IEEE Expert*, April 1997.
20. Jürgen Lind. The MASSIVE development method for multiagent systems. In *Proceedings of the Fifth International Conference on the Practical Application of Intelligent Agents and Multi-Agents*, Manchester, UK, 2000.
21. Jürgen Lind. MASSIVE*: Software Engineering for Multiagent Systems*. PhD thesis, University of the Saarland, 2000.
22. John McCarthy. Ascribing mental qualities to machines. In Martin Ringle, editor, *Philosophical Aspects in Artificial Intelligence*. Harvester Press, 1979.

23. Scott McNealy. Scott says... kick butt and have fun". *Sun Microsystems*, 1996. http://www.sun.com/960601/cover/.
24. Merriam-Webster. Wwwebster dictionary, 2000. http://www.m-w.com.
25. Microsoft Corporation. Visual c++, 2000. http://msdn.microsoft.com/visualc/.
26. Simon Miles, Mike Joy, and Michael Luck. Designing agent-oriented systems by analysing agent interactions. In *Proceeedings of the First International Workshop on Agent-Oriented Software Engineering (AOSE-2000) held at the 22nd International Conference on Software Engineering*, Limerick, Ireland, 2000.
27. J. P. Müller. Control Architectures for Autonomous and Interactin Agents: A Survey. In L. Cavedon, Anand Rao, and Wayne Wobcke, editors, *Intelligent Agent Systems: Theoratical and Practical Issues*, number 1209 in LNAI, 1996.
28. Jörg P. Müller. The Right Agent (Architecture) to do the Right Thing. In *Intelligent Agents V — Proc. of the ATAL-98*, volume 1555 of *LNAI*, 1998.
29. Hyacinth S. Nwana, Divine T. Ndumu, Lyndon C. Lee, and Jaron C. Collins. ZEUS: A tool-kit for building distributed multi-agent systems. *Applied Artifical Intelligence Journal*, 13(1):129–186, 1999.
30. James Odell, H. Van Dyke Parunak, and Bernhard Bauer. Representing agent interaction protocols in uml. In *Proceeedings of the First International Workshop on Agent-Oriented Software Engineering (AOSE-2000) held at the 22nd International Conference on Software Engineering*, Limerick, Ireland, 2000.
31. OMG and FIPA. Agent working group. `http://www.objs.com/isig/wg-agents06-minutes.html`, 1999.
32. Tom Ormerod. Human cognition and programming. In *Psychology of Programming*. Academic Press Ltd., London, 1990.
33. H. V. Parunak. Blue-Collar Agents: Keynote of the PAAM99 conference. http://www.erim.org/~van/Presentations, April 1999.
34. Programming Systems Lab. The mozart programming system. University of the Saarland, 1999. http://www.mozart-oz.org.
35. A. S. Rao and M. Georgeff. BDI Agents: from theory to practice. In *Proceedings of the First International Conference on Multi-Agent Systems (ICMAS-95)*, pages 312–319, San Francisco, CA, June 1995.
36. Stuart Russell and Peter Norvig. *Artificial Intelligence: A Modern Approach*. Prentice Hall, 1995.
37. M. Schillo, J. Lind, P. Funk, C. Gerber, and C. Jung. SIF - The Social Interaction Framework System Description and User's Guide to a Multi-Agent System Testbed. Technical Report TR-99-02, DFKI GmbH, 1999.
38. Bjarne Stroustrup. *The C++ Programming Language*. Addison-Wesley, Massachusetts, 1987.
39. Sun Microsystems. The Java Programming System, 1999. http://java.sun.com.
40. Sun Microsystems. Java Beans, 2000. http://java.sun.com/beans.
41. Alan M. Turing. On computable numbers, with an application to the entscheidungsproblem. *Proceedings of the London Mathematical Society*, 2(42), 1937.
42. Larry Wall, Randal L. Schwartz, and Tom Christiansen. *Programming Perl*. O'Reilly & Associates Inc., 2nd edition, 1996.
43. N. Wirth. A plea for lean software. *IEEE Computer*, 28(2):64–68, 1995.
44. M. Wooldridge and N. R. Jennings. Intelligent agents: Theory and practice. *The Knowledge Engineering Review*, 10(2):115–152, 1995.
45. M. Wooldridge, N. R. Jennings, and D. Kinny. The gaia methodology for agent-oriented analysis and design. *Journal of Autonomous Agents and Multi-Agent Systems*, 2000. to appear.
46. Frank Zappa. Joe's garage. Munchkin Music, 1979.

Agent-Based Software Engineering

Charles Petrie

Stanford Networking Research Center
350 Sera Mall
Stanford, CA 94305-2232
petrie@stanford.edu

Abstract. It has previously been claimed that agent technologies facilitate software development by virtue of their high-level abstractions for interactions. We address a more specific characterization and utility. We believe that it is important to distinguish agent technologies from other software technologies by virtue of a set of unique software characteristics. This is in contrast to much in the literature that concentrates on high-level characteristics that could be implemented with a variety of software techniques.

Agent-based software engineering (ABSE), for at least an important class of agents and applications, can be characterized by both model and inner/outer language components. Our experience in developing applications based on long-term asynchronous exchange of agent messages, similar to typical email usage, leads us to believe these unique characteristics facilitate useful software development practices. The utility derives from a stratification of change among the components, ease of collaborative change and debugging even during runtime due to asynchronous text parsing-based message exchange, and reuse of the outer language as well as generic agents as a programming environment.[1]

1 Agent Development Characteristics

Jennings and Wooldridge have described *Agent-Oriented Software Engineering* (AOSE)[19] [7]. AOSE effectiveness claims are based upon three strategies for addressing complex systems: *decomposition*, *abstraction*, and *organization* and that the "agent-oriented mindset" gives one an advantage in using these strategies. That agents have objectives gives one a clear way to decompose the problem into agents. That agent systems work largely by **emergent behavior** and handle errors gracefully reduces the need for detailed specifications, since not all interactions need be specified in advance, and allows more abstraction to be used in system building. And finally, agent systems are naturally hierarchical organizations themselves. Indeed, it is important to note that agent identity is a fundamental component of all agent languages and methodologies for interactions.

We agree with these points. In particular, the idea of engineering a system so that the correct emergent behavior results is the most critical idea in agent software engineering. We further agree with the notions introduced by Huhns[5] that one aspect of emergent

[1] A shorter version of this paper first appeared in *Proc. PAAM 2000*, Manchester, April, 2000.

behavior is having software modules being able to model themselves and other modules, which leads to modules that are able to attempt different methods of accomplishing a task based upon runtime data and these models, which in turn leads to flexibility and robustness without the necessity of the programmer having correctly considering every possibility. The fundamental idea here is that the programmer focuses on the types of interactions possible without specifying all possibilities in advance and one technique for doing this is modeling interaction behaviors. These notions are important and fundamental. This paper is also important because it points out that software engineering seems to have reached a plateau of results and has been stuck there for some time. Thus the agents approach is potentially very important.

However, we find the AOSE explanations lacking in the detail that would allow a software engineer to decide easily whether an AOSE approach was even being used or not. We describe *Agent-Based Software Engineering* (ABSE) here as a refinement of some aspects of AOSE, based upon our practical experience in agent building. We do not, though, attempt to describe how to practice ABSE. Our goal is rather show that ABSE could be distinguished objectively from other software techniques, which has not previously been done.

This is a topic that is frequently addressed with respect to languages. In fact, in the abstract of a recent paper on agent languages, M. Wooldridge said his intent was to develop "a semantics where conformance (or otherwise) to the semantics could be *determined by the independent observer*" [20]. Whether something is an agent or not, and whether a software engineering technology is agent-based or not, should also be verifiable by independent observers.

Further, we attempt to persuade the user that ABSE could be useful in practice and why, apart from the general potential of emergent behavior. We emphasize some particular aspects of agent models and languages that distinguish agent system development from other software technologies and make it useful. Our intent is to help bridge the gap between agent technology and software engineering.

1.1 Semantics-based Agenthood

Describing agent development requires distinguishing agents from other kinds of software. Unfortunately, definitions of agents most often differentiate the technology from other software technologies by anthromophising agents: ascribing human cognitive traits such as environmental awareness, autonomy, and intelligence. The AOSE view has its foundations in Yoav Shoham's "*Agent-Oriented Programming (AOP)*"[14] in which it is advocated that agents be directly programmed in terms of the mentalistic, intentional notions of agent theories. Similarly, Rao and Georgeff developed the "beliefs", "desires", and "intensions" (BDI)[13] theory of agenthood and developed both formalisms and programming technologies based on them. We call this a *semantic* view because it usually requires ascribing some meaning to the operation of each agent.

And while this early work was formal with distinct software technologies, it is clear that the difficult objectives of creating a programming environment were not completely reached. The programming languages and compilers generated were not generally useful. It has been critiqued as unhelpful by people attempting to use the technology[10]. But more important, this formal work has very limited scope in agent building, much as formal software methods in general have. Since useful languages and compilers were not forthcoming, proponents of agent technologies spoke more of the general characteristics of agents and how that influenced software practices.

These informal descriptions of agents as "autonomous" and "proactive" are useful. Courses on agents, such as "Intelligent Agents" [3], cover much important technical material. For instance, if one intends that agents follow goals without a lot of specific instructions, then one has to turn to the most sophisticated learning, planning, non-monotonic reasoning, and distributed constraint satisfaction techniques that have been developed by the Artificial Intelligence community. This is in fact the most important aspect of agents *per se*: that they perform such sophisticated reasoning, especially in collaboration with each other so that the desired behavior is emergent rather than specifically programmed.

But the less formal AOSE recent work does not describe mentalistic, intentional notions of agenthood in a way that would permit an objective observer to distinguish agents from other software technologies, at least not without a lot of persuasive discussion in each case. Shoham's definition of an agent as "an entity whose state is viewed as consisting of mental components such as beliefs, capabilities, choices, and commitments", and the similar BDI descriptions, are of little help in objectively defining agents apart from their specific formalisms. And it does not help to focus on one narrow theory of agents, such as BDI, as this tends not to generalize to a software engineering practice or methodology.

The informal interpretation of mentalistic agent theories is not sufficient to distinguish agent technology from other software technologies, much less provide practical specific techniques for agent building that would constitute *software engineering*. It is at least arguable that, say, object-oriented programming, could be used to implement non-monotonic reasoning, for instance, as well as any other. More to the point, how would one know if one is using agent technology as a software technique? The distinguishing factor cannot be just that the program can be interpreted as exhibiting a kind of autonomy using various sophisticated algorithms. This view of agents says nothing about programming practice, much less software engineering.

However, consider the use of AI techniques in building agents. At one time, "what is AI?" was an oft-asked question. The answer eventually turned out to be that AI was the use of AI techniques. This was a seemingly circular definition but it came to be accepted because they was a definite set of techniques that was developed by researchers and departments explicitly identified as "AI". The same idea can be used in the case of agents. It may be that emergent behavior system design is in its infancy, but based on experience, we can identify several general but distinguishing characteristics of agent software technology.

1.2 Agent Theory Modeling

The BDI theory is portrayed primarily in AOSE as a means of guiding agent software development. But BDI is only one type of agent semantics and to consider only it misses the abstraction of imposing any *agent theory* during development. This is especially important when one is converting legacy code into an agent capable of working with other agents to carry out a distributed computation. What one does in this case is to interpret the workings of the legacy code as an instance of a BDI theory that is then used as the common model upon which agent interactions are based, and which is thus the basis for the integration of the software components.

The Agent-Objection-Relationship model of [17] (similar to other work reported in this volume) is a clear example of an agent model, based more on entity-relationship models than on BDI, used for application-building. In our set of engineering applications, the *ProcessLink* framework used the *Redux* theory of design to characterize the acts of the engineering agents[12]. The Redux theory is quite different from the BDI theory and not at all anthromorphic. However, both are used in modeling: translation from legacy code into agent interactions.

The case is not that different with agents that are built "from scratch" rather than being legacy code conversions. One has a computation in mind and is then is careful to code it so that it ultimately conforms to the agent theory, whether it be BDI or Redux. Another example is Tate's O-Plan[16], which is similar to Redux in many respects, which was used in agents with the "Act" formalism[9].

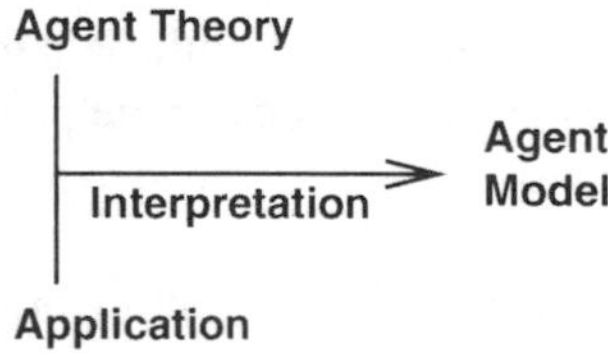

Fig. 1. Agent-based Modeling

As illustrated in Figure 1, the common characteristic of agent-based systems is that some agent theory is interpreted for some application to produce an agent model used for application development. This modeling is characteristic of many, if not all, agent systems, such as WARREN[1] (information ontology imposed on a BDI model), TIE-97[18] (O-Plan and Act), ProcessLink (Redux), and others. All of the ones referenced here are based on some version of hierarchical planning formalisms. For example, WARREN presumes a formal model in which goals are planed, actions to achieve them are scheduled, and execution of the actions is monitored. The links between goals and actions are further formalized, complete with constraints on action scheduling that further guides the development of the agents. The O-Plan and Act formalisms are even more detailed. Redux falls somewhere in between in complexity.

Thus, in both legacy code conversion and the pure agent development, for at least a very important class of agents, *agent construction is partially characterized by a modeling based on a common agent theory.*

1.3 Syntax-based Development

Jenning's ABSE paper[6], based largely upon [7], is also largely lacking in the detail necessary for objective determination of agent-based software engineering, with one important exception. Jennings, as have many others, notes that agents "have their own persistent thread of control" and notes later that this enables agents to select their actions based on "the agent's actual state of affairs". In comparison to remote procedure calls and the similar message passing of object-oriented programming, this is an important distinction, though it is frequently obscured with talk of "self-awareness".

Agents maintain state. This means that they can potentially model themselves and others, as Huhns points out. But the more important point, computationally, is that the response to a query or function call may be based not just on the state conveyed by the caller, but also based upon other information maintained by the agent from dynamic information sources. However, while this may distinguish agent technology from an important class of remote procedure calls, it does not distinguish it from, say, database queries against a database server with its own active thread of control. More important, it is difficult to objectively determine the state of "state". Something more is required.

While Shoham, Jennings, Wooldridge, and many others take the anthropomorphic semantic view of agents, this contrasts directly with the view of Genesereth and Ketchpel in which the distinguishing characteristic is the use of an Agent Communications Language (ACL)[4]. This alternative view is *syntactic* in that it only requires one to know something about the form of the communication among the software modules that are agent candidates. We have previously elaborated on this syntactic view by giving an operational definition for at least one type of agent: *typed-message agents*[11].

Our contribution was to add that if the computation could be performed just as well by a client-server architecture and protocol, then there is no need to call the software components "agents". The *requirement for a peer-to-peer protocol* is really a thesis that this objective indicator corresponds to the otherwise subjectively determined autonomous nature of agents, which maintain their own thread of control and state. This syntactic protocol and behavioral view requires no subjective interpretation in order to decide agenthood. And it clearly distinguishes agents not only from remote procedure calls, but also from databases that do not volunteer information and work with client-server protocols. Admittedly, one must additionally be able to evaluate whether the distributed computation being performed by the agents is better in one case or another, but we argue that without this degree of evaluation, one can say little about the efficacy of either agents or software engineering methods.

This distinction between a syntactic approach to agent definition, which permits an objective distinction between agent software and other kinds, and the semantic approach of ascribing mentalistic characteristics to some software models, is often conflated. For instance, in[17], it is asserted that one difference between the objects in Object-Oriented Programming and agents is that agents "can perceive events, perform actions, communicate, or make commitments. Objects are passive entities with no such capacities." Not only is this a claim that depends upon a subjective interpretation, the paper goes on immediately to point out that the distinction between ordinary object messages is that agent messages are typed. That is, the only objective difference between the two systems is that agent messages are typed, which is exactly the syntactic difference.

In addition to agent models, the language component of agent software plays an important role in development of agent-based systems. Typed-message agents communicate with inner and outer languages that characterizes most Agent Communication Languages (ACLs) today. So, after model translation, the other main ABSE task, for typed-message agents, is the development of the syntax for the outer and inner languages. In theory, this part of the development could require relatively little work. One could use one of the existing outer language ACL standards, like KQML or FIPA ACL, and then use KIF as the inner language, as KIF has all of the expressive power ever likely to be required by any agent application.

This scenario is of course naive. The various ACLs have not converged on a single all-purpose set of performatives and syntax after several years of use. In fact, the long experience of KQML applications and the constant invention of new performatives suggests that trying to define a single set of performatives that everyone will use is either futile or fascist. Similarly, the very expressiveness of KIF makes it sufficiently difficult to use that simpler inner languages are often developed for particular applications.

However, one only needs universal syntax if one really expects a universe of universal agents independently developed with different tools to speak the same language. But this (perhaps overly) ambitious goal is not necessary for agents to be a valuable software tool. And it is also likely that the more universal standards will be the exchange of HTML and XML documents via email and similar standard protocols more prosaic than multi-agent systems that typically are constructed to support some distributed but bounded complex computation. This does not mean that agent languages are not a useful methodology. And their ubiquitous use means that *agent technology is characterized by an ACL and inner language.*

2 ABSE Characteristics and Utility

Previously we have discussed some characteristics of at least a large class of agent systems: that they are based on agent theories, an ACL, and an agent inner language. We also require that the result be an agent system in the sense of requiring a peer-to-peer protocol. These are characteristics that can be objectively determined. We now describe how those characteristics map to characteristics of software engineering for agent systems.

2.1 Using Models for Control

Formalisms for agent control are obviously useful for the development of emergent behavior systems. The Distributed Artificial Intelligence community has been working on such formalisms for a number of years and the problems are far from resolved. This remains a research topic, characterized by Shoham's current economics and decision theoretic work[15]. This is indeed the crucial research topic, but since it is still research, it is difficult to make a claim that such control formalisms are characteristic of agent software development in general.

But we can claim that the formalisms in use today reduce the complexity of the agent interactions in some respect, and thus facilitate the engineering of emergent behavior, in addition to providing a guide for system development. If we look at the formal information ontology and architecture used for WARREN and other multi-agent systems, the planning and scheduling functions clearly organize the behaviors of the various information agents. Indeed, the agents can also monitor their own behavior and decide to clone themselves to offload work.

Another example is Redux. Given a constraint violation, Redux can advise, upon request, the logically consistent solutions to the problem. Further, Redux monitors the state of problem solving. If an agent attempts to make a move in the solution space that will cause a repetition of a cycle of moves by other agents, Redux will reply with a "SORRY" message and refuse the change in order to prevent thrashing of distributed design decisions. Moreover, Redux will tell designers when changes by other designers affect previously made decisions, even advising them to reconsider previously discarded choices.

This is not to say that these control functions could not be done with some other programming environment. But *ABSE is characterized by the commitment to some formal agent theory that reduces the complexity of anticipating the interactions of the agents for the programmer.*

2.2 Using Models and Languages as Guidelines

Modeling provides a template for agent development. It defines that kinds of conversations the agent could possibly have and thus what functions the programmer should provide. It is especially important for the transformation of legacy systems into agents. While this task necessarily requires a lot of intelligence on the part of the programmer, a model does provide a guide for the programmer.

For example, in Redux, a "decision" in a design problem consists of a "goal" and a result that is some non-empty conjunction of "subgoals" and "assignments". It is fairly easy for the programmer familiar with the Redux model to recognize what in the legacy code constitutes a decision being made. For instance, in a program for defining an electrical cable configuration given the parts and electrical requirements, the goal is the text or data specifying these and the result is a set of assignments of connections. The programmer adds software to the legacy system that can shape this data into a well-formed message to be sent to the other agents in the computation. This will occur automatically (subject to optional input from the engineer solicited at runtime) every time a new configuration is generated by the engineer.

This modeling adds an important dimension to especially the AOSE decomposition and abstraction strategies. One does not have merely the agent top-level objective (noted in AOSE) as a guide in agent building: one has a more elaborate model in each case that guides development of the interaction of the agents in the system. *This commitment to a common formal theory to guide development is a distinguishing characteristic of ABSE.*

The ACL also provides a cognitive guide for the programmer in anticipating the *kinds* of interactions among the agents. Some of the research in this is designed to implement strong conversational models, such as [2]. But apart from such conversational models, the profusion of dialects of ACLs and inner languages is confirming evidence that the simple *concept of outer and inner languages is not only characteristic of ABSE but also useful*. For example, many developers notice immediately that they could just use the KQML performatives "ASK" and "TELL" together with whatever inner language they choose to develop for their application. But it is usually the case, as with the ProcessLink (Electronic Project Language) (EPL)[2], that one uses some of the other standard ACL performatives and adds new ones.

However, the inner language is typically much more application-dependent and not as useful a guide to the developer as is the more application-independent ACL.An example of a simple inner language occurs in WARREN. Here is an instance of a query on IBM earnings from the Dow Jones news:

```
(monitor
:SENDER barney
:RECEIVER news-agent
:LANGUAGE simple-query
:ONOTOLOGY news
:REPLY-WITH ibm-query-2
:NOTIFICATION-DEADLINE (30 minutes)
:CONTENT (query news
:CLAUSES
(= $newsgroups ''dow-jones.indust.earnings-projections'')
(= subject ''IBM'')
:OUTPUT :ALL) )
```

Notice that the ACL performative "monitor" is a type of well-defined interaction among various agents in the distributed application. It defines a whole class of actions that can occur among the agents. The inner language (":content") refers to more specific types of functions and data. The "monitor" accepts, as content, the keywords "query", "news" "clauses", and "output". Further, "clauses" takes a particular set of feature/variable value assignments. The performative "monitor" is independent of the particular queries being made. *The commitment to some ACL in defining possible interactions and an inner language where domain-specific functions and data are specified is characteristic of ABSE.*

Figure 2 illustrates the basic three ingredients in agent construction, ignoring, for now the communications software. The agent theory is used to model the application. The theory is used to model the specific operations of the application. The ACL guides the formation of the basic agent interactions, and the inner language reflects the basic data exchange and functions. These elements help guide the system developer and also provide a measure of indirect control over the subsequent behavior of the agents.

The fact that one can apply a common theory to several components of an application, as well as at least an ACL, means that ABSE is also a way of integrating legacy applications. Not only can one "wrap" legacy code so that it corresponds to some programming methodology, such as objects, but the wrapping code further should also correspond to some common theory, which provides an extra "glue" for the integration. In our example systems, for instance, TIE97-1 agents included several agents developed at different sites in different countries. Redux has been used to integrate various engineering software in multiple disciplines. WARREN integrates agents working in multiple domains with different expertise and data sources.

---

[2] http://www-cdr.stanford.edu/ProcessLink/protocol/EPL-syntax.html

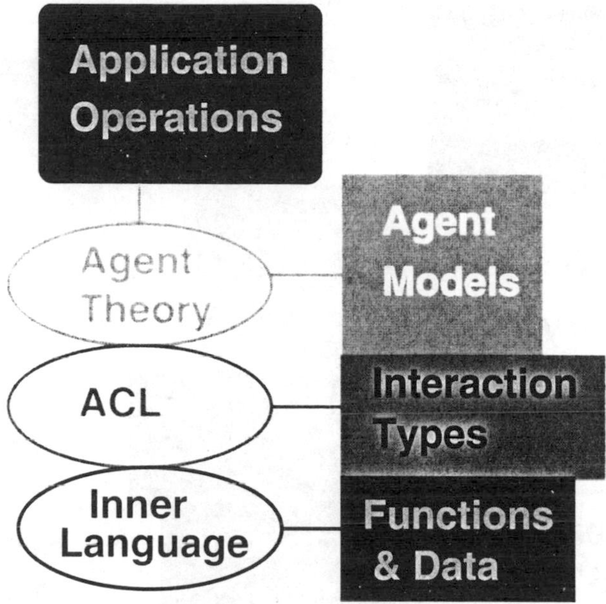

Fig. 2. Agent-based Construction Layers

2.3 Stratifying Rates of Change

The common model, ACL, and inner language are also useful because they allow the developer to stratify the change inherent in the development and maintenance of software systems. If one has designed the agent system well, then the model translation should be changed rarely if at at all, since this is the most difficult and fundamental change.

The set of performatives that comprise the ACL may change more often than the model translation and are, in an agent system, easier to change. Modifying an existing performative, or adding a new one, means changing the parsing of the syntax and possibly calling new functions. A well-designed set of performatives, for the class of applications, will change infrequently.

The inner language provides a more domain-task oriented language in which most of the development and maintenance change for a given application can occur.

As illustrated by Figure 3, changes in the translation into the agent model are fundamental. The degree of difficulty in managing such change in the agent system can be severe. However, typically, if the modeling has been done in an intelligent fashion, these changes are rare.

Since the ACL determines the kinds of interactions that can occur, changes in the ACL may be major, especially if a new performative is introduced. A well-designed ACL will introduce such change infrequently, though inevitably. The inner language provides a layer where change is more frequent but can be handled with less difficulty, realizing no change is trivial in any programming endeavor. In the last two cases, change

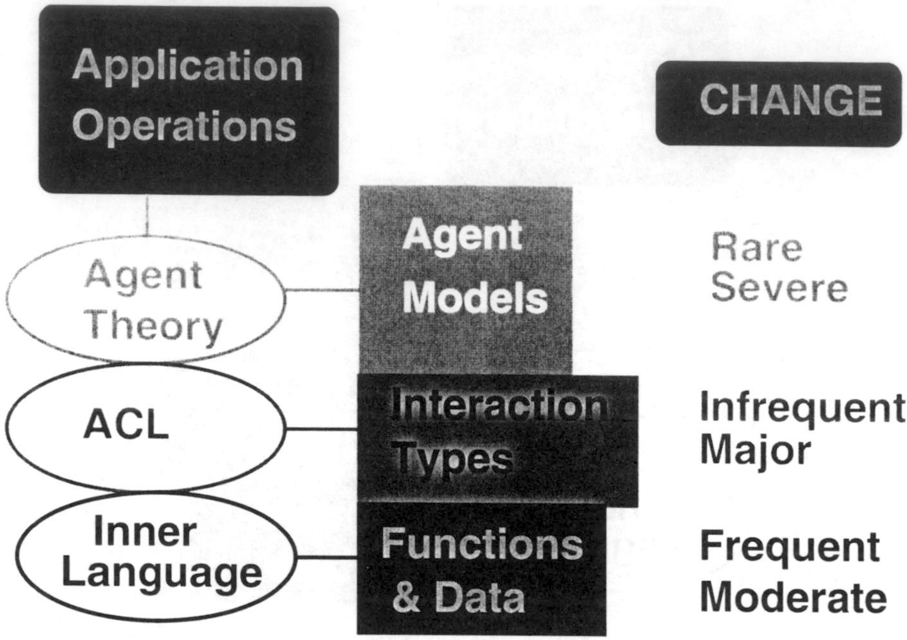

Fig. 3. Change Stratification

is largely communicated by changing the syntax of the languages - either in keywords, values allowed, or more complex changes.

ABSE is thus largely based on the syntax of the ACL and inner language. This means, unlike most other types of software, that message parsing is an intensive run-time computation. Apart from performance, this has a significant impact on distributed development.

Our own development methodology for ProcessLink reflects this. Each of the members of the development team "owns" and agent and may decide independently to change its functionality. However, the interface to each agent is defined by the set of messages it sends and receives and is documented on the web, which messages collectively describe the ProcessLink EPL. This means that the syntax of the ACL or the inner language is changed. Changes to the ACL are usually discussed beforehand in the group as these constitute part of the "jointly-owned" language. Changes to the inner-language are done first and the other team members notified of the change by email, with instructions to see the new web documentation.

2.4 Message-based Collaborative Change and Debugging

Debugging tools for agent systems are generally lacking with a few exceptions. On the other hand, the message-based nature of ABSE naturally provides some debugging functions. This is especially true for applications such as ours that is characterized by asynchronous message exchange among the software agents in which the response time may range from one second to over a day because the software agents depend heavily upon human response time and analysis. This is in contrast to agent applications in which the agents interact in real time without human intervention. The debugging characteristics described below may not be as useful in such applications.

There are three main aspects of agent messages that facilitate ABSE:

- Programming collaboration can occur at a common language level without requiring a common programming language.
- Application-level error messages are not generated by the programming language compilers (though this of course also occurs) but by the agents and their parsers, which provide useful information and quick fixes.
- With a store-and-forward message routing mechanism, message-based interactions provide new methods for debugging.

In ABSE, the programming of individual agents is well-separated from the collaborative programming. Individual agents may be written in the conventional programming language of choice - anything from Java to Smalltalk to Lisp. The collaborative programming is not done in any conventional programming language but rather in the shared ACL and inner language inherited and then refined during development using parsers. This means that there are no compiler constraints or messages of any sort generated by the system except for parser and network software failures, which are not at the level of the shared collaboration. *At the collaborative level, all messages are determined by the programmers,* including error messages.

If another team member does not change their parser to reflect the new syntax, if required, than an important feature of the language-based nature of ABSE is called into play. The parser of the agent receiving the new message will reject the message as being syntactically incorrect. It will return a standard "ERROR" message that includes the string that was not understood. For instance, one can type almost any string and send it to Redux and receive an error message with no code breakage. If one simply types a message with the performative "strange", one receives in reply an "ERROR" message with the text, in the inner language, "Performative 'strange' was unknown to Redux." Or the particular field in the inner language may be wrong: "ERROR RdxType was - *strange*" or even a particular syntax element was wrong: "ERROR in content parsing: content did not end with &. Last value parsed was 'weird'." Or "ERROR in content parsing: no match on any keyword for token 'badsyntax'." These last two illustrate how easy it is to get helpful information almost for free from the parser. It is also easy to have the agents note whether it was an ACL or inner language problem and include other helpful information. The agents do not break and the developers have a clear idea at runtime of the problem.

Some syntactic errors may also be treated the same way as are requests that cannot be fulfilled. Given a message that requires a response or an action, an agent may reply with a "SORRY" message indicating that for some reason, which may be given, the agent cannot properly process the message. This may be because of task data values, the state of problem solving, or even an unrecognized performative. For example, Redux may tell a designer, in the text part of the inner language, that the request to make a particular design decision cannot be fulfilled: " Sorry, this decision is inadmissible. Cause: the fact (IOU-2 is unavailable) is believed." A set of other examples follows:

- SORRY: Process-Controller cannot achieve goal of "schedule-meeting" Constraint-Manager reports "over-constrained"
- SORRY: Ticket-Agent does not understand query "best cost"
- SORRY: You do not have authority to reject decision Use-DOU. Only Optical-Designer can make that change.

Again, the agents do not break, the developers are provided with valuable information at runtime, and the agents can be easily modified to include as much information as desired in such problem messages.

There are many other examples of the ways in which agent messages are valuable for debugging and which use the standard ERROR and SORRY messages. Obviously, because these problem messages are part of the agent software, developers are free to include as much information as may be desired. Because the messages are parsed, providing such information is facilitated.

Agent messages also have other attributes that contribute to debugging. For instance, agents may be programmed to decide not to process a message because the the sender does not have the right authority. For example, Redux may tell a designer, in the text part of the inner language, " Sorry, but you do not have the authority to reject this decision.".

This is easy to determine since "SENDER" is a standard part of ACL syntax. Similarly, if there is a problem in even finding the correct name of the agent to be contacted, it is a simple matter to interpret the SORRY or ERROR messages from the agent name-server, request a list of all valid agents, and then use that information to find the right agent. These sorts of actions are quite typical of agent development, apart from any notions of automatic agent message routing based on content. The point here is that it is very easy to produce agents that degrade gracefully and provide as much information as desirable for development.

The message-based characteristic of agents can also help with debugging if a store-and-forward infrastructure, like that of the JATLite agent message router[8], is used. If a particular agent is having difficulty processing a sequence or set of messages from other agents, those other agents can be taken off-line and the set of messages replayed until the behavior of the agent is correct. We have found this capability to be very useful for debugging and it is dependent upon the unique message-passing nature of agents.

The message-based nature also facilitates runtime error correction. The engineering applications addressed by ProcessLink are long-lived and agent software may die or move during the project, which is characterized by asynchronous communications about design changes over a period of weeks. Errors in message processing are handled the same way as other agent errors or changes. The offending message is rejected by the agent with a "SORRY" or "ERROR" message that typically results in a message being sent to the developer of the sending agent.

At this point, the developers can decide whether the problem is in the sending agent, the receiver, or perhaps another. Now a change is made. If this should result in a different message being sent, the receiving agent simply deletes the last message from the message queue, maintained by the JATLite router, and awaits a new message. If the change is in the way the receiving agent should process the original message, it simply reconnects to the router using the new code and re-processes the original message, which has not been deleted. The computation then proceeds. There is no great

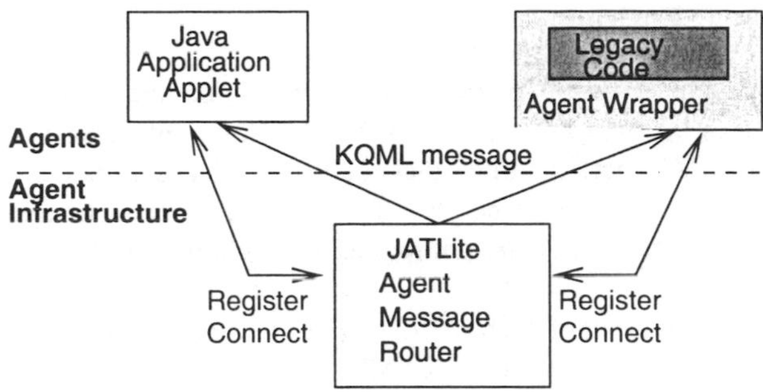

Fig. 4. JAT Agent Message Router

difference between correcting an error during development and during the application execution.

There is another important debugging benefit that can be derived from the asynchronous feature of agent messages if a JATLite-like store-and-forward router is used. Figure 4 illustrates the store-and-forward mechanism of the JATLite Agent Message Router (AMR). All messages go through the AMR and are then sent to the designated recipient. The messages are stored until the recipient signals they should be deleted. Since all messages go through a central point, one can use this characteristic for debugging.

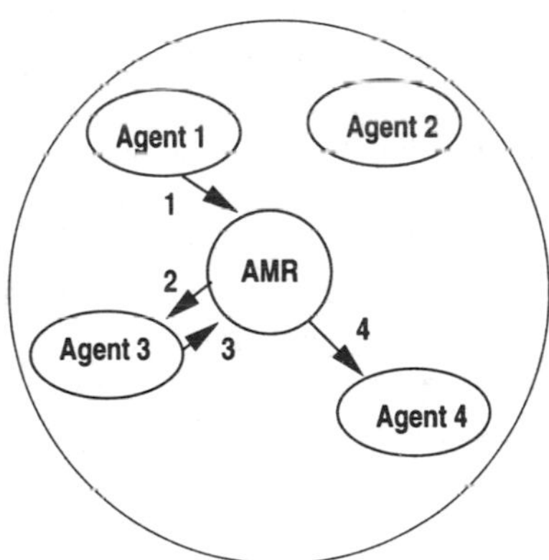

Fig. 5. Single-Stepping Message Delivery

One can build an administrative "agent", as illustrated in Figure 5, that displays the sending and receiving of messages among the agents. Further, since this agent is really a GUI applet tied to the router, one can use it to order the router to "single-step" message transfer and inspect the messages under a variety of conditions, based on regular expression matching on the ACL fields. This kind of debugging is important for system development but is only possible with a store-and-forward router.

2.5 Programming Environment

Since the models themselves are, or should be, general and ubiquitously applicable for many problems, they become a reusable basis for development. A well-designed system also identifies those ACL performatives that can be used largely unchanged not only for the life of a particular application but also for some large class of applications. This set of reusable agents and language components provides a high-level programming toolkit.

There is a well-known set of such performatives that occur and re-occur in different ACLs such as KQML and FIPA, such as "ASK", "TELL", "SORRY", "ERROR" and "REPLY". There are others that have yet to become standard. One we have discovered is the ProcessLink performative "TRACE". This performative, similar to the WARREN performative "monitor", is a request from one agent to another to track the status of an object: changes in values of particular properties or any at all. This is particularly useful for easily interfacing agents. Here is the (partial) BNF for the legal inner language component of this particular
performative:
```
:content := ''(''
   RdxType ''|'' <string> ''&''
   TargetName ''|'' <string> ''&''
   (AgentToNotify ''|'' <string>''&'')
```
where "RdxType" can be one of several types of objects in the Redux ontology. Other agents can respond with information about objects in their own ontology.

As an example in our application, the Redux agent tracks the validity of "constraints" while the Constraint Manager performs constraint satisfaction on those same constraints. Therefore, Redux should tell the Constraint Manager each time the validity of a constraint changes, among other things. Redux could be hard-coded to do so, requiring not only a check to see if there was an agent named "Constraint Manager" in the application, but also requiring that there be only one such Constraint Manager with the special name.

By using "TRACE", more than one Constraint Manager can dynamically make a request to Redux to track constraints, with no special hard coding other than the general ability to do the tracking. The Redux agent simply notes the name of the requesting agent and adds the request to the list of things to track. Notifications are then sent to the requesting agent as the object properties change with subsequent messages and computations. Adding a new agent means only that the new agent should send Redux a "TRACE" request. Integration does not require rewriting any Redux code. Notice also that both the characteristics of using an ACL and of agents having names make this capability possible.

The other characteristic of multi-agent systems that makes this kind of integration work is that the agents themselves are reusable. The Redux and Constraint Manger agents are two examples of generic agents that provide general functions useful for a large class of engineering applications. Thus a "library" of reusable agents is acquired. WARREN provides another good example of highly reusable generic agents for a large class of applications. However, unlike, say FORTRAN subroutines, the functionality of these software components is quite complex and they can volunteer messages to other software components and users unexpectedly.

3 Summary

We have presented a set of characteristics that may be used to objectively differentiate ABSE from other software technologies. One objection might be that the determination of whether a theory or a language is an "agent" theory or language is not objective. We appeal to the previous definition of AI. Agent theories and languages are those that are explicitly defined to be such by their developers. But we can do even better for agent languages: we can specify that they consist of a typed outer language (with specific characteristics such as explicit representations of the the sender and receiver and errors) and an inner content language, and that the communication protocol be peer-to-peer as previously discussed.

We have not done the differentiation with respect to other software technologies explicitly. We realize that ABSE can be compared to object-oriented programming, for instance, in which messages are also passed via the Internet to distributed code components. Beyond saying that agent messages have the characteristics described that distinguish them from remote procedure calls, which object messages resemble, we leave the detailed comparison of characteristics to experts in all of the other various software engineering technologies. Our goal was only to make such a comparison possible by providing agent software technology characteristics that can be objectively determined. Coverage is outside the scope and expertise of this paper.

We do note that a software technology is defined and differentiated by its commitments. ABSE is characterized by *agent theory modeling, an ACL, and an inner language*. It is defined further by the features of those languages, including the reusable but changeable ACL and the fact that these are text messages handled by agent parsers, as well as requiring a peer-to-peer protocol. Parsing is indeed critical to the utility of using these languages, as described above.

An ACL also has a kernel of reusable performatives, such as "ASK" and "TELL" together with a standard syntax and fields, such as "SENDER", "RECEIVER", and "ONTOLOGY" that reflect particular commitments, such as always declaring the identity of the sender and committing to a conversational mode of interaction that allows any agent to refuse processing of any message and providing for "ERROR" and "SORRY" messages. The import of the latter is that, unlike most software development systems where such errors are incorporated into a lower level of the infrastructure, these messages are generated by the software agents and provide very useful information for system development.

Certainly any programming language and methodology could be used to develop a system with these same commitments, perhaps easily. For instance, one could use the notion of object-oriented programming in combination with agent modeling and language parsing. But if the commitments above are part of the methodology, then we have ABSE.

We have speculated here about the utility of ABSE based upon our experience. We find the useful features of the ABSE characteristics to be:

- use of agent modeling to reduce the complexity of managing the emergent collective behavior of the agents.
- programming guidelines provided by the agent models and the ACL,

- stratification of change into model translation, the ACL, and the inner language,
- programming collaboration based upon asynchronous text message parsing, including error messages, and
- programming tools based upon reusable agents and language components.

Model translation provides both a guide to the developer and an anchor for that part of the software that should change the least. The use of parsed languages for interaction provides for late runtime evaluation of the software that changes the most. Error messages are particularly useful in this regard. And the use of asynchronous messages, together with this parsing, provides for a new mode of collaborative development.

ABSE is probably also a prototyping technique. Once an agent system is working, probably the system would be more efficient if it were compiled into a standard programming language such as one of the object-oriented languages. The agents become objects that pass methods to one another, with no need for an ACL or inner language, or any of the standard syntax and fields, or the required parsers. Parsing is an interpretative computation and once the languages and agent interactions are fixed, there is no reason why these should not be converted into code. Indeed, ABSE is waiting for a production compiler as envisioned by Shoham in the early 90's.

Acknowledgments

The ProcessLink experience is based upon work with Prof. Mark Cutkosky, Theresa Webster, Heecheol Jeon, Sigrid Goldmann, and Andreas Raquet. Barbara Dellen and Harold Holz also contributed to these ideas, Holz being especially responsible for noting that ACL fields such as "SENDER" are a special commitment of agent systems.

References

1. Decker, K., Sycara, K., Pannu, A., and Williamson, M., "Designing Behaviors for Information Agents," **Proc. First Internat. Conf. on Autonomous Agents (AGENTS-97)**, February, 1997.
   See also http://www.cs.cmu.edu/~softagents/papers/autoag96.ps.gz.
2. R. Elio and A. Haddadi, "Abstract Models and Conversation Policies", **Proc. Workshop on Specifying and Implementing Conversation Policies**, Autonomous Agents'99 Conference, Seattle, May, 1999. See also http://www.boeing.com/special/agents99/elio_a.pdf.
3. B. Faltings, O. Belakdar, S. Willmott,"Intelligent Agents", CS course at EPFL, Lausanne, 2000. See also http://nrc.stanford.edu/~petrie/agents/falt.html.
4. M. Genesereth and S. Ketchpel, "Software Agents"qq, *Communications of the ACM*, **37** (7), July 1994. See also http://logic.stanford.edu/papers/agents.ps.
5. M. Huhns, "Interaction-Oriented Programming", in this volume.
6. N. R. Jennings, "On Agent-Based Software Engineering", *Artificial Intelligence* **117** (2000), pp. 277-296, Elsevier Press, April, 2000.
7. N. R. Jennings, and M. Wooldridge "Agent-Oriented Software Engineering" in **Handbook of Agent Technology**, (ed. J. Bradshaw) AAAI/MIT Press, 2000.
   See also ftp://ftp.elec.qmw.ac.uk/pub/isag/distributed-ai/publications/agt-handbook.pdf.
8. H. Jeon, C. Petrie, and M/ R. Cutkosky, "JAT*Lite*: A Java Agent Infrastructure with Message Routing," *IEEE Internet Computing*, Mar/Apr 2000. See also http://www-cdr.stanford.edu/ProcessLink/papers/jat/jat.html.

9. K. L. Myers and D. E. Wilkins, "The Act Formalism", Version 2.2, SRI International Artificial Intelligence Center, Menlo Park, CA, September 1997.
See also http://www.ai.sri.com/~act/act-spec.ps.
10. D. Parks, "Agent-Oriented Programming : A Practical Evaluation", http://www.cs.berkeley.edu/~davidp/cs263/, 1997.
11. C. Petrie, "Agent-Based Engineering, the Web, and Intelligence", *IEEE Expert*, December, 1996. See also http://cdr.stanford.edu/NextLink/Expert.html.
12. C. Petrie, S. Goldmann, and A. Raquet, "Agent-Based Project Management", **Lecture Notes in AI 1600** pp. 339-362, Springer-Verlag, 1999.
See also http://cdr.stanford.edu/ProcessLink/papers/DPM/dpm.html.
13. A. S. Rao and M. P. Georgeff, "BDI agents: From theory to practice," Tech. Rep. 56, Australian Artificial Intelligence Institute, Melbourne, Australia, April 1995.
14. Y. Shoham, Y., "Agent-Oriented Programming" *Artificial Intelligence*, **60** (1), pp. 51-92, 1993.
15. "Control and Coordination of Multiple Agents through Decision Theoretic and Economics Methods", project. See also
http://coabs.globalinfotek.com/coabs_public/project_overview_pages/stanford.html.
16. A. Tate, B. Drabble, and J. Dalton, "The Open Planning Architecture and its Application to Logistics", in **Advanced Planning Technology** (ed. A.Tate), pp. 257-264, AAAI Press, 1996.
See also ftp://ftp.aiai.ed.ac.uk/pub/documents/1996/96-arpi-oplan-and-logistics.ps.
17. G. Wagner, "Agent-Oriented Analysis and Design of Organizational Information Systems", in **Proc. of Fourth IEEE International Baltic Workshop on Databases and Information Systems**, Vilnius (Lithuania), May 2000.
See also http://www.inf.fu-berlin.de/~wagnerg/BalticDB2000.ps.
18. The DARPA/Rome Laboratory Planning Initiative,
http://www.ai.sri.com/~wilkins/mpa/tie-97.html.
19. M. Wooldridge, and N. R. Jennings "Software Engineering with Agents: Pitfalls and Pratfalls" in *IEEE Internet Computing,* **3** (3), May/June 1999.
20. M. Wooldridge, "Verifiable Semantics for Agent Communication Languages", in **Proc. of ICMAS98**, pp. 349-356, IEEE Computer Society Press, May, 1998.

Software Architecture Attributes of Multi-agent Systems

Onn Shehory

IBM Research Lab in Haifa, the Tel-Aviv Site
IBM Building, 2 Weizmann St.
Tel-Aviv 61336, Israel
onn@il.ibm.com

Abstract. Multi-Agent Systems (MAS) introduce a unique software architecture style. MAS developed to date have several common architectural characteristics, even though differences in their design and implementation result in variations in their strengths and weaknesses. In this paper we study software-architectural properties of MAS to support the assessment of their suitability to the solution of computational problems. We present three MAS case-studies to demonstrate architectural properties and their effect on system functionality.

1 Introduction

Multi-Agent Systems (MAS), combining Distributed Artificial Intelligence (DAI) and software engineering, suggest solutions to highly distributed problems in dynamically changing and uncertain, open computational domains. It is increasingly understood that MAS have an important role as a software engineering approach, as suggested by the papers in this volume. Researchers in the field have developed agent-oriented methodologies that allow for agent and MAS specification and verification (e.g., [21]), design and analysis (e.g., [12]), and re-use (e.g., [2]). Although agents are already seen as a software engineering paradigm [8], the merit of *multi-agent systems* as a software architecture style [15] was only partly studied. In this paper we do not attempt to propose a new methodology or architecture. Instead, we examine architectural characteristics of multi-agent systems (and not the internal architecture of single agents) via a comparison between existing MAS architectures. We review commonalities and differences in the design and implementation of the MAS and the resulting strengths and weaknesses. MAS design research usually addresses issues such as the development of MAS, either from scratch, using agent specification and verification methodologies, or by re-use of existing MAS, to solve a given problem (e.g., in [7]). We examine MAS mainly with respect to their software architecture attributes such as robustness, flexibility and adaptability, code re-usability, etc. It is necessary to study the relation between the architecture of a MAS and its functionality to provide information upon which one may decide both whether a MAS may be an appropriate computational solution to given a problem, and if so, what type of MAS provides the most appropriate solution for this problem.

From a Software Architecture (SA) viewpoint, MAS are systems comprised from components, called agents. The agents are usually autonomous, where autonomy refers to a component not depending on the properties or the states of other components for its functionality. The components of the multi-component system are able to interact, usually by passing messages in a pre-defined high-level protocol (agent communication language, e.g., KQML [3]). In contrast to distributed object architectures (CORBA [13]), it is commonly assumed that no direct function call or implicit event invocation between the (component) agents are allowed. In particular, the autonomy of an agent a means that a has the sole control over the activation of its service and may refuse to provide it, or ask for a (monetary) compensation.

Solution design for computational problems is based on problem analysis, in an attempt to recognize typical patterns. These are compared to similar patterns of known SAs. Applying an appropriate SA will reduce the development time and increase the efficiency and adequacy of the solution. Due to their unique suitability to several classes of computational problems, it is important to characterize MAS as an SA style and to study their architectural properties. This may provide a family of solutions for highly distributed problems in open, heterogeneous, dynamic and information-rich environments. In this paper we make a first step in this direction.

1.1 Introduction to Software Architecture

The design and specification of overall system structure becomes dominant in software systems development as their size and complexity increase. Software architecture, a discipline within software engineering, discusses such issues. At the abstract level, SA involves the description of components from which systems are comprised, the interaction among these components and the patterns according to which the components are combined to form the whole system. At the practical level, SA refers to the design and specification of issues such as component decomposition and organization, communication protocols, control and data flow and structure, synchronization, etc. To differentiate between architectural styles, SA usually employs a common framework. The framework we adopt is based on treating a system as a collection of components and a set of interactions between these components. The framework determines what the components that construct instances of the architecture style are and constraints on the ways of combining them, e.g., constraints on the topology of the system. Once the framework is used to describe styles and systems, one can have a better understanding of the underlying computational model. This can be used to sort out the essentials of the style. It also supports comparison between styles and between systems within the style, thus evaluating advantages and drawbacks of the style.

1.2 MAS Terminology

MAS lack agreed upon terminology for describing systems, components and the relationships between them. We define several terms to be used in this paper.

- *Agent architecture:* describes the modules from which a single agent is comprised, the relationships between, and the interactions among these modules. For example, agents (in the context of MAS) usually have a communication module to enhance communication with users and other agents [16]. Some types of agents also have a planning module. Commonly, incoming messages arriving at the communication module affect the planning module by some connection (and with some restrictions), and the planning module may create outgoing messages to be handled by the communication module.

- *Multi-agent organization:* describes the way in which multiple agents are organized to form a MAS. Relationships and interactions among the agents and specific roles of agents within the organization are the focus of multi-agent organization. The agent architecture is not part of the multi-agent organization (although inter-relations between the two are common). For instance, agents may be organized in a fixed hierarchy, where the inter-relations are pre-defined, thus reducing the need to locate others and reason about them and the amount of communication necessary for system functioning.
- *Multi-agent infrastructure:* describes the agent architecture and the multi-agent organization, and possibly the dependencies between the two (when present), thus providing an infrastructure that enables constructing domain-specific MAS. The infrastructure may (and usually does) include services that enhance MAS activity and organization. Examples are agent naming service (ANS), agent location service (e.g. directory service), etc.
- *Multi-agent infrastructure services:* include services that are provided with the MAS infrastructure to support a variety of system needs. The following services may be found (or are desired) in MAS:
  - System design and development tools (e.g., agent editor, syntax checkers, system correctness verification tools).
  - System (dynamic) organizational activity enhancement such as agent location and coordination mechanisms (e.g., middle agents).
  - Tools for increasing system efficiency in resource utilization (e.g., mobility enhancement).
  - Agent and MAS activation, interfacing and testing tools.
  - Securing transactions of information, code and goods (via, e.g., security protocols).

The terms above will be used and elaborated upon in the following sections.

2 MAS Architectural Attributes

Using the terms above, we present and evaluate architectural properties of MAS. This presentation should allow for comparison between, and assessment of, different MAS infrastructures. Based on the attributes presented here we later present three MAS case studies, where we describe and analyze these MAS.

2.1 Agent Internal Architecture

In the last decade, a large number of agent architectures were introduced by both researchers and developers. When referring to agent architectures in the context of multi-agent systems, this number drops dramatically. In this work we discuss agent architectures only in the context of MAS. The types of agents that can be incorporated into

MAS include components that allow them for interaction with other agents and users (e.g., a communication component). However, regardless of their internal architecture, agents should be able to perform tasks or provide services. Ideally, one would prefer all the details of an agent's architecture to be hidden from other agents and users. This would allow entities with which the agent interacts to assume some capability of the agent and some interaction protocols, but will prevent the need that they know what methods and components are employed by the agent to perform its tasks. To date, this is only partly achieved, as research on MAS interoperation suggests [5].

2.2 Multi-Agent Organization

Broadly speaking, MAS are organized in one of the following ways: hierarchy, flat organization (sometimes referred to as democracy), subsumption, and a modular organization. Hybrids of these and dynamic changes from one organization style to another are also possible, though not very common in implemented MAS (probably due to the complexity of implementing dynamic re-organization). We summarize below the properties of these MAS organizational models.

Hierarchical MAS (e.g., federated MAS) are organized such that agents can only communicate subject to the hierarchical structure. The advantages of this restriction is that there is no need for a mechanism for agent location. In addition, the hierarchical structure significantly reduces communication in the system. Disadvantageous is the strict structure, which prohibits dynamic re-organization to best fit the needs of specific tasks. Also, hierarchy usually implies that the lower levels depend on the higher levels, and higher level may even be in partial or full control of the lower levels. This may be in contrast to a requirement for agent autonomy and self-interest. A hierarchical organization may also imply a somewhat centralized control. This is undesirable in systems which are comprised from components that belong to different organizations, and possibly geographically distributed.

Flat Organization of a MAS implies that each agent can directly contact any other agent. No fixed structure is applied on the system, however agents may dynamically form structures to perform specific tasks. In addition, no control of one agent by another is assumed. Such an organization requires either a closed system, so that each agent knows about all others ahead of time, or (when the system is open) an agent location mechanism must be provided as part of the infrastructure. A flat organization is advantageous since it fully supports autonomy and self-interest of agents as well as distribution and openness of MAS. It also allows for dynamic adjustments of the MAS organization to changes in tasks and environment. These openness and dynamism, however, result in communication overheads, the need for agent location mechanisms as well as mechanisms for dynamic MAS re-organization. The amount of reasoning (and computation) an agent performs with regards to other agents increases significantly in a flat organization.

Subsumption refers to MAS where some agents are components of other agents. These agents are subsumed by the container agents, which in turn may be components of larger container agents. The subsumption model is somewhat similar to the hierarchical model, however it takes it to the extreme by requiring that the subsumed agents completely surrender to the control of the container agent. From a software architectural viewpoint, such architecture resembles an inclusion of objects within a larger object, except for the (important) difference in the control methods. While objects are usually controlled and activated by (possibly remote) procedure call or event invocation, agents are activated by high-level communication. The strict control relationships in the subsumption organization results in efficient tasks execution and low communication overhead, however restricts the system to address a well defined set of tasks, with virtually no flexibility and adaptability. It is also not simple to modify a subsumption MAS (e.g., add a new component) in the face of long-term changes in tasks and environment of the system.

Modular MAS organization referes to MAS which are comprised from several modules, where each is virtually a stand-alone MAS. Typically, the partition of the system into modules is done along dimensions such as geographical vicinity or a need for intense interaction among agents and services within the same module. Often, the system is comprised of such parts as a result of its development process, during which new modules were gradually added to an already existing system. Modularity increases efficiency of task execution and reduces communication overhead. Also, within each module high flexibility, similar to flat organization flexibility, is usually enabled. On the other hand, re-organization across modules is rather complex, thus flexibility is limited. In addition, the given modularity implies constraints on inter-module communication.

Other properties play a role in MAS architecture and affect their performance. Among them are communication structures and protocols, degree of system openness, level of flexibility, infrastructure services, system robustness and code reusability. These are discussed below.

Communication Multiple MAS use a specially designed communication protocol, that best fits their agent architecture, MAS organization and the typical tasks of these systems. The advantage of such protocols is in their efficiency. Such systems, however, cannot converse with agents which do not support that specialized communication infrastructure. To avoid such limitations, several MAS support generic communication protocols such as KQML and FIPA-ACL and provide generic communication modules (e.g., in RETSINA [18] and D'Agents [6]).

Distributed computational systems implement several standard communication protocols. Three main attributes of such protocols are relevant to MAS:

1. **Symmetry:** In several MAS, client/server protocols are used for communication. Since these protocols are well supported by operating systems and programming languages, such implementations are simple and efficient. Their drawback is in the implied asymmetry between the communicating entities: one is in control of the communication whereas the other party can only respond upon request. In open

MAS with a flat organization asymmetry is inappropriate, and symmetric means of communication are implemented. This, however, increases protocol complexity and may slow down communication.
2. **Message recipients:** Messages in a network may be sent to a single addressee, to multiple ones (multicast) and to all (broadcast). In an open system, broadcast is impractical, since an agent does not know all of the other agents. Therefore, open MAS usually implement peer-to-peer or multi-cast communication. In closed MAS, however, broadcast is commonly used. The advantage of it is in the simplicity of the protocol. The disadvantage is that all agents receive the message, even when irrelevant for them, thus increasing network congestion.
3. **Connection type:** Connection-oriented and connectionless communication are both implemented in MAS. The advantages and drawbacks of these are not unique to MAS, though, and can be found in standard networks' text books (e.g., [19]). Typically, MAS implement connection-oriented communication, however in some cases connectionless protocols are supported as well. Connection-oriented communication is preferred when dependent tasks are performed concurrently by multiple agents, and coordination is necessary during execution. In such situations connectionless communication may prohibit coordination and proper task performance. In MAS where task execution is loosely coordinated and where concurrency is of minor importance, connectionless communication is sufficient.

System Openness The openness of a MAS refers to the ability of introducing additional agents into the system in excess to the agents that comprise it initially. In its basic level, MAS openness refers to the OSI definition of system openness. However in MAS, additional properties are considered. We categorize MAS opennes as follows:

1. **Dynamic openness:** MAS that allow agents to leave or enter the system dynamically, during run time, without explicit global notification, are the most open ones. The advantage of such openness is in the ability of the system to dynamically adjust itself to changes in the environment, tasks, and availability of capabilities and resources. This type of dynamism is important for MAS that are deployed in environments with high levels of uncertainty and changes. A major disadvantage of this extreme openness is the required additional services and computation. When agents can unpredictably appear and disappear, a robust agent location mechanism is a must. Also, agents must be provided with methods to alternate their tasks execution and planning, since availability of necessary capabilities and resources varies.
2. **Static openness:** Less dynamic, yet considered open, is the case where agents can be added to the system without re-starting it, but either all of the agents are notified on such an addition, or they all hold in advance a list of prospective additional agents. This type of openness eliminates the need for an agent location mechanism, and reduces the complexity of contingent execution and planning computation (although these are not eliminated). On the other hand, the flexibility of the system and its ability to adjust itself to dynamic changes is restricted. Such openness better fits cases of gradual and predictable changes.
3. **Off-line openness** The most restricted type of openness allows addition of new agents only off-line, by halting the system, adding agents, updating some connec-

tion information, and re-starting the system. This allows for changes in the system over time, though non-dynamic ones. However, excess infrastructure services and additional computation to handle dynamic changes are not necessary. Hence, such systems will perform more efficiently in cases of well defined, predictable problem domains.

The categories of MAS openness presented above can be shifted towards one another, thus gaining some advantages and compromising on others.

Infrastructure Services Infrastructure services are, in some MAS, inseparable from the system, whereas in others they are optional or unnecessary. We present some of these services:

1. An open MAS needs an Agent Naming Service (ANS), so that no two agents will have identical names, and the consequent confusion be avoided. Close or slightly open systems, where all of the agents (or the possible ones—in the latter systems) are known in advance do not need an ANS.
2. Open MAS require an agent location service (e.g., brokering or matchmaking). When the existence and availability of agents are not common knowledge, this service is a pre-condition to the ability of a MAS to perform its tasks. A centralized agent location service is simpler to implement and maintain, however more vulnerable and creates a single point of failure. Distributed location mechanisms (e.g., [9]) are much more complicated to design, implement and maintain, and increase communication and computation overheads, however provide a reliable, robust service.
3. An optional service useful in open MAS is a security service. In an open MAS, an agent may be uncertain with regards to the true identity and the trustworthiness of other agents. Security mechanisms (e.g., [11])can reduce the risks that stem from this uncertainty. These, however, increase computation (e.g., for encryption/decryption) and communication overheads, and may create bottlenecks at third parties' (e.g., certification authorities).
4. In MAS that allow for agent mobility (e.g. D'Agents [6]), an infrastructure service that supports mobility may be required. Commonly, this is provided via mobility servers, sometimes called agent docks. These run on machines where mobile agents arrive and provide interface and access to resources on these machines. Mobility servers increase computation overheads and pose security problems, however they provide an essential service in case that mobility is necessary.

System Robustness MAS allow for distribution of execution, which in turn allows for increase in system performance. In addition, failure of one agent does not necessarily imply a failure of the whole system. MAS robustness is further increased by replicated capabilities, enabled by multiple agents with similar capabilities. In such cases, when an agent that has some capability becomes un-available, another agent with a similar capability may be approached. Replicated capabilities are more natural (and useful) in open MAS, however can support robustness in close MAS as well. The disadvantage of this replication is in the resulting redundancy. The robustness of a MAS depends also on the type of services it uses and the way in which these are implemented, as mentioned above.

Code Reusability While some MAS are desinged as a domain specific solution, many others are more generic. They usually provide ready to use template agents, or at least components from which agents can be constructed, e.g., communication and reasoning modules. Using such components allows for easier development of new MAS, re-using existing code. However, this re-use introduces some code redundancy, since each agent replicates the generic parts of all agents. In a specially-designed system this redundancy can be avoided.

Although the properties discussed above are each not unique to MAS, combining them in a single system is unique to MAS. This results in the adequacy of MAS for solving problems where information, location and control are highly distributed, heterogeneous autonomous (self-controlled) components comprise the system, the environment is open and dynamically changing, and uncertainty is present. Note that if only a few of these problem domain characteristics are present, it may be advisable to consider other architectures as solutions. Given the limited development tools for MAS, the high complexity of such systems and the amount of code replication in them may result in excessive, unnecessary efforts in the development phase as well as inefficient solution and poor system performance.

3 MAS Case Studies

To illustrate the properties discussed above, we present present three case studies. More case studies, with more details on each, can be found in [17].

3.1 OAA and Federated MAS

The Open Agent Architecture (OAA) [10] is a multi-agent infrastructure designed and implemented based on the concepts of federated MAS. OAA provides a system infrastructure, an agent communication language (ACL), and a set of constructs from which agents can be built. An OAA MAS consists of a *facilitator* and multiple agents connected to it in a client/server fashion. By convention, these agents are categorized as user-interface agents, application agents, and meta-agents. The facilitator is a specialized server agent in charge of coordinating agent communication and cooperative problem solving. It also provides a global data store. OAA agents communicate using an ACL which is more expressive than KQML, though unique to OAA. All communications are done via the facilitator. The latter combines and decomposes messages and requests, directs them to the appropriate service provider agents, receivess and sends results to requesters. OAA exhibits a single layer hierarchical organization, however allows, conceptually, for multiple facilitators, among which a flat organization exists. OAA provides a library of agent components including tools for wrapping legacy systems to support MAS development and code re-use.

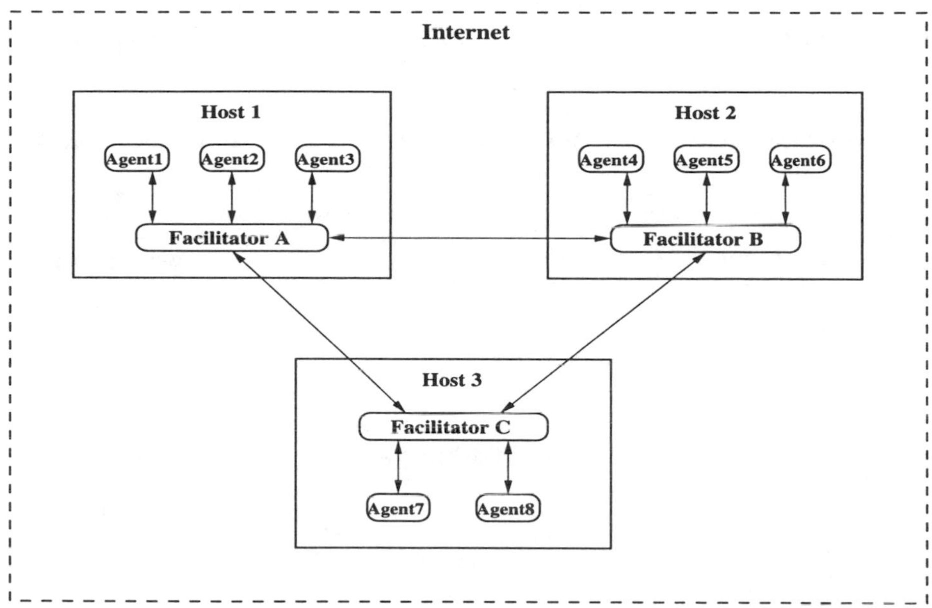

Fig. 1. The federated multi-agent organization.

As introduced in [4], the federated system organization consists of agents and facilitators as a means for achieving agent inter-operation. Facilitators and agents are organized into federations as illustrated in Figure 1. Agents do not communicate directly but via a local facilitator, and their messages are not addressed to a specific agent (as implemented in OAA). Facilitators direct messages to the most appropriate agents and communicate with one another. Within a federation (a group of agents facilitated by a single facilitator), an agent surrenders some of its autonomy to the facilitator. The number of facilitators is not bound, they may be running on multiple machines with an arbitrary network topology. In the federated organization, agents can dynamically connect and disconnect from a facilitator. Upon connection to a facilitator, an agent provides a specification of its capabilities and needs.

The federated organization facilitates application inter-operability. It also enhences system openness, allowing for dynamic agent connection and disconnection. Federated MAS allow, in concept, the inclusion of agents of heterogeneous architectures in a single system. This requires, however, rather sophisticated facilitators. The main drawbacks of federated MAS is the need to surrender agent autonomy, which may violate privacy and self-interest of agents, and the need to provide sufficiently sophisticated (and unbiased) facilitators.

3.2 RETSINA Multi-Agent Infrastructure

RETSINA (Reusable Task Structure based Intelligent Network Agents) [18] is a multi-agent infrastructure that includes a distributed MAS organization, protocols for inter-

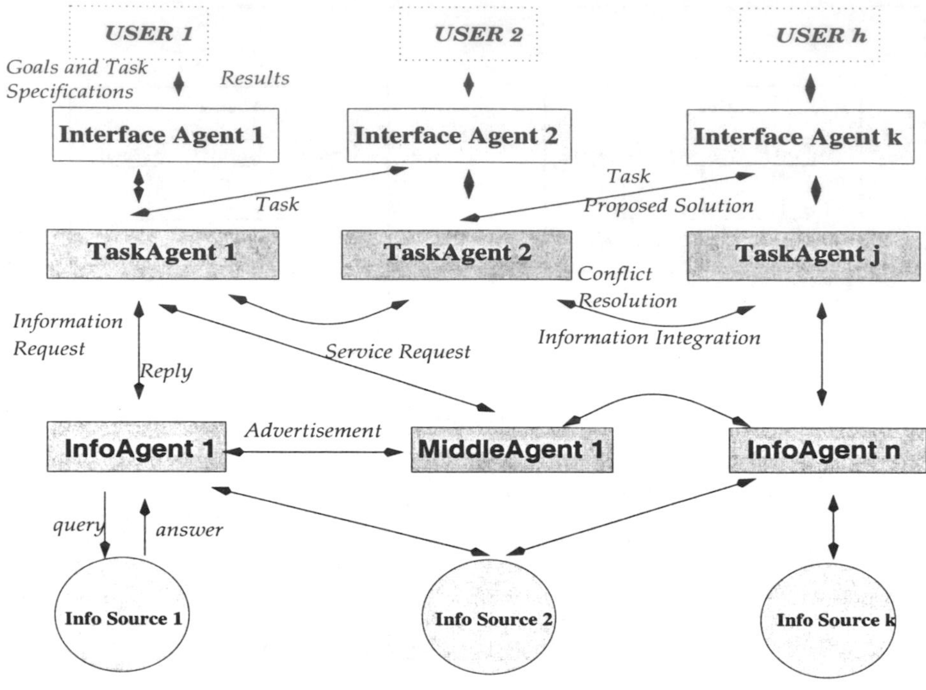

Fig. 2. The RETSINA multi-agent infrastructure

agent interaction and collaboration, and a reusable set of software components for constructing agents. It categorizes (only by convention) three types of agents (see Figure 2). *Interface agents* interact with users, *Task agents* support task performance and problem solving and *Information agents* provide access to information sources. A subcategory of information agents are middle agents, which handle information regarding other agents. Agents in RETSINA receive tasks, perform them or delegate them, possibly after decomposition, to other agents. Tasks that cannot be executed by a single agent are performed by teams that form dynamically, on demand.

Agents in RETSINA organize themselves to avoid processing bottlenecks and to address dynamic changes in information, tasks, number of agents and their capabilities. The agents are distributed over the Internet and run across different machines, communicating using KQML (though replacement to other languages is supported). Communication among agents is performed in a peer-to-peer fashion, supporting symmetry. In open MAS, agents must be able to locate one another. Distribution over the Internet and dynamic agent appearance and disappearance preclude broadcast communication solutions. In RETSINA this problem is solved by introducing matchmaking agents [1]. The process of matchmaking allows an agent A with some tasks, to learn the contact information and capabilities of another agent, B, who may be able to execute part of A's tasks via a matchmaker which is an agent that maintains the contact information of other agents. Agents that join the system advertise themselves and their capabilities to a matchmaker, and when they leave the agent society, they un-advertise. In search of other agents, agents approach a matchmaker and ask for names of relevant agents. After having acquired the information about other agents they can directly contact these agents and initiate cooperation as needed. To relax the problem of unavailable or overwhelmed single matchmaker, RETSINA provides a protocol for information coherence among multiple matchmaker agents [9]. By these means RETSINA supports dynamics openness. It also provides infrastructure services: an ANS and an agent editor. Altogether RETSINA exhibits a flat, dynamic system organization.

As part of the infrastructure, RETSINA provides an agent architecture which is based on a multi-module, multi-thread design. The modularity of the RETSINA agent architecture and having no direct interfaces between its functional modules results in code re-usability (e.g., the RETSINA communicator is used for multiple types of agents as well as non-agent applications that need to converse with agents). In addition, functional components can be easily replaced in a plug-in fashion.

To summarize, the RETSINA infrastructure supports flexible, dynamic organization (based on a flat organization) in an open environment. It also supports code re-usability and robustness and agent asynchrony. However, it introduces some code redundancy. This is an inevitable result of its adaptability to dynamic changes in tasks, agents and the working environment, which require duplicate expertise as well as multiple middle agents. The dynamic organization of RETSINA results in computation and communication overheads as well as additional code for the formation of teams on demand. Less flexible system organizations avoid this overhead (however they are less adaptable to changes).

3.3 The ADEPT Infrastructure

ADEPT (Advanced Decision Environment for Process Tasks) [14] is a multi-agent infrastructure, developed for the management of business processes. In ADEPT, the MAS is comprised of agencies, where each agency may either be a single agent or, recursively, a collection of several agencies (i.e., a subsumption organization). Communication and cooperative task execution are performed either within an agency, among its members, or between agencies, however not directly between members of an agency and agents or agencies outside this agency. Each agency is represented by a single responsible agent. This means that the ADEPT architecture can support hierarchical and flat organizational structure as well as a combination of these, however a specific organization style must be decided upon in advance and cannot be modified dynamically.

In the ADEPT system each agent provides a service. A service corresponds to either an atomic task or a composition of other services (which are provided by other agents). For each request for a service an agent decides whether to use the capabilities and resources of its own agency or to request services from other agents.

The ADEPT system organization is depicted in Figure 3. Agents and agencies can only communicate and (directly) cooperate with agents and agencies within their encapsulating agency. For example, agencies 5-8, which are sub-agencies of agency 4, cannot communicate with agencies 1-3. They can only use the responsible agent 4 to contact entities external to agency 4 (however they are not assumed to know these entities). In ADEPT, communication requires that agents, agencies and tasks, which are all objects,

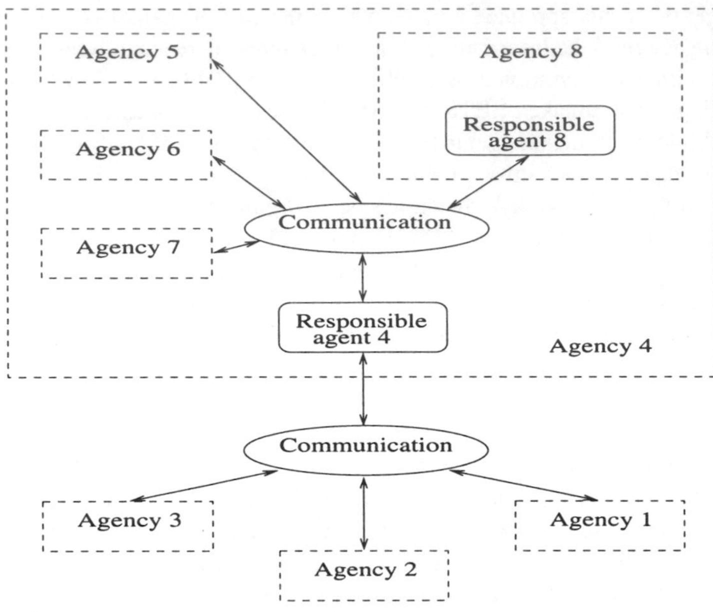

Fig. 3. The ADEPT multi-agent organization.

register themselves with an Object Request Broker (ORB) as defined in the specifications of CORBA [13]. For this DAIS, a commercial implementation of the CORBA specification, is used. DAIS distributes messages between registered objects. The ORB receives requests from agents or tasks and sends a message to another agent or task. The broker is responsible for locating the object referred to by a requester and delivering the requester's message to this object. DAIS supports registration, de-registration and message delivery via its ORB.

The ADEPT multi-agent infrastructure utilizes a well-known agent internal architecture, the ARCHON [20] agent architecture, with some modifications. The internal architecture of an ADEPT agent is comprised of several modules. Its modularity supports re-use, however some dependencies on the ARCHON architecture limit generality of the ADEPT modules. Nevertheless, ADEPT provides a more flexible organization than ARCHON does. It supports subsumption, hierarchical, flat and combined organizations. Yet, dynamic changes of the organization are not supported. An interesting property of the ADEPT infrastructure is of tasks being autonomous entities. This contributes to the mobility of tasks among agents and agencies, thus may increase the efficiency of task re-distribution. Issues of openness are not explicitly discussed in ADEPT, however it seems to allow for some, yet not dynamic, openness.

To summarize the above case studies, we compare the main architectural properties of OAA, RETSINA and ADEPT in Table 1.

Attribute	OAA	RETSINA	ADEPT
Organization	Hierarchy	Flat	Various
Control	Semi-centralized	Distributed	Partly distributed
Communication	Client/server	Symmetric	via the ORB
Commu. language	OAA specific	KQML, replaceable	Flexible
Openness	Partly dynamic	Fully dynamic	Partly dynamic
Services	Agent location	ANS, Location	Specification & verification
Re-use	OAA specific	Generic	Generic (requires CORBA)

Table 1. OAA/RETSINA/ADEPT architectural comparison.

4 Conclusion

In this research we make a first step in the direction of analyzing multi-agent systems as a *software architecture style*. Pursuing this direction shall make MAS more accessible to system designers and provide them with means for analyzing computational problems and considering MAS as one of the prospective solutions to these problems. As we have shown, MAS are a unique software architecture, distinguishable from other architectures, which provides solutions to a specific family of computational problems. Yet, further investigation of the properties of these systems is still necessary. Among others issues, efficiency properties of MAS, and in particular a rigorous comparison between MAS and other software architecture styles, were scarcely examined. Such additional research should allow for more adequate match between MAS and the problems they solve. In addition, it is necessary to be able to compare between different MAS and the solutions they provide to a given problem.

For multi-agent systems to succeed as a software architecture style, design methodologies, development tools, programming languages and evaluation criteria should become an inseparable part of this paradigm. In the last few years a significant research effort was aimed at these issues. In our work, we merely address design issues and evaluation criteria. Even here, we leave many open questions and a large amount of work for future research.

References

1. K. Decker, K. Sycara and M. Williamson. Middle-agents for the internet. In *Proceeding of IJCAI-97*, pages 578–583, Nagoya, Japan, 1997.
2. R. Erdur and O. Dikenelli. Agent oriented software reuse. In this volume.
3. T. Finin, R. Fritzon, D. McKay and R. McEntire. KQML – A language and protocol for knowledge and information exchange. In *Proceedings of the 13th International Workshop on Distributed Artificial Intelligence*, pages 126–136, Seatle, WA, July 1994.
4. M. Genesereth and S. Ketchpel. Software agents. *Communications of the ACM, Special Issue on Intelligent Agents*, 37(7):48–53, July 1994.
5. J. Giampapa, M. Paolucci and K. Sycara. Agent interoperation across multiagent system boundaries. In *Proceedings of Agents-00*, pages 179–186, Barcelona, Spain, 2000.

6. R. Gray, D. Kotz, G. Cybenko and D. Rus. D'agents: Security in a multiple-language, mobile-agent system. In Giovanni Vigna, editor, *Mobile Agent Security*, Lecture Notes in Computer Science. Springer-Verlag, 1998.
7. M. Huhns and M. Singh (editors). *Readings in agents*. Morgan Kaufmann, 1998.
8. N. Jennings. On agent based software engineering. *Artificial Intelligence*, 117(2):277–296, 2000.
9. S. Jha, P. Chalasani, O. Shehory, and K. Sycara. A formal treatment of distributed matchmaking. In *Proceeding of Agents-98*, pages 457–458, Minneapolis, Minnesota, 1998.
10. D. L. Martin, A. J. Cheyer and D. B. Moran. The open agent architecture: A framework for building distributed software systems. *Applied Artificial Intelligence*, 1999.
11. Y. Mass and O. Shehory. Distributed trust in multi-agent systems. In *Proceedings of Agents-00 Workshop on Trust, Deception and Fraud*, Barcelona, Spain, 2000.
12. S. Miles, M. Joy and M. Luck. Designing agent-oriented systems by analysing agent interactions. In this volume.
13. T. J. Mowbray and W. A. Ruh. *Inside CORBA - Distributed object standards and applications*. Addison Wesley, 1997.
14. T. Norman, N. Jennings, P. Faratin and E. Mamdani. Designing and implementing a multi-agent architecture for business process management. In J. Muller, N. Jennings and M. Wooldridge, editors, *Intelligent Agents 3*, Lecture Notes in Artificial Intelligence No. 1193, pages 261–275. Springer-Verlag, 1996.
15. M. Shaw and D. Garlan. *Software architecture : perspectives on an emerging discipline*. Prentice Hall, New Jersey, 1996.
16. O. Shehory and K. Sycara. The RETSINA communicator. In *Proceedings of Agents-00*, pages 199–200, Barcelona, Spain, 2000.
17. O. Shehory. Architectural properties of multi-agent systems. Technical Report CMU-RI-TR-98-28, The Robotics Institute, Carnegie Mellon University, December 1998.
18. K. Sycara, K. Decker, A. Pannu, M. Williamson and D. Zeng. Distributed intelligent agents. *IEEE Expert – Inteligent Systems and Their Applications*, 11(6):36–45, 1996.
19. A. S. Tanenbaum. *Computer networks*. Prentice Hall, 1988.
20. T. Wittig, editor. *ARCHON: an architecture for multi-agent systems*. Ellis Horwood, 1992.
21. M. Wooldridge. Agent-based software engineering. *IEE Proceedings on Software Engineering*, 144(1):26–37, 1997.

Agent UML: A Formalism for Specifying Multiagent Software Systems

Bernhard Bauer*, Jörg P. Müller*, James Odell[+]

* Siemens AG, ZT IK 6, D-81730 München, Germany
bernhard.bauer@mchp.siemens.de
joerg.mueller@mchp.siemens.de

[+] James Odell Associates, 3646 W. Huron River Dr,
Ann Arbor, MI 48103 USA
jodell@compuserve.com

Abstract. In the past, research on agent-oriented software engineering had been widely lacking touch with the world of industrial software development. Recently, a cooperation has been established between the Foundation of Intelligent Physical Agents (FIPA) and the Object Management Group (OMG) aiming to increase acceptance of agent technology in industry by relating to de facto standards (object-oriented software development) and supporting the development environment throughout the full system lifecycle. As a first result of this cooperation, we proposed AGENT UML [1; 20], an extension of the Unified Modeling language (UML), a de facto standard for object-oriented analysis and design. In this paper, we describe the heart of AGENT UML, i.e., mechanisms to model protocols for multiagent interaction. Particular UML extensions described in this paper include protocol diagrams, agent roles, multithreaded lifelines, extended UML message semantics, nested and interleaved protocols, and protocol templates.

1 Introduction

For the past decade, research on agent-oriented software engineering had suffered from a lack of touch with the world of industrial software development. Recently, it has been recognized that the use of software agents is unlikely likely to gain wide acceptance in industry unless it relates to de facto standards (object-oriented software development) and supports the development environment throughout the full system lifecycle.

Successfully bringing agent technology to market requires techniques that reduce the perceived risk inherent in any new technology, by presenting the new technology as an incremental extension of known and trusted methods, and by providing explicit engineering tools to support proven methods of technology deployment.

Applied to agents, these insights imply an approach that:

- introduces agents as an extension of active objects*: an agent is an object that can say "go"* (flexible autonomy as the ability to initiate action without external invocation) *and "no"* (flexible autonomy as the ability to refuse or modify an external request)[1];
- promotes the use of standard representations for methods and tools to support the analysis, specification, and design of agent software.

The former aspect of our approach leads us to focus on fairly fine-grained agents. More sophisticated capabilities can also be added where needed, such as mobility, mechanisms for representing and reasoning about knowledge, and explicit modeling of other agents. Such capabilities are extensions to our basic agents—we do not consider them diagnostic of agenthood.

To achieve the latter, three important characteristics of industrial software development should be addressed:

1. The scope of industrial software projects is much larger than typical academic research efforts, involving many more people across a longer period of time. Thus, communication is essential;
2. The skills of developers are focused more on development methodology than on tracking the latest agent techniques. Thus, codifying best practice is essential;
3. Industrial projects have clear success criteria. Thus, traceability between initial requirements and the final deliverable is essential.

The Unified Modeling Language (UML) is gaining wide acceptance for the representation of engineering artifacts in object-oriented software. Our view of agents as the next step beyond objects leads us to explore extensions to UML and idioms within UML to accommodate the distinctive requirements of agents. To pursue this objective, recently a cooperation has been established between the Foundation of Intelligent Physical Agents (FIPA) [7] and the Object Management Group (OMG). As a first result of this cooperation, we analyzed the requirements for such an endeavor and proposed the framework of AGENT UML [1].

In this paper, we describe a core part within AGENT UML, i.e., mechanisms to model protocols for multiagent interaction. This is achieved by introducing a new class of diagrams into UML: *protocol diagrams.* Protocol diagrams extend UML state and sequence diagrams in various ways. Particular extensions in this context include agent roles, multithreaded lifelines, extended message semantics, parameterized nested protocols, and protocol templates.

The model described in this paper has been proposed and accepted for inclusion into the upcoming FIPA'99 standard. It was invited to be submitted as a response to a Request for Information (RFI) issued by the OMG Analysis and Design Task Force for the next release of UML (v2.0).

The paper is structured as follows: In Section 2, we survey approaches to software specification, including UML. Section 3 specifies the extension of UML by multiagent interaction protocols. Section 4 discusses further details of the extensions. Section 5

---

[1] See [12], [16] for more comprehensive definitions of agents.

attempts a preliminary evaluation of the concepts, summarizes the results of the paper and discusses future research topics.

2 Software Specification Techniques

AGENT UML is an attempt to bring together research on agent-based software methodologies and emerging standards for object-oriented software development.

2.1 Methodologies for agent -based software development

There is a considerable interest in the agent R&D community in methods and tools for analyzing and designing complex agent-based software systems, including various approaches to formal specification (see [11] for a survey). Since 1996, agent-based software engineering has been a focus of the ATAL workshop series and was the main topic for MAAMAW'99 [9].

Various researchers have reported on methodologies for agent design, touching on representational mechanisms as they support the methodology. Our own report at [22] emphasizes methodology, as does Kinny's work on modeling techniques for BDI agents [14; 15]. The close parallel that we observe between design mechanisms for agents and for objects is shared by a number of authors, for example, [4; 6].

The GAIA methodology [25] includes specific recommendations for notation in support of the high-level summary of a protocol as an atomic unit, a notation that is reflected in our recommendations. The extensive program underway at the Free University of Amsterdam on compositional methodologies for requirements [10], design [3], and verification [13] uses graphical representations with similarities to UML collaboration diagrams, as well as linear (formulaic) notations better suited to alignment with the UML meta-model than with the graphical mechanisms that are our focus.

Our discussion of the compositionality of protocols is anticipated in the work of Burmeister et al. [5]. Dooley graphs [21] facilitate the identification of the *character* that results from an agent playing a specific role (as distinct from the same agent playing a different role).

The wide range of activity in this area is a sign of the increasing impact of agent-based systems, since the demand for methodologies and artifacts reflects the growing commercial importance of agent technology. Our objective is not to compete with any of these efforts, but rather to extend and apply a widely accepted modeling and representational formalism (UML) in a way that harnesses their insights and makes it useful in communicating across a wide range of research groups and development methodologies.

2.2 UML

The Unified Modeling Language (UML) [17] unifies and formalizes the methods of many object-oriented approaches, including Booch, Rumbaugh (OMT), Jacobson, and Odell. It supports the following kinds of models:

- *use cases:* the specification of actions that a system or class can perform by interacting with outside actors. They are commonly used to describe how a customer communicates with a software product.
- *static models:* describe the static semantics of data and messages in a conceptual and implementational way (e.g., class and package diagrams).
- *dynamic models:* include interaction diagrams (i.e., sequence and collaboration diagrams), state charts, and activity diagrams.
- *implementation models:* describe the component distribution on different platforms (e.g., component models and deployment diagrams).
- *object constraint language* (*OCL*): a simple formal language to express more semantics within an UML specification. It can be used to define constraints on the model, invariant, pre- and post-conditions of operations and navigation paths within an object net.

In this paper, we propose agent-based extensions to three following UML representations: packages, templates, and sequence diagrams. This results in a new diagram type, called *protocol diagram*, which we developed within FIPA 1999, and which will be considered for inclusion into UML version 2.0 by OMG. The UML model semantics are represented by a meta-model the structure of which is also formally defined by OCL syntax. Extensions to this meta-model and its constraint language are not addressed by this paper.

2.3 A rationale for AGENT UML

In a previous paper, we have argued that UML provides an insufficient basis for modeling agents and agent-based systems [1], see also [20]. Basically, this is due to two reasons: *Firstly*, compared to objects, agents are active because they can take the initiative and have control over whether and how they process external requests. *Secondly*, agents do not only act in isolation but in cooperation or coordination with other agents. Multiagent systems are social communities of interdependent members that act individually.

To employ agent-based programming, a specification technique must support the whole software engineering process—from planning, through analysis and design, and finally to system construction, transition, and maintenance.

A proposal for a full life-cycle specification of agent-based system development is beyond the scope for this paper. Both FIPA and the OMG Agent Work Group are exploring and recommending extensions to UML [1; 18]. In this paper, we will focus on a subset of an agent-based UML extension for the specification of *agent interaction protocols (AIP)*.

This subset was chosen because AIPs are complex enough to illustrate the nontrivial use of and are used commonly enough to make this subset of AGENT UML useful to other researchers. AIPs are a specific class of software design patterns in that they describe problems that occur frequently in multiagent systems and then describe the core of a reusable solution to that problem [8, p. 2].

The definition of interaction protocols is part of the specification of the dynamical model of an agent system. In UML, this model is captured by interaction diagrams, state diagrams and activity diagrams.

- *Interaction diagrams*, i.e. sequence diagrams and collaboration diagrams are used to define the behavior of groups of objects. Usually, one interaction diagram captures the behavior of one use case. These diagrams are mainly used to define basic interactions between objects at the level of method invocation; they are not well-suited for describing the types of complex social interaction as they occur in multiagent systems.
- *State diagrams* are used to model the behavior of a complete system. They define all possible states an object can reach and how an object's state changes depending on messages sent to the object. They are well suited for defining the behavior of one single object in different use cases. However, they are not appropriate to describe the behavior of a group of cooperating objects.
- *Activity diagrams* are used to define courses of events / actions for several objects and use cases. The work reported in this paper does not suggest modifications of activity diagrams.

3 AGENT UML Interaction Protocols

The definition of an agent interaction protocol (AIP) describes

- a communication pattern, with
  - an allowed sequence of messages between agents having different roles,
  - constraints on the content of the messages, and
- a semantics that is consistent with the communicative acts (CAs) within a communication pattern.

Messages must satisfy standardized communicative (speech) acts which define the type and the content of the messages (e.g. the FIPA agent communication language (ACL), or KQML). Protocols constrain the parameters of message exchange, e.g., their order or types, according to relationships between the agents or the intention of the communication.

The new diagram type introduced in this paper are *Protocol Diagrams*. Since interaction protocols, i.e. the definition of cooperation between software agents, define the exact behavior of a group of cooperating agents, we combine sequence diagrams with the notation of state diagrams for the specification of interaction protocols.

As an introductory example let us consider a surplus ticket market for flights. The example is taken from the PTA application (see Section 5). The auctioning of such tickets can be performed using, e.g. the FIPA English-Auction Protocol as shown in Figure 1. The auctioneer initially proposes a price lower than the expected market price, and then gradually raises the price. The auctioneer informs all participants that the auction has started (represented by the messages *inform(start-auction, departure, arrival)* in Figure 1) and announces the details of the flight. Each time a new price is announced (represented by *cfp(intial-price)* and *cfp(new-price)*), the auctioneer waits until a given *deadline* to see if any participants signal their willingness to pay the proposed price (*propose*) for the ticket. If a participant does not understand the ontology or syntax of the *cfp* it replies a *not-understood* communicative act. The diamond symbol with the 'x' in it indicates a decision resulting in zero or more communications being sent (see Section 4.2)). As soon as one participant indicates that it will accept the price, the auctioneer issues a new call for bids (*cfp(new-price)*) with an incremented price. The auction continues until no auction participants are prepared to pay the proposed price, at which point the auction ends. If the last price accepted by a buyer exceeds the auctioneer's reservation price, the ticket is sold to that participant for the agreed price (otherwise the auction fails). The participants are *informed* about the end of the auction and the buyer is *requested* to pay the price for the ticket.

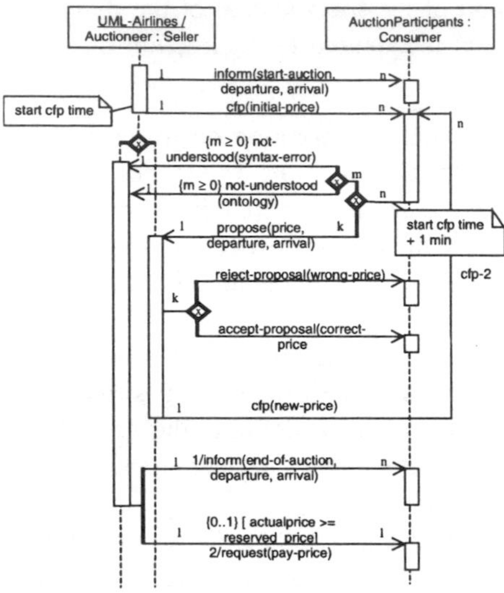

Figure 1. English-Auction protocol for surplus flight tickets

The diagram in Figure 1 provided a basic specification for a English Auction protocol. In [20] we have shown how such a specification can be gradually refined until the problem has been specified adequately to develop or generate code. Each level can express *intra-agent* or *inter-agent* activity.

4 Elements of Protocol diagrams

In the last chapter we gave an example how interaction protocols can be specified using the UML extension. In this chapter we will have a closer look at the different extensions.

4.1 Agent roles

In UML, *role* is an instance focused term. In the framework of agent oriented programming by *agent-role* a set of agents satisfying distinguished properties, interfaces, service descriptions or having a distinguished behavior are meant.

UML distinguishes between *multiple classification* (e.g., a retailer agent acts as a buyer *and* a seller agent at the same time), and *dynamic classification*, where an agent can change its classification during its existence.

Agents can perform various roles within one interaction protocol. E.g., in an auction between an airline and potential ticket buyers, the airline has the role of a seller and the participants have the role of buyers. But at the same time, a buyer in this auction can act as a seller in another auction. I.e., agents satisfying a distinguished role can support multiple classification and dynamic classification.

Therefore, the implementation of an agent can satisfy different roles. An agent role describes two variations, which can apply within a protocol definition. A protocol can be defined at the level of concrete agent instances or for a set of agents satisfying a distinguished role and/or class. An agent satisfying a distinguished agent role and class is called *agent of a given agent role* and *class*, respectively. The general form of describing agent roles in AGENT UML is

```
instance-1 ... instance-n / role-1 ... role-m : class
```

denoting a distinguished set of agent instances *instance-1,..., instance-n* satisfying the agent roles *role-1,..., role-m* with n, m ≥ 0 and *class* it belongs to. Instances, roles or class can be omitted, in the case that the instances are omitted the roles and class are not underlined. In Fig. 1 the auctioneer is a concrete instance of an agent named *UML-Airlines* playing the role of an *Auctioneer* being of class *Seller*. The participants of the auctions are agents of role *AuctionParticipants* which are familiar with auctions and of class *Consumer*.

4.2 Agent Lifelines and Threads of Interaction

The agent lifeline in protocol diagrams defines the time period during which an agent exists, represented by dotted vertical lines. The lifeline starts when the agent of a given agent role is created and ends when it is destroyed. For example, a user agent is created when a user logs on to the system and the user agent is destroyed when the user logs off. The lifeline may split up into two or more lifelines to show AND and OR parallelism and decisions, corresponding to branches in the message flow. Lifelines may merge at some subsequent point. In Figure 1 the lifeline splits in order to describe the different reaction of the agent depending on the incoming messages, here to handle proposals and not-understoods respectively. Figure 2 shows the graphical representations for the logical connectors AND, XOR, and OR.

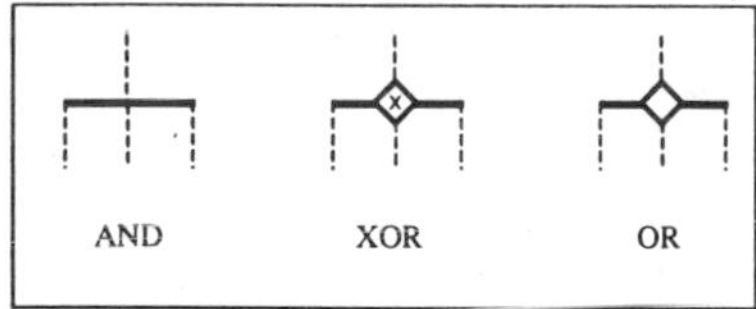

Figure 2. Connector types

The XOR can abbreviated by interrupting the *threads of interaction* as shown also in Figure 3 (right). The thread of interaction, i.e. the processing of incoming messages, is split up into different threads of interaction, since the behavior of an agent role depends on the incoming message. The lifeline of an agent role is split accordingly and the thread of interaction defines the reaction to different kinds of received messages.

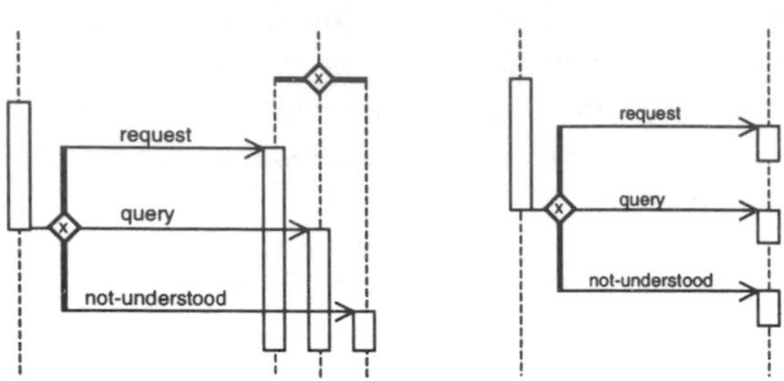

Figure 3. Full and abbreviated notation of XOR connection

The thread of interaction shows the period during which an agent role is performing some task as a reaction to an incoming message. It only represents the duration of the action, but not the control relationship between the sender of the message and its receiver. A thread of interaction is always associated with the lifeline of an agent role. Supporting concurrent threads of interaction is another recommended extension to UML .

4.3 Nested and Interleaved Protocols

Because protocols can be codified as recognizable patterns of agent interaction, they become reusable modules of processing that can be treated as first-class notions. For example, Figure 4 depicts two kinds of protocol patterns. The left part defines a nested protocol, i.e. a protocol within another protocol, and the right part defines an interleaved protocol, e.g. if the participant of the auction requests some information about his/her bank account before bidding. Additionally nested protocols are used for the definition of repetition of a nested protocol according to guards and constraints. The semantics of a nested protocol is the semantics of the protocol. If the nested protocol is marked with some guard then the semantics of the nested protocol is the semantics of the protocol under the assumption that the guard evaluates to true, otherwise the semantics is the semantics of an empty protocol, i.e. nothing is specified.

If the nested protocol is marked with some constraints the nested protocol is repeated as long as the constraints evaluate to true. In addition to the constraint-condition used in UML the description n..m, denoting that the nested protocol is

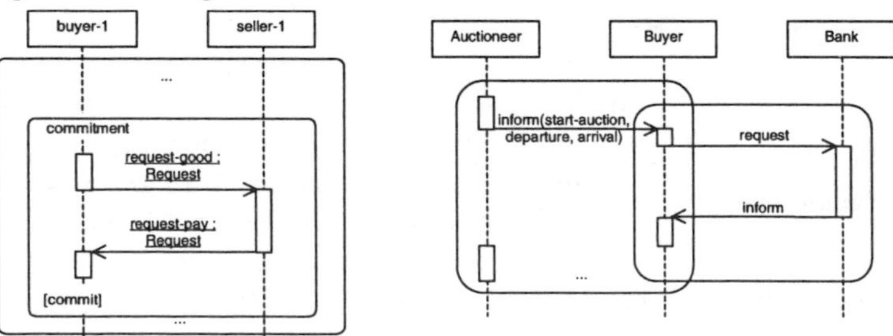

Figure 4. nested protocol and interleaved protocol

repeated n up to m times with $n \in N$, $m \in N \cup \{ * \}$, the asterisk denotes arbitrary times, is used as a constraint condition.

4.4 Extended Semantics of UML Messages

The main purpose of protocols is the definition of communicative patterns, i.e., patterns of messages sent from one agent role to another. This is described by various parameters, such as different cardinalities, depending on some constraints, or using AND / OR parallelism and decisions.

Sending a communicative act from one agent to another that conveys information and entails the sender's expectation that the receiver react according to the semantics of the communicative act. The specification of the protocol says nothing about how this reaction is implemented.

An asynchronous message is drawn as $\rightharpoonup$[2]. It shows the sending of the message without yielding control. A synchronous message is shown as $\rightarrow$. It shows the yielding of the thread of control (wait semantics), i.e. the agent role waits until an answer message is received and nothing else can be processed. Normally message arrows are drawn horizontally. This indicates the duration required to send the message is "atomic", i.e. it is brief compared to the granularity of the interaction and that nothing else can "happen" during the message transmission. If the messages requires some time to arrive, e.g. for mobile communication, during which something else can occur then the message arrow is shown as $\searrow$. The repetition of a part of a protocol is represented by an arrow or one of its variations usually marked with some guards or constraints ending at a thread of interaction which is, according to the time axis, before or after the actual time point, like the *cfp(new-price)* in Fig. 1. This repetition is another extension to UML messages

Each arrow is labeled with a message label[3]. The message label consists of the following parts, which can also be found in Fig. 1. The communicative act which is sent from one agent to another, like *cfp(initial-price)* with a list of arguments representing additional information for the characterization of the communicative act. The cardinality defines that a message is sent from one agent to n agents, like in the *cfp(new-price)* case. Constraints and guards, like {m >= 0 } and [actualprice >= reservedprice] respectively, can be added to define the condition when a message is sent. In addition to the constraint-condition used in UML the description n..m, denoting that the message is repeated n up to m times with $n \in N$, $m \in N \cup \{ * \}$, the asterisk denotes arbitrary times, is used as a constraint condition.

Messages may be sent in parallel or exactly one message out of a set of different messages should be sent. E.g., in Figure 1, exclusive sending is denoted as for the *reject-proposal* and *accept-proposal*. *inform(end-of-auction, departure, arrival)* and *request(pay-price)* are sent in parallel but *inform* is sent first (*1/inform-2*) and the

---

[2] Notation of UML v1.3.

[3] The message label is a special case of the message label presented in the UML 1.1 specification section 8.9.2.

request is sent as the second message (*2/request*). The request is also sent zero or one time {0..1}, depending on whether the reservation price was reached or not.

4.5 Input and Output Parameters for Nested Protocols

Nested Protocols can be defined either within or outside a protocol diagram where it is used or outside another protocol diagram. The input parameters of nested protocols are threads of interaction which are carried on in the nested protocol and messages which are received from other protocols.

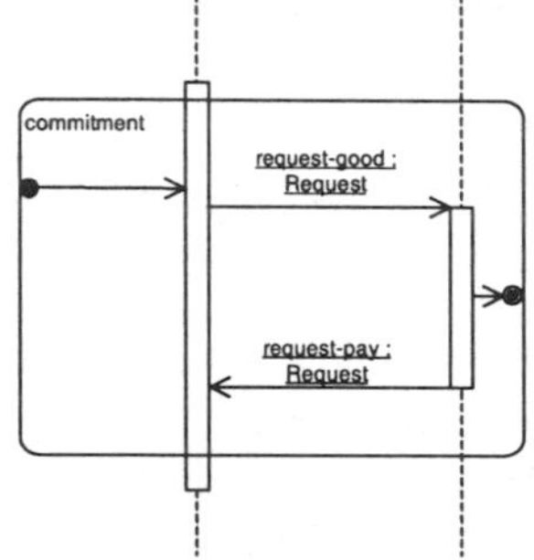

Figure 5. Input/output of nested protocols

The output parameters are the threads of interaction which are started within the nested protocol and are carried on outside the nested protocol and the messages which are sent from inside the nested protocol to agent roles not involved in the actual nested protocol. A message or thread of interaction ending at an input or starting at an output parameter of a nested protocol describes the connection of a whole protocol diagram with the embedded nested protocol.

The input and output parameters for the threads of interaction of a nested protocol are shown as in Figure 4 which is drawn over the top line and bottom line of the nested protocol rectangle, respectively. The input and output message parameters are shown as ⟼ and →◉, respectively.

The message arrows can be marked like usual messages. In this context the predecessor denotes the number of the input / output parameter. The input / output thread of interaction can be marked with natural numbers to define the exact number of the parameter.

4.6 Protocol Templates

The purpose of protocol templates is to create reausable patterns for useful protocol instances. E.g., Figure 6 shows a template for the FIPA-English-Auction Protocol from Figure 1. It introduces two new concepts represented at the top

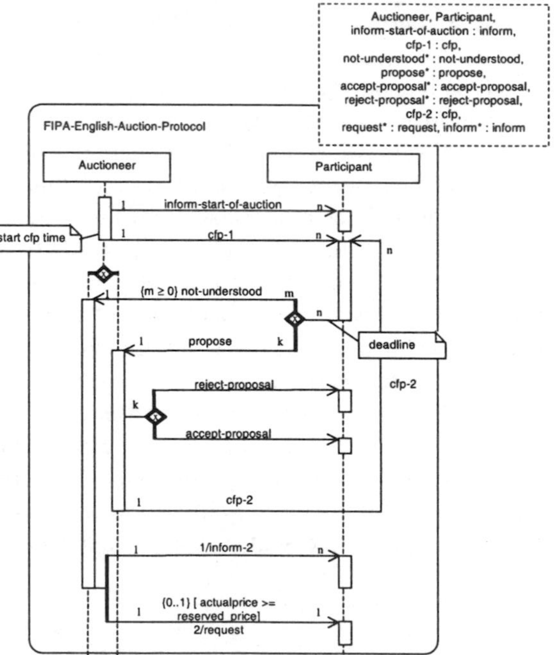

Figure 6. A generic AIP expressed as a template

of the sequence chart. First, the protocol as a whole is treated as an entity in its own right. The protocol can be treated as a pattern that can be customized for other problem domains. The dashed box at the upper right-hand corner declares this pattern as a *template* specification that identifies unbound entities (formal parameters) within the package which need to be bound by actual parameters when instantiating the package. A parameterized protocol is not a directly-usable protocol because it has unbound parameters. Its parameters must be bound to actual values to create a bound form that is a protocol. Communicative acts in the formal parameter list can be marked with an asterisk, denoting different kinds of messages which can alternatively be sent in this context. This template can be instantiated for a special purpose as shown in Figure 1[4]. Figure 7 applies the FIPA English Auction Protocol to a particular scenario involving a specific auctioneer *UML-Airlines* of role *Auctioneer* and Class *Seller* and *AuctionParticipants* of Class *Consumer*. Finally, a specific deadline has been supplied for a response by the seller. In UML terminology, the AIP package serves as a *template*. A template is a parameterized model element whose parameters are bound at model time (i.e., when the new customized model is produced).

```
FIPA-English-Auction-Protocol <
UML-Airlines / Auctioneer : Seller, AuctionParticipants : Consumer
start cfp time + 1 min
inform(start-auction, departure, arrival),
cfp(initial-price),
not-understood(syntax-error), not-understood(ontology),
propose(pay-price),
reject-proposal(wrong-price), accept-proposal(correct-price),
cfp(increased-price),
inform(end-of-action), request(pay-price, fetch-car)
```

Figure 7. Instantiation of a template

Wooldridge et al suggest a similar form of definition with their *protocol definitions* [25]. Here, they define packaged templates as "a pattern of interaction that has been formally defined and abstracted away from any particular sequence of execution steps." In contrast to their notation, we suggest a graphical approach that more closely resembles UML, while expressing the same semantics.

5 Evaluation and Conclusion

The artifacts for agent-oriented analysis and design were developed and evaluated in the German research project MOTIV-PTA (Personal Travel Assistant) [2, 23], aiming at providing an agent-based infrastructure for travel assistance in Germany (see www.motiv.de). MOTIV-PTA will run from 1996 to 2000. IT is a large-scale project involving approx. 10 industrial partners, including Siemens, BMW, IBM, DaimlerChrysler, debis, Opel, Bosch, and VW. The core of MOTIV-PTA is a multiagent system to wrap a variety of information services, ranging from multimodal route planning, traffic control information, parking space allocation, hotel reservation, ticket booking and purchasing, meeting scheduling, and entertainment.

From the end user's perspective, the goal is to provide a personal travel assistant, i.e., a software agent that uses information about the users' schedule and preferences in order to assist them in travel, including preparation as well as on-trip support. This requires providing ubiquitous access to assistant functions for the user, in the office, at

[4] This template format is not currently UML-compliant but is a recommendation for future UML extensions.

home, and while on the trip, using PCs, notebooks, information terminals, PDAs, and mobile phones.

From developing PTA (and other projects with corporate partners within Siemens) the requirements for artifacts to support the analysis and design became clear, and the material described in this paper has been developed incrementally, driven by these requirements. So far no empirical tests have been carried out to evaluate the benefits of the AGENT UML framework. However, from our project experience so far, we see two concrete advantages of these extensions: Firstly, they make it easier for users who are familiar with object-oriented software development but new to developing agent systems to understand what multiagent systems are about, and to understand the principles of looking at a system as a society of agents rather than a distributed collection of objects. Secondly, our estimate is that the time spent for design can be reduced by a minor amount, which grows with the number of agent-based projects. However, we expect that as soon as components are provided to support the implementation based on AGENT UML specifications, this will widely enhance the benefit.

Areas of future research include aspects such as

- description of mobility, planning, learning, scenarios, agent societies, ontologies and knowledge
- development of patterns and frameworks
- consideration of events
- real-time-constraints
- support for different agent communication languages and content languages

At the moment we plan to extend the presented framework towards inclusion of these topics. Moreover a project is on the way to refine the specification technique and generate code from such a specification for different agent platforms, e.g. for the MECCA system [2], based on a formal semantics of AGENT UML which is currently being developed.

References

[1] B. Bauer. *Extending UML for the Specification of Interaction Protocols*. submission for the 6th Call for Proposal of FIPA and revised version part of FIPA 99, 1999.

[2] B. Bauer, M. Berger: Agent-Based Personal Travel Assistance, submitted to MAMA 2000, 2000.

[3] F. M. T. Brazier, C. M. Jonkers, and J. Treur. *Principles of Compositional Multi-Agent System Development*. Proceedings 15th IFIP World Computer Congress, WCC'98, Conference on Information Technology and Knowledge Systems, IT&KNOWS'98, pages 347-360, Chapman and Hall, 1998.

[4] J. Bryson, and B. McGonigle. *Intelligent Agents IV: Agent Theories, Architectures, and Languages*. Proceedings ATAL 98, ed., Springer, 1998

[5] B. Burmeister, A. Haddadi, and K. Sundermeyer. *Generic, Configurable, Cooperation Protocols for Multi-Agent Systems*. Proceedings Fifth European Workshop on Modelling

Autonomous Agents in a Multi-Agent World, MAAMAW'93, pages 157-171, Springer, 1993.
[6] B. Burmeister. *Models and Methodology for Agent-Oriented Analysis and Design*. ed., 1996.
[7] http://www.fipa.org
[8] E. Gamma, R. Helm, R. Johnson, and J. Vlissides. *Design Patterns*. Addison-Wesley, 1997.
[9] F. J. Garijo, and M. Boman. *Multi-Agent System Engineering*. Proceedings of MAAMAW'99. Springer, ed., 1999.
[10] D. E. Herlea, C. M. Jonker, J. Treur, and N. J. E. Wijngaards. *Specification of Behavioural Requirements within Compositional Multi-Agent System Design*. Proceedings of Ninth European Workshop on Modelling Autonomous Agents in a Multi-Agent World, pages 8-27, Springer, 1999.
[11] C. A. Iglesias, M. Garijo, and J. C. González. *A Survey of Agent-Oriented Methodologies*. Proceedings of Fifth International Workshop on Agent Theories, Architectures, and Languages, pages 185-198, University Pierre et Marie Curie, 1998.
[12] N. R. Jennings, K. Sycara, and M.J.Wooldridge. *A Roadmap of Agent Research and Development*. Journal of Autonomous Agents and Multi-Agent Systems. 1(1), pages 7-36. July 1998.
[13] C. M. Jonker, and J. Treur. *Compositional Verification of Multi-Agent Systems: a Formal Analysis of Pro-activeness and Reactiveness*. Proceedings of International Workshop on Compositionality (COMPOS'97), Springer, 1997.
[14] D. Kinny, and M. Georgeff. *Modelling and Design of Multi-Agent Systems*. Intelligent Agents III, Springer, 1996.
[15] D. Kinny, M. Georgeff, and A. Rao. *A Methodology and Modelling Technique for Systems of BDI Agents*. 7th European Workshop on Modelling Autonomous Agents in a Multi-Agent World (MAAMAW'96)., pages 56-71. Springer, 1996.
[16] J. P. Müller. The Design of Autonomous Agents : A Layered Approach, volume 1177 of Lecture Notes in Artificial Intelligence. Springer-Verlag, Heidelberg, 1997.
[17] J. Odell and M. Fowler. *Advanced object-oriented analysis and design using UML*. SIGS Books / Cambridge University Press, 1998.
[18] J. Odell. *Agent Technology*, green paper, produced by the OMG Agent Working Group, ed., 1999.
[20] J. Odell, H. v. D. Paranuk, B. Bauer: *Representing Agent Interaction Protocols in UML*, in this volume.
[21] H. V. D. Parunak. *Visualizing Agent Conversations: Using Enhanced Dooley Graphs for Agent Design and Analysis*. Proceedings of Second International Conference on Multi-Agent Systems, pages 275-282, 1996.
[22] H. V. D. Parunak, and J. Odell. *Engineering Artifacts for Multi-Agent Systems*, ERIM CEC, 1999.
[23] Steiner D. MoTiV-PTA: Personal Travel Assistance for Germany, in Proceedings 4th World Congress on Intelligent Transport Systems. Berlin. Germany. October 21-24, 1997.
[25] M. Wooldridge, N. R. Jennings and D. Kinny. *The Gaia Methodology for Agent-Oriented Analysis and Design*. International Journal of Autonomous Agents and Multi-Agent Systems, 3:Forthcoming, 2000.

Agent-Oriented Modeling with Graph Transformation*

Ralph Depke Reiko Heckel Jochen Malte Küster

Dept. of Computer Science, University of Paderborn
Warburger Str. 100, D-33098 Paderborn
{depke,reiko,jkuester}@uni-paderborn.de

Abstract. The agent paradigm can be seen as an extension of the notion of (active) objects by concepts like autonomy, cooperation, and goal-oriented behavior. Mainstream object-oriented modeling techniques do not account for these agent-specific aspects. Therefore, dedicated techniques for *agent-oriented modeling* are required which are based on the concepts and notations of object-oriented modeling and extend these in order to support agent-specific concepts.
In this paper, an agent-oriented modeling technique is introduced which is based on UML notation. Graph transformation is used both on the level of modeling in order to capture agent-specific aspects and as the underlying formal semantics of the approach.

1 Introduction

As concepts and technologies of agent-based systems become part of more traditional software, agent-based software development is about to become one aspect of mainstream software engineering. Today, most software systems are implemented in an object-oriented programming language like C++ or Java, and the analysis and design of such systems is based on object-oriented modeling languages like the UML [16]. Thus, in order to incorporate agent concepts into mainstream software development, an integrated modeling approach for object- and agent-based systems is required.

As modeling concepts, agents and objects have complementary roles: agents act autonomously, driven by their goals and plans, thereby sensing and reacting to their environment and cooperating with other agents. Objects encapsulate data structures and operations and provide services to other objects. In this sense, Jennings, et al. [15] state that *"There is a fundamental mismatch between the concepts used by object-oriented developers ... and the agent view."* However, the view of objects as mere service providers has its origins in the paradigms of sequential OO programming, and is no longer adequate when considering concurrent languages like Java. As a modeling abstraction for concurrent objects, the concept of *active object* has been established [16] which has much similarity with the agent paradigm. What is still missing even in active objects is the idea of goal-driven behavior or *proactivity* of agents and the related concept of *autonomy*. Autonomy emphasizes the fact that an agent has control about its

* Research supported by the ESPRIT Working Group APPLIGRAPH.

operations: they are not called from outside like methods but are only invoked by the agent itself in order to reach a certain goal.

Still, object-oriented modeling languages like the UML provide a good basis for the modeling of agent-based systems. In fact, a number of authors propose extensions and adaptions of object-oriented modeling languages for agent-based systems [12, 21, 20]. Most approaches suffer from a problem which is also encountered in OO modeling languages: the lack of adequate means for describing the semantics of operations, their pre-conditions and effects on the system's configuration. In particular, the semantics of operations is relevant for the modeling of reactive behavior, i.e., for the way how agents sense and modify their environment.

Building upon the notation of the UML [16], in this paper we present an agent-oriented modeling technique which employs graph transformation rules[1] for specifying the effect of the agents' operations. We pay special attention to the modeling of co-operation and autonomy. Graph transformation rules in requirement specification and analysis allow us to capture the cooperation among several agents resulting in a joint activity. In the design phase, graph transformation rules specify the effect of the agents' local operations. Here, the non-determinism inherent to a rule-based approach provides a convenient model for the autonomy of agents. As underlying formal framework, typed graph transformation systems [2] provide a natural integration of structural and dynamic aspects as well as elaborate concepts for defining the consistency between requirements specification, analysis, and design (see [4]).

Next, we shall discuss in more detail the relevant properties of agent-based systems as well as the main concepts of our modeling approach. The following sections 3 to 5 are concerned with the three main phases of software modeling (i.e., requirements specification, analysis, and design). Section 6 reviews and discusses concepts of roles in object- and agent-oriented modeling, and Section 7 concludes the paper.

The paper continues previous work on agent-based systems which is documented in [3, 5, 14].

2 Agent-Oriented Modeling

In this Section, we outline our approach to agent-oriented modeling. First, we discuss typical aspects of agent-based systems like reactivity, autonomy, proactivity, and cooperation, and describe how these aspects are captured in our approach. Then, we survey the three main phases of system modeling, i.e., requirement specification, analysis, and design and explain how this general pattern is instantiated in our case.

Although it is difficult to find a general (technical) definition of the term *agent*, some important characteristics of agents can be identified which distinguish them from *programs* or *objects* [10]. *Reactivity* is the capability of an agent to perceive its environment and react to changes. This property can be considered as a prerequisite for purposeful autonomy of agents, and it is already captured within the concept of active objects. In our approach, agents perceive their environment by matching the left-hand

[1] See, e.g., [17, 6, 7] for a recent collection of surveys and [1] for an introductory text.

sides of their transformation rules against the current state of the system, thus searching for the occurrence of a certain pattern. Then, agents react to an occurrence by the application of the corresponding rule.

Autonomy is a property of agents that manifests in the nondeterminism of its behavior if the system is observed externally. Different to objects, agents possess *autonomous operations* that are not automatically triggered by messages but may be invoked by the agents themselves when a corresponding situation pattern occurs in their environment. If several autonomous operations are applicable in a particular situation, the decision which operation to apply is internal to the agent.

Agents are *proactive* meaning that their activities are directed towards a goal. In our approach, this goal-driven behavior is not explicitly modeled. However, there is a close relationship with the (external) nondeterminism of agents' behavior because the decision which operation to apply can be thought of as driven by the internal desire to reach a given goal. *Cooperation* among agents assumes a common goal which may be negotiated at run-time. In our approach, global graph transformation rules are used in order to describe the combined effect of negotiations and the resulting joint activities of a group of agents. The communication required is specified by means of UML sequence diagrams.

As a simple but typical example of an agent-based system we describe an online banking application where, in order to enable sophisticated services, customers may be assisted by a *personal banking agent* (PBA) which offers a range of advanced functionality. In particular, the PBA manages the payment of bills: When a bill is sent to the PBA by the merchant of a shop and the payment of this bill is initiated by the customer, the personal banking agent selects one of the customer's accounts of which the bill is to be paid. This selection takes into account the transaction cost of each account which is considered. Then, the amount specified in the bill is transfered from the selected account to the destination by *account agents* responsible for the individual accounts. The system just described has properties that are characteristic for an agent-based system [10]: The PBA reacts to changes in its environment (like the arrival of a bill) and it modifies this environment through its actions (by paying it). It acts autonomously on behalf of the customer by choosing the account the bill is to be paid from. The agent is goal-oriented in the sense that it aims at minimizing transaction costs by an appropriate account selection.

We divide the modeling process of agent-based systems in a typical sequence of activities which is already well known from the modeling of object-oriented systems. First, the requirements are specified by informal descriptions of the system's functionality and by scenarios of important interactions. The analysis of this specification results in a model where the requirements are captured more precisely. Thereafter, in the design model the behavior that has been described globally in the analysis model is expressed by the local behavior of objects and agents. Within the *requirements specification* (Section 3) we follow a use case-driven approach. Use cases representing the main external functions of the system as well as important internal interactions among agents are refined by typical scenarios which are described by means of global graph transformations and sequence diagrams. During *analysis* (Section 4) the agents and objects as well as their messages, attributes, and links, which are identified in the use cases and scenarios, are specified in an agent class diagram. The scenarios are analyzed in order to derive a more complete specification making explicit the different alternatives in the execution of a use case. The semantics of graph transformations and sequence diagrams thus shifts from optional to mandatory behavior: If the execution reaches a state satisfying a pre-condition (specified by the left-hand side of a graph transformation rule) the further interaction must follow one of the given alternatives.

The *design* (Section 5) refines the analysis model in such a way that globally described behavior is mapped to local specifications of the behavior of agents and objects. A refined class diagram introduces additional features, in particular, the signatures of the agents' autonomous operations. The local execution order of an agent's operations is determined by a state diagram associated to each agent class. The effect of these operations on the state of the system is described by local graph transformation rules.

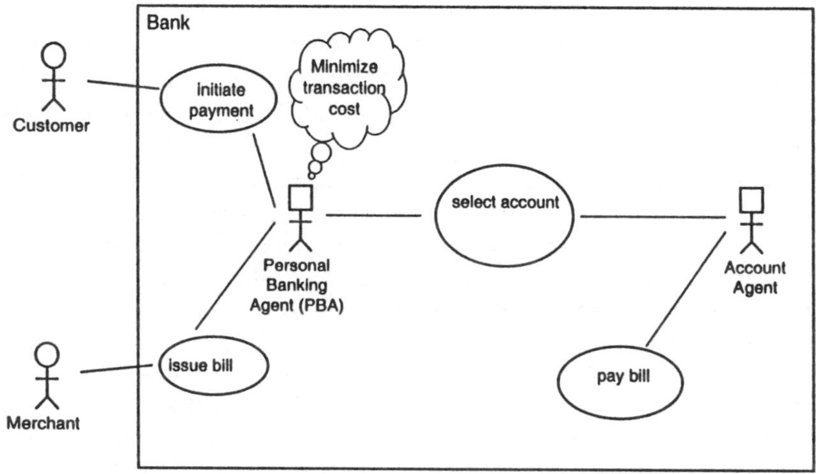

Fig. 1. Use case diagram for banking example

3 Requirements Specification

At the beginning of a development, customers and developers have to agree on the requirements a software product has to fulfill. These requirements are collected in a contract which has to be readable by the software developers as well as by customers which are typically not computer scientists. Therefore, a style of specification is appropriate which explains the functional and architectural requirements by means of informal diagrams and examples.

Use case diagrams are designed exactly for this purpose. They provide an abstract view of the system by identifying the main actors using it and the main functions that the system provides to them. In the context of agent-based systems, UML use case diagrams are extended by a special kind of actor (with square heads) representing agents. Goal cases (shown as clouds) are used in order to specify the goals of agents (cf. [12]).

The use case diagram of Figure 1, for example, identifies, besides two kinds of users, the agents PBA and AccountAgent. In this way, additional architectural requirements about the distribution of the system's functionality over different agents can be expressed. The use cases select account and pay bill that these agents participate in are internal to the system. They would not be shown in a typical UML use case diagram.

The abstract narrative description given by use cases is illustrated by typical examples, called *scenarios*, of how the system behaves when a use case is performed. In the methodology of this paper, scenarios are specified in two complementary ways. The overall effect of a use case like select account is described by a pair of instance diagrams as shown in Figure 2 modeling a *before-after* scenario of the use case. In the following section, this pair of diagrams shall be formally interpreted as an individual *graph transformation* representing the state change of objects and agents in the system.

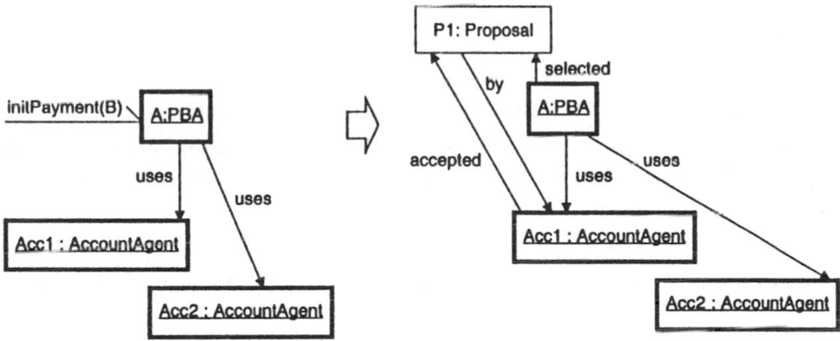

Fig. 2. Global graph transformation rule

In order to specify the communication between actors participating in a use case, UML *sequence diagrams* are used. The interaction that is necessary to select an account offering minimal transaction cost would typically be realized by the *contract net* protocol [9, 19] which describes the negotiation between a manager and a set of potential contractors about the delegation of a task. In terms of our example, a simplified version of this protocol may be informally described as follows.

> The Personal Banking Agent solicits proposals from the Account Agent by issuing a call for proposals, which specifies the interest in an account's transaction costs. Account Agent receiving the call for proposals are viewed as potential contractors, and are able to generate proposals to perform the task. Alternatively, account agents may refuse to propose. Once the Personal Banking Agent receives back replies from the Account Agent, it evaluates the proposals and makes its choice of which Account Agent will perform the task. The agent of the selected proposal will be sent an acceptance message, the others will receive a notice of rejection.

A typical scenario for two AccountAgents is depicted in Figure 3. Other scenarios for our example would include the possibility that no Account Agent makes a proposal or that no proposal is accepted.

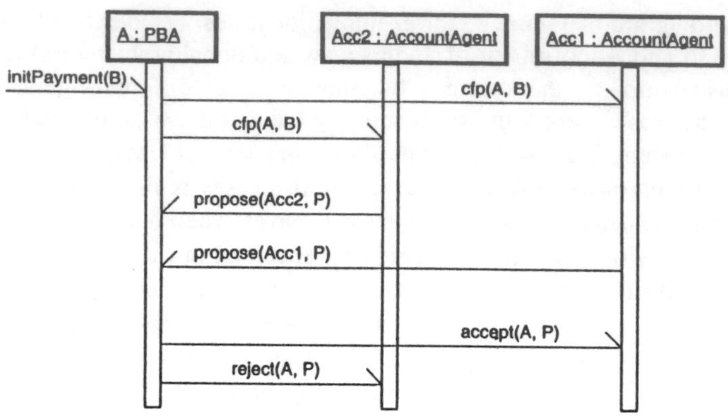

Fig. 3. Scenario for the banking example

4 Analysis

In order to serve as a basis for future design decisions, the requirements are analyzed and refined. Implementation-related issues are still avoided. Similar to object-oriented analysis, the refined model is structured into (sub)models [18], a *structural model*, a *dynamic model* and a *functional model*.

As *structural model*, an agent class diagram specifies the types of objects and agents, their attributes, associations, and messages. Notationally, we build on class di-

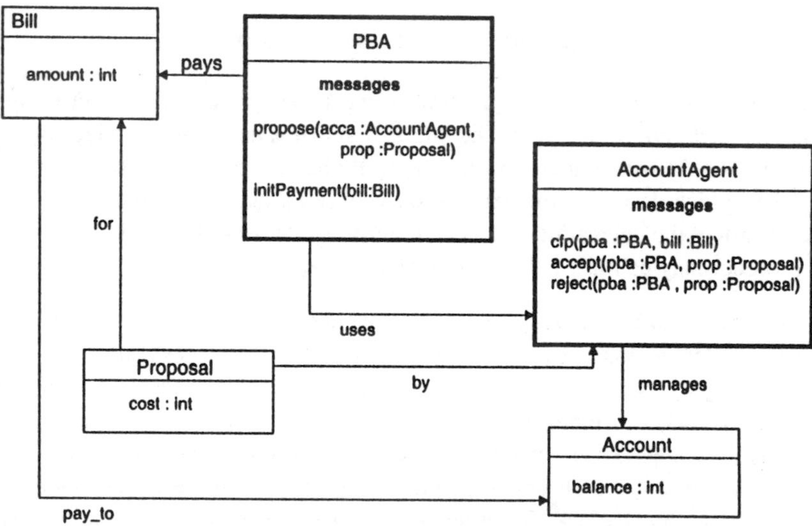

Fig. 4. Class diagram for banking example

agrams in UML [16] where agent classes are represented as active classes (with bold borders) that have an extra compartment for messages. In the agent class diagram in

Figure 4 we have agent classes PBA and AccountAgent and object classes Bill, Account and Proposal. Associations connect the PBAs to the Bills they have to pay and AccountAgents to the Accounts they manage. A Bill specifies an amount to be paid and the Account it is to be paid to. The messages correspond to those in the sequence diagram in Figure 3. They are modeled in the special message compartment of the agent class.

The *functional model* specifies the overall effect of a use case on the state of the system. In Section 3 this has been illustrated by a graph transformation, i.e., a pair of graphs modeling a *before-after* scenario of the use case. Formally, this scenario can be seen as an individual test case which has to be demonstrated by the implementation of the system. However, in order to have a complete view of the use case's overall effect, many such graph transformation pairs would be needed. Thus, a mechanism is required to specify (rather than to enumerate) pairs of graphs. The theory of graph transformation

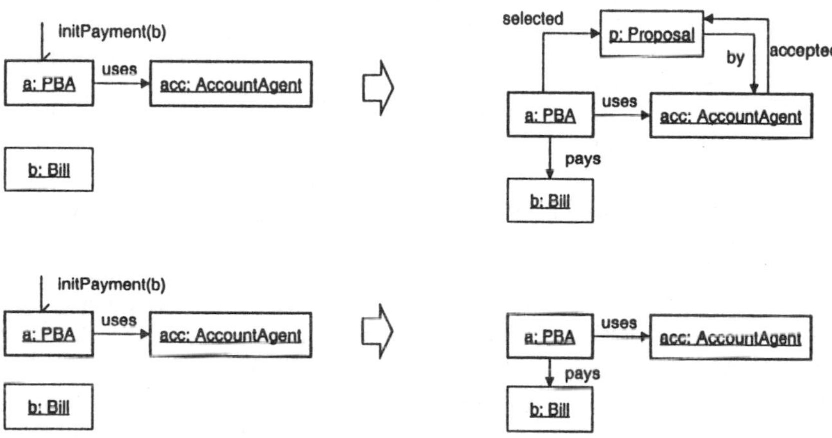

Fig. 5. Three rules specifying the possible result of each interaction

suggests a rule-based approach to this problem. A *graph transformation rule* $L \to R$ consists of a pair of graphs L, R such that the union $L \cup R$ is defined. (This ensures that, e.g., edges which appear in both L and R are connected to the same vertices in both graphs.) The left-hand side L represents the preconditions of the rule while the right-hand side R describes the postconditions. During analysis, rules are considered as incomplete specifications of the transformations to be performed, i.e., additional (unspecified) changes are permitted. This (quite liberal) notion of *graph transition* [8] shall be strengthened in the design model by the notion of *graph transformation* which assumes a complete specification of the changes during a step.

Figure 5 shows three rules specifying the possible effects of the use case select account. Each rule is only concerned with the interaction of one PBA with one of its AccountAgents during the execution of the contract net protocol. They specify the three possible results of each binary interaction.

The *dynamic model* complements the functional model by focusing on the communication required to execute a certain protocol. Like in the requirements specification, we use sequence diagrams to model the message flow between agents in the system. However, during analysis, we strengthen the semantics of these diagrams from an existential to a universal interpretation. This is analogous to the shift from individual transformations to universal transformation rules in the functional model. Thus, a sequence diagram associated with a graph transformation rule provides a complete specification of the interactions to be performed when the precondition is met. In Figure 6, the sequence diagrams for the banking example are presented. The first diagram models the case that the proposal of the AccountAgent is accepted by the PBA and the second one the rejection of the proposal. The third diagram depicts the case that the AccountAgent does not answer upon a call for proposal. They correspond to the three rules in Figure 5. A sequence diagram is activated when the precondition of the corresponding rule is met. For the rules in Figure 5 associated with the sequence diagrams in Figure 6, the precondition requires that the Account Agent is connected with the PBA by a uses link, and that the latter is activated by an initPayment message. Since the precondition is the same in all three cases, if the condition is met, the interaction between the two agents may conform to one of the three sequence diagrams.

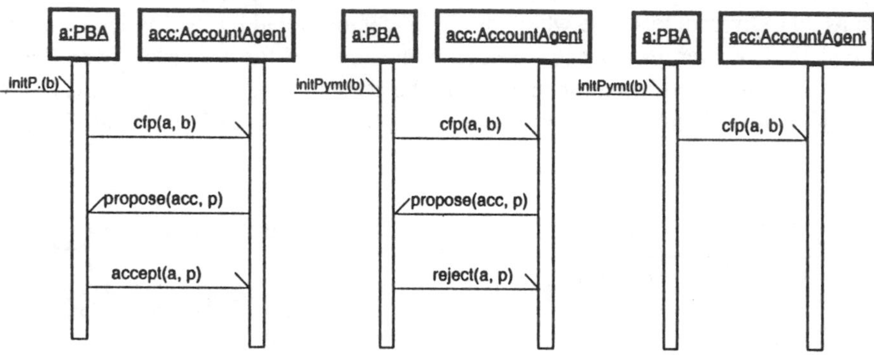

Fig. 6. Three sequence diagrams corresponding to the three rules in Figure 5

5 Design

The analysis phase is concerned with developing a model of what the system is supposed to do. The design model elaborates the analysis model concentrating on the question how the system will function. As a consequence, the focus of models is shifted from a global view on the system during analysis to a local view, thus providing the basis for an implementation. Like in analysis, we distinguish a structural model, a dynamic model, and a functional model.

In the *structural model*, the class diagram of the design phase refines the class diagram of the analysis adding, in particular, the signatures of the agent's autonomous operations for which an extra compartment is provided. Notice the difference with

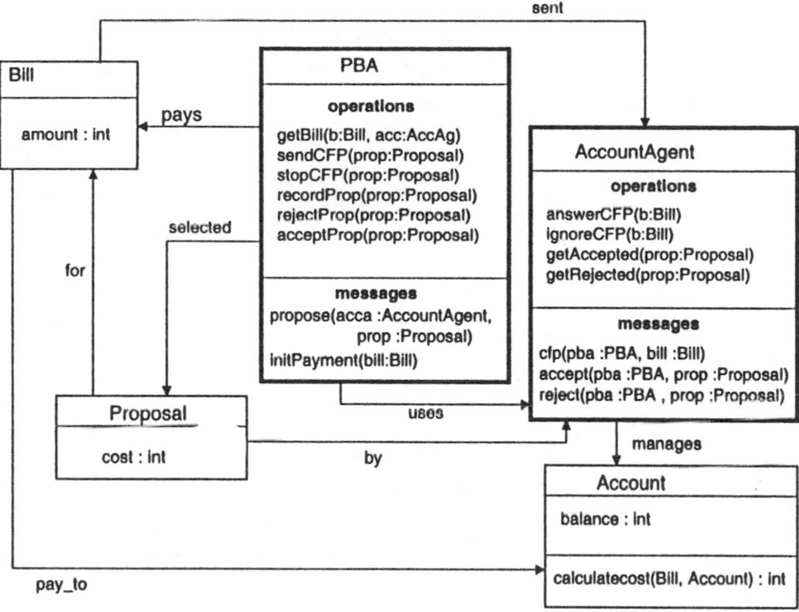

Fig. 7. Agent class diagram

methods as specified in the method compartment of objects: agent's operations are *autonomous*, that is, they are never called by another object or agent but only executed under control of the agent itself (cf. Section 2). As a consequence, we distinguish agent's messages and operations while in the case of objects, both notions are integrated in the notion of a method.

By a state diagram for each agent class, the *dynamic model* specifies the ordering of operations an agent of this class may perform. As agents do not automatically react to events of their environment but decide autonomously when and how to react, transitions are not labeled with an event and an action but only with the name of the operation. This usage of statecharts is semantically different from traditional approaches [11]. The notion of a protocol state machine [16] comes closest to our understanding. Consider, as an example, the statechart for the AccountAgent. From the first state, this agent may either proceed to the *proposed* state by answering a call for proposal or it may decide not to propose and proceed to the final state. The agent decides what to do based on an internal strategy that is not part of the model.

In the *functional model*, the operations declared in the structural model are specified by graph transformation rules. Whereas the dynamic model is concerned with the order of operations, the functional model shows how operations change the state of the system. As agent's operations may only affect that part of the state which can be accessed locally, we require that all objects in the left-hand side of a rule are reachable via a path originating at the *self* agent. For example, in Figure 9 the operations getBill and sendCFP of the PBA are specified. The first operation triggers the agent to issue requests for proposals for a given bill. If a PBA has not yet sent a call to a particular AccountAgent (expressed by the negative context condition for the sent link) the PBA

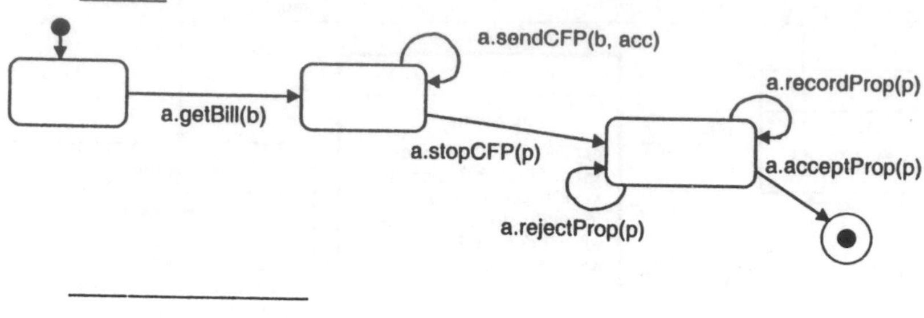

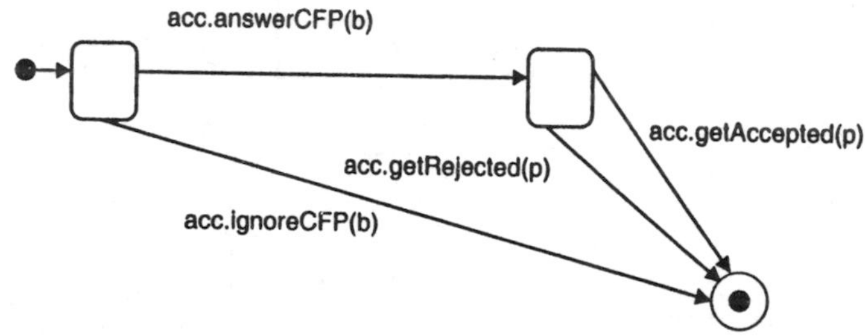

Fig. 8. Statecharts for agents *PBA* and *AccountAgent*

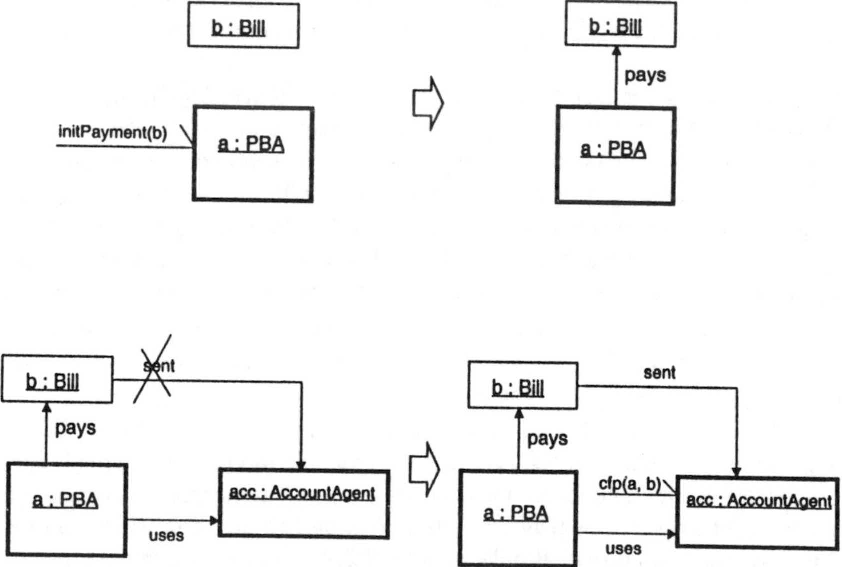

Fig. 9. Graph transformation rules getBill and sendCFP

may use the second rule for issuing the call. On reception of a call for proposal mes-

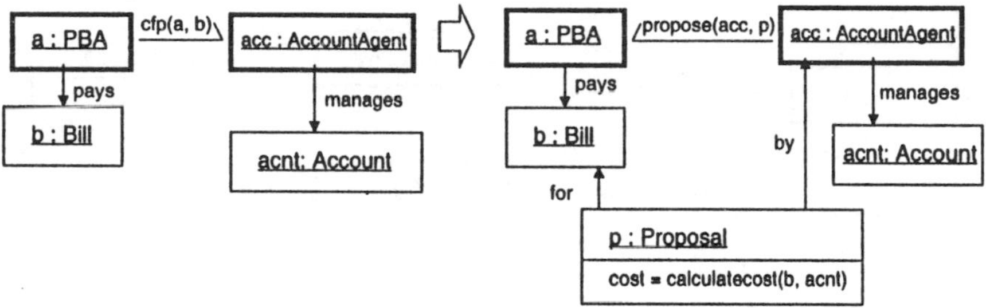

Fig. 10. Graph transformation rule answerCFP

sage, an AccountAgent may decide to send a Proposal specifying the costs for the required transaction as described by the rule answerCFP in Figure 10. The alternative rule for ignoreProp is not shown. It has the same pre-condition and the only effect of removing the cfp message. Receiving a proposal, the PBA may either reject it if it

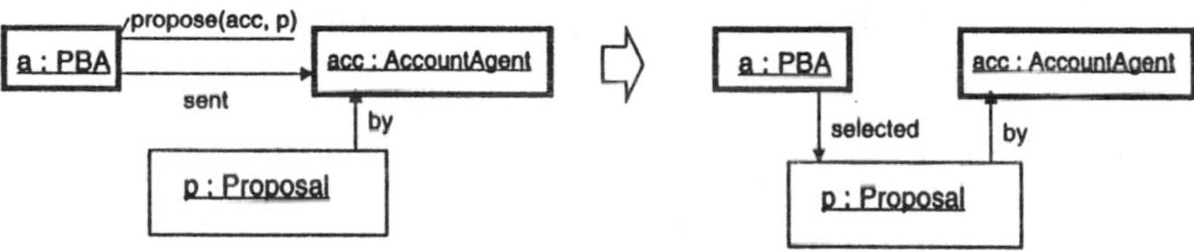

Fig. 11. Graph transformation rule stopCFP

has bigger cost than the best proposal received so far or it may record this proposal as its current favorite. The first proposal is recorded when the agent stops sending calls. The operations stopCFP and recordProp are specified in Figure 11 and 12. The rule for rejectProp is not shown. When the PBA decides to have received enough proposals, it sends the current best an accept message. Upon reception of this message, the AccountAgent records its proposal as accepted. When rejected, the agent deletes its proposal.

6 Roles in Agent-Oriented Modeling

The concept of roles is well-established in object-oriented modeling [13]. During its life-time, an object may play one or several roles encapsulating a certain functionality which may change dynamically when the object evolves. The operations and attributes required to play a role are represented by a role type. The existence of an object's role

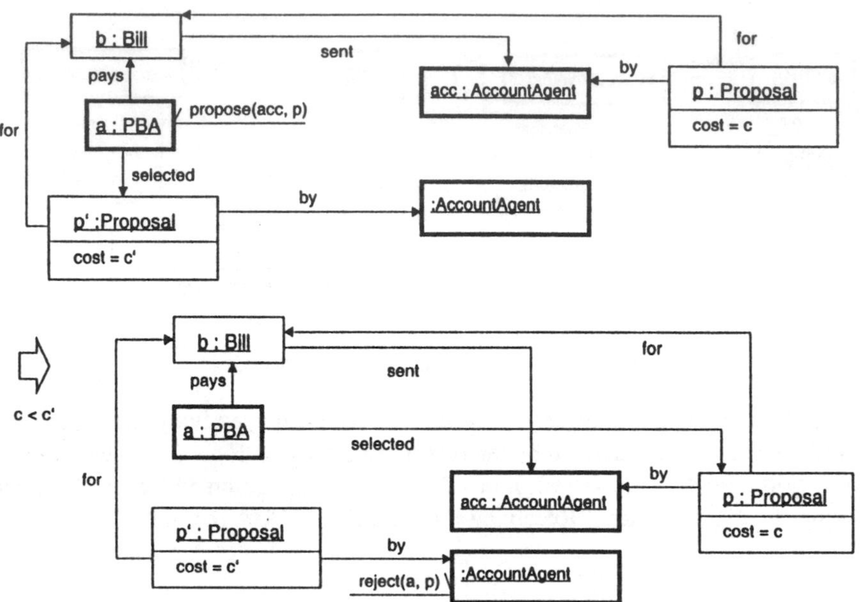

Fig. 12. Graph transformation rule recordProp

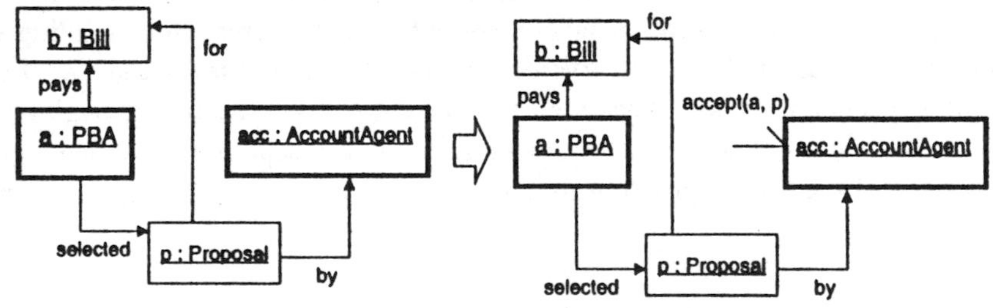

Fig. 13. Graph transformation rule acceptProp

depends on that of the object itself. Roles restrict the visibility of an object or agent if associations to other objects or agents only exist via attached roles.

In agent-oriented modeling, agent roles are used for capturing goals, tasks, or functions exhibited by the agent. According to Wooldridge et al. [21], a role has associated to it responsibilities, permissions, activities, and protocols which are defined by specific role schemata. Responsibilities comprise lifeness conditions like the execution of a prescribed sequence of protocols. In this way the interaction of roles is specified. Wood et al. [20] introduce a Multi-agent Systems Engineering (MaSE) methodology where roles are introduced as more fine-grained building blocks of agent classes which capture agent goals during the design phase. A role serves as an abstract description for the functions it is responsible to fulfill in order to reach an assigned goal.

Both object and agent roles restrict the behavior and state of an entity to the part which is necessary to reach a goal, to fulfill a single task, or to participate in a specific interaction. Next, we sketch in which way roles would be integrated in our methodology. In the requirements specification, an actor's interactions are determined by the use cases it is participating in. Each interactions defines a role of the actor, encapsulating the agent's behavior during the corresponding use case. The personal banking agent, for example, assumes the role of an *account selector* when interacting with the select account use case in Figure 1. Relative to this use case, the *account agent* takes the role of a possible contractor for the selection of an account. Another role of the account agent is that of a *bill payer* transferring money to another account. When global graph transformation rules and sequence diagrams are used to describe the functional behavior of use cases, each occurrence of an agent in a rule or a diagram corresponds to a different role.

Thus, in the early stage of development, roles simplify the transition from requirement specification to analysis. In fact, the classes in the analysis model can be derived by integrating *role classes* that encapsulate the state and behavior necessary to participate in the interactions associated with the use cases. Role classes can be instantiated like object or agent classes, but their instances do only exist in connection with an agent or object. That means, a role instance automatically disappears together with the object, agent or role it depends on. Thus, from a structural point of view, this *role-of relationship* is similar to a composition in UML. Considering the behavior of roles, it resembles inheritance because roles can access their parent's features as if they were their own.

Roles also make more systematic the transition from analysis to design because each role contributes only to one global interaction. Thus, interactions can be realized one by one. In a second step, the behavior of the corresponding roles can be coordinated yielding the behavior of the entire class. In this way the complexity of the total behavior of a class participating in many different interactions can be structured, e.g., by attaching statecharts to the individual roles and synchronizing theses statecharts afterwards.

In order to make this concept of roles more useful it has to be integrated syntactically and semantically in a formal agent model like the one presented in [4].

7 Conclusion

In this paper, we have presented an approach to agent-oriented modeling based on UML notation and concepts of typed graph transformation systems [2]. Extending the notion of active object from object-oriented modeling, specific support is provided for characteristic aspects of agent-based systems like autonomy, goal-driven behavior, and cooperation of agents.

The theory of graph transformation also provides the mathematical background for the formalization of the approach. In [4], for example, *graph processes* [2] and concepts of views of graph transformation systems [8] are used in order to formalize the consistency between requirement specification, analysis and design in agent-oriented modeling.

References

1. M. Andries, G. Engels, A. Habel, B. Hoffmann, H.-J. Kreowski, S. Kuske, D. Plump, A. Schürr, and G. Taentzer. Graph transformation for specification and programming. *Science of Computer Programming*, 34:1–54, 1999.
2. A. Corradini, U. Montanari, and F. Rossi. Graph processes. *Fundamenta Informaticae*, 26(3,4):241–266, 1996.
3. R. Depke, R. Heckel, and J. M. Küster. Integrating visual modeling of agent-based and object-oriented systems. In *Proc. Fourth Intern. Conference on Autonomous Agents (AGENTS-2000)*, Barcelona, Spain, June 2000.
4. R. Depke, R. Heckel, and J. M. Küster. Modeling agent-based systems with graph transformation. Technical Report No. 213, University of Paderborn, Dep. of Comp. Sci., August 2000. `http://www.uni-paderborn.de/cs/ag-engels/Papers/Depke2000TR.pdf`.
5. R. Depke, R. Heckel, and J.M. Küster. Modeling agent-based systems with graph transformation and UML: From requirement specification to object-oriented design. In *GRATRA 2000: Joint APPLIGRAPH/GETGRATS Workshop on Graph Transformation Systems*, pages 87–95, Berlin, Germany, March 2000. Proceedings available at `http://tfs.cs.tu-berlin.de/gratra2000/`.
6. H. Ehrig, G. Engels, H.-J. Kreowski, and G. Rozenberg, editors. *Handbook of Graph Grammars and Computing by Graph Transformation, Volume 2: Applications, Languages, and Tools*. World Scientific, 1999.
7. H. Ehrig, H.-J. Kreowski, U. Montanari, and G. Rozenberg, editors. *Handbook of Graph Grammars and Computing by Graph Transformation, Volume 3: Concurrency and Distribution*. World Scientific, 1999.
8. G. Engels, R. Heckel, G. Taentzer, and H. Ehrig. A combined reference model- and view-based approach to system specification. *Int. Journal of Software and Knowledge Engeneering*, 7(4):457–477, 1997.
9. Foundation for Intelligent Physical Agents (FIPA). Agent communication language. In *FIPA 97 Specification, Version 2.0*, `http://www.fipa.org`. FIPA, 1997.
10. S. Franklin and A. Graesser. Is it an agent, or just a program?: A taxonomy for autonomous agents. In J.P. Müller, M.J. Wooldridge, and N.R. Jennings, editors, *Proc. ECAI'96 Workshop on Agent Theories, Architectures, and Languages: Intelligent Agents III*, volume 1193 of *LNAI*, pages 21–36. Springer-Verlag, August 12–13 1997.

11. D. Harel. Statecharts: A visual formalism for complex systems. *Science of Computer Programming*, 8:231–274, 1987.
12. C. A. Iglesias, M. Garijo, J. C. González, and Juan R. Velasco. Analysis and design of multiagent systems using MAS-CommonKADS. In M.P. Singh, A. Rao, and M.J. Wooldridge, editors, *Proc. 4th Int. Workshop on Agent Theories, Architectures, and Languages (ATAL-97)*, volume 1365 of *LNAI*, pages 313–328. Springer-Verlag, July 24–26 1998.
13. Bent B. Kristensen. Object Oriented Modeling with Roles. In *Proc. 2nd International Conference on Object-Oriented Information Systems (OOIS'95), Dublin, Ireland, 1995*, pages 57–71, London, 1996. Springer.
14. J.M. Küster. Visual modeling of agent-based systems: A role-oriented approach using the UML. diploma thesis, University of Paderborn, Germany, 2000.
15. N. Jennings M. Wooldridge and D. Kinny. A methodology for agent-oriented analysis and design. In *Proceedings of the third annual conference on Autonomous Agents*, pages 69–76, Seattle, WA USA, May1–5 1999. ACM.
16. Object Management Group. UML specification version 1.3, June 1999. `http://www.omg.org`.
17. G. Rozenberg, editor. *Handbook of Graph Grammars and Computing by Graph Transformation, Volume 1: Foundations*. World Scientific, 1997.
18. J. Rumbaugh, M. Blaha, W. Premerlani, F. Eddy, and W. Lorensen. *Object–oriented Modelling and Design*. Prentice–Hall, 1991.
19. R. G. Smith. The contract net protocol: High-level communication and control in a distributed problem solver. In *IEEE Transaction on Computers*, number 12 in C-29, pages 1104–1113, 1980.
20. M. Wood and S. A. DeLoach. An Overview of the Multiagent Systems Engineering Methodology. In *Proc. 1st International Workshop on Agent-Oriented Software Engineering (ICSE-2000 Workshop), Limerick, Ireland, 2000.*
21. M. Wooldridge, N. R. Jennings, and D. Kinny. The Gaia methodology for agent-oriented analysis and design. *Journal of Autonomous Agents and Multi-Agent Systems*, 3(3):285–312, 2000.

Representing Agent Interaction Protocols in UML

James J. Odell[*] H. Van Dyke Parunak[†] Bernhard Bauer[‡]

[*] James Odell Associates, 3646 W. Huron River Dr., Ann Arbor, MI 48103 USA
jodell@compuserve.com

[†] ERIM Center for Electronic Commerce, P.O. Box 134001, Ann Arbor, MI 48113 USA
vparunak@erim.org

[‡] Siemens, ZT IK 6, D-81730 München, Germany
bernhard.bauer@mchp.siemens.de

Abstract. Gaining wide acceptance for the use of agents in industry requires both relating it to the nearest antecedent technology (object-oriented software development) and using artifacts to support the development environment throughout the full system lifecycle. We address both of these requirements using AUML, the Agent UML (Unified Modeling Language)—a set of UML idioms and extensions. This paper illustrates the approach by presenting a three-layer AUML representation for agent interaction protocols: templates and packages to represent the protocol as a whole; sequence and collaboration diagrams to capture inter-agent dynamics; and activity diagrams and state charts to capture both intra-agent and inter-agent dynamics.

1 Introduction

Successful industrial deployment of agent technology requires techniques that reduce the risk inherent in any new technology. Two ways that reduce risk in the eyes of potential adopters are:

- to present the new technology as an incremental extension of known and trusted methods, and
- to provide explicit engineering tools that support industry-accepted methods of technology deployment.

We apply both of these risk-reduction insights to agents.

To leverage the acceptance of existing technology, we present agents as an extension of active objects, exhibiting both dynamic autonomy (the ability to initiate action without external invocation) and deterministic autonomy (the ability to refuse or modify an external request). Thus, our basic definition of an agent is "an object that can say 'go' (dynamic autonomy) and 'no' (deterministic autonomy)." This approach leads us to focus on fairly fine-grained agents. More sophisticated capabilities can also be added, such as mobility, BDI mechanisms, and explicit modeling of other agents. Such capabilities are extensions to our basic agents, that is, they can be applied where needed, but are not diagnostic of agenthood.

Accepted methods of industrial software development depend on standard representations for artifacts to support the analysis, specification, and design of agent software. Three characteristics of industrial software development require the disciplined development of artifacts throughout the software lifecycle. The scope of industrial software projects is much larger than typical academic research efforts, involving many more people across a longer period of time, and artifacts facilitate communication. The skills of developers are focused more on development methodology than on tracking the latest agent techniques, and artifacts can help codify best practice. The success criteria for industrial projects require traceability between initial requirements and the final deliverable—a task that artifacts directly support.

The Unified Modeling Language (UML) is gaining wide acceptance for the representation of engineering artifacts in object-oriented software. Our view of agents as the next step beyond objects leads us to explore extensions to UML and idioms within UML to accommodate the distinctive requirements of agents. The result is Agent UML (AUML). This paper reports on one such area of extension—the representation of agent protocols.

Section 2 provides background information on agent design methods in general, on UML, and on the need for AUML. Section 3 introduces a layered approach to representing agent protocols in AUML. Templates and packages provide a high-level summary (Section 4), sequence diagrams and collaboration diagrams furnish alternative views of the interactions among agents (Section 5), and state diagrams and activity diagrams detail the internal behavior of individual agents in executing protocols (Section 6). Section 7 summarizes our contribution.

2 Background

Agent UML (AUML) synthesizes a growing concern for agent-based software methodologies with the increasing acceptance of UML for object-oriented software development.

2.1 Agent Software Methodologies

The agent R&D community is increasingly interested in design methods and representational tools to support the associated artifacts (see [12] for a helpful survey). Multi-Agent System Engineering was the focus of a session at ATAL'97 [5, 10, 13, 17, 19, 23, 25, 26] and the entire MAAMAW'99 [9].

A number of groups have reported on methodologies for agent design, touching on representational mechanisms as they support the methodology. Our own report [23] emphasizes methodology, as does the work by Kinny and colleagues [15, 16] on modeling techniques for BDI agents. The close parallel that we observe between design mechanisms for agents and for objects is shared by a number of authors, for example [5, 6].

The GAIA methodology [28] includes specific recommendations for notation that supports the high-level summary of a protocol as an atomic unit, a notation that is reflected in our recommendations. The extensive program underway at the Free University of Amsterdam on compositional methodologies for requirements [11], design [4], and verification [14] uses graphical representations with strong links to UML's collaboration diagrams, as well as linear (formulaic) notations better suited to alignment with UML's metamodel than with the graphical mechanisms that are our focus. Our discussion of the compositionality of protocols is anticipated in the work of Burmeister et al. [7], though our notation differs widely from hers. Dooley graphs facilitate the identification of the "character" that results from an agent playing a specific role (as distinct from the same agent playing a different role) [21, 27]. We capture this distinction by leveraging UML's existing name/role:class syntax in conjunction with collaboration diagrams.

This wide-ranging activity is a healthy sign that agent-based systems are having an increasing impact, since the demand for methodologies and artifacts reflects the growing commercial importance of our technology. Our objective is not to compete with any of these efforts, but rather to extend and apply a widely accepted modeling and representational formalism (UML)—one that harnesses insights and makes them useful for communicating across a wide range of research groups and development methodologies.

2.2 UML

During the seventies, structured programming was the dominant approach to software development. Along with it, software engineering technologies were developed in order to ease and formalize the system development lifecycle: from planning, through analysis and design, and finally to system construction, transition, and maintenance. In the eighties, object-oriented (OO) languages experienced a rise in popularity, bringing with it new concepts such as data encapsulation, inheritance, messaging, and polymorphism. By the end of the eighties and beginning of the nineties, a jungle of modeling approaches grew to support the OO marketplace. To make sense of and unify these various approaches, an Analysis and Design Task Force was established on 29 June 1995 within the OMG. By November 1997, a de jure standard was adopted by the OMG members called the Unified Modeling Language (UML).

The UML unifies and formalizes the methods of many approaches to the object-oriented software lifecycle, including Booch, Rumbaugh (OMT), Jacobson, and Odell [18]. It supports the following kinds of models:

- **static models**- such as class and package diagrams describe the static semantics of data and messages. Within system development, class diagrams are used in two different ways, for two different purposes. First, they can model a problem domain conceptually. Since they are conceptual in nature, they can be presented to the customers. Second, class diagrams can model the implementation of classes—guiding the developers. At a general level, the term class refers to the encapsulated unit. The conceptual level models types and their associations; the implementation level models implementation classes. While both can be more generally thought of as classes, their usage as concepts and implementation notions is important both in purpose and semantics. Package diagrams group classes in conceptual packages for presentation and consideration. (Physical aggregations of classes are called components which are in the implementation model family, mentioned below.)

- **dynamic models-** including interaction diagrams (i.e., sequence and collaboration diagrams), state charts, and activity diagrams.
- **use cases-** the specification of actions that a system or class can perform by interacting with outside actors.
- **implementation models-** such as component models and deployment diagrams describing the component distribution on different platforms.
- **object constraint language (OCL)-** is a simple formal language to express more semantics within an UML specification. It can be used to define constraints on the model, invariant, pre- and post-conditions of operations and navigation paths within an object net.

In this paper, we are suggesting agent-based extensions to the following UML representations: packages, templates, sequence diagrams, collaboration diagrams, activity diagrams, and statecharts. The UML model semantics are represented by a metamodel whose structure is also formally defined by OCL syntax. OCL and the metamodel offer resources to capture the kinds of logical specifications anticipated in (for example) [4, 11, 14, 15, 16, 28], but space does not permit exploring this use of UML in this paper.

2.3 AUML

Compared to the traditional approach to objects, agents are autonomous and interactive. Based on internal states, their activities include goals and conditions that guide the execution of defined tasks. While objects need outside control to execute their methods, agents know the conditions and intended effects of their actions and hence take responsibility for their needs. Furthermore, agents act both alone and with other agents. Multiagent systems can often resemble a social community of interdependent members that act individually.

However, no formalism yet exists to sufficiently specify agent-based system development. To employ agent-based programming, a specification technique must support the whole software engineering process—from planning, through analysis and design, and finally to system construction, transition, and maintenance.

A proposal for a full life-cycle specification of agent-based system development is beyond the scope of this paper. Both FIPA and the OMG Agent Work Group are exploring uses of and recommending extensions to UML [1, 20]. Depke *et al* [29] discuss graph transformation and roles in an agent-baseed UML. We are working on a comprehensive scheme for AUML [22]. In this paper, we indicate how UML can be used to express *agent interaction protocols* (AIP), as well as express where extensions to the standard UML (AUML) AIPs might be appropriate.

This subset was chosen because interaction protocols are complex enough to illustrate the nontrivial use of AUML and are used commonly enough to make this subset of AUML useful to other researchers. Agent interaction protocols are a good example of software patterns which are ideas found useful in one practical context and probably useful in others. A specification of an AIP provides an example or analogy that we might use to solve problems in system analysis and design.

We want to suggest a specification technique for AIPs with both formal and intuitive semantics and a user-friendly graphical notation. The semantics allows a precise definition that is also usable in the software-engineering process. The graphical notation provides a common language for AIP communication—particularly with people not familiar with the agent approach.

Before proceeding, we need to establish a working definition. An agent interaction protocol (AIP) describes a communication pattern as an allowed sequence of messages between agents and the constraints on the content of those messages.

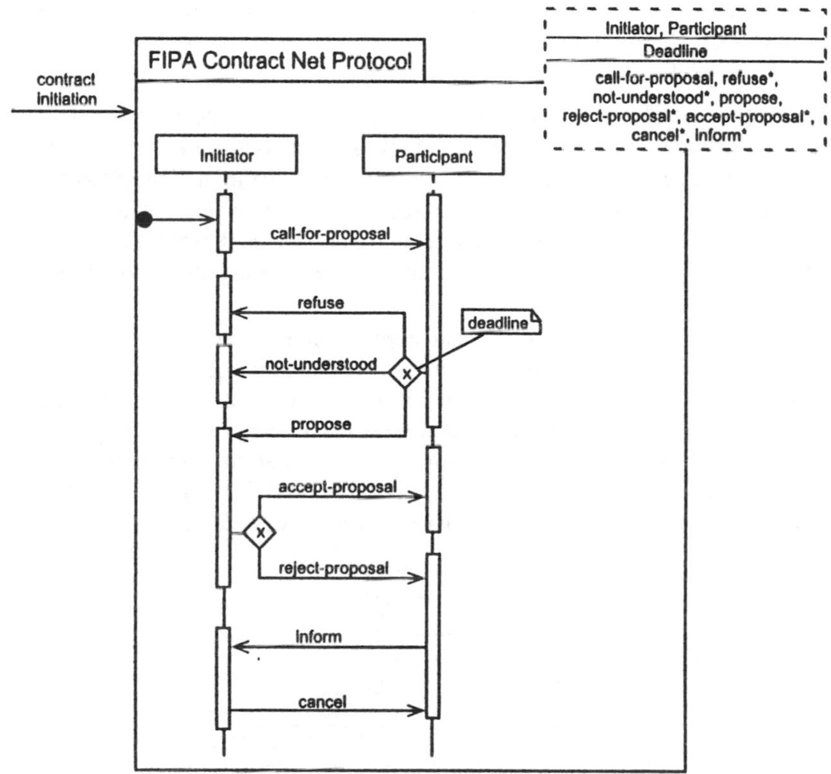

Fig. 1. A generic AIP expressed as a template package.

3 A Layered Approach to Protocols

Figure 1 depicts a protocol expressed as a UML *sequence diagram* for the contract net protocol. When invoked, an Initiator agent sends a call-for-proposal to an agent that is willing to participate in providing a proposal. The Participant agent can then choose to respond to the Initiator before a given deadline by: refusing to provide a proposal, submitting a proposal, or indicating that it did not understand. (The diamond symbol indicates a decision that can result in zero or more communications being sent—depending on the conditions it contains; the "x" in the decision diamond indicates an *exclusive or* decision.) If a proposal is offered, the Initiator has a choice of either accepting or rejecting the proposal. When the Participant receives a proposal acceptance, it will inform the Initiator about the proposal's execution. Additionally, the Initiator can cancel the execution of the proposal at any time.

This figure also expresses two more concepts represented at the top of the sequence chart. First, the protocol as a whole is treated as an entity in its own right. The tabbed folder notation at the upper left indicates that the protocol is a *package*, a conceptual aggregation of interaction sequences. Second, the packaged protocol can be treated as a pattern that can be customized for analogous problem domains. The dashed box at the upper right-hand corner expresses this pattern as a *template* specification that identifies unbound entities within the package which need to be bound when the package template is being instantiated.

The original sequence diagram in Fig. 1 provides a basic specification for a contract net protocol. More processing detail is often required. For example, an Initiator agent requests a call for proposal (CFP) from a Participant agent. However, the diagram stipulates neither the procedure used by the Initiator to produce the CFP request, nor the procedure employed by the Participant to respond to the CFP. Yet, such details are important for developing detailed agent-based system specifications.

Figure 2 illustrates how *leveling* can express more detail for any interaction process. For example, the process that generated the communication act CA-1 could be complex enough to specify its processing in more detail using an activity diagram. The agent receiving CA-1 has a process that prepares a response. In this example, the process being specified is depicted using a sequence diagram, though any modeling language could be chosen to further specify an agent's underlying process. In UML, the choice is an interaction diagram, an activity diagram, or a statechart.

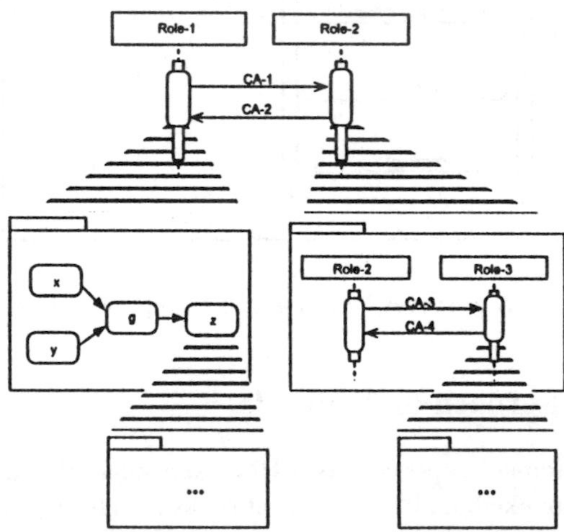

Fig. 2. Interaction protocols can be specified in more detail (i.e., leveled) using a combination of diagrams.

Finally, leveling can continue "down" until the problem has been specified adequately to develop or generate code. So in Fig. 2, the interaction protocol at the top of the diagram has a level of detail below, which in turn has another level of detail. Each level can express *intra-agent* or *inter-agent* activity.

In summary, these two examples illustrate several features of our approach:

- The protocol as a whole is an entity. This top level is discussed further in Section 4.
- The sequence diagram itself describes the inter-agent transactions needed to implement the protocol. Section 5 further discusses this notation and an alternative (the collaboration diagram).

In addition to inter-agent transactions, complete specification of a protocol requires discussion of intra-agent activity and is supported by UML's activity diagrams and statecharts (discussed in Section 6).

4 Level 1: Representing the Overall Protocol

Patterns are ideas that have been found useful in one practical context and can probably be useful in others. As such, they give us examples or analogies that we might use as solutions to problems in system analysis and design. Agent interaction protocols, then, provide us with reusable solutions that can be applied to various kinds of message sequencing we encounter between agents. There are two UML techniques that best express protocol solutions for reuse: *packages* and *templates*.

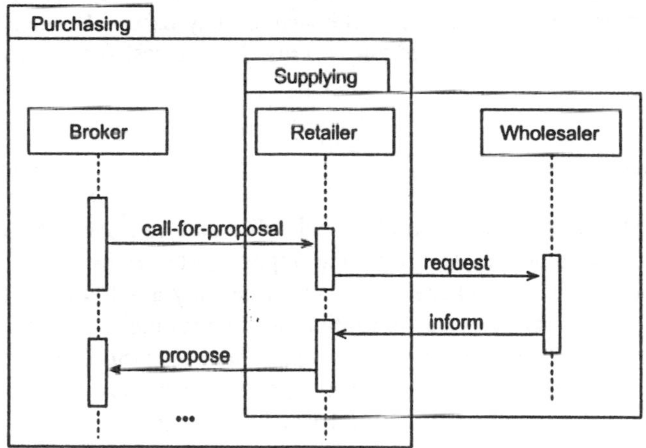

Fig. 3. Using packages to express nested protocols.

4.1 Packages

Since interaction protocols are patterns, they can be treated as reusable aggregates of processing. UML describes two ways of expressing aggregation for OO structure and behavior: *components* and *packages*. Components are physical aggregations that compose classes for implementation purposes. Packages aggregate modeling elements into conceptual wholes. Here, classes can be conceptually grouped for any arbitrary purpose, such as a subsystem grouping of classes. Since AIPs can be viewed in conceptual terms, the package notation of a tabbed folder was employed in Fig. 1.

Because protocols can be codified as recognizable patterns of agent interaction, they become reusable modules of processing that can be treated as first-class notions. For example, Fig. 3 depicts two packages. The Purchasing package expresses a simple protocol between a Broker and a Retailer. Here, the Broker sends a call for proposal to a Retailer and the Retailer responds with a proposal. For certain products, the Retailer might also place a request with a Wholesaler regarding availability and cost. Based on the return information, the Retailer can provide a more accurate proposal. All of this could have been put into a single Purchasing protocol package. However, many businesses or departments may not need the additional protocol involving the Wholesaler. Therefore, two packages can be defined: one for Purchasing and one for Supplying. When a particular scenario requires the Wholesaler protocol, it can be nested as a separate and distinct package. However, when a Purchasing scenario does not require it, the package is more parsimonious.

Burmeister et al. suggest a similar construct when they describe their *complex cooperation protocols* [7]. Their three primitive protocols—offering, requesting, and proposing—"are general enough to be used in a large number of interaction situations." Their approach "allows for the construction of (more complex) application or task protocols." In addition to their three primitive protocols, we advocate a pragmatic approach where the analyst may extend Burmeister's general set to include any protocols that might be reused for a nested specification—using AUML.

4.2 Templates

Figure 1 illustrates a common kind of behavior that can serve as a solution in analogous problem domains. In Fig. 3, the Supplying behavior is reused exactly as defined by the Supplying package. However, to be truly a pattern—instead of just a reusable component—package customization must be supported. For example, Fig. 4 applies the FIPA Contract Net Protocol to a particular scenario involving buyers and sellers. Notice that the Initiator and Participant agents have become Buyer and Seller agents, and the call-for-proposal has become the seller-rfp. Also in this scenario are two forms of refusal by the Seller: Refuse-1 and Refuse-2. Lastly, an actual deadline has been supplied for a response by the seller.

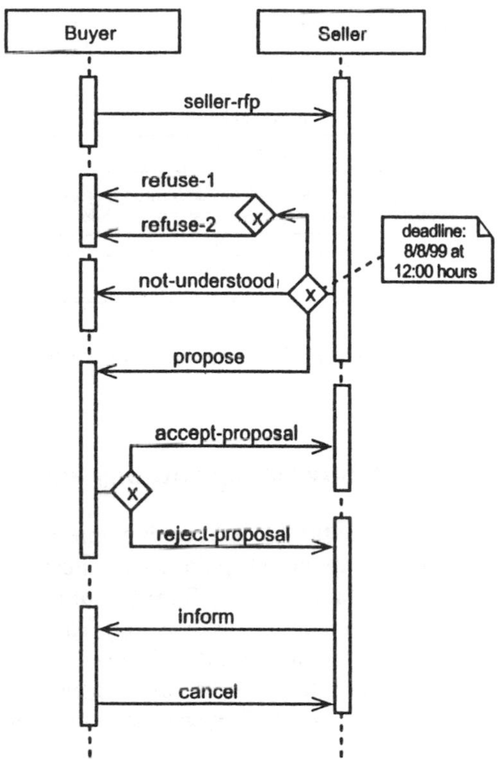

Fig. 4. Applying the template in Fig. 1 to a particular scenario involving buyers and sellers.

In UML argot, the AIP package serves as a *template.* A template is a parameterized model element whose parameters are bound at model time (i.e., when the new customized model is produced). In Fig. 1, the dotted box in the upper right indicates that the package is a template. The unbound parameters in the box are divided by horizontal lines into three categories: role parameters, constraints, and communication acts. Figure 5 illustrates how the new package in Fig. 4 is produced using the template definition in Fig. 1.[1] Wooldridge et al. suggest a similar form of definition with their *protocol definitions* [28]. In their packaged templates "a pattern of interaction . . . has been formally defined and abstracted away from any particular sequence of execution steps. Viewing interactions in this way means that attention is focussed on the essential nature and purpose of interaction rather than the precise ordering of particular message exchanges." Instead of the notation illustrated by Wooldridge et al., our graphical approach more closely resembles UML, while expressing the same semantics.

---

[1] This template format is not currently UML compliant, but is recommended for future UML extensions.

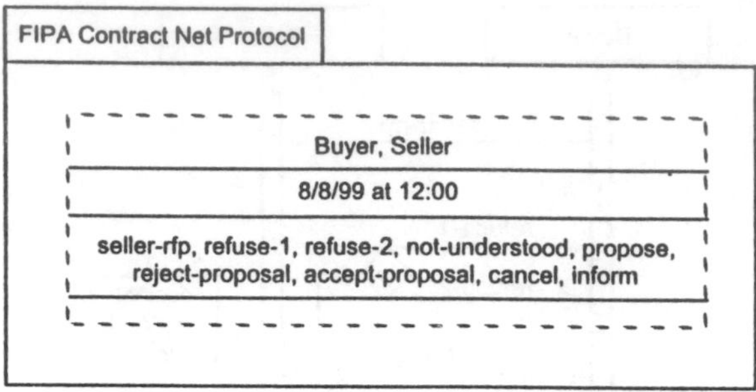

Fig. 5. Producing a new package using the Fig. 1 template; Fig. 4 is the resulting model.

5 Level 2: Representing Interactions among agents

UML's *dynamic models* are useful for expressing interactions among agents. *Interaction diagrams* capture the structural patterns of interactions among objects. Sequence diagrams are one member of this family; collaboration diagrams are another. The two diagrams contain the same information. The graphical layout of the sequence diagram emphasizes the chronological sequence of communications, while that of the collaboration diagram emphasizes the associations among agents. *Activity diagrams* and *statecharts* capture the flow of processing in the agent community.

5.1 Sequence Diagrams

A brief description of sequence diagrams using the example in Fig. 1 appeared above. (For a more detailed discussion of sequence diagrams, see Rumbaugh [24] and Booch [3].) In this section, we discuss some possible extensions to UML that can also model agent-based interaction protocols.

Figure 6 depicts some basic elements for agent communication. The rectangle can express individual agents or sets (i.e., roles or classes) of agents. For example, an individual agent could be labeled Bob/Customer. Here Bob is an instance of agent playing the role of Customer. Bob could also play the role of Supplier, Employee, and Pet Owner. To indicate that Bob is a Person—independent of any role he plays—Bob could be expressed as Bob:Person. The basic format for the box label is agent-name/role:class. Therefore, we could express all the various situations for Bob, such as Bob/Customer:Person and Bob/Employee:Person. (Note that when an individual agent is specifed, the label is underlined, e.g., <u>Bob/Customer:Person</u>. See Fig. 9.)

The rectangular box can also indicate a general set of agents playing a specific role. Here, just the word Customer or Supplier would appear. To specify that the role is to be played by a specific class of agent, the class name would be appended (e.g., Employee:Person, Supplier:Party). In other words, the agent-name/role:class syntax is used without specifying an individual agent-name.

Agent-1/Role:Class
Agent-2/Role:Class
CA-1
CA-2

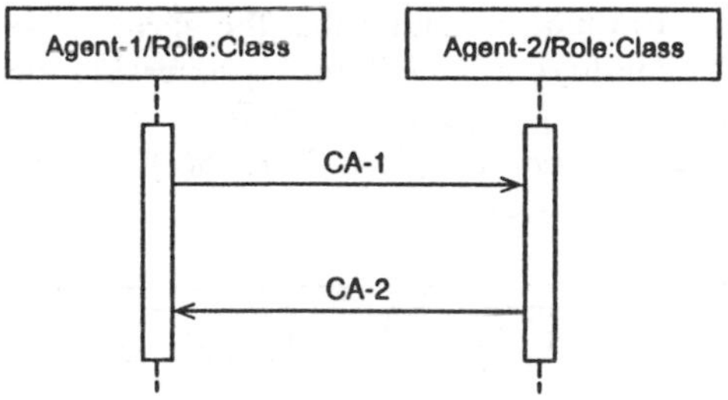

Fig. 6. Basic format for agent communication.

The agent-name/role:class syntax is already part of UML (except that the UML syntax indicates an object name instead of an agent name). Figure 6 extends UML by labeling the arrowed line with an agent *communication act* (CA), instead of an OO-style *message*.

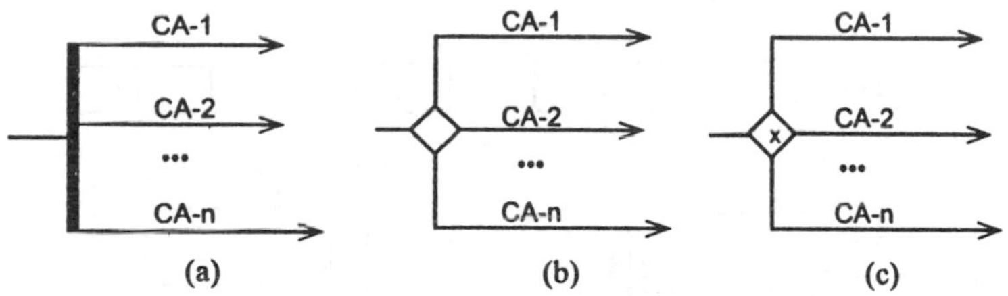

CA-1
CA-2
•••
CA-n
(a)
CA-1
CA-2
•••
CA-n
(b)
CA-1
x
CA-2
•••
CA-n
(c)

Fig. 7. Some recommended extensions that support concurrent threads of interaction.

Another recommended extension to UML supports concurrent threads of interaction. While UML does support asynchronous messages, multiple concurrent threads are directly expressed.[2] Figure 7 depicts three ways of expressing multiple threads. Figure 7(a) indicates that all threads CA-1 to CA-n are sent concurrently. Figure 7(b) includes a decision box indicating that a decision box will decide which CAs (zero or more) will be sent. If more than one CA is sent, the communication is concurrent. In short, it indicates an *inclusive or*. Fig. 7(c) indicates an *exclusive or*, so that exactly one CA will be sent. Figure 7(a) indicates an *and* communication.

Figure 8 illustrates one way of using the concurrent threads of interaction depicted in Fig. 7. Figures 8(a) and (b) portray two ways of expressing concurrent threads sent from agent-1 to agent-2. The multiple vertical, or *activation*, bars indicate that the receiving agent is processing the various communication threads concurrently. Figure 8(a) displays parallel activation bars and Fig. 8(b) activation bars that appear on top of each other. A few things should be noted about these two variations:

- The semantic meaning is equivalent; the choice is based on ease and clarity of visual appearance.

---

[2] As OO implementations become more advanced, such an extension would be considered useful in any case.

- Each activation bar can indicate either that the agent is using a different role or that it is merely employing a different processing thread to support the communication act. If the agent is using a different role, the activation bar can be annotated appropriately. For example in Figs. 8(a) and (b), CA-n is handled by the agent under its role-1 processing.

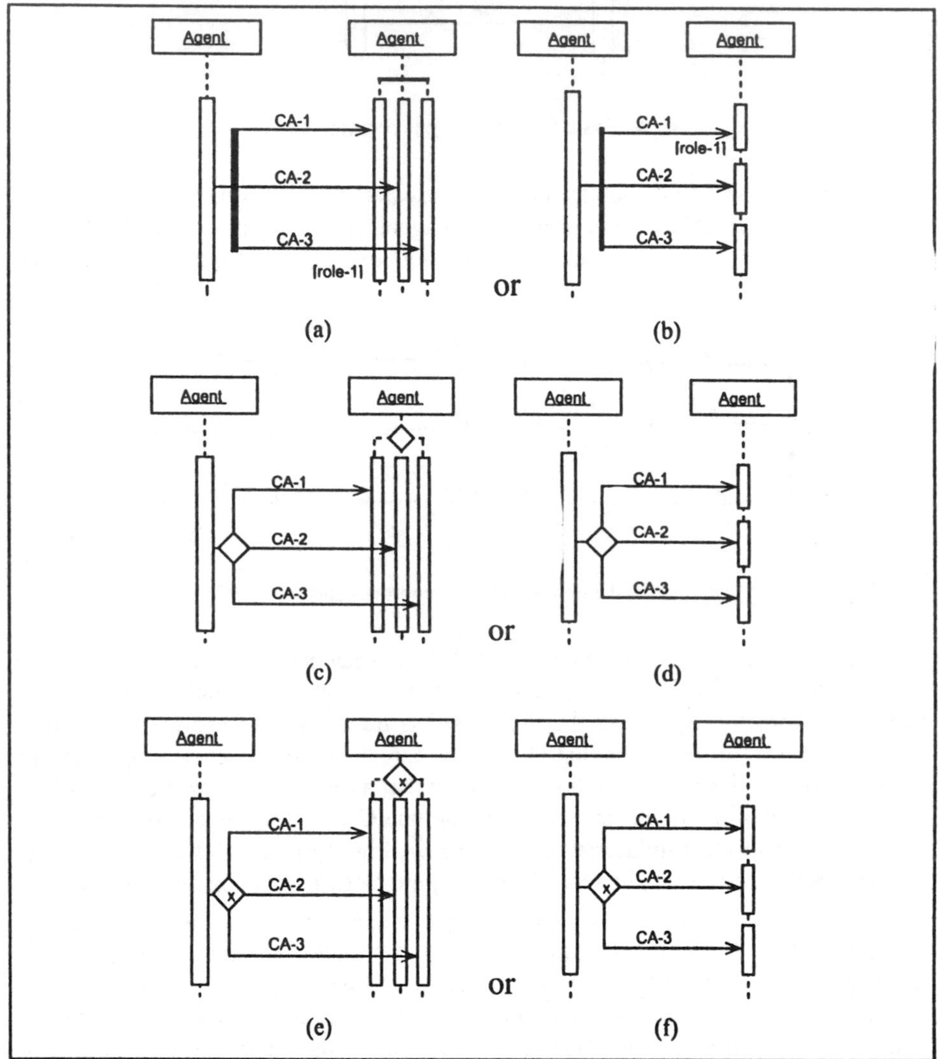

Fig. 8. Multiple techniques to express concurrent communication with an agent playing multiple roles or responding to different CAs.

These figures indicate that a single agent is concurrently processing the multiple CAs. However, the concurrent CAs could *each* have been sent to a *different* agent, e.g., CA-1 to agent-2, CA-2 to agent-3, and so on. Such protocol behavior is already supported by UML; the notation in Fig. 7, on the other hand, is a recommended extension to UML.

(For more detailed treatment of these extensions to the UML sequence diagram for protocols, see [1, 2].)

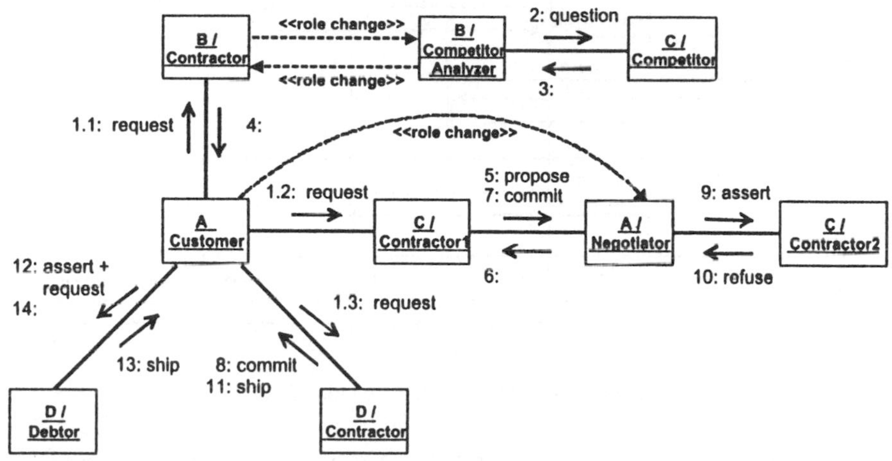

Fig. 9. An example of a collaboration diagram depicting an interaction among agents playing multiple roles.

5.2 Collaboration Diagrams

Figure 9 is an example of a collaboration diagram and depicts a pattern of interaction among agents. One of the primary distinctions of the collaboration diagram is that the agents (the rectangles) can be placed anywhere on the diagram; whereas in a sequence diagram, the agents are placed in a horizontal row at the diagram's top. The sequence of interactions are numbered on the association lines in a collaboration diagram; whereas on the interaction diagram, a timed sequence of interaction is basically read from the top down. If the two interaction diagrams are so similar, why have both? The answer lies primarily on the person and interaction protocol being described—for that person, one diagram type might provide a clearer, more understandable representation over another. Semantically, they are almost equivalent; graphically they are similar. For example, Fig. 10 expresses basically the same underlying meaning as Fig. 9 using the sequence diagram. Experience has demonstrated that agent-based modelers can find both types of diagrams useful.

Dooley Graphs [21] are isomorphic to collaboration diagrams. The critical distinction is that a single agent can appear as multiple nodes in a Dooley Graph. The ICMAS paper calls these nodes *characters*. The intuition in the terminology is that a character is a specific agent playing a specific role. The role is an abstraction over several characters with similar patterns of interaction. Inversely, each node is an agent in a specific role, where "role" is here defined fairly narrowly (not just purchaser, for example, but purchaser under a renegotiated contract in contrast with the same purchaser's role in the original contract).

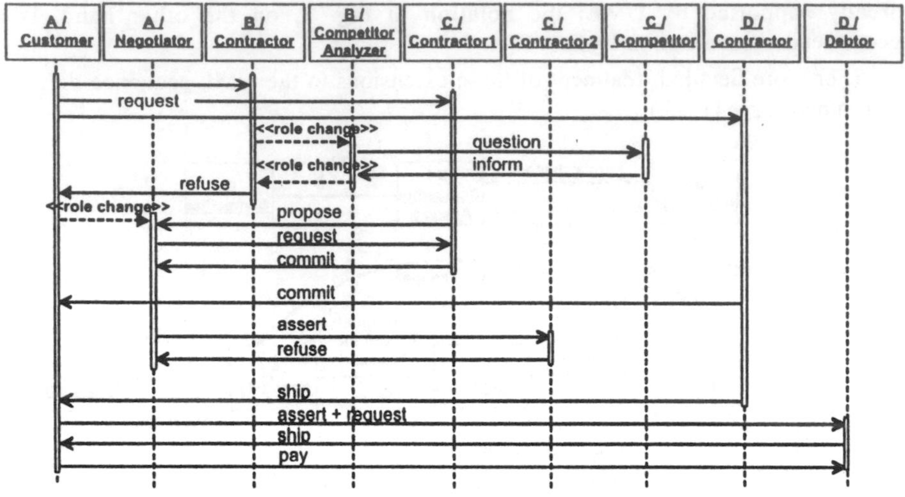

Fig. 10. A sequence diagram version of Fig. 9.

Given our notation for an agent playing a role and having a precise enough definition of roles, we could construct a collaboration diagram that has the same semantic content as a Dooley Graph.

5.3 Activity diagrams

Agent interaction protocols can sometimes require specifications with very clear processing-thread semantics. The *activity diagram* expresses operations and the events that trigger them. (For a more detailed treatment, see Odell's description of activity diagrams in [18].) The example in Fig. 11 depicts an order processing protocol among several agents. Here, a Customer agent places an order. This process results in an Order placed event that triggers the Broker to place the order, which is then accepted by an Electronic Commerce Network (ECN) agent. The ECN can only associate an order with a quote when both the order and the market maker's quote has been accepted. Once this occurs, the Market Maker and the Broker are concurrently notified that the trade has been competed. The activity diagram differs from interaction diagrams because it provides an explicit thread of control. This is particularly useful for complex interaction protocols that involve concurrent processing.

Activity diagrams are similar in nature to colored Petri nets in several ways. First, activity diagrams provide a graphical representation that makes it possible to visualize processes simply, thereby facilitating the design and communication of behavioral models. Second, activity diagrams can represent concurrent, asynchronous processing. Lastly, they can express simultaneous communications with several correspondents. The primary difference between the two approaches is that activity diagrams are formally based on the extended state-machine model defined by UML [24]. Ferber's BRIC formalism [8] extends Petri nets for agents-based systems; this paper extends UML activity diagrams for the same purpose.

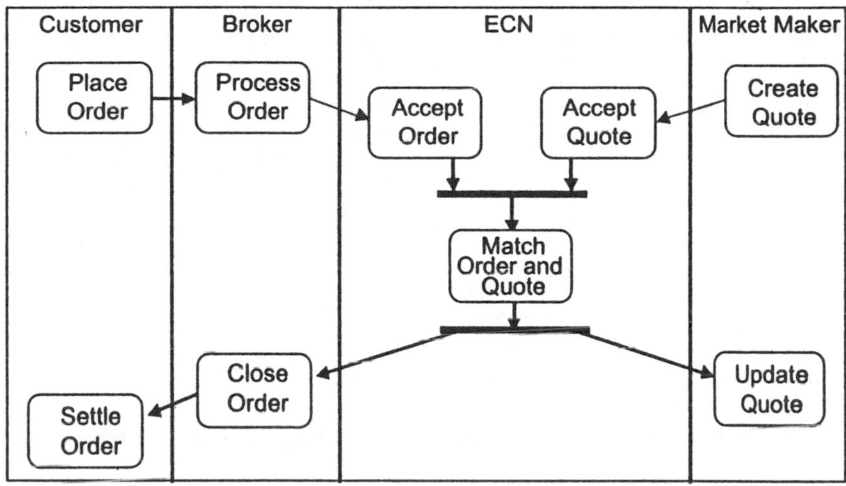

Fig. 11. An activity diagram that depicts a stock sale protocol among several agents.

5.4 Statecharts

Another process-related UML diagram is the *statechart*. A statechart is a graph that represents a state machine. States are represented as round-cornered rectangles, while transitions are generally rendered by directed arcs that interconnect the states. Figure 12 depicts an example of a statechart that governs an Order protocol. Here, if a given Order is in a Requested state, a supplier agent may commit to the Requested negotiation—resulting in a transition to a Committed negotiation state. Furthermore, this diagram indicates that an agent's commit action may occur only if the Order is in a Requested state. The Requested state has two other possible actions besides the commit: the supplier may refuse and the consumer may back out. Notice that the supplier may refuse with the order in either the Proposed or the Requested states.

The statechart is not commonly used to express interaction protocol because it is a state-centric view, rather than an agent- or process-centered view. The agent-centric view portrayed by interaction diagrams emphasizes the agent first and the interaction second. The process-centric view emphasizes the process flow (by agent) first and the resulting state change (i.e., event) second. The state-centric view emphasizes the permissible states more prominently than the transition agent processing. The primary strength of the statechart in agent interaction protocols is as a constraint mechanism for the protocol. The statechart and its states are typically not implemented directly as agents. However, an Order agent could embody the state-transition constraints, thereby ensuring that the overall interaction protocol contraints are met. Alternatively, the constraints could be embodied in the Supplier and Customer roles played by the agents involved in the order process.

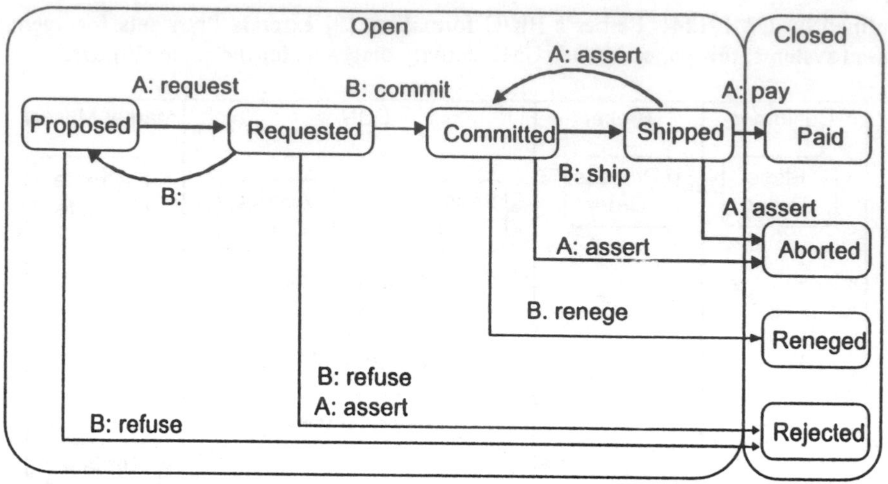

Fig. 12. A statechart indicating the valid states and transitions governing an Order protocol.

6 Level 3: Representing Internal Agent Processing

At the lowest level, specification of an agent protocol requires spelling out the detailed processing that takes place within an agent in order to implement the protocol. In a holarchic model, higher-level agents (holons) consist of aggregations of lower-level agents. The internal behavior of a holon can thus be described using any of the Level 2 representations recursively. In addition, state charts and activity diagrams can also specify the internal processing of agents that are not aggregates, as illustrated in this section.

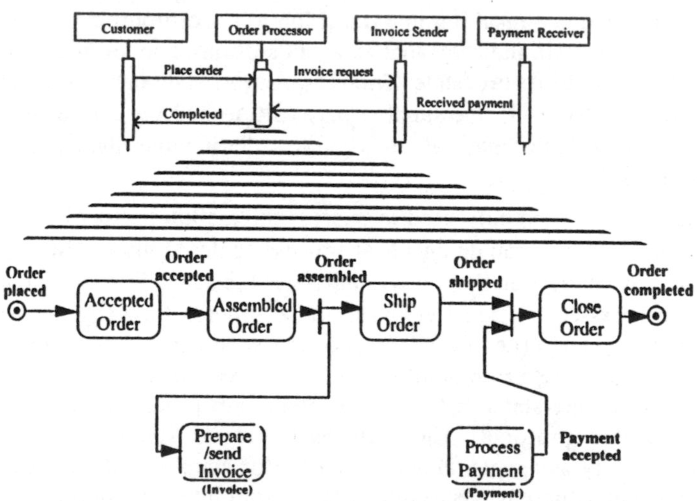

Fig. 13. An activity diagram that specifies order processing behavior for an Order agent.

6.1 Activity Diagrams

Figure 13 depicts the detailed processing that takes place within an Order Processor agent. Here, a sequence diagram indicated that the agent's process is triggered by a Place Order CA and ends with an order completed event. The internal processing by the Order Processor is expressed as an activity diagram, where the Order Processor accepts, assembles, ships, and closes the order. The dotted operation boxcs represent interfaces to processes carried out by external agents—as also illustrated in the sequence diagram. For example, the diagram indicates that when the order has been assembled, both Assemble Order and Prepare/send Invoice actions are triggered concurrently. Furthermore, when both the payment has been accepted and the order has been shipped, the Close Order process can only then be invoked.

6.2 Statecharts

The internal processing of a single agent can also be expressed as statecharts. Figure 14 depicts the internal states and transitions for Order Processor, Invoice Sender, and Payment Receiver agents. As with the activity diagram above, these agents interface with each other—as indicated by the dashed lines. This intra-agent use of UML statecharts supports Singh's notion of agent skeletons [27].

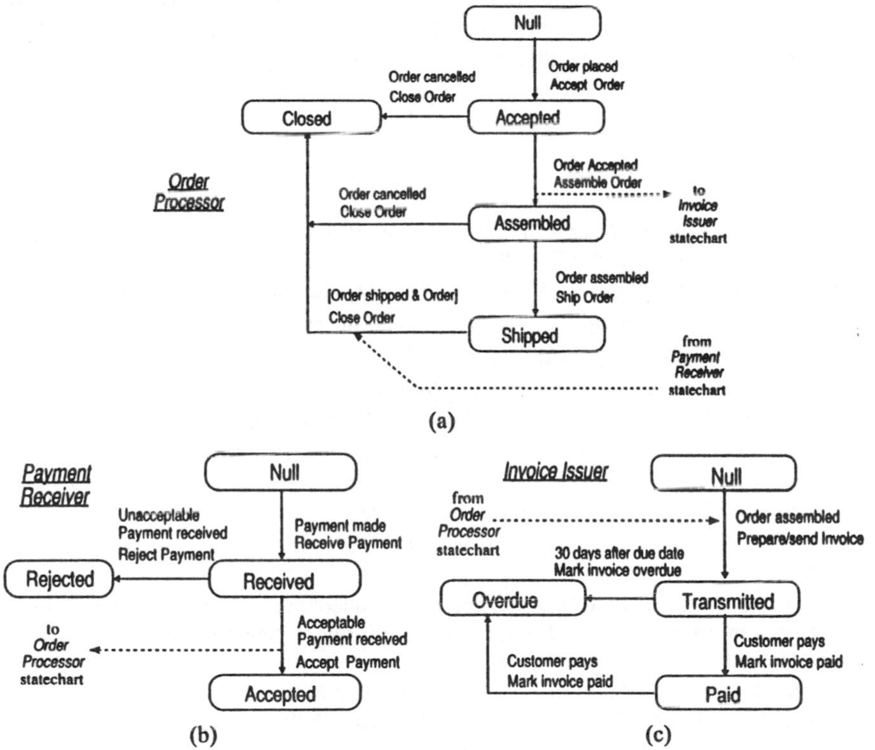

Figure 14. Statechart that specifies order processing behavior for the three agents.

7 Conclusion

UML provides tools for specifying agent interaction protocols at multiple levels:

- specifying a protocol as a whole, as in [28];
- expressing the interaction pattern among agents within a protocol, as in [1, 8, 21]; and
- the internal behavior of an agent, as in [27].

Some of these tools can be applied directly to agent-based systems by adopting simple idioms and conventions. In other cases, we suggest several straightforward UML extensions that support the additional functionality that agents offer over the current UML version 1.4. Many of these proposed extensions are already being considered by the OO community as useful extensions to OO development on UML version 2.0. Furthermore, many of the AUML notions presented here were developed and applied within the MoTiV-PTA projects [http://www.motiv.de/], an agent-based realization of a personal travel assistant, supported by the German Ministry of Technology.

Agent researchers can be gratified at the increasing attention that industrial and business users are paying to their results. The transfer of these results to practical application will be more rapid and accurate if the research community can communicate its insights in forms consistent with modern industrial software practice. AUML builds on the acknowledged success of UML in supporting industrial-strength software engineering. The idioms and extensions proposed here for AIP's—as well as others that we are developing—are a contribution to this objective.

References

1. Bauer, B., *Extending UML for the Specification of Interaction Protocols*, submitted for the 6th Call for Proposal of FIPA, 1999.
2. Bauer, B., *Extending UML for the Specification of Interaction Protocols*, in this volume.
3. Booch, Grady, James Rumbaugh, and Ivar Jacobson, *The Unified Language User Guide*, Addison-Wesley, Reading, MA, 1999.
4. Brazier, Frances M.T., Catholijn M. Jonkers, and Jan Treur, ed., *Principles of Compositional Multi-Agent System Development* Chapman and Hall, 1998.
5. Bryson, Joanna, and Brendan McGonigle, "Agent Architecture as Object Oriented Design," *Intelligent Agents IV: Agent Theories, Architectures, and Languages. Proceedings of ATAL'97.*, ed., Springer, Berlin, 1998.
6. Burmeister, B., ed., *Models and Methodology for Agent-Oriented Analysis and Design* 1996.
7. Burmeister, Birgit, Afsaneh Haddadi, and Kurt Sundermeyer, ed., *Generic, Configurable, Cooperation Protocols for Multi-Agent Systems* Springer, Neuchâtel, Switzerland, 1993. (Programmable model of interaction)
8. Ferber, Jacques, *Multi-Agent Systems: An Introduction to Distributed Artificial Intelligence*, Addison Wesley Longman, Harlow, UK, 1999.
9. Garijo, Francisco J., and Magnus Boman ed., *Multi-Agent System Engineering: Proceedings of MAAMAW'99*, Springer, Berlin, Germany, 1999.

10. Gustavsson, Rune E., "Multi Agent Systems as Open Societies," *Intelligent Agents IV: Agent Theories, Architectures, and Languages*, ed., Springer, Berlin, 1998.

11. Herlea, Daniela E., Catholijun M. Jonker, Jan Treur, and Niek J.E. Wijngaards, ed., *Specification of Behavioural Requirements within Compositional Multi-Agent System Design* Springer, Valencia, Spain, 1999.

12. Iglesias, Carlos A., Mercedes Garijo, and José C. González, ed., *A Survey of Agent-Oriented Methodologies* University Pierre et Marie Curie, Paris, FR, 1998.

13. Iglesias, Carlos A., Mercedes Garijo, José C. González, and Juan R. Velasco, "Analysis and Design of Multiagent Systems using MAS-CommonKADS," *Intelligent Agents IV: Agent Theories, Architectures, and Languages*, Munindar P. Singh *et al.* ed., Springer, Berlin, 1998, pp. 313-328.

14. Jonker, Catholijn M., and Jan Treur, ed., *Compositional Verification of Multi-Agent Systems: a Formal Analysis of Pro-activeness and Reactiveness* Springer, 1997.

15. Kinny, David, and Michael Georgeff, "Modelling and Design of Multi-Agent Systems," Intelligent Agents III: Proceedings of the Third International workshop on Agent Theories, Architectures, and Languages (ATAL'96), ed., Springer, Heidelberg, 1996.

16. Kinny, David, Michael Georgeff, and Anand Rao, "A Methodology and Modelling Technique for Systems of BDI Agents," *Agents Breaking Away. 7th European Workshop on Modelling Autonomous Agents in a Multi-Agent World (MAAMAW'96).*, Walter VandeVelde and John W. Perram ed., Springer, Berlin, 1996, pp. 56-71. .

17. Lee, Jaeho, and Edmund H. Durfee, "On Explicit Plan Languages for Coordinating Multiagent Plan Execution," *Intelligent Agents IV: Agent Theories, Architectures, and Languages*, ed., Springer, Berlin, 1998, pp. 113-126.

18. Martin, James, and James J. Odell, *Object-Oriented Methods: A Foundation*, (UML edition), Prentice Hall, Englewood Cliffs, NJ, 1998.

19. Nodine, Marian H., and Amy Unruh, "Facilitating Open Communication in Agent Systems: the InfoSleuth Infrastructure," *Intelligent Agents IV: Agent Theories, Architectures, and Languages*, Munindar P. Singh *et al.* ed., Springer, Berlin, 1998, pp. 281-296.

20. Odell, James ed., *Agent Technology*, OMG, green paper produced by the OMG Agent Working Group, 1999.

21. Parunak, H. Van Dyke, ed., *Visualizing Agent Conversations: Using Enhanced Dooley Graphs for Agent Design and Analysis* 1996.

22. Parunak, H. Van Dyke, and James Odell, *Engineering Artifacts for Multi-Agent Systems*, ERIM CEC, 1999.

23. Parunak, H. Van Dyke, John Sauter, and Steven J. Clark, "Toward the Specification and Design of Industrial Synthetic Ecosystems," *Intelligent Agents IV: Agent Theories, Architectures, and Languages*, Munindar P. Singh *et al.* ed., Springer, Berlin, 1998, pp. 45-59.

24. Rumbaugh, James, Ivar Jacobson, and Grady Booch, *The Unified Modeling Language Reference Manual*, Addison-Wesley, Reading, MA, 1999.

25. Schoppers, Marcel, and Daniel Shapiro, "Designing Embedded Agents to Optimize End-User Objectives," *Intelligent Agents IV: Agent Theories, Architectures, and Languages*, Munindar P. Singh *et al.* ed., Springer, Berlin, 1998, pp. 3-14.

26. Singh, Munindar P., "A Customizable Coordination Service for Autonomous Agents," *Intelligent Agents IV: Agent Theories, Architectures, and Languages*, Munindar P. Singh *et al.* ed., Springer, Berlin, 1998, pp. 93-106.

27. Singh, Munindar P., ed., *Developing Formal Specifications to Coordinate Heterogeneous Autonomous Agents* IEEE Computer Society, Paris, FR, 1998.

28. Wooldridge, Michael, Nicholas R. Jennings, and David Kinny, "The Gaia Methodology for Agent-Oriented Analysis and Design," International Journal of Autonomous Agents and Multi-Agent Systems, 3:Forthcoming, 2000.
29. Depke, Ralph, Reiko Heckel, Jochen Malte Küster, "Requirement Specification and Design of Agent-Based Systems with Graph Transformation, Roles, and UML," in this volume.

On the Identification of Agents in the Design of Production Control Systems

Stefan Bussmann[1], Nicholas R. Jennings[2], and Michael Wooldridge[3]

[1]DaimlerChrysler AG, Research and Technology 3
Alt-Moabit 96A, 10559 Berlin, Germany.
Stefan.Bussmann@daimlerchrysler.com

[2]Dept. of Electronics and Computer Science, University of Southampton
Southampton SO17 1BJ, United Kingdom.
nrj@ecs.soton.ac.uk

[3]Dept. of Computer Science, University of Liverpool
Liverpool L69 7ZF, United Kingdom.
M.J.Wooldridge@csc.liv.ac.uk

Abstract. This paper describes a methodology that is being developed for designing and building agent-based systems for the domain of production control. In particular, this paper deals with the steps that are involved in identifying the agents and in specifying their responsibilities. The methodology aims to be useable by engineers who have a background in production control but who have no prior experience in agent technology. For this reason, the methodology needs to be very prescriptive with respect to the agent-related aspects of the design.

1 Introduction

Software agents are on the verge of becoming a key control technology for large-series production control systems. With ever shorter product life-cycles, decreasing product launch times, and increasing product variety, manufacturing processes must provide more product flexibility and higher volume scalability while maintaining high product quality and low manufacturing costs. Agent technology is well suited to addressing the control aspects of these new manufacturing requirements [2]. As autonomous decision-makers, agents are able to dynamically react to unforeseen events, exploit different capabilities of components, and adapt flexibly to changes in their environment. The ability of agents to adapt their behaviour at run-time reduces the need for the designer to foresee all possible scenarios and changes that the system will encounter: agents automatically adapt to changing products or varying volumes.

After more than a decade of research, the potential of agent technology has been demonstrated in the context of large-series production. The DaimlerChrysler prototype for manufacturing cylinder heads is controlled by a completely decentralised agent-based system, which provides unprecedented flexibility and scalability [3]. The system has been installed as a bypass to an existing transfer line and was evaluated through exhaustive performance tests. The performance tests, as well as the on-going operation of the prototype, proved the industrial feasibility and underlined the competitive advantage of agent-based control. The technology is now ready to be exploited in industrial production.

The widespread use of agent-based control, however, will require software engineering methods and tools that support the development of industrial-strength control systems. Although we have some experience in the application of agent technology to cylinder head production, the application of agent technology to different production processes (such as engine assembly or car painting) will still require a major engineering effort. Such an engineering effort has to move agents out of the laboratory and into the planning teams designing manufacturing systems. Planning engineers, however, usually have no degree in agent technology or artificial intelligence. Therefore to make the technology accessible to them, agent-based control must provide a methodology that includes all the agent-related design rationales necessary to apply an agent-based approach to a manufacturing system. These design rationales tell a software engineer with no prior experience in agent development how to make agent-related design decisions. To this end, many software design methodologies have been developed, including object-oriented and even agent-oriented approaches (see [6,9] for an overview). But none of these methodologies is applicable to the design of agent-based production control systems; they either provide analysis models that are inappropriate for production control or else they lack comprehensive design rationales.

The aim of our research work is therefore to extend the state-of-the-art by proposing a methodology for the design of agent-based production control systems that can be successfully applied by an engineer with no prior experience in agent technology. To this end, the methodology should provide: (i) a model of the decision making necessary in production control in order to enable the designer to directly move from the domain to the agent-oriented design aspects; and (ii) a set of criteria for the design of the agent-related aspects which guide the designer with no prior agent-related experience. In this paper, we take the first significant step towards this goal by proposing a design method for identifying the agents of a production control system. The identification of agents is central to the methodology. It allows the designer to move from pure domain concepts (such as production processes), to agent-oriented concepts (such as agents and decision responsibilities). In addition, the identification of agents provides the basis for all other subsequent design steps, such as interaction design or agent programming.

The presentation of the design method for agent identification is organised as follows. The remainder of this section introduces the notion of a methodology and the basic concepts of production control. Section 2 briefly discusses why existing methodologies are not sufficient for the design of agent-oriented production control systems. Section 3 then gives an overview of the design method proposed, and sections 4 and 5, respectively, describe the analysis and design steps of the method. Section 6, finally, draws some conclusions.

1.1 What is a methodology?

A methodology is a recipe that enables an engineer to find a solution to a specified set of problems. It should be sufficiently precise to enable any engineer with a standard education to successfully apply the recipe to a suitable problem, while at the same time it should leave enough room for creativity. A *methodology* always consists of the following components [8].

- A definition of the problem space to which the methodology is applicable.
- A set of models that represent different aspects of the problem domain or the solution at different stages.
- A set of methods that transform instances of one model into another model.
- A set of procedural guidelines that define an order for the systematic application of the methodological steps.

The application of a methodology starts with a problem statement and ends with a solution to the problem. Methods and guidelines tell the designer how to go from the problem statement to the solution. An *agent-oriented design methodology* for production control is consequently a methodology that explains how to go from a specification of a production control problem to an agent-oriented design of a control system. However, for such a methodology to be widely used, the methodology must provide *all* necessary methods and guidelines such that an engineer with only minimal training and experience in agent development is able to successfully derive an agent-oriented design. This is achieved if the concepts of the methodology are *intuitively* related to the relevant concepts of the problem domain and if the methodology includes *all the (agent-related) rationales* necessary to derive the agent-oriented design. In terms of the above definition of a methodology, this translates into the following requirements.

Model appropriateness. The models of a methodology should be easily related to the relevant concepts of the problem domain. The initial model should be based on domain concepts and any new concepts should be put into relation to concepts already introduced. This applies in particular to the introduction of agent-oriented concepts.

Method prescriptiveness. The methods of the methodology should be prescriptive in the sense that they define each step the designer has to go through, and for each step clearly identify what the task of the designer is and – at least for any agent-oriented aspect – explain how the task should be performed. The methods must therefore clearly distinguish between domain and agent-oriented design reasoning.

As will be discussed in subsequent sections, the method for agent identification presented in this paper fulfils the above requirements and can therefore be seen as a first step towards an industrially relevant methodology for production control.

1.2 Production control

Production systems for discrete manufacturing usually consist of processing components, such as machining or assembly stations, which are connected by a transportation system consisting of conveyor belts and switches (see Figure 1). During the operation of the production system, work pieces associated with specific jobs are fed into the production system, transported to the next station, processed by the station, moved to the next station, processed again and so on until the work pieces are finished and leave the system.

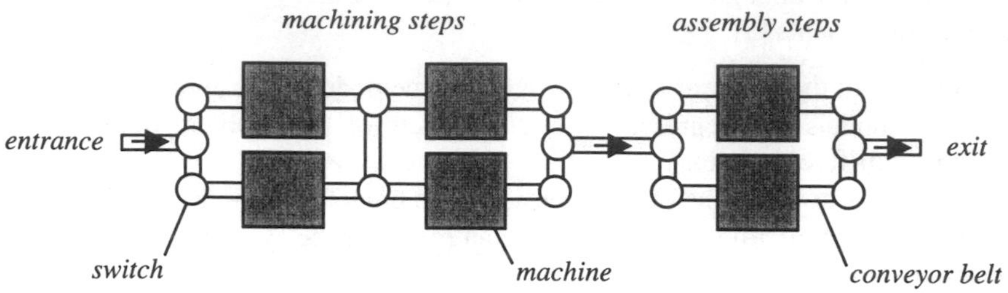

Fig. 1. Example production system.

For such a production system, the task of the control system is to assign jobs to stations (resource allocation) and to manage the material flow (transportation allocation). To date, the pre-dominant approaches to performing these tasks in practice have been to create a schedule beforehand, which is then simply executed at run-time by the local controllers of the production components. This approach works well if actions are executed as planned, but fails completely otherwise. In case of a disturbance, a controller is unable to execute its actions or has to postpone them. Since production operations are optimised in order to maximise productivity and minimise costs, resource capacities are fully utilised and buffer sizes are reduced to a minimum. As a consequence, any deviation from the schedule quickly affects neighbouring units resulting in a cascading effect of the disturbance. Since the schedule-driven control does not support re-scheduling, the impact of a disturbance on production cannot be constrained. As every real production system is regularly affected by disturbances, production operations soon deviate from the production schedule. It is even "proverbial among shop foremen that the schedules produced by the front office are out of date the moment they hit the floor" [19, p. 303].

To overcome this limitation of the current approach, it is necessary to interleave scheduling and execution, i.e., to enable the local controllers to autonomously perform the resource and transportation allocation. With more autonomy, the local controller is able to choose the right action in its current situation. As before, the controller is triggered by a sensor signal indicating that an action is required. But in contrast to the schedule-driven approach, the controller now has to first choose an appropriate action. To achieve this, the controller must first determine the set of possible actions that can be performed in this situation (referred to as the *decision space*). The controller then collects all decision-relevant information (the *decision input*), and finally chooses an action according to a *decision rule* that evaluates the different alternatives with respect to their goal achievement (see Figure 2). During this decision process, the controller may interact with other controllers if necessary. Once the decision has been made, the controller can initiate the action and monitor the execution just as in the schedule-driven approach.

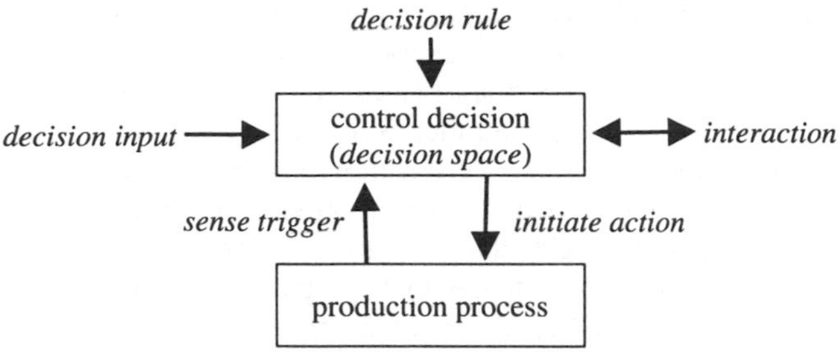

Fig. 2. Abstract model of control decisions.

This abstract model of a control decision is an obvious starting point of any design methodology for production control, since it describes the basic task of the controller and how it interfaces with the production process.

2 Related Work

With the shift from laboratory to industrial applications, it has become increasingly apparent that existing methodologies, such as purely object-oriented approaches, are insufficient to capture the key features of agent-based systems [1,14]. This experience has led to the development of distinctively agent-oriented design methodologies over the last few years. Most agent-oriented methodologies have been extensions of existing methodologies, in particular knowledge-oriented and object-oriented approaches. Only recently have methodologies based on purely agent-oriented concepts been proposed.

The knowledge-oriented methodologies proposed for designing agent-based systems are extensions of the knowledge-engineering methodology CommonKADS [22], to which agent-oriented concepts are added. The CoMoMAS methodology [7] extends CommonKADS by adding a social analysis model, identifying social competencies of agents in terms of goals, intentions, and roles; and a co-operative analysis model, modeling co-operation and conflict resolution methods. MAS-CommonKADS [10] also extends CommonKADS by adding an agent, a co-ordination, and an organisation model. Because of the underlying knowledge-engineering approach, however, both methodologies view an agent system as a problem solving system decomposing the system task into subtasks. In this way they identify agents on the basis of task hierarchies and knowledge requirements. This model is inappropriate for the decision-centric view of production control.

Several agent-oriented approaches have been inspired by object-oriented approaches, such as OMT [21] and OOSE [11]. The methodology of Kendall, Malkoun and Jiang [12] for manufacturing applications, for instance, creates first an object-oriented and a manufacturing model of the system to be designed, and then identifies agents in these two models. However, even though Kendall et al. view an agent as an autonomous decision maker, their methodology identifies agents (in both models) on the basis of their *activeness*, that is, whether a component pro-actively performs or initiates an operation. Activeness, though, is also a property of conveyor belts or lifts, which actively move work pieces, but which do not decide whether or not to act. The activeness criterion can therefore identify as agents some entities that are not autonomous decision makers. This critique also applies to the methodology of Burmeister [1], which solely relies on object-oriented techniques to identify agents.

The limitations of methodologies that are based on concepts from other fields have led to the development of methodologies that are purely (or mostly) based on agent-oriented concepts. The dominant agent-oriented concept used is that of a role. Kendall [13] defines a role as an abstraction of agent behaviour modelled in terms of responsibilities, possible collaborators, required expertise, and co-operation mechanisms used. The most important advantage of the concept of a role is that it can be freely assign and reassigned to agents, as long as the agent assigned to the role fulfils the role's requirements. Role-based methodologies, e.g., [5,14,15,17,18,23], use this abstraction to create a model of system behaviour, and then identify agents by mapping the roles to agent instances. The Gaia methodology [23], for instance, aggregates roles into agent types and instantiates as many agents as necessary in a given scenario.

Most role-based methodologies, however, require that the designer is able to directly identify the roles in an application. However, this is not possible in production control. A requirements specification of a production control system consists only of a description of the physical components of a production system and the production goals to be achieved. The specification of the physical components, in turn, only describes a sensor and actuator interface to each component. To identify roles in a specific production application, it is therefore necessary to derive an understanding of the required control process first. None of the methodologies, however, explain how the decision making should be modelled or combined to form roles. For production control, it is therefore necessary to extend these methodologies by a preceding analysis step that derives roles from the production control problem.

Parunak, Sauter, and Clark [20] take a different approach to building multi-agent systems. They view a multi-agent system as consisting of many simple, interacting agents which exhibit social coherence. In their methodology, Parunak et al. base the identification of agents on a linguistic case analysis of the problem description. As with the criterion of activeness, a linguistic case analysis may identify agents that have no decisions to make, such as conveyor belts or lifts. Even the level of abstraction is pre-determined by the system description. If the description speaks of spindle, machining space, positioning and tools to describe the processing of work pieces, a machine agent cannot be identified, even though such a level of abstraction is more appropriate in many cases. Parunak et al. try to reduce the risk of identifying inappropriate agents by providing a set of pre-defined agent types, such as unit, resource, manager, part, customer and supplier agents. However, it is not clear whether this pre-defined set is appropriate for all manufacturing applications or which subtypes should be identified in one category. An agent-based production control system will certainly have resource agents, but the pre-defined set of agent types does not prescribe how the different resources should be assigned to agents. Finally, Parunak et al. discuss principles for validating candidate agents that are useful and relevant. Such principles include identifying things not functions, identifying small agents, and determining where there is decentralisation. Given our experience in this area, however, these principles are not sufficiently prescriptive to guide a designer in identifying agents.

To summarise, there is currently no methodology for the design of an agent-based production control system that satisfies the requirements stated in section 1.1. First of all, most methodologies provide analysis models unsuitable for representing the problem domain, i.e., to model the decision making necessary to control a production process. Second, nearly all methodologies provide criteria for agent identification that lead to an inappropriate set of agents for production control. It is therefore necessary to extend existing design methodologies by developing a design method that captures decision-making in its models and provides a comprehensive list of criteria for identifying agents. Such a design method could be used, for example, to identify (decision-based) roles of a production control application as required by the role-based methodologies.

3 Overview of the Design Method

The design method proposed in this paper identifies the agents necessary to control a given production process. The design method consists of two main steps: an *analysis* step and an *identification* step. The analysis step creates a decision-based model of the control task that contains all the decisions necessary to control the production process. On the basis of this model, the identification step assesses the suitability of an agent-based approach and identifies the agents of the system. The result of the method is a list of agents and their associated decision responsibilities.

This section gives an overview of the design method. It specifies the design input, as well as the design output, and outlines the two main steps of the method. The subsequent sections then present each step of the method. This section also defines a simple production system, which will be used to illustrate the design method.

3.1 Design input

The input to the design method is a requirements specification of the production control problem. It must consist of two parts:

1. A specification of the (physical) production system to be controlled.
2. A specification of the production operation conditions and production goals.

The first part specifies the (mechanical) components of the production system and their arrangement on the factory floor. Furthermore, the specification defines for each component its physical behaviour and, optionally, its control interface. The control interface provides information about the status of the production component to the control system (through sensors) and allows actions to be executed by the component (through actuators). Examples of components are machines, assembly stations, conveyor belts, lifts, transportation switches, and buffers.

Example. Throughout this paper, the following simple production system will be used to illustrate the design method. This simple production system consists of one loading unit, several transportation switches, two flexible machining stations, one unloading unit, and several conveyor belts (see Figure 3). The flexible machines are able to process a wide range of products. Their capabilities are overlapping, but not identical.

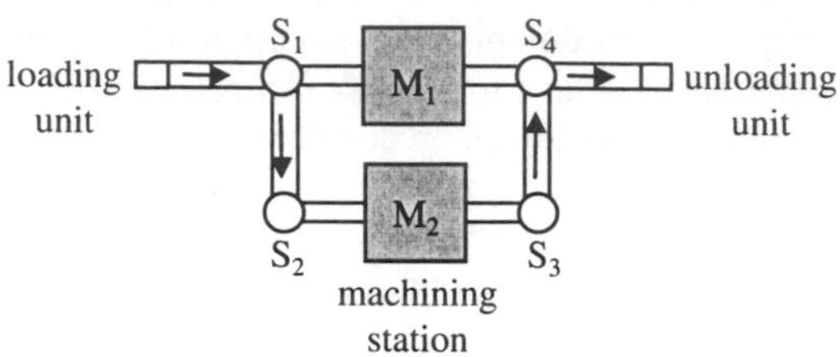

Fig. 3. Simple production system example.

The loading unit puts work pieces on the first conveyor belt as prescribed by the order input stream. The transportation switches distribute the work pieces onto the two machines. The machines process the work pieces if they have the requested capabilities. A work piece may only enter a machine if operations requested by the work piece are a subset of the machine's capabilities. After processing, the work pieces are moved to the unloading unit.

The second part of the problem specification defines conditions and goals for the production process. The *operation conditions* specify the order mix fed into the production system and the spectrum of possible changes and disturbances to the production system during operation. Disturbances are unanticipated breakdowns of components, while changes are induced by the production management and may affect components or the input of the production system. The specification of the *production goals* describes the expected behaviour of the production system under the specified conditions. Examples of production goals are maximal throughput, minimal investment costs, flexibility with respect to component or order changes, robustness with respect to mechanical or control failures, volume scalability, and reconfigurability of components.

Example. The input stream of the simple production example is an arbitrary mix of different products to be produced. Changes to the production process are not expected and the only possible disturbances are sudden breakdowns of machining stations. The goal of the simple production system is to maximise the throughput and to be robust against station failures.

3.2 Design output

The output of the design method is a list of the agents necessary to control the production system specified. Each agent is defined by the decision tasks for which it is responsible. Furthermore, the method specifies any dependencies between any decision tasks of different agents.

The list of agents defines the global structure of the agent-based control system. It serves as the basis for further design steps specifying the interactions or the agent reasoning (these subsequent steps are not dealt with in this paper).

3.3 Design steps

The design method prescribes two major steps in order to go from the design input to the desired design output.

1. *Analysis of decision making* – The decisions necessary during the control process are identified and analysed. The result of this step specifies the constraints that any control system supposed to achieve the production goals must satisfy.
2. *Identification of agents* – The overall structure of the agent-based system is designed. In particular, this step identifies the agents of the system, the decisions for which they are responsible, and the need for interactions between the agents.

Each step of the design method is described in the following sections; section 4 describes the analysis of the decision making, and section 5 presents the agent identification method.

4 Analysis of the Decision Making

The aim of the analysis phase is to develop a model of the control task that can be used as a basis for the identification of the control agents. To achieve this, the analysis step must model the decision making of the control process. A control system controls a production system by monitoring the production process through sensors and by commanding actions to be executed by the actuators of the production components. Because of the discrete nature of most production systems, the operation to be executed by a component can be chosen from a discrete set of possible operations (cf. section 1.2). The analysis step therefore derives decision tasks and decision constraints from the specification of the production control problem and creates a decision model consisting of a set of decision tasks and dependency relations between them. The resulting decision model then serves as a basis for the subsequent design steps.

However, the decision model should only include those decision tasks and constraints that all solutions to the control problem must make or satisfy. Imposing tasks or constraints that do not apply to all potential solutions would limit the space of possibilities in the subsequent design steps and could lead to sub-optimal design decisions. Tasks and constraints that apply to all solutions, though, do not fully determine the control process. The decision model therefore has to be completed in a later design step in order to represent a full control strategy that is capable of achieving the production goals.

The analysis is performed in three steps. First, all decisions at the control interface which any control system has to make in order for the production process to advance are collected. These decisions are called *effectoric* because of their immediate execution by an actuator. Although a control system can make (preparatory) decisions that are not immediately executed by a component, any decision must eventually influence an effectoric decision in order to become effective in the production process. It is therefore appropriate to start the analysis with the effectoric decisions. Second, the possible dependencies between control decisions are identified and modelled in a dependency diagram. Third, the decision dependencies are classified with respect to their importance for the production goals and their intensity during operation.

4.1 Identification of effectoric decisions

Effectoric decisions can be identified by looking at the possible choices a component has for its behaviour. There must be more than one alternative in order to require a real decision.

Example. Transportation switch S_1 has two alternatives for any work piece reaching it; move the work piece to machine M_1 or to the switch S_2. Transportation switch S_2 has no choice. Theoretically, the switch could delay transportation, but there is no reason to do so. Practically, therefore, switch S_2 has no choice but to allow the work piece to proceed immediately.

Each identified decision task is characterised according to the following pre-defined schema (Table 1). The parameters of a decision task characterise the subject and object of the decision, i.e., who is deciding about whom; in other words, who performs the action and who is affected by the action. The trigger slot specifies the situation in which the decision becomes necessary. The decision space represents the set of possible choices the component has in that particular situation. Finally, a unique identifier for the decision task facilitates later reference.

Slot	Description
id	unique identifier
params	subject and object of decision
trigger	situation that triggers decision
decision space	set of possible choices

Table 1. Schema for effectoric decisions.

Example. In the case of switch S_1, a decision is required every time a work piece reaches the switch (the switch is the subject and the work piece the object) (see table 2). The switch must then choose one of the two possible exits and transfer the work piece to this exit. This decision has to be made immediately in order not to block the entry. Note that in this particular case, the switch can make its decision earlier if it anticipates a work piece. The trigger is simply the latest possible moment to make the decision.

Slot	Description
id	#2
params	switch S_1, work piece
trigger	work piece at entry
decision space	{left, right}

Table 2. Example effectoric decision at switch S_1.

The set of decision tasks can be represented in a trigger diagram where arrows indicate the temporal sequence of the decisions. An arrow expresses the fact that the physical action enacted because of the first decision eventually or necessarily leads to a situation triggering the second decision. The arrows thus identify all possible causal relationships between decision tasks.

Example. Any decision taken at switch S_1 leads to a decision about how to process the work piece at one of the two succeeding machines (because the work piece will either arrive at machine M_1 or (via switch S_2) at machine M_2). In the decision diagram there is therefore one arrow from the decision task of the switch S_1 to the decision task of machine M_1 and one to the decision task of machine M_2 (see Figure 4).

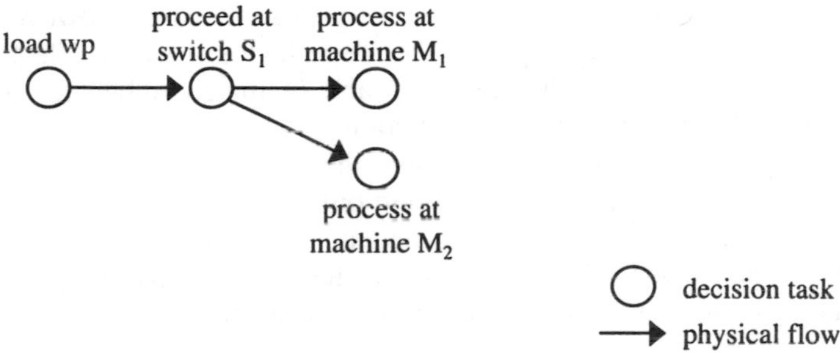

Fig. 4. The trigger diagram for the simple production system.

The trigger diagram illustrates the temporal sequence of decisions (as they are triggered by the physical process) and it can be used as a visual aid in the following analysis (and design) steps.

4.2 Identification of decision dependencies

As stated, the decision model only covers the purely local aspects of a decision. It specifies the situation at the component that triggers the decision and lists the possible reactions of which the component is capable. But it does not specify how to react, i.e., which action to choose. How to decide in a particular situation is determined by the decision rule (cf. section 1.2).

Example. Transportation switch S_1 has to choose one of the exits for each work piece at its entry. Which exit it chooses is irrelevant to the switch. It can move a work piece equally well to either of the exits (as long as they are both free). From the point of view of system performance, however, it is by no means irrelevant onto which exit a work piece is moved. First of all, a work piece may only be moved to a machine that is able to process it. Secondly, the switch determines the distribution of work pieces onto the machines and thus influences the workload on each machine.

A decision task is called *dependent* on another decision if the former cannot be made (optimally) without some kind of interaction with the latter. Two (or more) decision tasks are called *dependent (on each other)* if one decision task depends on the other and vice versa. Several researchers have looked at different types of dependencies between tasks in order to derive necessary interactions (e.g., [4,16,25]). For the following analysis, though, it is sufficient to detect that there is some kind of dependency between two decision tasks.

In this domain, the identification of dependencies is usually straightforward (as in the previous example). Many dependencies can be identified simply by studying the trigger diagram since this represents (most of) the effects of the decisions in the production process. Other dependencies can be identified by studying the related decision parameters of the decision tasks. If two tasks refer to the same parameters, it is likely that their decisions will be dependent. In the working example, for instance, the transportation switch and the machine both make decisions about the same work piece and are consequently linked in some way. In some cases, however, it can be quite difficult to identify and prove the dependence between decision tasks. Nevertheless, it is assumed that the designer is able (with acceptable effort) to identify all *relevant* dependencies in the given production system.

The set of dependencies can also be represented in a diagram. A dependency arrow spans from one decision task to another if and only if the former is dependent on the latter. A dependency arrow is double-headed if and only if the decision tasks are mutually dependent. Dependencies between more than two decision tasks are represented by an arrow with more than one head (on each side).

Example. The decision of a transportation switch to move a work piece onto a specific exit is highly dependent on the decision with respect to how to process a work piece at a machine. As already pointed out, a work piece should only proceed to a machine at which it can be processed. It is therefore necessary to decide which machine is able and willing to process this work piece before the work piece can proceed to the switch. The decision about which operations to apply to the work piece can be delayed until the entry of the work piece into the machine, but the choice of a suitable machine must be made beforehand. Consequently, the decision at switch S_1 is dependent on the decision whether to process the work piece either at machine M_1 or machine M_2 (see Figure 5).

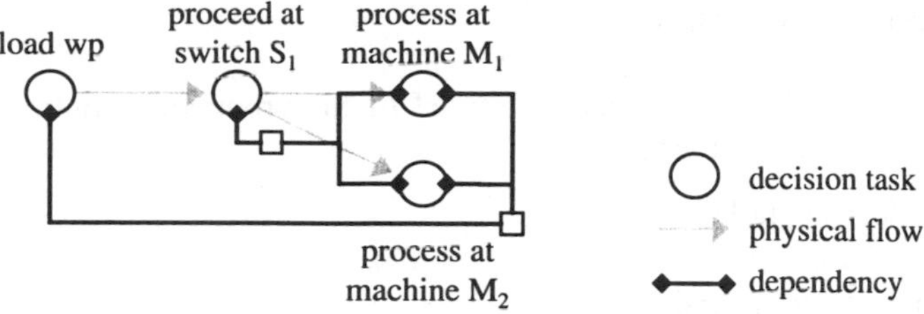

Fig. 5. The dependency diagram for the simple production system.

4.3 Classification of decision dependencies

Each dependency identified in the decision model is characterised quantitatively according to its intensity and its importance. This allows subsequent design steps to uniformly assess the required interactions between decision tasks. The intensity of a dependency indicates how intense an interaction has to be in order to cope with a dependency. The importance of a dependency tells the designer whether it is necessary to cope with the dependency at all.

Intensity: The intensity of a dependency is uniformly characterised by the degree of the required interaction. The degree of a dependency measures the percentage of a decision space that is affected by the dependency. A choice taken from the affected decision space without interaction with the other decision tasks will affect the system performance.

Example. The transportation switch is fully affected by the dependencies. It can only choose an exit, if the next machine has also been determined. The machines, on the other hand, are only partly affected. They can still decide how to process the work piece once it has reached the machine entry. However, a machine must decide whether or not to process a work piece before the work piece leaves a switch.

Importance: The importance of a dependency can be rated from 0 to 1 by the consequences on the system performance if the dependency is ignored during the control process. If the consequences lead to the non-performance of the production system, the importance is set to 1. If no consequences can be detected, the importance is 0. In between, it is up to the designer to assign an appropriate value. Ideally, the importance measure should be directly linked to a significant performance value (e.g., throughput).

Example. All dependencies are important because ignoring any of them would lead to non-performance as soon as a work piece reaches a machine that cannot process it.

4.4 Output of analysis phase

The result of the analysis is a decision model of the production control tasks. The decision model consists of four parts:

- a list of all decision tasks;
- a trigger diagram;
- a dependency diagram; and
- a classification of each dependency.

The decision model contains all the decisions that any control system must make in order to solve the control problem. However this model is incomplete in the sense that it fails to represent a full control strategy. The missing information has to be completed in subsequent design steps.

5 Identification of the Agents

After analysing the decision making, it is possible to start the design process by identifying the agents of the control system. The agents have to be identified first as they are the basic building blocks of an agent-based control system; they define the overall architecture of the system. Interactions can only be defined by specifying which agent is interacting with which other. At the same time, however, the system architecture also restricts the set of possible interactions, since it specifies the set of agents existing in the control system. It is therefore crucial to identify a set of agents that optimally supports the task of achieving the production goals.

Here an agent is viewed as an interacting decision maker that is able to pro-actively achieve its goals while it is adapting to its dynamic environment. Consequently, it is straightforward to identify an agent by assigning it a set of tasks from the decision model for which it will be solely responsible. Unfortunately, not every assignment of agents to decision tasks will lead to a well-defined agent-based system. For example, if two agents are each responsible for controlling the same actuator, the agents are not fully autonomous (in their behaviour). Only one agent may have full control over the actuator, while the other must request the controlling agent to execute the desired action. Moreover, not every decision network is equally suitable for agent identification. The analysis focused on the decision aspects and deliberately did not take into account any criteria for structuring an agent-based system. It must therefore be possible to reorganise the decision network isomorphically (i.e., without changing the semantics of the decision process) such that it becomes more suitable for agent identification. To this end, section 5.2 describes allowable operations on the decision network.

But even after a substantial reorganisation of the decision network according to agent-oriented criteria, it may still be impossible to identify agents simply because an agent-based approach is inappropriate for the given control problem. Section 5.3 therefore lists necessary criteria on the decision network that helps assess the suitability of an agent-based approach. If a decision network fails to meet (most of) the criteria, an agent-based approach is not appropriate and the (agent-oriented) design process should terminate. If, on the other hand, the applicability of the agent-based approach is confirmed, the assignment of decision tasks to agents can begin. This assignment process is described in section 5.4.

The very first step, however, is to complete the decision network. The analysis only includes those decision tasks in the decision model that all solutions to the control problem must make (cf. section 4). As a consequence, though, the decision model is incomplete. Section 5.1 therefore adds the missing decision aspects such that the completed decision model represents a full control strategy capable of achieving the production goals.

5.1 Completion of the decision network

The decision network is incomplete if any of the decision tasks are not fully specified. According to the decision making model described in section 1.2, a decision task consists of

1. a trigger, specifying the situation that activates the decision;
2. the decision space, specifying the set of possible choices;
3. the decision input, specifying the information necessary to make a decision; and
4. the decision rule, specifying how to make a decision (based on the decision input).

During the analysis process, the designer is only obliged to specify the trigger and the decision space of a decision task. All other slots may be left unspecified. At this point of the design process, however, the decision model must be completed such that all mandatory slots are fully specified. It is therefore necessary to fill in the decision input and decision rule slots (if they have not been specified so far). This can be done in two ways:

1. The decision input only refers to information that can be provided by the sensors of the production system, and the decision rule specifies how to make the decision based on this information.
2. The decision input refers to sensory information and to the results of other decisions that will be used as a basis for the decision rule to make its decision.

The second option allows additional decision tasks to be introduced that prepare effectoric decisions. The effectoric decision tasks use the non-effectoric decisions to simplify their own computation. Usually, these decisions cover decision aspects that are common to several decision tasks and thus they increase the overall modularity of the decision process.

Example. The decision task of transportation switch S_1 can be greatly simplified if the next machine is chosen before the work piece reaches the switch S_1 (see Figure 6). Based on this abstract decision, the switch can immediately decide whether the work piece must be moved onto the left or right exit. The corresponding dependency diagram is shown in Figure 7.

Non-effectoric decisions can themselves use other decisions to prepare their own decision, leading to an arbitrary hierarchy of decisions. The depth of this hierarchy depends on the complexity of the decision process. The introduction of new decision tasks, of course, requires that the dependency diagram is updated, and is eventually extended by any new dependencies.

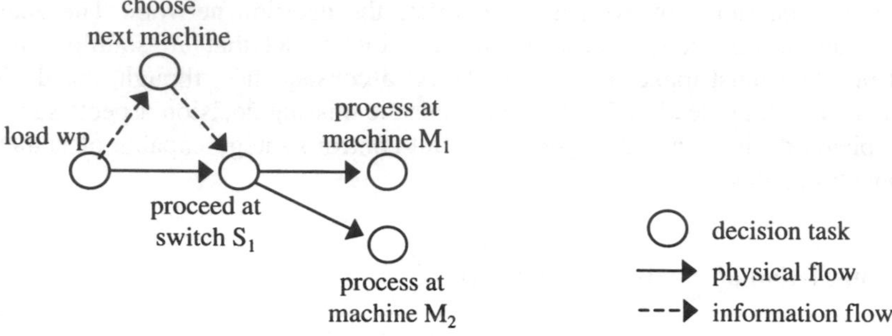

Fig. 6. Introduction of abstract decision *Choose next machine.*

It should be noted that the process of completing the decision model is non-trivial. The decision model must be completed in such a way that the resulting decision making process achieves the production goals. In particular, the decision tasks must take into account the different dependencies that were identified in the analysis phase. The development of a control strategy, however, depends strongly on the kind of production process to be controlled and is therefore application-dependent. It is assumed that the designer is able to find a control strategy that is capable of achieving the production goals under the specified operation conditions.

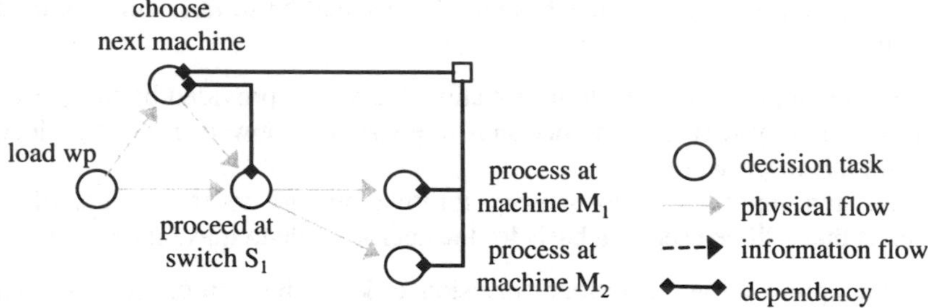

Fig. 7. The extended dependency diagram.

5.2 Operations on the decision network

The decision network is developed in the analysis phase without any consideration of criteria for structuring an agent-based system. It may therefore be difficult to identify agents on the basis of this representation of the decision process. This section presents a set of allowable operations on the decision network that improve the representation of the decision process, but leave its semantics unchanged. That is, the modified decision network executes the same control command as the original one and consequently achieves the same goal satisfaction as the first. In this regard, the original and the modified decision models are isomorphic.

A decision network is unsuitable for the identification of agents if – according to the criteria for a well-formed agent-based system – a decision task must be assigned to different agents. Such a situation is not permissible because it violates the autonomy and integrity of an agent. In such cases the decision task must be split into different aspects of the original decision that of course share a strong dependency. The different aspects may then be assigned to different agents. There are two ways to split a decision task:

- `divide` splits a decision task into independent aspects of the decision that are considered in parallel (see Figure 8). Each new decision task has the same decision space, but different criteria for making the decision.

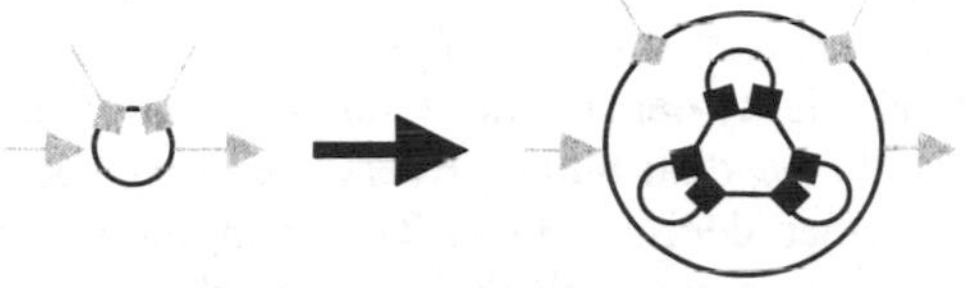

Fig. 8. The `divide` operation.

- `expand` splits a single decision task into subsequent decision (sub)tasks. The result of one decision is the input to another decision task (see Figure 9). Except for the last, every decision subtask formally requires a new decision space and a new decision rule.

Fig. 9. The `expand` operation.

After each operation, the dependency links must be adjusted accordingly. After a split, a new decision task must inherit any dependency link if the dependency applies to its (sub)task. Each dependency link must be inherited by at least one (sub)task. Additionally, any dependencies between the newly introduced decision tasks must be identified and characterised according to the schema described in section 4.3.

The operations described above may be applied in subsequent design steps in order to make the decision network more suitable for agent identification.

5.3 Assessment of the suitability of an agent-oriented approach

Before the actual identification of the agents can start, it is necessary to assess whether an agent-based approach is appropriate to the specific production control problem. Not every control problem is appropriate for an agent-based, or even a distributed, approach. A control problem must fulfil several criteria in order to be appropriate. These criteria do not guarantee that an agent-based approach will be successful, or that it is better than other approaches. However the criteria do rule out applications that are obviously inappropriate.

For an agent-oriented approach to be adequate, the decision network must fulfil three conditions:

1. *There are multiple decision tasks.*
   An agent-based system is always distributed (at least logically). If there is only one decision task, the decision process cannot be distributed. This condition is therefore mandatory.
2. *The decision process is dynamic.*
   A control system that has to make all decisions at once cannot make use of the full power of agent technology. However, this does not rule out the use of agents. The condition is therefore optional. If it is fulfilled, it supports the agent case.
3. *The decisions are at least partly independent.*
   If the decisions are all highly dependent on each other, it is difficult to see how the decision process could be distributed. Every decision task would communicate heavily with every other decision task. This condition is therefore mandatory. However, the condition is not "black and white". No application has purely dependent or purely independent decision tasks. How much dependence is acceptable depends on the particular agent techniques used and is therefore ultimately left to the designer.

If the decision network scores low on the above conditions, the designer may still be able to transform the decision network into a more suitable form by using the allowable operations described in section 5.2. If, after extensive improvements, the decision network still scores low on the above conditions, the control system should not be developed as a (pure) agent-based system. This does not imply that it is impossible to use an agent-based approach. Rather it only suggests that the designer should reflect very carefully about what other (possibly application-dependent) reasons are in favour of agent technology and why it is not more appropriate to use other approaches.

Example. Despite its simplicity, the simple production example scores high on the necessary conditions. First, the decision network has more than one decision task. Second, the decision process is dynamic. There is a constant flow of (different) work pieces into the system that must be distributed to the machines depending on their current availability. Third, the decision tasks are partly independent, even though they all relate to the same task: distributing work pieces onto two machines.

5.4 Clustering of decision tasks

After confirming the applicability of agent technology to the given control problem, the agents of the production control system can finally be identified. Here an agent is identified by creating a cluster of decision tasks for which the agent is solely responsible. Since every decision task should be assigned to an agent, the identification of agents is essentially a problem of partitioning the decision network.

However, in order to create a well-formed agent-based system, the resulting clusters should fulfil the following two modularity criteria (cf. also [24]):

1. The decision tasks of a cluster should be coherent.
2. There should be no strong coupling (dependence) between any two clusters.

Strong cohesion and low coupling for clusters of decision tasks can be achieved in three ways:

- **interface cohesion**
  All decision tasks in one cluster access the same sensors and effectors, whereas decision tasks in different clusters do not access the same physical interface.
- **responsibility cohesion**
  The responsibility for a local state of a production object (e.g., a machine or work piece) is assigned to at most one cluster. Decision tasks in another cluster may not directly alter this state.
- **low interactive coupling**
  There is no strong coupling (i.e., dependence) between the decision tasks of different clusters.

Note that the above criteria can be in conflict. It is a design decision to resolve a conflict by preferring one particular criterion. Moreover, it may not be possible to cluster the decision network created in the analysis phase according to any of the above criteria. In such cases, the network first has to be transformed by the operations described in section 5.2 before the clustering can be performed successfully.

Once the decision network has a suitable form for clustering, the following strategies can be employed to cluster the decision model:

- **Interface clustering**
  Cluster decision tasks that access the same physical interfaces. Several interfaces may end up in one cluster, but an interface should never belong to more than one cluster. In case of a conflict, a decision task can be split and the sub-decisions assigned to different clusters.
- **Data / State clustering**
  Cluster decision tasks which access and change the same logical data or status of the production system (e.g., the work piece status).
- **Dependence clustering**
  Cluster decision tasks which have a strong dependence.
- **No bottleneck clustering**
  Distribute decision tasks such that the system has no bottlenecks.

Example. In the decision model of the simple production system, agents can be identified in a straightforward fashion. First of all, a switch agent and a machine agent are associated with each switch or machine respectively and they become responsible for the decision task associated with the particular component. Likewise, a loading agent is assigned to the loader and its decision task. All these agents are static.

The decision task *choose next machine*, though, is not directly associated with a single component. It involves all possible machines and the work piece that is supposed to be processed. This decision task is therefore divided into several aspects: A decision aspect for each machine and one for the work piece. The work piece agent responsible for this decision task is created by the loading agent when the corresponding work piece is put on the first conveyor belt. This work piece agent then interacts with the machine agents in order to choose the next machine and informs the switch agent of switch S_1 about the next goal machine.

As with the modularity criteria, the above strategies can be in conflict too. Again it is a design decision about which strategy should be preferred when there is a conflict.

Clustering strategies (in combination with the allowable operations) are applied to the decision network until a satisfactory partitioning has been found. Even though the modularity criteria indicate the quality of the partitioning, it is ultimately left to the designer to decide whether the achieved quality is sufficient.

5.5 Output of the agent identification phase

The results of the first design step are twofold. First of all, an assessment of the decision model created in the analysis phase indicates the suitability of an agent-oriented approach to the particular production control problem. Secondly, in cases where the suitability is confirmed, the design step identifies a list of agents, each associated with a subset of the decision tasks. The agents are solely responsible for the execution of their decision tasks, but depend on other agents whenever decision dependencies exist between decision tasks that are assigned to different agents.

6 Conclusions and Future Work

This paper has presented a design method for the identification of agents in production control systems. The design method consists of two main steps. First, the decision making necessary to control the given production system is analysed. This step identifies the decisions necessary to achieve the production goals and the dependencies between these decisions. Second, the necessary agents to control the production system are identified. This step transforms the decision network into a more suitable form for an agent-oriented approach, assesses the appropriateness of an agent-oriented approach and identifies the agents as well as the required interactions. The result of the method is a set of agents associated with control responsibilities and dependencies.

The proposed design method fulfils the requirements put forward in section 1.1. First of all, the design process is based on models that are appropriate for production control. The analysis model is centered on the concept of control decisions that are central to the problem of controlling a production process. Likewise, decision dependencies are derived by relating this notion to the effects on the production performance. Finally, agents are identified by clustering decision tasks. Second, the design method is prescriptive with respect to its agent-related aspects. The analysis step clearly defines which information to provide in the analysis model. The design step provides criteria for re-organising and clustering the decision network in order to identify agents. Finally, the design method provides criteria for assessing the suitability of an agent-oriented approach for the given production control problem. In summary, the design method fulfils both requirements put forward in section 1.1. Thus it allows an engineer with no prior experience in agent technology to successfully apply the design method to a production control problem.

The next stage of this work is to complete the design method by dealing with the interactions that occur between the agents. These interactions stem from the dependencies that exist between the agents' decision making responsibilities. To this end, many interaction formalisms and design approaches have been proposed to date. However none of these approaches addresses the question of how protocols are derived from a problem description.

References

1. B. Burmeister: "Models and Methodology for Agent-Oriented Analysis and Design". In K. Fischer (ed.): *Working Notes of the KI'96 Workshop on Agent-Oriented Programming and Distributed Systems*, pages 7 – 17. Document D-96-06. DFKI: Saarbrücken, Germany, 1996.
2. S. Bussmann, D.C. McFarlane: "Rationales for Holonic Manufacturing Control". In *Proc. of Second Int. Workshop on Intelligent Manufacturing Systems*, pages 177 – 184, Leuven, Belgium, 1999.
3. S. Bussmann, K. Schild: "Self-Organizing Manufacturing Control: An Industrial Application of Agent Technology". In *Proc. of the Fourth Int. Conf. on Multi-Agent Systems*, pages 87 – 94, Boston, MA, USA, 2000.
4. K.S. Decker: *Environmental Centered Analysis and Design of Coordination Mechanisms*. PhD Thesis, University of Massachusetts, MA, USA, 1992.
5. M. Wood, S.A. DeLoach: "An Overview of the Multiagent Systems Engineering Methodology". In this volume.
6. R.G. Fichman, C.F. Kemerer: "Object-Oriented and conventional analysis and design methodologies – comparison and critique". In *IEEE Computer*, Vol. 25, No. 10, pages 22 – 39, 1992.
7. N. Glaser: "The CoMoMAS Methodology and Environment for Multi-Agent System Development". In C. Zhang, D. Lukose (eds.), *Multi-Agent Systems – Methodologies and Applications*, LNAI 1286, pages 1 – 16. Springer-Verlag: Berlin, Germany, 1997.
8. H. Hußmann: *Formal Foundations for Software Engineering Methods*. LNCS 1322, Springer-Verlag: Berlin, Germany, 1997.
9. C.A. Iglesias, M. Garrijo, J.C. Gonzalez: "A survey of agent-oriented methodologies". In *Pre-Proc. of the 5th Int. Workshop on Agent Theories, Architectures and Languages*, Paris, France, 1998.
10. C. A. Iglesias, M. Garijo, J.C. Gonzalez, J.R. Velasco: "Analysis and Design of Multiagent Systems Using MAS-CommonKADS". In M.P. Singh, A. Rao, M.J. Wooldridge (eds.), *Intelligent Agents IV (ATAL'97)*, LNAI 1365, pages 314 – 327. Springer-Verlag: Berlin, Germany, 1998.
11. I. Jacobson: *Object-Oriented Software Engineering: A Use Case Driven Approach*. Addison-Wesley, 1992.
12. E.A. Kendall, M.T. Malkoun, C.H. Jiang: "A Methodology for Developing Agent Based Systems". In C. Zhang, D. Lukose (eds.), *Distributed Artificial Intelligence – Architecture and Modelling*, LNAI 1087, pages 85 – 99. Springer-Verlag: Berlin, Germany, 1996.

13. E.A. Kendall: "Agent Software Engineering with Role Modelling". In this volume.
14. D. Kinny, M. Georgeff: "Modelling and Design of Multi-Agent Systems". In J.P. Müller, M.J. Wooldridge, N.R. Jennings (eds.), *Intelligent Agents III (ATAL'96)*, LNAI 1193, pages 1 – 20. Springer-Verlag: Berlin, Germany, 1997.
15. J. Lind: *MASSIVE: Software Engineering for Multiagent Systems*. PhD thesis, University of Saarbrücken, Germany, 1999.
16. F. von Martial: *Coordinating Plans of Autonomous Agents*, LNAI 610. Springer-Verlag: Berlin, Germany, 1992.
17. B. Moulin, M. Brassard: "A Scenario-Based Design Method and an Environment for the Development of Multiagent Systems". In C. Zhang, D. Lukose (eds.), *Distributed Artificial Intelligence – Architecture and Modelling*, LNAI 1087, pages 216 – 232. Springer-Verlag: Berlin, Germany, 1996.
18. A. Omicini: "SODA: Societies and Infrastructure in the Analysis and Design of Agent-based Systems". In this volume.
19. H.V.D. Parunak: "Manufacturing Experience with the Contract Net". In M.N. Huhns (ed.), *Distributed Artificial Intelligence*, pages 285 – 310. Pitman: London, UK, 1987.
20. V. Parunak, J. Sauter, S. Clark: "Toward the Specification and Design of Industrial Synthetic Ecosystems". In M.P. Singh, A. Rao, M.J. Wooldridge (eds.), *Intelligent Agents IV (ATAL'97)*, LNAI 1365, pages 45 – 59. Springer-Verlag: Berlin, Germany, 1998.
21. J. Rumbaugh, M. Blaha, W. Premerlani, F. Eddy, W. Lorensen: *Object-Oriented Modeling and Design*. Prentice-Hall: Englewood Cliffs, NJ, USA, 1991.
22. G. Schreiber, B.J. Wielinga, R. de Hoog, H. Akkermans, W. Van de Velde: "CommonKADS: A comprehensive methodology for KBS development". In *IEEE Expert*, Vol. 9, No. 6, pages 28 – 37, 1994.
23. M. Wooldridge, N.R. Jennings, D. Kinny: "The Gaia Methodology for Agent-Oriented Analysis and Design". In *Autonomous Agents and Multi-Agent Systems*, Vol. 3, No. 3, pages 285 – 312, 2000.
24. E. Yourdon, L.L. Constantine: *Structured Design*. Prentice Hall: Englewood Cliffs, NJ, USA, 1979.
25. E.S.K. Yu, J. Mylopoulos: "Understanding the 'Why' in Software Process Modelling, Analysis, and Design". In *Proc. of the 16th Int. Conf. on Software Engineering*. Sorrento, Italy, 1994.

Agent Software Engineering with Role Modelling

Elizabeth A. Kendall

School of Network Computing, Monash University
McMahons Rd., Frankston, VIC 3199 Australia
kendall@infotech.monash.edu.au

Abstract . Due to their autonomy and social behavior, agents will play important roles in future emerging enterprises. They will fill key positions and provide essential capabilities. We propose role modelling as a software engineering technique for specifying, analyzing, and designing systems on the basis of the roles that the agents will play. Our approach builds on our earlier research in patterns [4, 5] of agent systems. Object-oriented role models can be extended to represent *patterns* of agent interaction that can then be employed to engineer agent systems.

1 Role Models in Object-oriented Software Engineering

In object-oriented software engineering, a ***role model*** identifies and describes a structure of interacting objects [1, 7, 11]. Often the structure is archetypal or recurring. The description is comprised of roles. A ***role*** defines a position and a set of responsibilities within a role model; roles are assigned to objects in an application. The responsibilities in a role are made up of services and tasks. The services are externally accessible, through an interface; tasks yield results that are utilised within the role itself. A role has collaborators; these are other roles that it interacts with.

A role model representation of a pattern of interaction is shown in Figure 1, where a rounded box is a role, and the solid arrows indicate collaboration paths between the roles. The direction of the arrow represents the direction of messaging, and the solid circle on the link from the Mediator to the Colleague indicates that there is more than one Colleague. As can be seen from Figure 1, the Colleague roles do not interact directly with each other. All collaboration occurs through the Mediator role.

Once a role model has been captured, it can be instantiated, as needed, in any application. The five object instances in the enterprise application (shown as rectangles in the bottom half of Figure 1) can be assigned to play the various roles, as indicated by the dashed arrows.

The full semantics of the role model for the Mediator pattern can be detailed in additional views and notation that are provided in [1]. The important distinction between a UML collaboration diagram and the role model in Figure 1 is that the role model is an abstraction; the instance collaboration diagram is merely an instantiation of it.

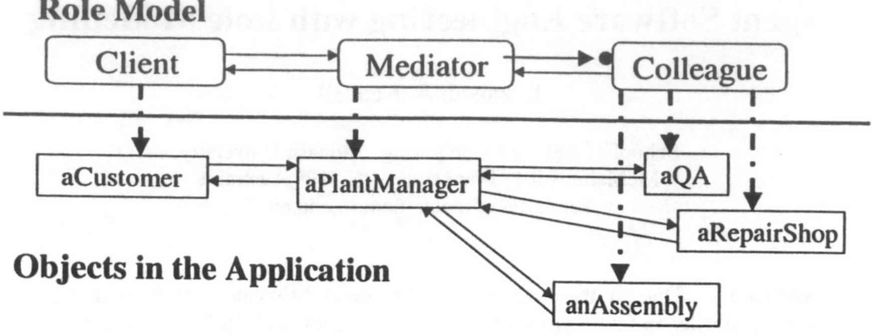

Figure 1:. Role Model for the Mediator Pattern and Role Assignments

2 Role Models of Agent Systems

2.1 Overview

Over the last few years, we have completed research in how object-oriented techniques can be utilised and extended for agents systems [4-7]. We feel that role modelling offers a promising approach for agent analysis and design because of the following [7]:

- *Social:* The emphasis is on social or interactive behavior
- *Proactive:* Roles in a role model can work together to accomplish a goal.
- *Reuse:* Roles may move shared representations for agents from the data or ontology level up to the collaboration and interface levels.
- *Patterns:* Role models are reoccurring or archetypical structures of interacting objects or elements; they are patterns that should be documented and transferred.
- *Unified Model:* Role models provide a new abstraction that can unify diverse aspects of an agent system. For example, facets of an agent's expertise, such as its generic tasks, can be described more easily with role models than with an object model. Also, agents, objects, and people can play roles.
- *Partitioning Agent Behavior:* Roles have been used to partition an object's behavior [12]. Barbuceanu [2] partitions an agent's beliefs, goals, and behavior according to the roles that it plays to facilitate context switching and to decompose sophisticated agent behavior.
- *Design:* Role model synergy or synthesis, which involves integrating roles, is valuable for agent design.
- *Implementation:* There are several object oriented design patterns for roles [7].
- *Role Dynamics:* Role models are not static; they can have various forms of dynamic behavior. Role model dynamics may be valuable for modelling mobility, adaptive behavior, context switching, and other aspects of agent systems.
- *Documentation:* Roles and role models provide documentation for agent patterns and frameworks that is independent of the implementation.

Object roles have the facets or dimensions listed in Table 1.

Table 1. Facets of an Object Role

role model	context
responsibilities	services, tasks
collaborators	roles it interacts with
external interfaces	access to services
relationships to other roles	aggregation, generalization, refinement, role sequences

As agents are extensions of objects, they encompass all the features that objects have, adding autonomous, proactive, social, reactive, and intelligent behavior (Table 2).

Table 2. Facets of an Agent Role

role model	context
responsibilities	services, tasks, goals, obligations, interdictions
collaborators	roles it interacts with
external interfaces	access to services
relationships to other roles	aggregation, specialization, generalization, role sequences
expertise	ontology, inferencing, problem solving knowledge
coordination and negotiation	protocol, conflict resolution, knowledge of why other roles are related, permissions
other	resources, learning/ adaptability

2.2 Example Agent Role Model: Supply Chain with Service Provisioning

A supply chain is a common pattern of collaboration for agents [2]. A supply chain is comprised of suppliers and consumers. The head of the supply chain is only a consumer, while the tail is only a supplier. An internal link in the chain must be both a consumer and a supplier. A consumer can have many suppliers, but a supplier usually only has one consumer in a given supply chain. (The supplier will typically be involved in several supply chains, however.)

We have represented the Supply Chain pattern of interaction in terms of role models. At the highest level, a Supply Chain is made up of three roles: Supply Chain (SC) Head, SC Tail, and SC Participants. The relationships between the links in the chain can be captured in terms of another role model: Predecessor-Successor. A Predecessor can have many Successors, but a Successor has only one Predecessor. As shown in the role model in Figure 2, an SC Participant is both a Predecessor and a Successor. The SC Participant role merges the roles of Predecessor and Successor, refining the behavior of both. An SC Head is a specialization of a Predecessor, and an SC Tail refines the role of Successor.

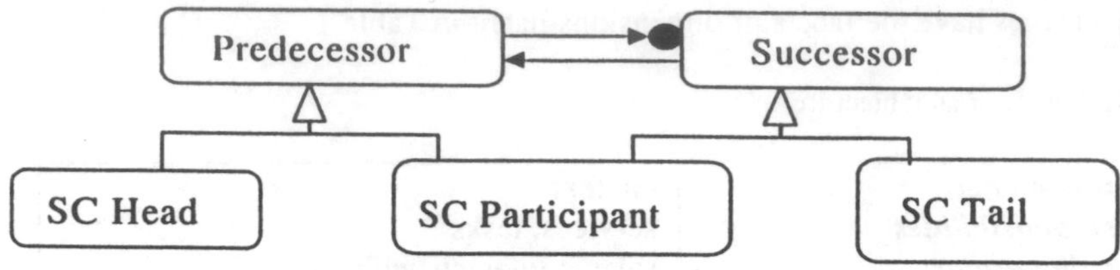

Figure 2: Supply Chain: Top Level Role Model

We have documented many detailed supply chain role models that consider service provisioning and the phases of negotiation, delivery, and payment. Figure 2-2 considers negotiation and delivery in a supply chain with just two elements. Because of the phases, role sequences are required, with nested or contained roles. A SC Head goes from being a Customer who negotiates for services to a User who utilises them. An SC Tail is first a Provider and then an Operator. During negotiation, the Customer in the head negotiates with the Provider in the tail. During delivery, the Operator in the successor delivers supplies to the User in the predecessor.

Additional notations and formalisms for role models can be found in [1]; we have introduced Role Responsibility (RRC) cards [6, 7] as a simple way to document the key facets of an agent role in a given role model (Table 2).

3 Role Models during Agent System Analysis

3.1 Agent Role Models as Patterns

Analysis should begin with goal centric use cases [5]. Goals should be partitioned, which means that they should be assigned to individual roles. Any agent application will in fact encompass many role models. During analysis, relevant role models should be identified. This can be done from scratch by identifying the agents in an application and their collaborations.

Alternatively, a role model catalog can be used; this provides commonly occurring agent role models. A role model catalog resembles a set of patterns or a pattern language [4], and role model catalogs are being used at BT for downstreaming agent technology. A pattern language has been shown to be valuable for transferring experience. Alexander initially developed the concept of patterns in his work on architecture and urban planning. Patterns are masterful solutions that take time to evolve or develop; they can be identified once the level of understanding is deep and comprehensive enough to uncover invariants.

The role model catalog developed at BT includes approximately 60 role models, including those from agent enhanced workflow, flexible manufacturing, electronic commerce, agent based information management and retrieval, and the FIPA protocols (contract net, auctions, etc.). As discussed in sections 1 and 2, these role models are patterns of interaction. The patterns in the BT catalog were mined from numerous existing agent frameworks or specifications. This includes Zeus, FIPA, Single Function Agents, and KADS.

The BT catalog provides concrete details about the roles and the role models. All of the facets from Table 2 are considered, in addition to interactions and protocols. For example, the supply chain roles can employ certain techniques for negotiation and coordination, such as a contract net or an auction; further, some of the role models involve ontologies

When presented with a new application, analysts should go through the role model catalog to identify which patterns of interaction appear. To facilitate dissemination and proper use, full pattern format has been used for the role model documentation. That is, the role models are fully motivated solutions for application analysis models.

3.2 Illustration from an Agent Application

As an illustration, consider an application in agent enhanced workflow (AEW) [7] or flexible manufacturing. The agents can be arranged in such a way that each agent is dependent upon one other agent to deliver work or supplies to them. For example, four agents may represent an end customer and three enterprises, respectively. The Customer deals directly only with Enterprise 1. Enterprise 1 depends on Enterprise 2 for supplies or work, and Enterprise 2 in turn depends on Enterprise 3. At the highest level, the application is an instantiation of the Supply Chain role model. The Customer is the SC Head, Enterprise 1 and Enterprise 2 are both SC Participants, and Enterprise 3 is an SC Tail. Enterprise 1 is an SC Successor to the Customer, but it is a SC Predecessor to Enterprise 2.

However, each enterprise in the supply chain can be made up of several entities. For example, Enterprise 1 may be a manufacturing company with a hierarchical structure and agents to represent each domain. In this case, both the Bureaucracy [10] and Supply Chain role models appear, to yield Figure 3. It is the responsibility of the Plant Manager to be the SC Successor to the Customer, but it is the Assembly (for example) functional group that requires input from Enterprise 2, so it is the SC Predecessor in that context.

aPlantManager must play all of the roles found in a Successor, in addition to the role of a Manager. Likewise, anAssembly must be a Predecessor in addition to satisfying the responsibilities of a Subordinate. If negotiation and delivery are considered, the internal roles appear as well. Both entities must appropriately address context switching as they go from role to role.

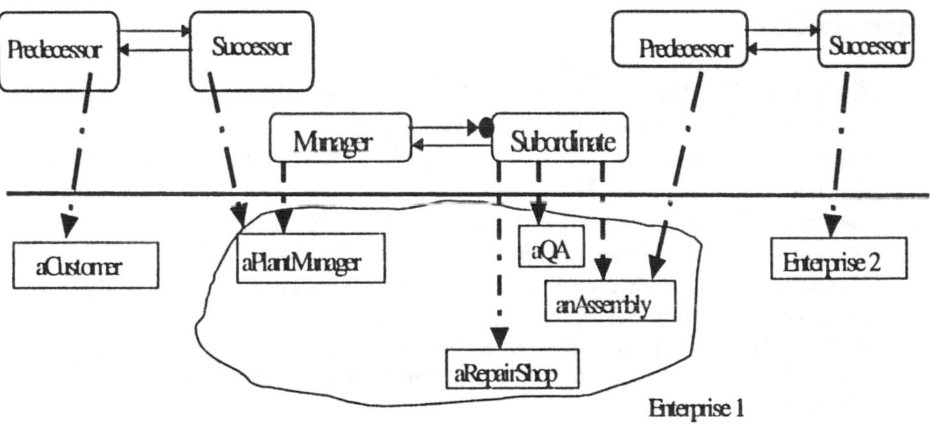

Figure 3. Bureaucracy with Supply Chain Model for Agent Enhanced Workflow

4 Agent Design with Role Models

Role models are also useful during agent system design. Basically, the roles that a given agent needs to play have to be identified and composed during design. This approach has been utilized in object oriented software engineering, in particular during framework design [11]. A software engineer can design an agent class by composing or assembling all of the responsibilities, interfaces, expertise, and protocols from the individual roles, following the documentation provided in tables 1 and 2. For example, if an agent can be found in a Supply Chain and also as a Manager, Subordinate, or Client (Director Client and Clerk Client are considered together for simplicity) of a Bureaucracy, then the agent must be capable of playing the seven roles shown in Figure 4. Each of these roles would be fully specified, per tables 1 and 2.

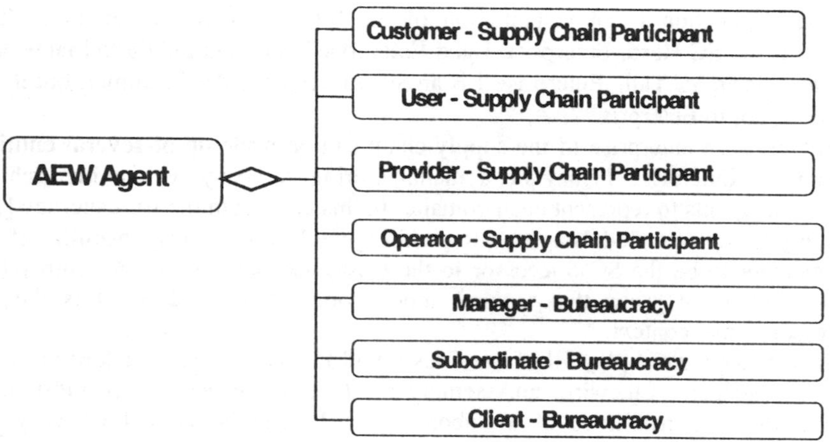

Figure 4. Role Composition during Design

References

1. Andersen, E. (Egil), *Conceptual Modeling of Objects: A Role Modeling Approach*, PhD Thesis, University of Oslo, 1997.
2. Barbuceanu, M., Gray, T., Mankovski, S., "Coordinating with Obligations," Agents '98, Minneapolis, May, 1998, p. 62 - 69.
3. Gamma, E.R., R. Helm, R. Johnson, and J. Vlissides, *Design Patterns: Elements of Reusable Object-Oriented Software.* Addison-Wesley, 1994.
4. Kendall, E. A., P.V. Murali Krishna, Chirag V. Pathak, C.B. Suresh, "Patterns of Intelligent and Mobile Agents," Agents '98, May, 1998.
5. Kendall, E. A., U. Palanivelan, S. Kalikivayi, "Capturing and Structuring Goals: Analysis Patterns," EuroPlop'98, European Pattern Languages of Programming, Germany, July, 1998.
6. Kendall, E. A., "Agent Roles and Role Models: New Abstractions for Multiagent System Analysis and Design," International Workshop on Intelligent Agents in

Information and Process Management, German Conference on Artificial Intelligence, Bremen, Germany, September, 1998.

7. Kendall, E. A., "Role Modelling for Agent System Analysis and Design," ASA/MA'99, November, 1999.
8. Rational Software, "UML Documentation: Behavioral Elements Package: Collaboration Overview," http://www.rational.com/uml/resources/index.html
9. Riehle, D., "Composite Design Patterns", *OOPSLA '97, Proceedings of the 1997 Conference on Object-Oriented Programming Systems, Languages and Applications*, ACM Press, Page 218-228, 1997.
10. Riehle, D., "Bureaucracy", in *Pattern Languages of Program Design* 3, R. Martin, D. Riehle, F. Buschmann (Ed.), Addison Wesley, 1998, pp. 163 - 185.
11. Riehle, D., T. Gross, "Role Model Based Framework Design and Integration," *OOPSLA'98, Proceedings of the 1998 Conference on Object- oriented Programming Systems, Languages and Applications*, ACM Press, 1998.
12. M. T. Tu, F. Griffel, M. Merz, W. Lamersdorf, "A Plug- In Architecture Providing Dynamic Negotiation Capabilities for Mobile Agents," Mobile Agents: Second International Workshop (MA'98), Stuttgart, Germany, September, 1998, pp. 222 - 236.

Designing Agent-Oriented Systems by Analysing Agent Interactions

Simon Miles Mike Joy Michael Luck

Department of Computer Science, University of Warwick
Coventry, CV4 7AL, United Kingdom

smiles@dcs.warwick.ac.uk

Abstract. We propose a preliminary methodology for agent-oriented software engineering based on the idea of *agent interaction analysis*. This approach uses interactions between undetermined agents as the primary component of analysis and design. Agents as a basis for software engineering are useful because they provide a powerful and intuitive abstraction which can increase the comprehensiblity of a complex design. The paper describes a process by which the designer can derive the interactions that can occur in a system satisfying the given requirements and use them to design the structure of an agent-based system, including the identification of the agents themselves. We suggest that this approach has the flexibility necessary to provide agent-oriented designs for open and complex applications, and has value for future maintenance and extension of these systems.

1 Introduction

The agent paradigm has, over recent years, given rise to a large amount of research on the internal structure of agents as general problem-solvers capable of effective intelligent behaviour in dynamic environments. This concentration of work on the development of *agent architectures* has been just one side of the many aspects illuminated by the agent metaphor. More recently, however, agents have been used as an abstraction for general software engineering. This paper explores the rôle of agent-oriented methods for just such a purpose, and introduces a preliminary methodology that may be used as a basis for designing agent-based systems.

The full potential of agent-based systems in solving problems in complex domains depends upon the systems themselves, and the designs from which they are constructed, being tailored to the conditions that vary across the domain. They also need to be sufficiently adaptable and fault tolerant to cope with changes in the domain that arise due to maintenance, extension and so on [12, 24]. To achieve this, a methodology that produces agent-based designs must be flexible enough to describe these varying requirements and their interconnections. In particular, the significant area of open systems should be addressed [26].

An abstraction of the social aspects of an agent can be given as a system *rôle*, and this concept is used in many of the emerging agent-oriented methodologies [13, 17, 27]. Rôles are useful as they provide a way to describe a multi-agent system as analogous to an organisation without placing heavy restrictions on the behaviour of concrete agents at runtime. The usefulness of this approach can be extended by identifying organisational patterns using rôle modeling [16] which can then be used repeatedly as the basis for new systems.

However, the choice of organisation or rôle models will effect the performance of the system [7, 23, 29]. The applicability of the organisation to the domain and the effects of changes in connected systems over time must be accounted for. One way of doing this is to analyse and tailor the behaviour of groups of agents to the domain either by providing *coordination media* to societies of agents [23] or *organisational rules* to the system which influence the dynamic form of the organisation [29]. While these approaches provide appropriately constrained flexibility to the organisations, the constraints and infrastructures which are appropriate to the particular domain must be identified.

We explore a different approach, named *agent interaction analysis*, based on using the interactions between agents as a primary component of analysis. As with the MaSE methodology [7, 25], this approach does not constrain the organisation or rôle model until late in the analysis, after domain-specific requirements have been identified. *Agent interaction analysis*, by translating requirements into agent interactions rather than rôles, also allows for the system behaviour to be flexibly distributed between the designed system and connected systems. The product of the steps described in this paper is an organisational structure and justifications for that structure. This allows for other rôle-based methodologies to continue the design process from that organisation to an implementation.

The next section provides detail on some of the terms used in, and sets the scene for, the rest of this paper. Section 3 provides an overview of *agent interaction analysis*. Later sections then look at each step of this process in turn. Section 4 examines the initial analysis of the system requirements and explains what information is necessary for *agent interaction analysis*. Next, Section 5 describes how the system aims can be decomposed into a structure which represents the system functionality in a modularised way. Section 6 describes the concept of an *interaction* between agents and details the part it plays in the design process. The next stage, described in Section 7, derives useful design information from the interactions and system requirements. Finally, Section 8 shows how the design is reduced to a form which is implementable and more comprehensible as a whole. The final two sections describe how the process is useful for maintenance and extension, and then mention the other work done on this project.

2 Agents and Goals

The term *agent* is used in a variety of related ways in the literature surrounding agent-based systems[10]. On the one hand, it is used to describe software artefacts that satisfy certain architectural requirements in order to achieve particular functionality. On the other, as in this paper, agents are used as a software engineering abstraction that enables complex software to be decomposed into a collection of sophisticated interacting components (that may also share the qualities of the previous view). In developing a methodology for agent-oriented design, we aim for it to be sufficiently flexible and general to apply to designs using a wide range of entities, but there are certain properties that we assume system components will have or can be thought of as having. These assumptions enable the designer to develop systems with those properties implicit, thus making the rest of the design easier to comprehend.

The properties are fairly standard (e.g., see [15]): the agents are considered to be *autonomous*, *decision making*, *social*, *flexible* and *reactive* entities. *Agent interaction analysis* is concerned with the social aspects of agents and, therefore, doesn't directly address the analysis of reaction to a non-autonomous environment in the system design.

These properties describe the broad expectations we have in all the agents in systems resulting from our design approach. We do not require any further particular architectural implementation constraints; indeed it should not impose any further constraints since we cannot know in advance the form agents will take in an open system.

In this paper we describe the direction agents have in their autonomy in terms of declarative *goals* possessed by the agents. To increase the flexibility and range of systems which the methodology can produce, we also allow that goals can have a variety of solutions with different quantative *worths* [6].

3 Overview of Agent Interaction Analysis

The primary building blocks used by our approach are *interactions* between agents. The approach of *agent interaction analysis* is as follows.

- We assume the system contains an arbitrary number of flexible agents with the properties described in the next section (and no other details known as yet).
- We interpret the system requirements as goals and preferences for their achievement.
- We decompose the system goals into independent hierarchies of goals, comparable to hierarchical plans, and actions which achieve the lowest level goals.
- We treat the successful *engagement* of one or more agents to pursue a goal as an interaction.
- From the particular requirements of each interaction and the system preferences we derive the forms of architecture and particular coordination mechanism to make agents taking part in the interaction behave in a way that fits the preferences well.

The overall structure of the agent interaction analysis process is shown in Figure 1, in which the primary entities are written in larger letters. The arrows indicate the transformations between entities which make up the design process.

Requirements The requirements must be analysed to extract the structure of a multi-agent system which will usefully implement them.

Goals As described above, goals describe desired states of the system.

Preferences Preferences denote an encompassing concept that includes different constraints relating to the other significant information in the requirements aside from goals. Particular types of preferences are recognised in *agent interaction analysis*, such as quality of goals, but they can also represent other domain restrictions and desired system properties that require taking account of.

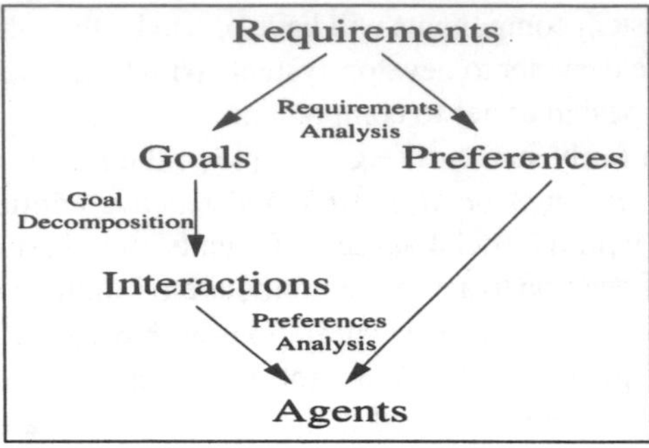

Fig. 1. The transformations involved in agent interaction analysis

Interactions Agreements on coordination between agents (or *place-holders* for where agents will exist) are known as *interactions*. Section 6 expands further on the meaning of interactions.

Agents Agents, or rôles which agents can take, are derived from the other entities and implemented.

While this process is not a fully defined or mature methodology, it does describe a part of such a methodology with beneficial properties for agent-oriented design. The remainder of this paper describes the details of how such a process works and contains arguments for why it is useful.

4 Agent Interaction Analysis Requirements

As with every development methodology, an early stage of the design process is to derive the needed information, in a useful form, from the given requirements. This stage is the first of relevance to *agent interaction analysis* and, in this case, what we want are *goals* and *preferences*. The goals may be continuous over the system lifetime or dependent on context, e.g., at regular intervals or invoked by a user. The preferences may take different forms determining, for instance, the measures of success for goals or restrictions on resources. Examples of preferences are given below.

Now, traditional *requirements analysis* attempts to decompose systems into objects, functions and states so as to understand the problem [5]. *Agent interaction analysis*, however, is concerned with design, i.e., reaching an implementable solution. Therefore, the technique and end product of the artefacts derived from the requirements may be very different. Nevertheless, regardless of the way in which *agent interaction analysis* produces a useful decomposition, the requirements analysis should at least indicate the highest level of system goals, the contexts in which they can occur, and the preferences attached to them. In terms of requirements analysis, this means clarification of definite states which functions should achieve. Importantly, because of the attention to the high-level and the goal-orientation, this stage of the design process can usefully borrow from requirements analysis ideas.

A range of requirements analysis techniques are available (with several being described in [5], and one aimed at agent-based systems described in [1]). It is interesting to note that these techniques derive relations between agents both internal and external to the system being designed and, because we are concerned primarily with interactions, there is no explicit distinction between these different classes of agent.

As an example of the products of the analysis, the following simplistic translations could be made.

- "When a user clicks on a button in the graphical interface the document being edited should be saved" translates to an interaction in which agents cooperate on the goal to save the document. It also states a fact about the interface, i.e., that pressing the button is one way of causing this interaction. This is the *context-based* appearance of goals.
- "The temperature should not go above 100 degrees" places a restriction on the system and describes a system goal to keep the temperature below 100. The goal is considered to be part of an interaction (as they all are) but is likely to be implemented by a single agent repeatedly cooperating with itself. This concept of an agent cooperating with itself reduces to the internal processing of the agent and, while a valuable way to provide an overarching framework for design, is only cooperation in the broadest sense.
  The 100 degrees part describes the measure of quality for the goal, which is high when the temperature is below 100 degrees and low when it is above. A different application might have a wider range of qualities, e.g., "the cooler the better." This is is the *continuous* appearance of goals.
- Aside from context-based and continuous appearance of goals, another possibility is *regular* appearance, e.g., "Back up the system at midnight every night." This sort of interaction is described by the (very simple) cooperation between a clock and another agent.
- "The transferred file should contain the least amount of corruption as possible given other preferences, such as sufficient rapidity" describes a set of preferences concerning the result of a process, which are the quality measures of the goal to transfer the file.

5 Goal Decomposition

Once the system goals are known, we need to examine how the system could be broken up to enable the designer to identify agents and their properties, as well as allowing a division of labour in designing the system [18]. Decomposing goals means finding states that allow the goal state to be achieved more easily or finding independent parts of the goal state such that when the parts are achieved the whole is achieved.

An example of a graphically represented goal decomposition is given in Figure 2. In this diagram, *Goal 1* has been decomposed into three independent goals which, if achieved in some specified order, will cause the achievement of *Goal 1*. Similarly, *Goal 4* has also been decomposed. A real world example which would follow this structure is if the goals were representing the following environment states. *Goal 1* is the state in which a table has been moved to another location, *Goal 2* is the state where one end has been lifted in the air, *Goal 3* is the state where the other end has been lifted, *Goal 4* is the state where the lifted table has been moved to another location, *Goal 5* is the state where one end has been moved along, and *Goal 6* is the state where the other end has been moved. Some of these decomposed goals must be done in parallel, some sequentially.

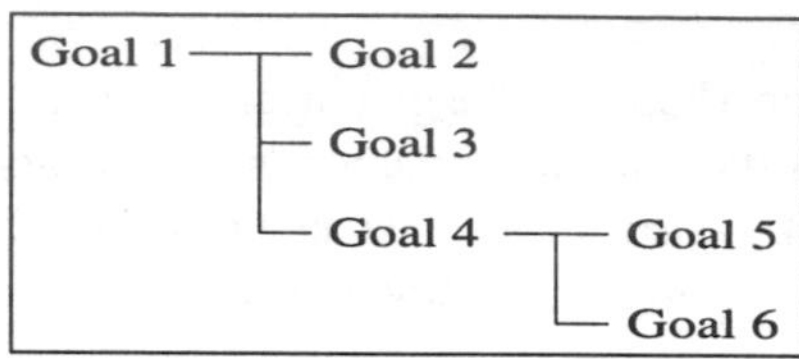

Fig. 2. An example of goal decomposition

This task of decomposition is similar to the production of hierarchical plans. Goals reduce to a series, or some other combination, of subgoals. Unlike a hierarchical plan, this structure is not necessarily possessed by an individual or a group of agents, and it does not require the decomposed system goal to be achieved in this way when the system is running. At this stage, the decomposition only allows us to state that the enactment of that decomposition *could* occur in the system if circumstances were correct. The weakness of the implications of the decompositions is essential to retain the system and agent flexibility as far as possible, with the tightening of the design coming at later stages. Importantly, multiple decompositions can be developed for the same goal. Now, although it may appear that the decomposition produces a full design itself, this may lose the benefits of the agent-oriented approach. In particular, if the fully decomposed subgoals can be translated into actions, then that series of actions achieves the system goal. However, without the agent-based system, or another form of system, to execute them in a flexible manner, we could lose the benefits of such systems such as loss of robustness, decisions on the use of one connecting system or another, reactions to the state of the domain and scope for extension. It could also leave the system as a whole harder to comprehend.

In a full object-oriented design, for instance, we would construct entities and describe message passing between them. What is needed in such a design and not in goal decomposition is the specification of both how to achieve aims at a high level and the mechanisms to allow those functions to happen (and happen robustly in a well designed system). In goal decomposition we have ignored all description of underlying structure and decision-making, leaving that to the agent-based system.

6 Interactions

At this stage of the process we have:

- an assumed multi-agent system with an arbitrary number of minimally defined agents;

- a set of goal hierarchies suggesting ways to decompose the goals in the system requirements so as to hopefully be able to implement them; and
- a set of preferences or restrictions derived from the requirements.

The next step is to combine the first two of the above, i.e., state how a multi-agent system would enact the goal decompositions. In doing this, it is important to retain the whole tree of subgoals from the decompositions. This allows agents to share sections of a problem so that the system remains efficient, robust and conforms to other system preferences. It also allows for high level goals to be delegated to externally connected systems where we may not need to be concerned with how they are further decomposed or otherwise achieved. The notion of goal decomposition in this way means that we wish goals to be passed around the multi-agent system involving cooperation between agents. The agreed cooperation between agents on a goal is called an *interaction*. However, this cooperation is not between particular agents as they have not yet been defined, regardless, we do not necessarily know which agents will cooperate to achieve a goal. Therefore, to define interactions without agents we use *place-holders* for agents. Figure 3 illustrates the structure of an interaction with three rôles for cooperating agents to take in achieving the labeling goal.

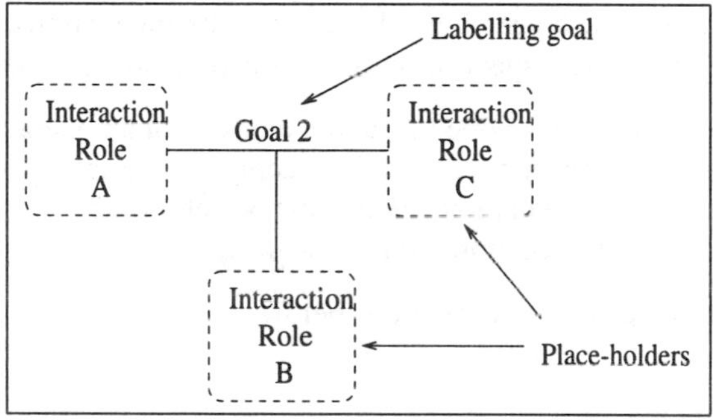

Fig. 3. The structure of an example interaction

Each interaction is labeled by a goal. There is more complexity to interaction than message passing between objects but it has a similar eventual effect in that control is transferred between system components in a limited and meaningful way. Before cooperation can take place for a goal, one of the agents involved must possess that goal, so that interactions have *originators* of the labeling goal which is one of the place-holders involved. The other place-holding agents in an interaction also have rôles within that interaction such as being delegated goals, acting in parallel, monitoring the appropriate execution of the goal, and so on, with the exact roles depending on the goal. Part of the flexibility achieved by not specifying the agents involved in an interaction can mean that the agents filling the interaction rôles may be inside or outside of the designed system or may, in fact, be the same agent. It is important to note that, due to the fact that agents may refuse to cooperate, an interaction only illustrates the successful case where the originator has eventually found a cooperator. It could also represent a chain of delegations where only the last agent in the chain knows how to continue its decomposition or completion [20].

At this point we can start to refine the design of the system. We have a possible, but not mandatory or inflexible, way of decomposing system goals so as to achieve them. The interactions specify what must be possible and the preferences specify what it means for them to be achieved well. From these we can derive a form of multi-agent system which will behave in a way that is both flexible and consistent with requirements.

The other important aim of a methodology is to make the design comprehensible at the implementation level. As a result of the potential division into several pieces developed by separate people and consisting of complex hierarchies, at this stage the design may be hard to comprehend as a whole or implement efficiently. This will be addressed later: for now the different areas of functionality described by goals can be understood and developed separately.

7 Preference Analysis

Continuing the process of agent interaction analysis, we now develop the design of agents, or system rôles which agents can hold, from the interactions we would like to be possible. There are several aspects of these interactions we can take into account.

1. Which agents should be developed from the analysis of an interaction?
2. How can the agents coordinate so as to best achieve the goal?
3. How can we ensure a system goal *will* always be achieved?
4. How can preferences be accounted for in the design?

Each of these is discussed in the subsections below.

7.1 Classes of Agents

The first aspect above concerns the set of agents to which the results of the other three aspects are to be applied; different sets of agents may be applicable to different rôles in an interaction. The sets can be restricted by a number of factors as follows.

Comprehensibility Restricting the set of agents designed to take part in an interaction could aid the understanding of the resulting system.

Preferences on available resources Restricting or expanding the sets of agents may be desirable to reduce complexity or the number of agents in the system.

Preferences on the monitoring of conflicting goals The best way to resolve conflicts between goals may be to have single agents with multiple goals able to decide actions based on their combination of goals. This requires overlapping sets between interactions.

Preferences on limiting function availability For efficiency or security reasons the designer may wish to limit the number of agents with the ability to achieve a goal.

Restrictions from external systems Only some external agents may be able to complete the goal.

Preferences on state of agents The state of an agent may restrict which classes it can belong to. For example, local mobile agents may be suitable for an interaction while non-local ones aren't.

Likelihood of high load If the goal is going to be required to be achieved repeatedly or requires a lot of resources to complete, the designer may want to expand the set of agents available to distribute the task more widely.

We can also distinguish between those agents designed to achieve success in a particular interaction and those which *may* be able to do so. In some systems it may be preferable for most or all agents to be able to adopt a goal even if they will not achieve it as effectively or efficiently as those specifically designed to. This may be the case when these latter agents already have other goals to achieve so that the system is better balanced by others adopting the goal. Similarly, a further distinction can be made between agents designed for an interaction and those *compelled* to adopt such goals. This is discussed further below in Section 7.3.

7.2 Assurance Analysis

Much work has gone into the development of coordination mechanisms. In the broadest sense we can include commitments [14], trust [21], contracts, system roles [3, 28], social laws [11] and so on. Different mechanisms are suitable for different preferences on coordination; some are more rapid while others are more secure or robust. Different goals in a system may be best served by different mechanisms.

In *agent interaction analysis* we need to find suitable mechanisms for agents without knowing in all cases which agents are taking part. For this reason, we need a set of design tools for examining, from the point of view of a single agent in an interaction, how best to fulfill the goal and system preferences. We call this *assurance analysis* as it examines how an agent can measure or alter the likelihood of success for a particular interaction, e.g., if A delegates to B what *assurance* does A have that B will achieve the goal as A would prefer it to be achieved?

Due to space limitations we will not discuss assurance analysis further here, except to list below some of the things that it should address.

- The *priority* at which the cooperators place a goal, relative to other goals.
- The methods used to complete goals and their side-effects.
- Use of resources, allocated for one goal, in pursuit of other goals.
- Errors in communication.
- Quality of the solution of a goal (as measured by preferences).

7.3 Satisfaction

There is one preference which will generally be implicit in the requirements: that the system goals always *will* be achieved when they should. Of course, the designer can't decide how external systems will behave but it should be possible, in a lot of cases, to restrict the design so that the system will always achieve the goals, even if to minimal standards in certain circumstances.

If a goal is possessed by an agent it will act towards it at some stage because it is pro-active and continuous. However, if an agent cannot complete a goal by itself it will need to cooperate. Unfortunately, a request for cooperation may be rejected by all possible cooperators so that the goal is never achieved.

To address this, the designer may want to make it mandatory for particular agents to take on particular goals if no other agent is doing so. This is an extreme form of assurance where the minimum standards are guaranteed. Such a restriction is comparable to *services* in other methodologies [9, 19, 26] but we note that, while these agents must take on the goals if required, they might not be the agents that actually do so at run-time. It is also one reason why agents should often be able to possess and deal with multiple goals.

7.4 Preferences

While it appears that a vast amount of analysis would be done for the system because of all the interactions within it, many interactions will have a similar form and suggest a certain structure for the agents and overall system [2]. For example, certain things can be assumed about an interaction which we restrict to occurring within the designed system, such as honest communication of information; or a goal which requires rapidity over all else, which may require low communication costs.

8 Design Collation

Agent interaction analysis can provide a justified structure for a flexible multi-agent system. The result of the above design methods is a set of designs leading from the goals and preferences of requirements to the desirable properties of sets of agents involved in particular interactions. The final stage is to reach a design which is coherent and comprehensible enough to implement.

The preference analysis produces descriptions of agents with restrictions on their architecture and the system in which they exist, possibly including physical location in a highly distributed system. This collection of agents needs to be reduced to a set that is useful to implement. We identify some criteria for situations in which agents or systems may be most suitable for being merged, as follows.

- Where the assurance analysis suggests that two agents in an interaction must have such high assurance that it would be best to make them the same agent, the interaction will become an internal processing of the goal (perhaps implicit).
- Where functionality of, and requirements on, agents are similar or the same.
- Where assurance analysis suggests similar coordination mechanisms for agents in different interactions, it may be suitable to merge those place-holders. For instance, a single agent may act as a gateway to less reliable connected systems to provide especially secure coordination.
- Where the low level goals place-holders are dealing with require similar actions to be performed.

After this iterative collation we should be left with a multi-agent system which is implementable and justified in its design. The latter property refers to the fact that the designer can indicate where the system has been tailored to the likely demand the application will place on it to improve its efficiency and has maintained flexibility to increase robustness.

9 Maintenance and Extension

One obvious use of the flexibility of agent-based systems is to ease the incorporation of changes. This helps both in repairing faulty software and in extending the requirements of the system. There are two aspects to this robustness: within the design and during use.

The methodology used affects how easily the design can be altered. Object-oriented designs provide highly cohesive, separated entities which can be altered individually so changes that fall in the bounds of a single object will be relatively simple to make. Agent interaction analysis offers a comparable division in terms of goals. Changes are applied to the design early in its documentation, usually at the goal decomposition stage. At this point the functionality is divided allowing targeting of changes, and there are only very few assumptions or restrictions making it unlikely for features of the system to conflict. After these changes have been made we can follow the documentation from the early to late stages, examining design decisions and replacing them where necessary. Finally the alterations will be merged into the final version of the design with minimal effect on the rest of the system.

At execution time multi-agent systems have an advantage over most other forms of system in adapting to change [12]. By having multiple independently running, decision-making, reactive, communicating and balancing entities, changes can be adapted to by being treated as differences in options available and then taken advantage of. To provide most scope for this adaptation the agents should remain as flexible as the system requirements permit. By emphasizing the interactions between agents and not limiting the interactions too much, agents within the system are free to choose good coordination strategies that the current form of the system allows.

10 Summary and Conclusion

In this paper we have proposed the idea of a form for agent oriented software engineering methodologies, *agent interaction analysis*, which takes abstract interactions between agents as its primary components of analysis. By decomposing the system requirements into interactions, based around the exchange of goals, we suggest that a more robust design, and one that is well tailored to maintenance and changes in the domain, can be produced.

We have shown how the interactions can be examined to determine efficient forms for the participating agents, and have used the idea of *assurance* to examine the requirements of individual roles in interactions, particularly in terms of extracting helpful information to allow designers to choose effective coordination mechanisms.

Clearly, this work only introduces the general principles of the approach, and there are many issues remaining to be tackled. One is creation of techniques for assurance analysis, so that coordination can be described and judged with respect to the rest of the design. We have done work on a range of specific techniques for assurance analysis in BDI agents. One such technique uses a generalised agent architecture which can be used to express and compare a variety of coordination mechanisms such as trust and basic commitments. Another technique measures the cost, as given by preferences, of using mechanisms between many agents such as brokers, references to agents to static rôles and commitments with or without reference to the committing agents. This work is left for discussion elsewhere due to space limitations.

As this paper only describes a framework, a full methodology can only be produced together with detailed techniques for suitably documenting these designs. The approach presented in this paper is deliberately distinguished from any notation that it may use. As a foundation, some of the concepts may be best illustrated in the recent work on agent-oriented extensions to UML [4, 8, 22]. We have done work on adapting UML diagrams for documenting *agent interaction analysis*. For example, collaboration diagrams can be easily adapted to express the structure of interactions.

In future work, we aim to develop a fully usable methodology which uses agent interaction analysis, and test it in the production of suitable applications. We are also working on using assurance analysis to describe and assess coordination mechanisms to help in the development of other such mechanisms tailored to particular domains.

The approach of agent interaction analysis, as suggested in this paper, clears the way for general effective methodologies targeted at the design of multi-agent systems for complex and open applications flexible enough to cope with a wide range of uncertainty and dynamism.

References

1. D. Amyot, L. Logrippo, R. J. A. Buhr, and T. Gray. Use Case Maps for the capture and validation of distributed systems requirements. In *Fourth International Symposium on Requirements Engineering (RE-99)*, 1999.
2. Y. Aridor and D. B. Lange. Agent design patterns: Elements of agent application design. In *Proceedings of the Second International Conference on Autonomous Agents (Agents-98)*, Minneapolis, USA, 1998.
3. M. Barbuceanu. Coordinating agents by role based social constraints and conversion plans. In *Proceedings of the Fourteenth National Conference on Artificial Intelligence (AAAI-97)*, pages 16–21, 1997.
4. B. Bauer, J. P. Müller, and J. Odell. Agent uml: A formalism for specifying multiagent software systems. In *this volume*.
5. A. M. Davis. *Software Requirements: Objects, States and Functions*. Prentice Hall, 1993.
6. K. S. Decker and V. R. Lesser. Designing a family of coordination algorithms. In *Proceedings of the First International Conference on Multi-Agent Systems (ICMAS-95)*, pages 73–80, 1995.
7. S. A. DeLoach and M. Wood. Developing multiagent systems with agenttool. In *Proceedings of the Seventh International Workshop on Agent Theories, Architectures and Languages (ATAL-00)*, 2000.

8. R. Depke, R. Heckel, and J. M. Küster. Requirement specification and design of agent-based systems with graph transformation, roles and uml. In *this volume*.
9. Elammari, M. and Lalonde, W. An agent-oriented methodology: High-level and intermediate models. In *Proceedings of Agent-Oriented Information Systems 1999 (AOIS-99)*, 1999.
10. S. Franklin and A. Graesser. Is it an agent, or just a program?: A taxonomy for autonomous agents. In J.P. Müller, M.J. Wooldridge, and N.R. Jennings, editors, *Intelligent Agents III: Proceedings of the Third International Workshop on Agent Theories, Architectures and Languages (ATAL-96)*, pages 21–35. Springer-Verlag, 1997.
11. C. V. Goldman and J. S. Rosenschein. Mutual adaptation enhanced by social laws. Technical Report CS98-5, The Hebrew University, Israel, 1998.
12. M. N. Huhns. Interaction-oriented programming. In *this volume*.
13. C. A. Iglesias, M. Garijo, and J. C. Gonzalez. A survey of agent-oriented methodologies. In J. P. Müller, M. P. Singh, and A. S. Rao, editors, *Intelligent Agents V: Proceedings of the Fifth International Workshop on Agent Theories, Architectures and Languages (ATAL-98)*, 1998.
14. N. R. Jennings. Commitments and conventions: The foundation of coordination in multi-agent systems. *Knowledge Engineering Review*, 8(3):223–250, 1993.
15. N. R. Jennings, K. Sycara, and M. Wooldridge. A roadmap of agent research and development. *Autonomous Agents and Multi-Agent Systems*, 1(1):275–306, 1998.
16. E. A. Kendall. Agent software engineering with role modelling. In *this volume*.
17. E. A. Kendall. Role modelling for agent system analysis and design. In *Proceedings of the First International Symposium on Agent Systems and Applications (ASA/MA'99)*, November 1999.
18. D. Kinny, M. Georgeff, and A. Rao. A methodology and modelling technique for systems of BDI agents. In Walter Van de Velde and J.W. Perram, editors, *Agents Breaking Away: Proceedings of the Seventh European Workshop on Modelling Autonomous Agents in a Multi-Agent World (MAAMAW-96)*, January 1996.
19. C. Landauer and K. Bellman. Agent-based information infrastructure. In *Proceedings of Agent-Oriented Information Systems 1999 (AOIS-99)*, 1999.
20. M. Luck and M. d'Inverno. Engagement and cooperation in motivated agent modelling. In C. Zhang and D. Lukose, editors, *Distributed Artificial Intelligence Architecture and Modelling: Proceedings of the First Australian DAI Workshop*, pages 70–84. Springer-Verlag, 1996.
21. S. P. Marsh. *Formalising Trust as a Computational Concept*. PhD thesis, Department of Computing Science and Mathematics, University of Stirling, 1994.
22. J. Odell, H. V. D. Parunak, and B. Bauer. Representing agent interaction protocols in uml. In *this volume*.
23. A. Omicini. Soda: Societies and infrastructures in the analysis and design of agent-based systems. In *this volume*.
24. I. Sommerville. *Software Engineering*. Addison-Wesley, fifth edition edition, 1995.
25. M. Wood and S. A. DeLoach. An overview of the multiagent system engineering methodology. In *this volume*.
26. M. Wooldridge, N. R. Jennings, and D. Kinny. A methodology for agent-oriented analysis and design. In *Proceedings of the Third International Conference on Autonomous Agents (Agents-99)*, Seattle, USA, 1999.
27. M. Wooldridge, N. R. Jennings, and D. Kinny. The Gaia methodology for agent-oriented analysis and design. *Journal of Autonomous Agents and Multi-Agent Systems*, 3, 2000.
28. L. Yu and B. F. Schmid. A conceptual framework for agent oriented and role based workflow modeling. In *Proceedings of Agent-Oriented Information Systems 1999 (AOIS-99)*, 1999.
29. F. Zambonelli, N. R. Jennings, and M. Wooldridge. Organisational abstractions for the analysis and design of multi-agent systems. In *this volume*.

SODA: Societies and Infraestructures in the Analysis and Design of Agent-Based Systems

Andrea Omicini

LIA, Dipartimento di Elettronica, Informatica e Sistemistica, Università di Bologna
Viale Risorgimento 2, I-40136 Bologna, Italy

aomicini@deis.unibo.it

Abstract. The notion of society should play a central role in agent-oriented software engineering as a first-class abstraction around which complex systems can be designed and built as multi-agent systems. We argue that an effective agent-oriented methodology should account for *inter-agent* aspects by providing engineers with specific abstractions and tools for the analysis and design of *agent societies* and *agent environments*.

In this paper, we outline the SODA agent-oriented methodology for the analysis and design of Internet-based systems. Based on the core notion of *task*, SODA promotes the separation of individual and social issues, and focuses on the social aspects of agent-oriented software engineering. In particular, SODA allow the agent environment to be explicitly modelled and mapped onto suitably-defined agent infrastructures.

1 Introduction

The engineering of complex applications in the Internet era raises new problems which require new models, languages and methodologies. Agent-based approaches [21] exploit the agent abstraction to address issues like distribution, heterogeneity, decentralisation of control, unpredictability, and need for intelligence [22]. Agents situatedness and their reactivity help to deal with dynamic and unpredictable environments; their pro-activeness in pursuing goals makes it possible to abstract away from the control issue and to easily deal with decentralisation of control; and so on.

However, the most mature approaches to agent-oriented engineering have till now concentrated on *intra-agent* aspects – how to build an individual agent, starting from *ad hoc* agent languages, architectures, and methodologies. These approaches implicitly promote methodologies for the engineering of multi-agent systems where systems are built as a sum of separately engineered agent components, which are then put together by exploiting some technology or infrastructure for interoperability – like ACL, mediation services, brokers, and so on.

According to the most recent research trends, this neglects one of the most relevant aspects of agent-based systems, that is, the social ones [9, 18, 19]. Agents are not simple software components to be first built, then combined: they are goal-driven individuals, who assume to live and interact with other individuals within a *society*. In the same way as human ones, agent societies exhibit global behaviours which cannot be reduced to the mere sum of the behaviours of their individual components. As a result, societies should be considered as first-class components of multi-agent systems, and specific models, abstractions, languages, and methodologies have to be provided for their engineering [11, 13, 14, 25].

Even more, the *agent environment*, that is, the space where agents live and interact, is not neutral with respect to system design and development. Building a MAS in an open, distributed, decentralised, heterogeneous, dynamic, and unpredictable environment obviously affects the way in which such a system is conceived and deployed. As a peculiar example, think of an open system where some resources have to be made available to explorer agents coming from unknown sources – like buyer agents, for instance. The engineering of such a system would simply amount to designing the agent environment in terms of available resources and services, and deploying a suitably-configured infrastructure – possibly, without writing a single line of agent code. As a result, also the structure of the agent environment should be adequately modelled through specific abstractions, and taken into account at every step of the engineering process of a multi-agent system.

In this context, this paper outlines the SODA agent-oriented methodology for the analysis and design of Internet-based systems, aimed at defining abstractions and procedures specifically tailored to the engineering of agent societies and environments. Based on primitive notion of *task*, SODA promotes the separation of individual and social issues since the very early analysis phase. Since it intentionally does not address intra-agent issues, SODA is not a complete methodology, and focuses instead on the social aspects of agent-oriented software engineering, by exploiting *coordination models* and *technologies* [15]. In particular, SODA allow the agent environment to be explicitly modelled and mapped onto suitably-defined agent infrastructures.

2 Society and environment in agent systems

Till now, agent-oriented engineering [21] has been mainly concerned with intra-agent aspects, that is, the analysis, design and development of individual agents. This is basically a *computational* issue [20], which involves the way in which each agent works when seen as an individual (software) system.

As suggested by many recent research efforts [9, 18, 19], inter-agent issues should instead be considered at least as relevant as intra-agent one, and handled as that. In particular, by taking *interaction* as an independent dimension for the analysis, design and development of multi-agent system, it should be made clear how such a dimension should affect the methodologies for the engineering of complex software systems as a multi-agent one [10]. For instance, Miles, Joy, and Luck [13] present a methodology for agent-oriented software engineering based on the analysis of agent interaction.

Agents in a multi-agent system interact by living and working within their environment, and by relating with other agents. Correspondingly, inter-agent aspects in multi-agent systems basically amount to two strongly related issues: the social and the environment one.

2.1 Society

Agents are individual entities with social abilities [22]. In general, they have a partial representation of the world around them, a limited ability to sense and change it, and typically rely on other agents for anything falling outside of their scope or reach. So, agents are to be thought as living dipped into societies: the behaviour of an individual agent is often not understandable outside its social structure. The behaviour of a buyer agent in an auction is difficult to be explained out of the context of the auction itself and of the rules that govern it. Dually, the behaviour of a society of agents cannot generally be expressed in terms of the behaviour of its composing agents. So, the rules governing an auction, in conjunction with the behaviour of the individual agents participating to it, lead to a global behaviour that could not be reduced to the mere composition of the individual's behaviour [20]. Social rules harness agent interaction, and drive the global behaviour of a society towards the accomplishment of its global goals.

So, societies should be no longer built by merely combining a number of separately engineered agents. Instead, agent-oriented methodologies should adopt agent societies as first-class abstractions to be exploited in the analysis, design, and development of complex software systems. For this purpose, agent-oriented methodologies should supply specific models, abstractions, and technologies for the engineering of agent societies. In particular, a methodology should help engineers to determine the social structures required, the social laws they need, how social rules should be designed, and how they should be enforced. For instance, one should be able to determine how much of a social behaviour should be embodied in agents, and how much should be instead charged upon social infrastructures – a particularly relevant issue when open systems are concerned.

2.2 Environment

When looking at agents as *situated entities*, which cannot be thought separately from the environment they live in, the idea of modelling a software system as a multi-agent system without modelling the agent *environment* seems to be ineffective from its very ground. Generally speaking, agents and societies live in environments that may be heterogeneous, dynamic, open, distributed, and unpredictable – like the Internet. The properties of the environment obviously affect the way in which agents represent the world they live in, and how they plan and deliberate their course of actions. So, agent-oriented methodologies should make it possible to model the agent environment from the earliest phases of the engineering process, and to express dependencies within the agents and the environment itself.

Even more, the features of the agent environment are often not completely predetermined, but may be partially defined according to the systems needs. So, the environment of a multi-agent system may be subject to an engineering process, aimed at shaping and configuring the environment itself. For instance, one may think of directory services, shared knowledge bases, authentication services, and so on: how they are built and made available to the agents of a multi-agent system both affects and depends on the way in which the system and its agents are engineered. So, agent-oriented methodologies should help not only to model the agent environment, but also to shape and build it.

3 SODA

SODA (Societies in Open and Distributed Agent spaces) is a methodology for the analysis and design of Internet-based applications as multi-agent systems. The goal of SODA is to define a coherent conceptual framework and a comprehensive software engineering procedure that accounts for the analysis and design of individual agents, agent societies, and agent environments. SODA is not concerned with intra-agent issues: designing a multi-agent system with SODA leads to define agents in terms of their required observable behaviour and their role in the multi-agent system. Then, whichever methodology one may choose to define the agent structure and inner functionality, it could be easily used in conjunction with SODA.

Instead, SODA concentrates on inter-agent issues, like the engineering of societies and infrastructures for multi-agent systems. Since this conceptually covers all the interactions within an agent system, the design phase of SODA deeply relies on the notion of *coordination model* [2, 16, 17]. In particular, as discussed in [4, 7], coordination models and languages are taken as the sources of the abstractions and mechanisms required to engineer agent societies: social rules are designed as coordination laws and embedded into coordination media, and social infrastructures are built upon coordination systems.

3.1 Analysis

During the analysis phase, the application domain is studied and modelled, the available computational resources and the technological constraints are listed, the fundamental application goals and targets are pointed out. The result of the analysis phase is typically expressed in terms of high-level abstractions and their mutual relationships, providing designers with a formal or semi-formal description of the intended overall application structure and organisation.

Since by definition agents have goals that they pursue pro-actively, agent-oriented analysis can rely on agent *responsibility* to carry on one or more *tasks*. Furthermore, agents live dipped into an environment, which may be distributed, heterogeneous, dynamic, and unpredictable. So, the analysis phase should explicitly take into account and model the required and desired features of the agent application environment, by modelling it in terms of the required *resources* and the *services* made available to agents. Finally, since agents are basically interactive entities, which depend on other agents and available resources to pursue their tasks, the analysis phase should explicitly model the interaction protocols in terms of the information required and provided by agents and resources.

So, the SODA analysis phase exploits three different models:

- the *role model* – the application goals are modelled in terms of the *tasks* to be achieved, which are associated to *roles* and *groups*
- the *resource model* – the application environment is modelled in terms of the *services* available, which are associated to abstract *resources*
- the *interaction model* – the interaction involving roles, groups and resources is modelled in terms of *interaction protocols*, expressed as *information* required and provided by roles and resources, and *interaction rules*, governing interaction within groups.

The above models represent the basis of the SODA analysis phase. Even though conceptually distinct, they are obviously strictly related, and should be defined in a consistent way.

The role model *Tasks* are expressed in terms of the responsibilities they involve, of the competences they require, and of the resources they depend upon. Responsibilities are expressed in terms of the state(s) of the world that should result from the task accomplishment.

Tasks are classified as either *individual* or *social* ones. Typically, social tasks are those that require a number of different competences, and the access to several different resources, whereas individual ones are more likely to require well-delimited competence and limited resources (see [4] for an example).

Each individual task is associated to an individual *role*, which by consequence is first defined in terms of the responsibilities it carries. Analogously, social tasks are assigned to *groups*. Groups are defined in terms of both the responsibility related to their social task, and the *social roles* participating in the group. A social role describes the role played by an individual within a group, and may either coincide with an already defined (individual) role, or be defined *ex-novo*, in the same form as an individual one, by specifying its task as a sub-task of its group's one.

The resource model *Services* express functionalities provided by the agent environment to a multi-agent system – like recording an information, querying a sensor, verifying an identity. In this phase, each service is associated to an abstract *resource*, which is then firstly defined in terms of the service it provides.

Each resource defines abstract *access modes*, modelling the different ways in which the service it provides can be exploited by agents. If a task assigned to a role or a group requires a given service, the access modes are determined and expressed in terms of the granted *permission* to access the resource in charge of that service. Such a permission is then associated to that role or group.

The interaction model Analysing the interaction model in SODA amounts to the definition of *interaction protocols* for roles and resources, and *interaction rules* for groups.

An interaction protocol associated to a role is defined in terms of the *information* required and provided by the role in order to accomplish its individual task. An interaction protocol associated to a resource is defined in terms of the information required to invoke the service provided by the resource itself, and by the information returned when the invoked service has been brought to an end, either successfully or not. An interaction rule is instead associated to a group, and governs the interactions among social roles and resources so as to make the group accomplish its social task.

It is worth to be noted that this approach ensures a form of uncoupling: each interaction protocol is not specifically bounded to any other, and can be defined somehow independently – by simply requiring the specification of the information needed, but not its source. Obviously, the final outcome of the analysis phase should account for this, too, by ensuring that for any information required by any protocol, there is at least one entity in the system in charge of supplying such information.

The outcome In all, the results of the SODA analysis phase are expressed in terms of roles, groups, and resources. To summarise,

- a role is defined in terms of its individual task, its permissions to access the resources, and the corresponding interaction protocol
- a group is defined in terms of its social task, its permissions to access the resources, the participating social roles, and the corresponding interaction rule
- a resource is defined in terms of the service it provides, its access modes, the permissions granted to roles and groups to exploit its service, and the corresponding interaction protocol.

3.2 Design

Design is concerned with the representation of the abstract models resulting from the analysis phase in terms of the design abstractions provided by the methodology. Differently from the analysis phase, a satisfactory result of the design phases is typically expressed in terms of abstractions that can be mapped one-to-one onto the actual components of the deployed system.

The SODA design phase is based on three strictly related models:

- the *agent model* – individual and social roles are mapped upon *agent* classes
- the *society model* – groups are mapped onto *societies* of agents, which are designed and organised around *coordination abstractions*
- the *environment model* – resources are mapped onto *infrastructure* classes, and associated to *topological abstractions*.

The agent model An *agent class* is defined as a set of (one or more) roles, both individual and social ones. As a result, an agent class is first characterised by the tasks, the set of the permissions, and the interaction protocols associated to its roles. Agent classes can be further characterised in terms of other features: their *cardinality* (the number of agents of that class), their *location* (with respect to the topological model defined in this phase – either fixed, for static agents, or variable, for mobile agents), their *source* (from inside or outside the system, given the assumption of openness).

The design of the agents of a class should account for all the specifications coming from the SODA analysis phase – but may exploit in principle any other methodology for the design of individual agents, since this issue is not covered by SODA. What is determined by SODA is the outcome of this phase, that is, the *observable behaviour* of the agent in terms of all its interactions with the surrounding environment. Such a behaviour is defined by the interaction protocols, delimited by the permission sets, and finalised to the achievement of the agent tasks.

The society model Each group is mapped onto a *society of agents*. So, an agent society is first characterised by the social tasks, the set of the permissions, the participating social roles, and the interaction rules associated to its groups.

The agent model also assigns social roles to agents, so that the main issue in the society model is how to design interaction rules so as to make societies to accomplish their social tasks. Since it deals with managing agent interaction, the problem of achieving the desired social behaviour by means of suitable social rules is basically a *coordination* issue [12]. As a result, societies in SODA are designed around *coordination media*, that is, the abstractions provided by coordination models for the coordination of multi-component systems [3].

So, the first point in the design of agent societies is the choice of the fittest coordination model – that is, the one providing the abstractions that are expressive enough to model the society interaction rules [6]. Thus, a society is designed around coordination media [7] embodying the interaction rules of its groups in terms of *coordination rules*. The behaviour of the suitably-designed coordination media, along with the behaviour of the agents playing social roles and interacting through such media, makes an agent society pursue its social tasks as a whole. This allows societies of agents to be designed as first-class entities, as shown in [4] where an example is also discussed.

The environment model Resources are mapped onto *infrastructure classes*. So, an infrastructure class is first characterised by the services, the access modes, the permissions granted to roles and groups, and the interaction protocols associated to its resources. Infrastructure classes can be further characterised in terms of other features: their *cardinality* (the number of infrastructure components belonging to that class), their *location* (with respect to topological abstractions), their *owner* (which may be or not the same as the one of the agent system, given the assumption of decentralised control).

The design of the components belonging to an infrastructure class may follow the most appropriate methodology for that class – since SODA does not specifically address these issues, components like databases, expert systems, or security facilities, can all be developed according to the most suited specific methodology. Again, what is determined by SODA is the outcome of this phase, that is, the services to be provided by each infrastructure component, and its *interfaces*, as resulting from its associated interaction protocols.

Finally, SODA assumes that a topological model of the agent environment is provided by the designer – but does not provide for topological abstractions by its own, since any system and any application domain may call for different approaches to this problem. However, as an example of an expressive set of topological abstractions that may easily fit many Internet-based multi-agent systems, one may look to *places*, *domains* and *gateways* as defined by the TuCSoN model for the coordination of Internet agents [5].

The outcome In all, the results of the SODA design phase are expressed in terms of agent classes, societies of agents, and infrastructure classes. To summarise,

- an agent class is defined in terms of its individual and social roles, as well as its cardinality, location, and source

- a society of agents is defined in terms of its groups, as well as its corresponding coordination abstraction(s)
- an infrastructure class is defined in terms of its resources, as well as its cardinality, location, and owner.

4 Related works and conclusions

The main reference for the development of SODA is represented by the pioneering work on Gaia [23]. Gaia, to our knowledge, is the first agent-oriented software engineering methodology that explicitly takes into account societies (there, mainly referred to as *organisations*) as first-class entities, by providing a coherent conceptual framework for the analysis and design of multi-agent systems. Even though at an early stage of its development, SODA addresses some of the shortcomings of Gaia, which does not suit well open systems, and cannot easily deal with self-interested agents [24]. In addition, SODA is the first agent-oriented methodology to our knowledge to explicitly take the agent environment into account, and provide engineers with specific abstractions and procedures for the design of agent infrastructures.

Zambonelli, Jennings, and Wooldridge [25] also try to address Gaia shortcomings, by putting the notion of organisation at the core of their agent-oriented methodology. A similar approach is proposed by Kendall [11], which adopts *role models* as the main organisational abstraction for modelling multi-agent systems. There, however, the notion of role is taken as primitive, whereas SODA considers role as a derived notion, and task and service as primitive ones. In turn, Blanzieri and Giorgini [1] address the openness issue by proposing a conceptual infrastructure based on the notion of *implicit culture*.

Early versions of the SODA methodology have already been used for the analysis and design of Internet-based multi-agent systems [7, 8]: however, the methodology was never explicitly neither formalised nor named before. In the near future, we intend to exploit SODA in the design of real Internet-based multi-agent systems so as to further verify its effectiveness.

References

1. Enrico Blanzieri and Paolo Giorgini. Implicit culture and multi-agent systems. In this volume.
2. Nadia Busi, Paolo Ciancarini, Roberto Gorrieri, and Gianluigi Zavattaro. *Coordination Models: A Guided Tour*, chapter 1. In Omicini et al. [15], December 2000.
3. Paolo Ciancarini. Coordination models and languages as software integrators. *ACM Computing Surveys*, 28(2):300–302, June 1996.
4. Paolo Ciancarini, Andrea Omicini, and Franco Zambonelli. Multiagent system engineering: the coordination viewpoint. In Nicholas R. Jennings and Yves Lespérance, editors, *Intelligent Agents VI — Agent Theories, Architectures, and Languages*, volume 1767 of *LNAI*, pages 250–259. Springer-Verlag, February 2000.
5. Marco Cremonini, Andrea Omicini, and Franco Zambonelli. Multi-agent systems on the Internet: Extending the scope of coordination towards security and topology. In Francisco J. Garijo and Magnus Boman, editors, *Multi-Agent Systems Engineering – Proceedings of the 9th European Workshop on Modelling Autonoumous Agents in a Multi-Agent World (MAMAAW'99)*, volume 1647 of *LNAI*, pages 77–88. Springer-Verlag, June 30–July 2 1999.

6. Enrico Denti, Antonio Natali, and Andrea Omicini. On the expressive power of a language for programming coordination media. In *Proceedings of the 1998 ACM Symposium on Applied Computing (SAC'98)*, pages 169–177. ACM, February 27 - March 1 1998. Track on Coordination Models, Languages and Applications.
7. Enrico Denti and Andrea Omicini. Designing multi-agent systems around an extensible communication abstraction. In John-Jules Ch. Meyer and Pierre-Yves Schobbens, editors, *Formal Models of Agents – ESPRIT Project ModelAge Final Report*, volume 1760 of *LNAI*, pages 90–102. Springer-Verlag, 1999.
8. Enrico Denti and Andrea Omicini. Engineering multi-agent systems in LuCe. In Stephen Rochefort, Fariba Sadri, and Francesca Toni, editors, *Proceedings of the ICLP'99 International Workshop on Multi-Agent Systems in Logic Programming (MAS'99)*, Las Cruces (NM), November 30 1999.
9. Fumio Hattori, Takeshi Ohguro, Makoto Yokoo, Shigeo Matsubara, and Sen Yoshida. Socialware: Multiagent systems for supporting network communities. *Communications of the ACM*, 42(3):55–61, March 1999. Special Section on Multiagent Systems on the Net.
10. Michael N. Huhns. Interaction-oriented programming. In this volume.
11. Elizabeth A. Kendall. Agent software engineering with role modelling. In this volume.
12. Thomas Malone and Kevin Crowstone. The interdisciplinary study of coordination. *ACM Computing Surveys*, 26(1):87–119, 1994.
13. Simon Miles, Mike Joy, and Michael Luck. Designing agent-oriented systems by analysing agent interactions. In this volume.
14. James Odell, H. Van Dyke Parunak, and Bernhard Bauer. Representing agent interaction protocols in UML. In this volume.
15. Andrea Omicini, Franco Zambonelli, Matthias Klusch, and Robert Tolksdorf, editors. *Coordination of Internet Agents: Models, Technologies and Applications*. Springer-Verlag, December 2000.
16. George A. Papadopoulos. *Models and Technologies for the Coordination of Internet Agents: A Survey*, chapter 2. In Omicini et al. [15], December 2000.
17. George A. Papadopoulos and Farhad Arbab. Coordination models and languages. *Advances in Computers*, 46:The Engineering of Large Systems:329–400, August 1998.
18. Joav Shoham and Moshe Tennenholtz. Social laws for artificial agent societies: Off-line design. *Artificial Intelligence*, 73, 1995.
19. Munindar P. Singh. Agent communication languages: Rethinking the principles. *IEEE Computer*, 31(12):55–61, December 1998.
20. Peter Wegner. Why interaction is more powerful than computing. *Communications of the ACM*, 40(5):80–91, May 1997.
21. Michael J. Wooldridge. Agent-based software engineering. *IEE Proceedings on Software Engineering*, 144(1):26–37, February 1997.
22. Michael J. Wooldridge and Nicholas R. Jennings. Intelligent agents: Theory and practice. *The Knowledge Engineering Review*, 10(2):115–152, 1995.
23. Michael J. Wooldridge, Nicholas R. Jennings, and David Kinny. The Gaia methodology for agent-oriented analysis and design. *Autonomous Agents and Multi-Agent Systems*, 3(3):285–312, September 2000.
24. Franco Zambonelli, Nicholas R. Jennings, Andrea Omicini, and Michael J. Wooldridge. *Agent-Oriented Software Engineering for Internet Applications*, chapter 13. In Omicini et al. [15], December 2000.
25. Franco Zambonelli, Nicholas R. Jennings, and Michael J. Wooldridge. Organisational abstractions for the analysis and design of multi-agent systems. In this volume.

A Modelling Approach for Agent Based Systems Design

Omer F. Rana

Department of Computer Science,
Cardiff University, POBox 916,
Cardiff CF24 3XF, UK.
o.f.rana@cs.cf.ac.uk

Abstract. A modelling approach based on the Soft Systems Methodology (SSM) is proposed as a first stage in developing agent based systems. The SSM approach enables a better conceptualisation of the system being developed, and enables each stake holder to evaluate the system from their particular viewpoints. Such an approach can also support the decomposition of an information system into a set of collaborating agents. We suggest that this is a more intuitive approach to designing agent based systems, and one which can be used as a first step to other work centered on the Unified Modelling Language (UML). A methodology for translating systems requirements into a set of collaborating agents is presented.

1 Introduction

Many approaches to facilitate object based design have been proposed in the recent past, such as the Unified Modelling Language (UML) and the Shlaer-Mellor methodology, for instance. Such techniques are centered on the role of an "object" as the unit of abstraction, requiring the decomposition of a particular problem into a set of interacting objects. Extending this approach to objects which are supported by generic object management services, has led to the concept of *components*. Component based software development (CBD) has proven to be a useful approach for building large-scale information systems. The promised benefits of components for improved code re-usability and customisation, however, has failed to materialise. It is often just too difficult to create truly re-usable business logic, and building generalised components that can be usefully employed in a wide range of applications, and give good performance, has proven to be very difficult. One of the reasons for this is the problem of guessing what features will be potentially useful in the future, and the changing nature of user requirements and the environment in which a component operates, often leading to even well-designed components quickly being overtaken by events. There are also organisational difficulties, associated with changing the behaviour of developers and their managers, which have often proven insurmountable [4].

Perhaps the principle benefit that component technology has introduced is the discipline of "modularity" it imposes on large information systems development. Enabling designers and implementors to think in terms of modular functionality, CBD allows developers to create transparent interfaces, that isolate component usage from implementation. Also, there are numerous software tools to support assembling applications from components: ranging from infrastructure technologies providing runtime execution environments for integrating components of different kinds, support for component packaging and distribution, managing transactions between a collection of components, handling asynchronous invocation and message passing between components, to security management and event handling. These features are supported to varying levels of maturity in currently available industry standard implementations such as Microsoft's COM+, OMG's CORBA and Sun's JeanBeans and Enterprise JavaBeans. Hence, the three key elements that provide the focus for CBD are: component functionality, interfaces, and component assembly/connectivity [1]. A strong overlap exists between concepts in CBD and object oriented development, and often design techniques overlap between these two areas. A key requirement of developing information systems with components is the necessity to translate business needs into a collection of off-the-shelf or custom components. Developers must be able to answer the key question of how to design solutions that target this technology to meet particular business needs more effectively. UML is a popular notation for describing the architecture of applications constructed from components. In UML five views of a system can be constructed: a "Use-case" giving the perspective of an external user, a "Logical" perspective giving a functional view of the system, a "Component" view for identifying the architectural blocks that make up the system, system "Concurrency" for describing coordination mechanisms, and a "Deployment" view which provides a mapping between system parts onto a physical architecture.

Defining system behaviours using UML is unflexible, and a UML design cannot easily capture modifications to requirements for the system being modelled. It is also very complex, and cannot be used to model subjective information in an efficient manner. Hence, although UML is useful for modelling precise system behaviours, and prevent "requirements creep", it may not be useful if components being modelled can vary their behaviour over time. What is needed is support for "dynamic" components, which can better capture the the dynamic aspects of an information system. Such dynamic components may have behaviour, albeit subject to constraints, to model a functionality that may vary based on changes in the business environment. A design methodology that is more intuitive to system users, and enables developers to capture subjective requirements is essential to develop scalable systems, where components can adjust their behaviour to changing requirements. Checkland's Soft Systems Methodology (SSM) [5] offers one such modelling approach, and combined with the emerging area of agent based information management, offers an adaptive, dynamic and user-centric approach to developing large scale information systems. We view agents as flexible components that have behaviour, and communicate with each other through a specialised language based on speech act theory [13]. Each component now contains a set of rules for interacting with its environment, having a set of pre-defined "beliefs" about the environment in which it operates, a set of "desires" on what it wants to achieve in the near term (supported, perhaps, by a planning engine), a set of "commitments" it can make to other components with which it is interacting, and a long term set of goals or "intentions" it is trying to achieve. The "desires" and "commitments" of the agent can vary over time, and are determined by the number and types of interactions that the agent has with other components. Hence, each component is dynamic, in that it can change its behaviour over time and can react to changes in its environment.

The need to decompose a complex system into a hierarchy of interacting sub-systems has been identified by Wooldridge, Jennings and Kinny [9]. They suggest the need for modularity, and propose a software lifecycle based on executable specifications. How the decomposition of a system is to be achieved is not specified in their work, and no support is provided for identifying possible sub-divisions within the system. Similarly, Brazer, Jonker and Treur [10] identify a composition approach to constructing agent based systems, provided the constituent roles are known in advance. Such roles are often hard to determine, and modelling a complex system as a collection of compositional sub-systems is not always obvious.

A design methodology for assembling flexible components, to build dynamic information systems is described. Our proposed approach goes beyond existing work on extending UML for agents (AUML) [8], as proposed by Odell and others. We believe that extending UML to support agent development is a useful technique, however it is limited by the need to define precise assumptions about the modelled system. UML also does not allow the role of particular stake holders within a modelled system to be investigated. We suggest a phased approach, where the first phase involves the use of SSM as a system modelling approach, followed by translating an SSM description into UML, or an alternative approach which can facilitate an implementation of the system. Our main contribution is the importance of thinking about the components of an information system in a more flexible manner, and involve the users and their specific expectations of the system in the modelling process. Such expectations can be used to identify the role that each agent much support within the system. We suggest that it is important to work with a methodology that helps conceptualise business need, rather than constraints imposed by a design approach, as with object oriented approaches such as UML and Shlaer-Mellor [14]. We discuss lessons learned, and the benefit of combining SSM with adaptive components in section 3.2.

2 Previous Work and Motivation for Modelling with SSM

SSM is a seven stage methodology, as illustrated in figure 1, where five stages are associated with *real world* thinking, three of which are for deriving change recommendations and taking action to alter the situation. The other two stages are involved with developing "root definitions" and "conceptual models". Root definitions enable the users of this methodology to place a particular emphasis on the system being developed, and "conceptual models" define activities necessary to achieve the emphasis. Users of SSM formulating the root definition must identify the following: (1) beneficiaries or victims of the system, called "Customers", (2) the entities that carry out the main activities of the system or lead to them, called "Actors", (3) the process of transforming inputs to desired outputs, called "Transformations", (4) a particular emphasis or viewpoint, image or purpose which makes the root definition meaningful, called "Weltanschauung", (5) the entity who has authority to start or stop a system, called "Owner", and (6) the external influences that affect the operation of a system, called "Environment". The entities within the system need not necessarily be humans – the same definition can apply to systems where all entities are software components. However, separation between what is required from the system being developed from some requirements perspective, to how it is eventually achieved, lends SSM the ability to involve subjectivity into the modelling process. Checkland and Holwell [6] indicate that the aim of SSM is not to ape the natural sciences, which involve positivistic testing of hypothesis to destruction – calling this "hard" systems thinking. The social world, within which an information system operates is assumed to be more fluid, and one which both persists and changes. This suggests that research seek both interpretation and learning, rather than purely an optimisation.

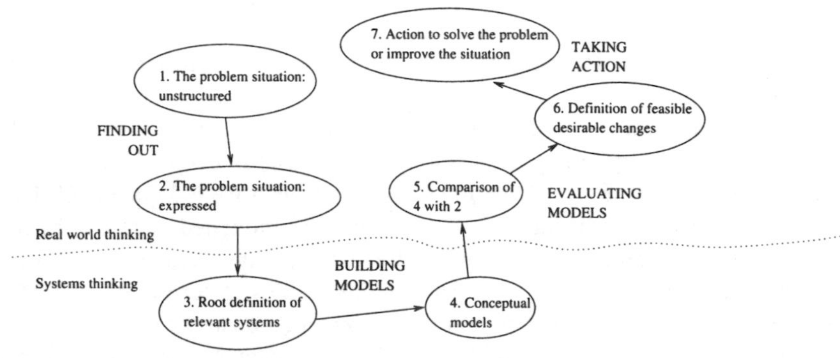

Fig. 1. Checkland's Soft System Methodology

A root definition is usually presented in a single statement, and combines the six components specified above. For example, for an e-commerce application, it could be:

> A Telecomms Provider (TP) owned charging system, to facilitate internet enabled users arriving over TP owned ISDN lines to make travel ticket purchases at lower costs than other internet service provers, and at a faster speed, using SoftwareA

where, Customers are "internet enabled users", Actors include "SoftwareA" and "ISDN line" operators, Transformations correspond to business transactions of "purchasing tickets", Weltanschauung is to facilitate the use of TP charging system for internet enabled users over TP ISDN lines, the Owner is the 'TP' and the Environment can be other competitors in the area providing a similar service. Similarly, other root definitions can be derived, based on the particular viewpoint, or business need being investigated. Each viewpoint therefore provides a perspective of system usage for a given stake holder, and must identify activities that need to be undertaken to achieve some objective. Each root definition is expanded into a conceptual model, to identify activities necessary for a business to meet the specified purpose, and to identify the relationships between these activities. Figure 2 illustrates the conceptual model, where the semantics of each activity is informally defined and is aimed, primarily, to facilitate discussion about how a business should be managed. In many ways, the relationships between activities are presented to enable an exploration of possible scenarios and likely outcomes that could have been ignored. The objective of developing the conceptual model therefore being an exploration of possible activities that could be undertaken to achieve a result in a given instance. This informal approach is much more intuitive to the users of a system, and allows first a focus on particular root definitions with a particular "Weltanschauung", followed by a conceptual model with a wider scope. Conceptual models can also be represented in a hierarchic form, enabling high-level models to be refined with additional activities, also illustrated in figure 2, as activities A4.1 and A4.2.

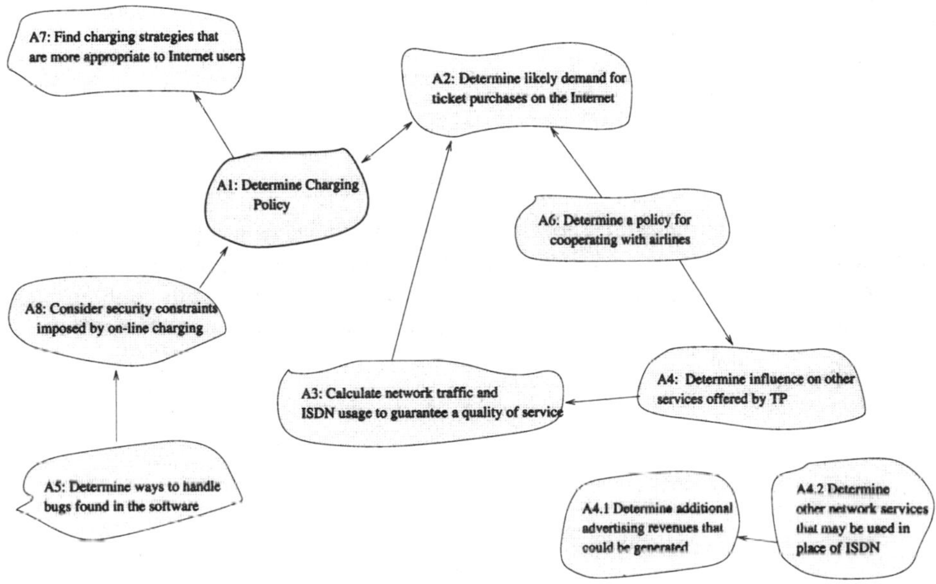

Fig. 2. Conceptual Model for TP Travel Services

SSM therefore provides a more informal method to capture system requirements, and studies on linking SSM with UML use-cases have been investigated in [2],[3]. In such studies the emphasis is generally on developing a first pass at systems design using SSM, followed by validating system models by UML, often by finding correspondences between UML and SSM terminology, such as linking SSM root-definition to UML Use-case actors.

3 Demonstration of Approach

Our design approach is illustrated in figure 3, and contains three phases: (1) Analysis of the business model, by considering various "views" of information system requirements, and expressed as root-definitions. A conceptual model is constructed for each root definition, relating activities necessary to achieve a "view". SSM Actors and Customers are identified, followed by the construction of a "sequence" and "collaboration" diagram between these entities, the former showing a temporal exchange of messages between entities in the system, and the latter displaying associations between the entities. Finally, based on collaborations thus defined, rules for Actors and Customers are derived, based on the BDI model. Each behaviour rule is defined using the template in Code Segment 1.

```
WHEN
 Messages Arrive with Particular Condition(s)
IF
 { Belief(s) & Commitment(s) & Intention(s) & Capability }
THEN
 Update
 { Belief(s) & Commitment(s) & Intention(s) }
 Send Message(s) to Other Entitie(s)
```

Code Segment 1

The "Capability" of an agent does not change with time, however its ability to perform a given action is determined by its 'Beliefs', and 'Commitments' it has made to perform a given task, within a given time interval, to other components – both 'Beliefs' and 'Commitments' vary over time, based on interactions between agents.

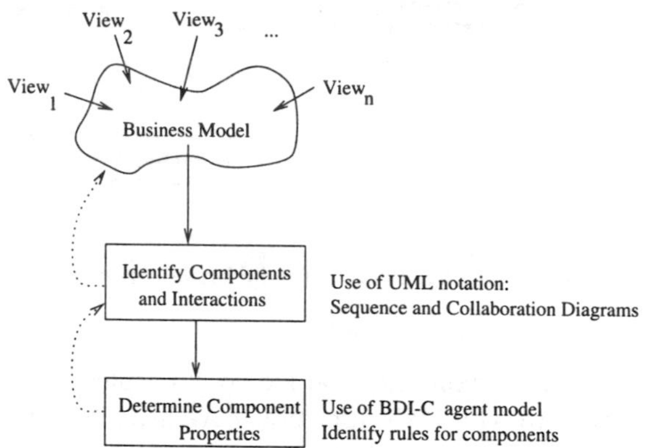

Fig. 3. Design Approach based on SSM and dynamic components

Consider a system for business to business e-commerce, for purchasing airline tickets over the Internet, comprising of buyers, sellers and various intermediate roles. A root definition for such a system can be:

> A Telecomms Provider (TP) owned charging system, to encourage airlines X and Y to provide their inventories on-line in the format required by SoftwareA, increasing revenues for airlines X and Y, and increasing user traffic on TPs network

in this instance, the TP is the Customer, Actors are airlines “X”, “Y”, and SoftwareA operators, Transformations correspond to debits on TP account, and credits to “X” and “Y” accounts, Weltanschauung is the set of processes required to increase revenues for airlines “X” and “Y” and traffic on TPs network, and Environment includes other airlines, and other network operators. In this case the root definition describes the viewpoint of the network operator over which e-commerce transactions are to take place. Similarly, other root definitions can be specified, such as:

> A purchasing system owned by A, to enable finding the lowest price flight tickets from the nearest airport to A

in this case, the viewpoint (or Weltanschauung) is based on the perspective of a buyer “A”. Different buyers could have different viewpoints however, as some may require an intermediate leasing service with which they can interact, rather than directly owning a purchasing system. Hence, another root definition for a buyer could be:

> A leasing system owned by B, to facilitate the discovery of merchants selling flight tickets with car rental and holiday homes.

Root definitions are therefore subjective, and reflect the particular needs or viewpoints of a user within the system. Root definitions for the sellers can be similarly described, based on their particular perspective or objective in using the information system. A conceptual model is subsequently derived for each root definition, indicating activities that need to be performed to achieve the viewpoints identified in the root definition. A set of common themes should now be explored between root definitions, to find overlap between the viewpoints, as illustrated in figure 4, and identified by various users. Such overlaps illustrate common services or roles that must be supported within an information system, and together with the “Actors” lead to the description of initial “beliefs” and required “capabilities” for agents. The “Actors” definition can also be used to find supported relationships between collaborating participants. For instance, in the travel agent example, airlines need to interact with buyers directly or via intermediate agents. Also, both airlines and buyers need to interact with the Telecomms Providers. Additional roles can be isolated based on differences in root definitions, and activities identified within the conceptual model.

Subsequently, the roles and interactions derived from the SSM model are translated into collaboration and sequence diagrams. Each sequence diagram represents a shared activity based on overlaps in conceptual models of different users. The approach is very general to this point, and particular details, such as the actual number of buyers and sellers, the number of intermediate agents etc, is not specified. Subsequently, a more specific description of the system is necessary, such as the physical number of buyers and sellers – as this is necessary before making use of UML. An example for 2 buyers, 2 sellers and an intermediate facilitator is illustrated in figure 5, showing that first buyers and sellers register their vocabulary (ontology) with the facilitator, followed by requests for information using ‘askone’, ‘askall’ and ‘tell’ messages. Figure 5(b) models one possible scenario, and the order of messages can vary, as agents are operating asynchronously. This arrangement corresponds to the root definition where intermediate agents are leased to obtain seller details.

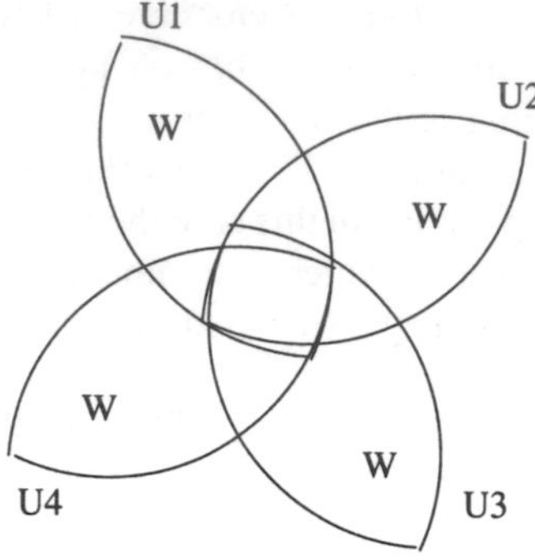

Fig. 4. Overlap between Weltanschauung of different users. *U*: User, *W*:Weltanschauung

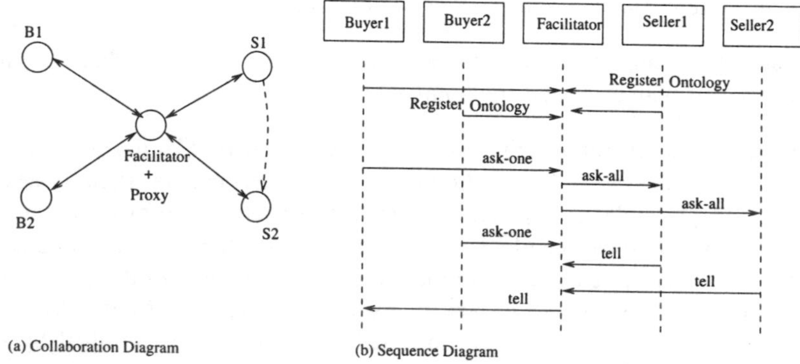

Fig. 5. (a) Collaboration diagram, (b) Sequence diagram, for 5 agents

As described previously, behaviour rules for components are defined with an `WHEN-IF-THEN` combination, where the `WHEN` portion relates to new events occurring in the environment of an agent, the `IF` portion compares the current state of the component with conditions that are required to make the rule applicable, and the `THEN` portion corresponds to actions that are taken by the component as a result of the rule firing. The `IF` portion is a generic mechanism to match against the beliefs, commitments, capabilities and intentions, enabling these to be combined in different ways.

3.1 Design Methodology

The design methodology comprises of the following phases:

1. Identify stake holders within the system. These are individuals who will be users of the system in the future, or will be affected by it in some way. A set of representative users must be identified, and interviewed to determine their particular requirements and expectations from the system. It is useful to note here that requirements of users can range from technical concerns to political and social concerns from a

system. Most existing design methodologies do not concentrate on the latter, and are primarily concerned with supporting technical objectives.

2. Based on user requirements and expectations, derive a root definition for each user, or a group of users.
3. A conceptual model of the required system must be then be developed from root definitions obtained in (2). The conceptual model must describe a set of activities or actions, as identified by a stake holder, required to achieve their Weltanschauung.
4. Steps (2) and (3) are used to find overlap in Weltanschauung and outlined activities across the different stake holders. These common activities are enumerated, and combined into a set of "roles". Each "role" must specify a set of pre-conditions that need to be validated to active it, and the transformations that are performed by it to other roles within the system. A pre-defined template specifying roles may also be used, as identified in the "market place" paradigm for e-commerce [10].
5. A rule base is developed based on actions to be performed within a given role, as identified by the activities defined in the conceptual models. These rules represent the initial beliefs and capabilities of each agent within the system. Each rule should also enable assertion or retraction of facts relating to it. Each rule may follow the general format identified in code segment 1.
6. Interactions between agents are also specified based on the conceptual model and root definition. Hence, in order to achieve a particular viewpoint, it may be required for a group of agents to interact. For instance, in the airline example, the airlines must be able to communicate with the Telecomms Provider.
7. Interactions between agents are modelled using UML sequence diagrams. Each diagram illustrates a given activity outlined in the conceptual model. The Weltanschauung for a particular user will involve multiple interactions, each of which can be represented as a sequence diagram.
8. The rules defining agent behaviours and the UML sequence diagrams may then be implemented using various agent development toolkits, or directly in a particular programming language such as Java.
9. The system is then monitored by each user to evaluate its behaviour with respect to their particular root definitions. An acceptance test is undertaken to measure how effective a system has been to meet the original user need. Based on feedback from users, the root definition needs to be updated and the process repeated.

The proposed methodology is user centered, and enables agent roles to more closely reflect user needs. It accounts for the different perspectives each user has about the system, and which requires a system to be adaptive. Hence, SSM can capture both changes in user perceptions, as well as changes in the environment within which the system operates. Both of these are reflected in the the root definitions for each user. Figure 6 illustrates the decomposition approach, where overlapping activities between conceptual models identify common agent services.

3.2 Benefits and Pitfalls

SSM appears an obvious complement to agent oriented information systems design, primarily because of the ability to capture subjective system requirements, subsequently

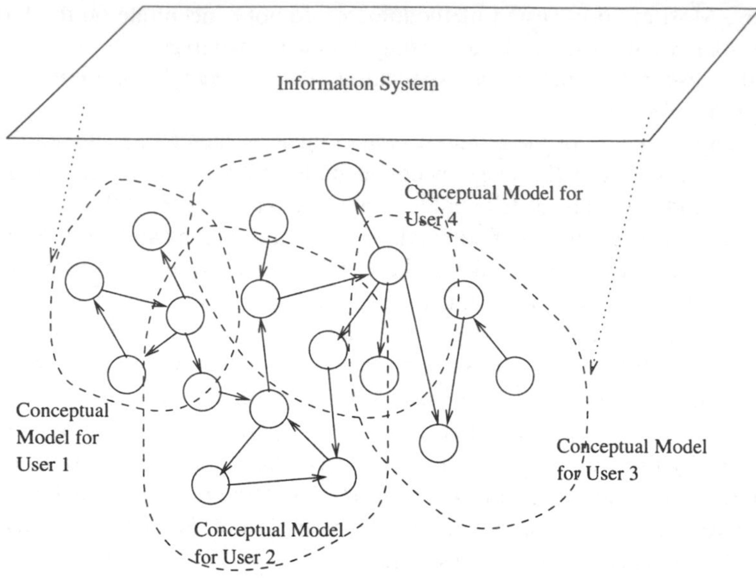

Fig. 6. System Decomposition into overlapping conceptual models

enabling a developer to capture system needs more intuitively. Our design approach illustrated in figure 3 is top-down, however if templates are available from an existing business scenario, pre-defined agent-based components may be used. Since components can vary their behaviour over time, using `ASSERT` and `RETRACT` to add and remove rules for instance, it is possible for components to start with pre-defined knowledge and modify it based on changes in root-definition, and usage. Use of some UML notation as an intermediate step can help validate SSM models, at the same time overcome the complexity of UML. To facilitate a unified view, all components are agents, and legacy information systems can be 'wrapped' as agents. Hence, the granularity of a component can be a complete information system, an operation performed by the information system, or as a bridge to enhance the functionality of the information system, albeit dictated by a system model in SSM. In this instance, each agent is undertaking a role which contributes towards the objectives of all stake holders within the system. An agent can subsequently adapt its role based on preference to a particular category of users.

The pitfalls with this approach relate to the difficulty of verifying the behaviour of an agent system, as interactions between agents can lead to complex behaviours which are hard to predict. Safety critical systems may not be amenable to such a design approach, unless constraints on agent behaviours are very stringent, which would approximate a traditional object oriented model in the limiting case. It may be difficult to determine intermediate roles for agents, due to conflicting root definitions. In this instance, the users will be required to vary their root definitions to find roles. In this case, a feedback mechanism must support users to change their particular emphasis. If only a few intermediate roles are identified, such as using a single facilitator to find merchants for buyers, a bottleneck may exist within the system, suggesting the use of a more open communication model where agents could send messages to each other directly. This cannot be detected with the SSM model, but can with the UML collaboration diagrams. SSM also has limitations, in that it may be difficult to combine root-definitions to give an aggregate utility measure that could be used to construct behaviour rules. At present, these have to be combined, or correlated in some way by the developer, and the methodology does not provide an automatic way to achieve this. Mechanisms for optimising root definitions, by using weight factors are obvious extensions, but these could eradicate the simplicity benefits of using SSM. Other issues such as security are beyond the scope of this paper, but can also be identified as concerns within a root definition. Such an approach would necessitate 'trust-relationships' to be established between agents, to ensure that messages are only processed from trusted hosts/agents, and others discarded.

4 Conclusion

A methodology based on SSM for developing information systems, composed of adaptive agents, is described. The use of SSM enables developers to communicate requirements with business users in a more intuitive manner. SSM facilitates the improvement of existing information system usage, and can incorporate "best practise" within a relevant industry into a model. Templates or "patterns" thus obtained may be re-used to identify agent roles in a related discipline, by analysing similarities in usage derived from the conceptual model. Although former approaches centered on the object oriented paradigm also provide useful abstractions, these are generally quite inflexible, and cannot easily relate the particular business processes being modelled by the agent system. With an SSM approach the root definitions provide a good mechanism to related business process management with agent behaviours. We propose the use of SSM as a first step in analysing business models, and explore possible ways of improving information usage, using different root definitions, based on particular concerns of each stake holder within a system. These models are then translated into a design composed of components, a set of interaction patterns between components, and subsequently into an architecture for components based on the BDI model.

Acknowledgements

I am grateful to Steve McIntosh and Brian Wilson for some very enthusiastic and engaging discussions on SSM.

References

1. A. W. Brown. Moving from Components to CBD. *Component Strategies*, April 1999.
2. D. W. Bustard, Z. He, and F. G. Wilkie. Soft Systems and Use-Case Modelling: Mutually Supportive or Mutually Exclusive? *Proceedings of the 32nd Hawaii International Conference on System Sciences (HICSS-32)*, January 1999.
3. D.W. Bustard, T.J. Dobbin, and B.N Carey. Integrating Soft Systems and Object-Oriented Analysis. *IEEE International Conference on Requirements Engineering*, April 1996.
4. D. Chappell. Taking Stock of Component Technology. *Component Strategies*, June 1999.
5. P. Checkland. *Systems Thinking, Systems Practice*. John Wiley and Sons, 1981.

6. P. Checkland and S. Holwell. *Information, Systems and Information Systems*, John Wiley and Sons, 1998.
7. P. Chen. The Entity-Relationship model – Towards a Unified View of Data. *ACM Transactions on Database Systems*, 1(1):9–36, 1976.
8. James Odell, H. Van Dyke Parunak, and Bernhard Bauer, "Extending UML for Agents," AOIS Worshop at AAAI 2000. Also available at: `http://www.jamesodell.com/publications.html`
9. M. Wooldridge, N.R. Jennings, and D. Kinny. "A Methodology for Agent-Oriented Analysis and Design", in Proceedings of the third International Conf. on Autonomous Agents, ACM Press, 1999.
10. F.M.T. Brazier, C.M. Jonker, and J. Treur. "Principles of Compositional Multi-Agent System Development", Proceedings of IFIP'98 Conference on Information Technology and Knowledge Systems, in J. Cuena (ed.), Chapman and Hall, 1998.
11. C. Landauer and K. Bellman. Agent-Based Information Infrastructure. *Proceedings of workshop on Agent Oriented Information Systems, at third annual conference on Autonomous Agents*, May 1999.
12. P. Heymans M. Petit and P-Y. Schobbens. Agents as a Key Concept for Information Systems Requirements Engineering. *Proceedings of workshop on Agent Oriented Information Systems, at third annual conference on Autonomous Agents*, May 1999.
13. Y. Shoham. Agent-Oriented Programming. *Artificial Intelligence*, 60:51–92, 1993.
14. L. Starr. *How to build Shlaer-Mellor object models*. Yourdon Press, 1996.
15. G. Wagner. Towards Agent-Oriented Information Systems and Agent-Object-Relationship Modelling. *Preliminary Report, Institut für Informatik, Freie Universität Berlin, Germany*, August 1999.

An Overview of the Multiagent Systems Engineering Methodology

Mark F. Wood Scott A. DeLoach

Department of Electrical and Computer Engineering
Air Force Institute of Technology
2950 P Street, Wright-Patterson AFB, OH, USA 45433-7765
woodm@stratcom.mil scott.deloach@afit.edu

Abstract. To solve complex problems, agents work cooperatively with other agents in heterogeneous environments. We are interested in coordinating the local behavior of individual agents to provide an appropriate system-level behavior. The use of intelligent agents provides an even greater amount of flexibility to the ability and configuration of the system itself. With these new intricacies, software development is becoming increasingly difficult. Therefore, it is critical that our processes for building the inherently complex distributed software that must run in this environment be adequate for the task. This paper introduces a methodology for designing these systems of interacting agents.

1. Introduction

The advent of multiagent systems has brought together many disciplines in an effort to build distributed, intelligent, and robust applications. They have given us a new way to look at distributed systems and provided a path to more robust intelligent applications. However, many of our traditional ways of thinking about and designing software do not fit the multiagent paradigm. Over the past few years, there have been several attempts at creating tools and methodologies for building such systems. Unfortunately, many of the tools focused on specific agent architectures [1, 12] or have not gone to the necessary level of detail to adequately support complex system development [8, 24]. In our research, we have been developing both a complete-lifecycle methodology and a complimentary environment for analyzing, designing, and developing heterogeneous multiagent systems. The methodology we are developing is Multiagent Systems Engineering (MaSE).

Constructing multiagent systems is difficult. They have all the problems of traditional distributed, concurrent systems, plus the additional difficulties that arise from flexibility requirements and sophisticated interactions. Sycara states in [21] that there are two technical hurdles to the extensive use of multiagent systems. First, there is a lack of a proven methodology enabling designers to clearly structure applications as multiagent systems. Second, there are no general case industrial-strength toolkits that are flexible enough to specify the numerous characteristics of agents.

This paper addresses the first technical hurdle by proposing a methodology for the design of multiagent systems. The focus is on the construction of a multiagent system through an entire software development lifecycle from problem description to implementation. Research into multiagent system methodologies, for the most part, has focused more on high-level descriptions and concepts than on an actual design methodology. Other design paradigms - object-oriented systems in particular - do exist as general-case solutions, but these are neither tuned for, nor particularly useful in creating a system that is intended to take full advantage of agent capabilities. Object-oriented design has achieved some maturity and provides a stable foundation upon which to build. However, object-oriented methodologies are not directly applicable to agent systems - typical agents are significantly more complex in both design and behavior than objects.

1.1 Scope

Because of assumptions made to simplify the research, MaSE has a few limitations. First, we assume that the system being created is closed and that all external interfaces are encapsulated by an agent that participates in the system communication protocols. Second, the methodology does not consider dynamic systems where agents can be created, destroyed, or moved during execution. Third, inter-agent conversations are assumed to be one-to-one, as opposed to multicast. However, substituting a series of point-to-point messages can be used to fulfill the requirement for multicast. Finally, it is assumed that the systems designed with MaSE would not be very large; the target is ten or less software agent classes. This is not a hard constraint, but simply indicates that no verification or validation of larger systems was done and that no thought was given to the potential problems of such systems.

Work is ongoing at the Air Force Institute of Technology (AFIT) to extend this methodology in these and other areas. Both the problems of dynamic systems and multicast conversations appear to be relatively straightforward extensions using predefined *move* activities and special multicast conversations. While not designed for open systems, MaSE can also be used to design agents that operate in an open environment as long as there are appropriately define protocols for the agent to use.

1.2 Related Work

There have been several proposed methodologies for analyzing, designing, and building multiagent systems [8]. The majority of these are based on existing object-oriented or knowledge-based methodologies. In fact, the syntax of many of the models was taken from the Unified Modeling Language even though the methodology itself is dissimilar to most object-oriented approaches.

Actually, MaSE builds upon the work of many agent-based approaches; it takes many ideas and combines them into a complete, end-to-end methodology. For instance, work on goals and roles by Kendall [11] influenced the initial MaSE analysis steps while the mapping of roles to agent classes builds off the concepts presented by Kinny, Georgeff, and Rao [12]. Only the Gaia approach [24] attempts to encompass the entire life cycle, although the authors admit to its shortcomings. The main advantage of MaSE over previous methodologies is its scope and completeness.

2. Multiagent Systems Engineering Methodology

The Multiagent System Engineering (MaSE) methodology, takes an initial system specification, and produces a set of formal design documents in a graphically based style. The primary focus of MaSE is to guide a designer through the software lifecycle from a prose specification to an implemented agent system. MaSE is independent of a particular multiagent system architecture, agent architecture, programming language, or message-passing system. A system designed in MaSE could be implemented in several different ways from the same design. MaSE also offers the ability to track changes throughout the process. Every design object can be traced forward or backward through the different phases of the methodology and their corresponding constructs. MaSE is described in more detail in [4, 22]. An overview of the methodology and models is shown in Figure 1.

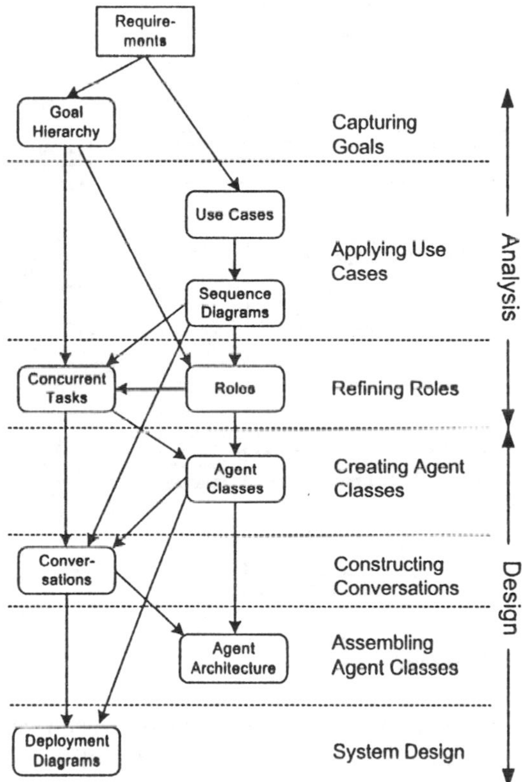

Fig. 1. The MaSE Methodology

The general operation of MaSE follows the progression of steps shown in Figure 1, with outputs from one section becoming inputs for the next. The methodology is iterative across all phases with the intent that successive "passes" will add detail to the models described later. The gray boxes denote models used within the methodology and the phases are listed down the right side of the figure. The arrows indicate how the models influence each other.

2.1 Capturing Goals

The first phase in MaSE is Capturing Goals, which takes the initial system specification and transforms it into a structured set of system goals as shown in a Goal Hierarchy Diagram (Figure 2). This phase of MaSE is drawn in a large part from analysis patterns in [11]. In the MaSE methodology, a goal is always defined as a system-level objective. Lower-level constructs may inherit or be responsible for goals, but goals always have a system-level context.

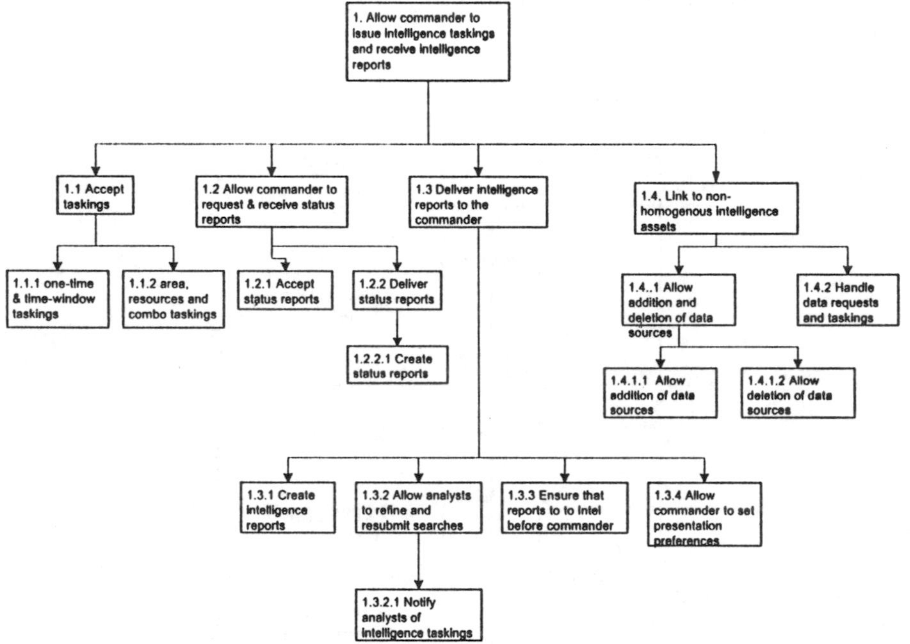

Fig. 2. Goal Hierarchy Diagram

There are two parts of the Capturing Goals phase: identifying and structuring goals. The goals are identified by distilling the essence of the set of requirements. These requirements may include detailed technical documents, user stories, or formalized government specifications. Once these goals have been captured and explicitly stated, they are less likely to change than the detailed steps and activities involved in accomplishing them.

The goals are then analyzed and structured into a form that can be passed on and used in the design phases of the MaSE methodology. In a Goal Hierarchy Diagram, goals are organized by importance. The main sequences of interaction and subordinate details must be distinguishable from one another. Each level of the hierarchy contains goals that are roughly equal in scope and all sub-goals relate functionally to their parent.

2.2 Applying Use Cases

It is the conversations between agents that are the real backbone of a multiagent system, as they enable the distributed operation that is the strength of agent technology. The second phase of MaSE looks down the road toward constructing these conversations and creates use cases to ease this difficulty.

The Applying Use Cases phase captures use cases from the initial system requirements and restructures them as a Sequence Diagram (Figure 3). A sequence diagram depicts a sequence of messages between multiple agent roles.

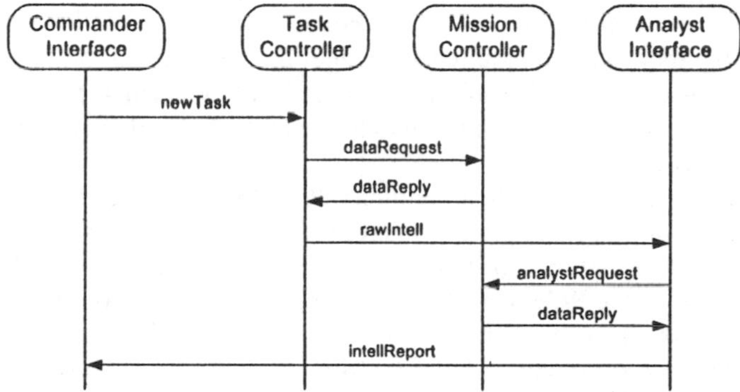

Fig. 3. Sequence Diagram

First, use cases are drawn from the system requirements. Use cases are narrative descriptions of a sequence of events that define desired system behavior. They are examples of how the user (or the requirements document editor) thinks the system should behave in a given case.

A Sequence Diagram is used to determine the minimum set of messages that must be passed between roles. If a message is passed between two roles, then there must be a corresponding communication path between them. A communication path between roles played by separate agent classes means that a conversation must exist between the two agent classes to pass the message. The agent class playing the role that initiated the communication becomes the initiator of that conversation, while the receiving agent class becomes the responder. Typically, we create at least one sequence from a use case. If there are several possible scenarios, multiple Sequence Diagrams are created.

2.3 Refining Roles

The third step of MaSE is to transform the structured goals of the Goal Hierarchy Diagram into a form more useful for constructing multiagent systems: roles. Roles are the building blocks used to define agent's classes and capture system goals during the design phase. We guarantee that system goals are accounted for by ensuring that every goal is associated with a role and that every role is played by an agent class.

A role is an abstract description of an entity's expected function and encapsulates the system goals that it has been assigned the responsibility of fulfilling. Roles are created to do something. They are similar to the notion of an actor in a play or an office within an organization. Roles are described in detail in [10,12,24].

The general case transformation of goals to roles is one-to-one; each goal maps to a role. However, there are many exceptional situations where it is useful to combine goals. Similar or related goals may be combined into single roles for the sake of convenience or efficiency. Goals that share a high degree of cohesion as described in [16] can be combined into a single role.

Some goals imply distributed roles. Any mention of separate machines or other distribution requires one role for each "side" of the distributed relationship. Interfacing with an external source is the same. One role must interface with the source while another may be required to bridge the gap back to the system. This is also true for any database, file interface, or user interface in the system. A user interface implies a role by itself and should be separate from other roles as if it were a separate data source.

Role definitions are captured in a traditional Role Model [10] as shown in Figure 4. MaSE also allows a more complete version of a Role Model, as shown in Figure 5, which includes information on interactions between role tasks. However, the traditional version of the Role Model is more useful at the outset of the role definition process before tasks have been defined, as well as later in the analysis to provide a high-level view of the system. In the traditional Role Model, lines between roles denote possible communications paths between roles. These paths are derived from the Sequence Diagrams developed in the previous step.

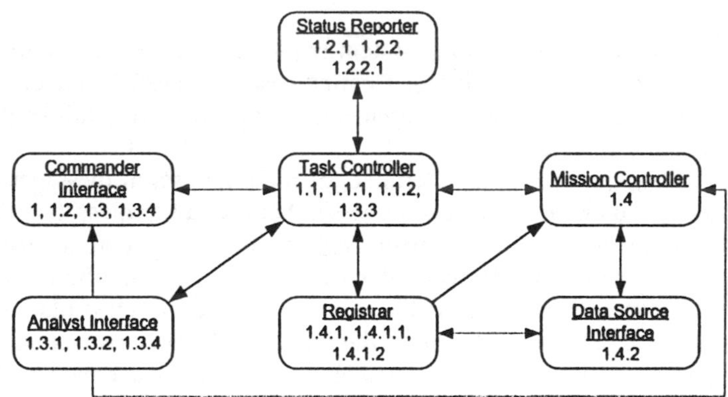

Fig. 4. Traditional Role Model

In MaSE, roles are typically documented in a more detailed version of a Role Model as shown in Figure 5. First, the goals associated with each role are listed under the role name. It also shows the set of tasks associated with each role, which are used to define the role's behavior. Roles are denoted by rectangles, while the role tasks are denoted by ovals attached to the role. Tasks are simply identified in the MaSE Role Model. The detailed description of a task's definition is provided in the next section. Lines between tasks denote communications protocols that occur between the tasks. The arrows denote the initiator/responder relationship of the protocol with the arrow pointing from the initiator to the respondent. Solid lines indicate peer-to-peer communications, which are generally implemented as external communications protocols. External protocols involve message passing between roles that may become actual messages if their roles end up being implemented in separate agents. Dashed lines denote communication between concurrent tasks within the same role. A lined is dashed if it will only occur within the same instance of the role in the final system. Roles may not share or duplicate tasks. Sharing of tasks is a sign of improper role decomposition. Shared tasks should be placed in a separate role, which can be combined into various agent classes in the Design phase.

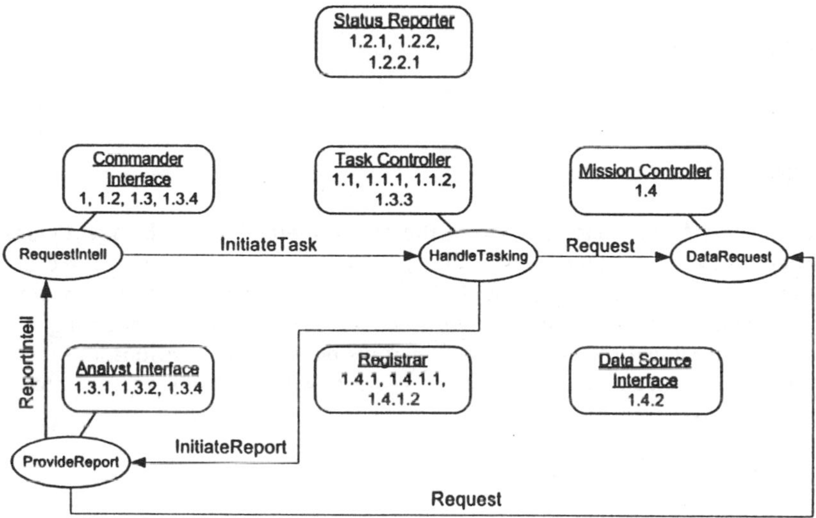

Fig. 5. MaSE Role Model

After roles are created, tasks are associated with each role. Every goal associated with a role can have a task that details how the goal is accomplished. This must be done after role creation since tasks communicate with tasks in other roles. A MaSE task, which captures a bidder's behavior in a Contract Net Protocol, is shown in Figure 6. A task is a structured set of communications and activities, depicted as a state diagram.

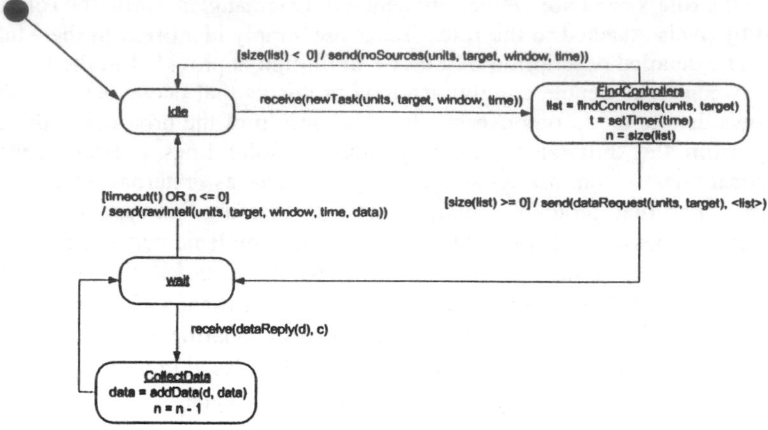

Fig. 6. MaSE Task

2.4 Creating Agent Classes

In the Creating Agent Classes phase of the MaSE methodology, the agent classes are identified from component roles. The product of this phase is an Agent Class Diagram, shown in Figure 7, which depicts agent classes and the conversations between them. The boxes in the figure are the agent classes, containing the class name and its assigned roles. Lines with arrows denote conversations and point from the initiator of the conversation to the responder, with the name of the conversation written either over or next to the arrow.

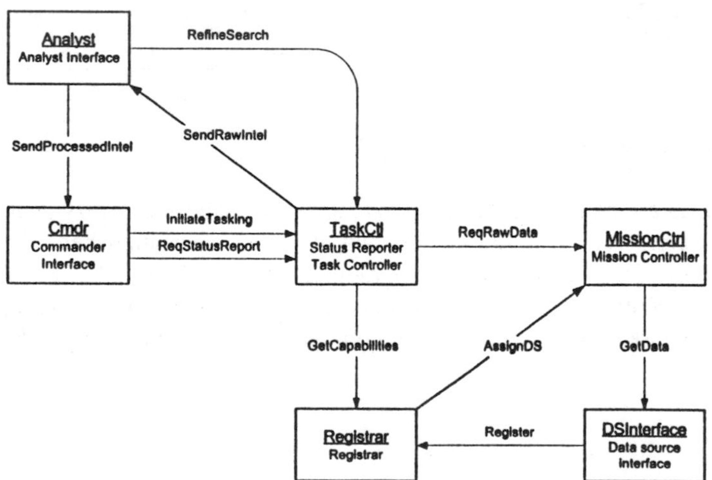

Fig. 7. Agent Class Diagram

During this phase of MaSE, agent classes consist of two components: roles and conversations. In a later MaSE phase, internal details are added to agent classes. The conversations of an agent class are those that it participates in, either as an initiator or responder.

The primary difference between the Agent Class Diagram and similar object diagrams is the semantics of the relationships between agent classes. In Agent Class Diagrams, these relationships define conversations that are held between agent classes. In fact, the primary purpose of this phase is to identify the agent classes that "anchor" each side of a conversation.

Just as before, when mapping goals to roles, there is generally a one-to-one mapping between roles and agent classes. However, the designer may combine multiple roles in a single agent class or map a single role to multiple agent classes. Since agents inherit the communication paths between roles, any paths between two roles become a conversation between their respective classes. As such, it is desirable, where possible, to combine two roles that share a high volume of message traffic. When determining which roles to combine, size and frequency of communications are important, not just the number of communication paths.

2.5 Constructing Conversations

Constructing Conversations is the next phase of MaSE. It is closely linked with the phase that follows it, Assembling Agents. As will be discussed later, it is often beneficial to alternate between the two phases. A MaSE conversation defines a coordination protocol between two agents. Specifically, a conversation consists of two Communication Class Diagrams, one each for the initiator and responder. A Communication Class Diagram is a pair of finite state machines that define the conversation states of the two participant agent classes. The *initiator* side of a conversation is shown in Figure 8 with its associated *responder* side shown in Figure 9. The initiator begins the conversation by sending the first message.

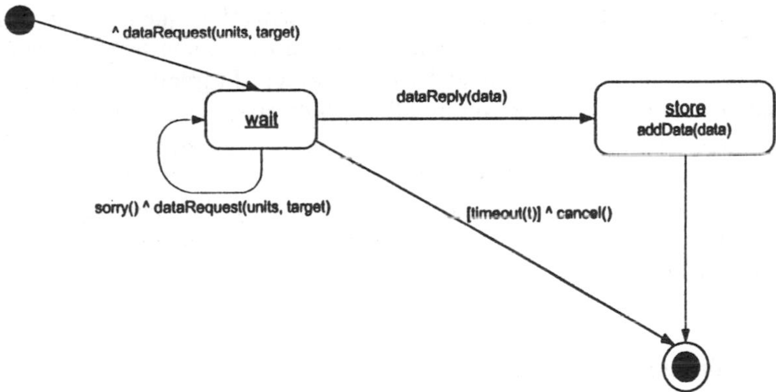

Fig. 8. Initiator Communication Class Diagram

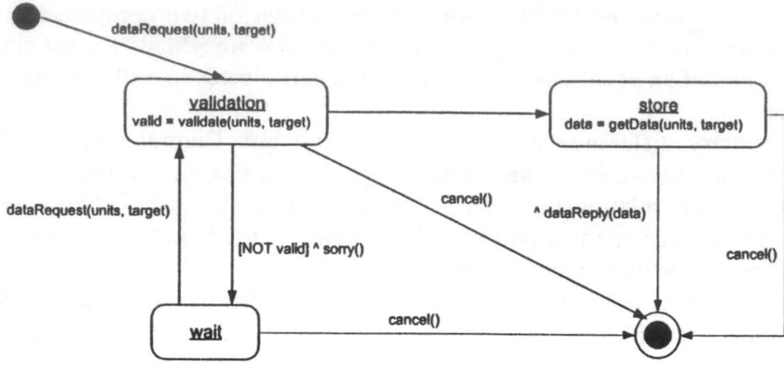

Fig. 9. Responder Communication Class Diagram

When an agent receives a message, it compares it to its active conversations. Upon a match, the agent transitions the appropriate conversation to a new state and performs any required activities from either the transition or the new state. Otherwise, the agent compares the message to all possible conversations that it may participate in with the agent that sent the message, and begins a new conversation if the message matches a transition from the start state. Any activities in a conversation, which may occur in a state or on a transition, are mapped to methods in the corresponding agent classes. The syntax of a transition follows conventional UML notation as shown below, and described in [3].

```
rec-mess(args1) [cond]/activity^trans-mess(args2)
```

While the operation of a conversation is relatively simple, its design can be quite complicated. Conversations are defined at a high level. Specifically, the initiator and responder agent classes are specified for each conversation in the system. The problems encountered in this phase deal with building the finite state automata that define the operation and protocol of conversations.

Conversations must support and be consistent with all sequence diagrams derived earlier. They may also incorporate states from tasks. Some tasks, in fact, operate entirely over single conversations and can be designed directly. In general though, conversations are built by first adding all possible states and transitions that can be derived from the Sequence Diagrams and tasks. At this point, much of the conversation often exists. For the rest of the conversation design, it is a matter of adding states and transitions as necessary to convey the required messages and provide robust operation. Automatic verification of conversation correctness is addressed by Lacey in [13].

2.6 Assembling Agent Classes

In this phase of MaSE, the internals of agent classes are created. Work by Robinson [18] describes the details of assembling agents from a component-based architecture. He defines five different architectural style templates: Belief-Desire-Intention (BDI), reactive, planning, knowledge based, and a user-defined architecture. Each architecture template has a specific set of components. For example, a reactive architecture includes a Controller, MessageInterface, RuleContainer, and Effectors.

A designer can either define components from scratch or use pre-existing components. Furthermore, components may have sub-architectures containing components. Components are joined with either inner- or outer-agent connectors. Inner-agent connectors (thin arrows) define visibility between components while outer-agent connectors (thick dashed arrows) define connections with external resources such as other agents, sensors and effectors, databases, and data stores. Internal component behavior may be represented by formal operation definitions as well as state-diagrams that represent events passed between components. An example of a component-based architecture is shown in Figure 10.

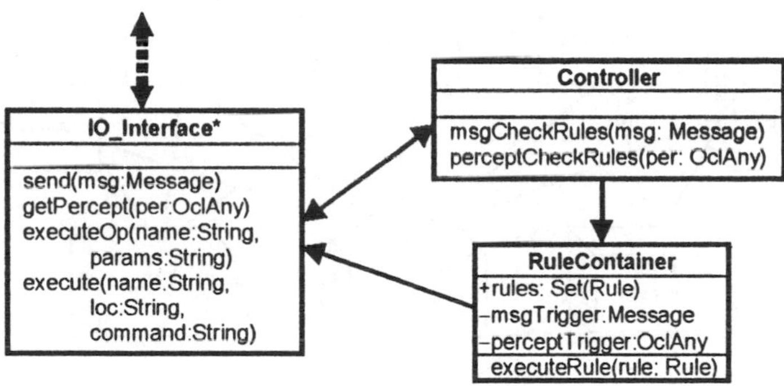

Fig. 10. Generic Reactive Agent Class Architecture

2.7 Constructing Conversations versus Assembling Agent Classes

As discussed in their respective sections, constructing conversations and agent class assembly are closely related activities. In practice, it is useful to alternate between these phases while staying within one functional area of the design. The question of which to do first is answered best by the style of conversations the system uses. In particular, is the system communication-heavy? Are the communications relatively complex? The designer should design conversations first if the system consists of many simple conversations, or if the initial context of the system includes many use cases. It is generally better to define the agents first if there are complex conversations, or if many of the agent classes are being reused.

2.8 System Design

The final phase of the MaSE methodology takes the agent classes and instantiates them as actual agents. It uses a Deployment Diagram to show the numbers, types, and locations of agents within a system. System design is actually the simplest phase of MaSE, as most of the work was done in previous steps. The idea of instantiating agents from agent classes is the same as instantiating objects from object classes in object-oriented programming.

Deployment Diagrams are used to define a system based on agent classes defined in the previous phases of MaSE. Deployment Diagrams define system parameters such as the actual number, types, and locations of the agents within the system. Figure 11 shows an example Deployment Diagram. The three dimensional boxes are agents, and the connecting lines represent conversations between agents. The agents are named either after their agent class, or in the form of "designator: class" if there are multiple instances of a class. A dashed-line box indicates that agents are housed on the same physical platform.

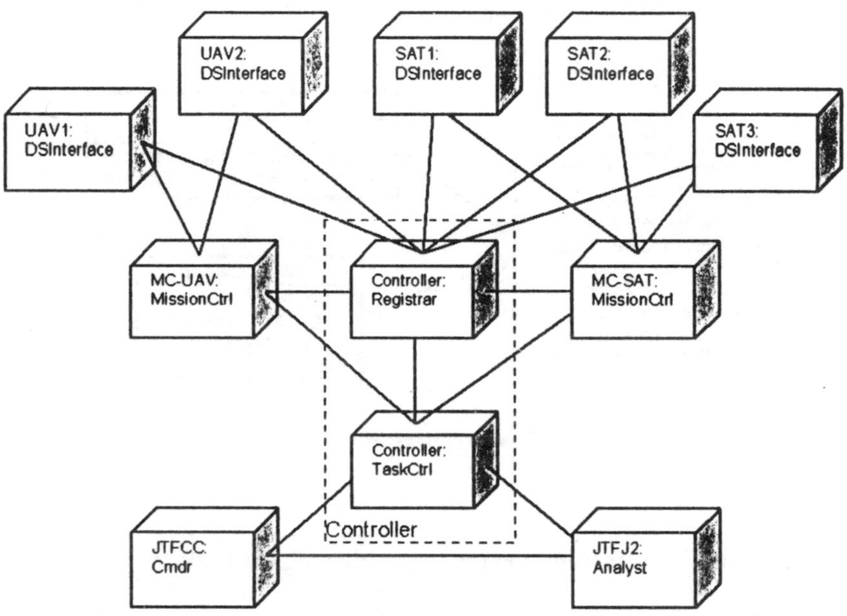

Fig. 11. MaSE Deployment Diagram

A system must be arranged in a Deployment Diagram before it can be implemented in code. This is due to the differences between agents and agent classes. An agent requires information such as a hostname or address to participate in a multiagent system. A Deployment Diagram also offers another opportunity for the designer to tune the system. Agents can be arranged among various machine configurations to take advantage of the available processing power of network bandwidth.

A final element to consider is automatic code generation. The MaSE methodology is concerned with actually engineering agent systems. As such, all of the steps of the methodology work toward that end. It is our vision that code generation be a largely automatic process. Code generation is not a part of MaSE at this time, but is assumed to happen just after this phase.

3. Contributions

MaSE guides a multiagent system designer through the entire software development lifecycle, beginning from a textual system representation and proceeding in a structured manner toward a working implementation. MaSE combines several pre-existing models into a single structured methodology. Most of the models used within the methodology have therefore been already justified and validated within the realm of agents and multiagent systems. A sequence of guided transformations connects the elements of this strong foundation together into a clear high-level picture of how a designer should go about creating a multiagent system.

In conjunction with the MaSE methodology, we have developed a tool, called agentTool, to support the development of multiagent systems using MaSE [5]. The agentTool system currently supports the entire lifecycle from the Goal Hierarchy diagram down to code generation. Developing the methodology and tool together allowed us to focus the methodology toward automation. Focusing on automation forced us to define an unambiguous semantics for the models as well as the relationships between the models. Using MaSE and agentTool we have shown that you can develop a multiagent systems development methodology, along with an automated toolset, that supports multiple types of agent architectures, languages, and communications frameworks.

4. MaSE Applications

MaSE has been successfully applied in numerous graduate-level projects as well as several research projects. The Multi-Agent Distributed Goal Satisfaction project [20] is a collaborative effort between AFIT, the University of Connecticut, and Wright State University where MaSE is being used to design the collaborative agent framework to integrate different constraint satisfaction and planning systems. The Agent-Based Mixed-Initiative Collaboration project [2] is also using MaSE to design a multiagent system focused on distributed human and machine planning. MaSE has been used successfully to design an agent-based heterogeneous database integration system [14] as well as a multi-agent approach to a biologically based computer virus immune system [7].

5. Acknowledgements

This research was supported by the Air Force Office of Scientific Research (99NM097) and the Dayton Area Graduate Studies Institute (HE-WSU-99-09). The views expressed in this article are those of the authors and do not reflect the official policy or position of the United States Air Force, Department of Defense, or the US Government.

References

[1] Brazier, F., Jonker C., Treur, J.: Principles of Compositional Multi-Agent System Development. Proceedings of the IFIP'98 Conference (1998).

[2] Cox, M., Kerkez, B., Srinivas, C., Edwin, G., Archer, W.: Toward Agent-Based Mixed-Initiative Interfaces. In Proceedings of the 2000 International Conference on Artificial Intelligence. CSREA Press (2000).

[3] DeLoach, S.A.: Multiagent Systems Engineering: a Methodology and Language for Designing Agent Systems. Proceedings of Agent Oriented Information Systems '99 (1999) 45-57.

[4] DeLoach, S. A., Wood M. F.: Multiagent Systems Engineering: the Analysis Phase. Technical Report, Air Force Institute of Technology, AFIT/EN-TR-00-02, June 2000.

[5] DeLoach, S.A., Wood, M.F.: Developing Multiagent Systems with agentTool. The Seventh International Workshop on Agent Theories, Architectures, and Languages, (2000).

[6] Drogoul, A., and Collinot A.: Applying an Agent Oriented Methodology to the Design of Artificial Organizations: A Case Study in Robotic Soccer. Autonomous Agents and Multi-Agent Systems, 1(1), 113-129.

[7] Harmer, P.K., Lamont, G.B.: An Agent Architecture for a Computer Virus Immune System. Genetic and Evolutionary Computation Conference (2000).

[8] Iglesias, C., Garijo, M., Gonzalez, J.: A Survey of Agent-Oriented Methodologies. In: Müller, J.P., Singh, M.P., Rao, A.S., (Eds.): Intelligent Agents V. Agents Theories, Architectures, and Languages. Lecture Notes in Computer Science, Vol. 1555. Springer-Verlag, Berlin Heidelberg (1998) 185-198.

[9] Jennings, N. R., Sycara, K., and Wooldridge, M. 1998 "A Roadmap of Agent Research and Development" Autonomous Agents and Multi-Agent Systems, 1(1), 7-38.

[10] Kendall, Elizabeth A.: Agent Software Engineering with Role Modelling. In this volume (2000).

[11] Kendall, Elizabeth A., and Zhao, L.: Capturing and Structuring Goals. Workshop on Use Case Patterns, Object Oriented Programming Systems Languages and Architectures (1998).

[12] Kinny, D., Georgeff, M., Rao, A.: A Methodology and Modelling Technique for Systems of BDI Agents. Agents Breaking Away: Proceedings of the Seventh European Workshop on Modelling Autonomous Agents in a Multi-Agent World, MAAMAW '96. Lecture Notes in Artificial Intelligence, Vol. 1038. Springer-Verlag, Berlin Heidelberg (1996) 56-71.

[13] Lacey, T., DeLoach, S.A.: Automatic Verification of Multiagent Conversations. Proceedings of the Eleventh Annual Midwest Artificial Intelligence and Cognitive Science Conference, (2000) 93-100.

[14] McDonald, J.T., Talbert, M.L., DeLoach, S.A.: Heterogeneous Database Integration Using Agent Oriented Information Systems. Proceedings of the International Conference on Artificial Intelligence (2000).

[15] Nwana, H. S.: Software Agents: An Overview. Knowledge Engineering Review. 11(3): 205-244 (1996).

[16] Pressman, R.S.: Software Engineering: A Practitioners Approach, 3rd ed. McGraw-Hill Inc., New York (1992).

[17] Raphael, Marc J., DeLoach, S.A.: Marc J. Raphael & Scott A. DeLoach. A Knowledge Base for Knowledge-Based Multiagent System Construction. Proceedings of the National Aerospace and Electronics Conference (2000).

[18] Robinson, D.J.: A Component Based Approach to Agent Specification. MS thesis, AFIT/ENG/00M-22. School of Engineering, Air Force Institute of Technology (AU), Wright-Patterson Air Force Base Ohio, USA (2000).

[19] Rumbaugh, J.: Object-Oriented Modeling and Design, Prentice-Hall Inc., Englewood Cliffs, New Jersey (1992).
[20] Saba, G.M., Santos, E.: The Multi-Agent Distributed Goal Satisfaction System. Submitted to International ICSC Symposium on Multi-Agents and Mobile Agents in Virtual Organizations and E-Commerce (MAMA'2000).
[21] Sycara, K. P.: Multiagent Systems. AI Magazine 19(2): 79-92 (1998).
[22] Wood, M. F.: Multiagent Systems Engineering: A Methodology for Analysis and Design of Multiagent Systems. MS thesis, AFIT/GCS/ENG/00M-26. School of Engineering, Air Force Institute of Technology (AU), Wright-Patterson AFB Ohio, USA (2000).
[23] Wooldridge, M., and Jennings, N.: Intelligent Agents: Theory and Practice. Knowledge Engineering Review, 10(2): 115-152 (1995).
[24] Wooldridge, M., Jennings, N., Kinny, D.: The Gaia Methodology for Agent-Oriented Analysis and Design. Autonomous Agents and Multi-Agent Systems. 3 (3): (2000).

Security for Mobile Agents

Nobukazu Yoshioka* Yasuyuki Tahara*
Akihiko Ohsuga* Shinichi Honiden†

* Corporate Research & Development Center, TOSHIBA Corp.
1, Komukai Toshiba-cho, Saiwai-ku, Kawasaki-shi, Japan.
{nobukazu.yoshioka,yasuyuki.tahara,akihiko.ohsuga}@toshiba.co.jp

† National Institute of Informatics
2-1-2 Hitotsubasi, Chiyoda-ku, Tokyho, Japan.
honiden@nii.ac.jp

Abstract. In view of the proliferation and expansion of wide-area open networks such as the intranets and extra-nets, agent technology is attracting greater attention. However, as yet there is well-established and widely used method of developing safe and secure agent systems. In this paper, we propose a methodology that supports the step-by-step development of mobile agent systems while ensuring consideration of security issues. This approach results in a robust infrastructure for practical system development, and by supporting calculation of various costs allows efficiency and security tradeoffs to be objectively evaluated.

1 Introduction

In view of the mounting use of computer networks such as the intranets and extra-nets between organizations, and the expansion of such networks, the software that supports these networks is becoming increasingly important. It is this context that the concept of mobile agents is attracting attention. However, mobile agents suffer from insufficiencies respecting developmental methodology and security. Until these problems are solved, widespread adoption of agents is unlikely. In particular, this is because it is difficult to build practical large-scale systems in the absence of rigorous developmental methodologies.

In this paper, we propose a methodology that supports the step-by-step development of mobile agent systems while ensuring consideration of security issues. The methodology revolves around the use of patterns that take these issues into account.

Our methodology has the following features. Firstly, it is a concrete development method with security concerns fully integrated. Secondly, we can easily construct a suitable computation model by examining the patterns and their costs. The pattern approach was originally conceived as an aid to object-oriented software development. In this paper we apply the same concept to the development of agent systems. This results in a robust infrastructure for practical system development, and by supporting calculation of various costs allows efficiency and security tradeoffs to be objectively evaluated. Such tradeoffs and methodologies are important because the system that concerns the security by ad-hoc method may be too slow and have security hole.

In addition, software for intranets/extra-nets recently should be adopted dynamical changes safely and quickly, when the structure of organization changes for innovation. Our methodology allows us such changes because it uses not only structure of agents but also organization and control information of hardware.

Previous work has included proposals for safety and security techniques for mobile agent systems [8]. However, these proposals did not incorporate a concrete methodology, and focused on only parts of the overall system rather than taking the necessary holistic approach. This state of affairs is reflected in the absence of any general guidelines for mobile agent systems. Tahara [13] proposed mobile agent patterns. Other approaches have also been proposed, but without the integration of security and safety issues. Additionally the absence of objective cost guidelines was a problematic omission. We have developed more abstract patterns in order to avoid the domain-specificity of other work.

The contribution of this work can be viewed from a variety of different perspectives. From the software engineering point of view, (1) our work provides a basis for CASE and IDE tool design, (2) agent migration necessity can be discussed formally, and (3) security can be maintained while integrating legacy applications. From the system management perspective, it provides a mechanism for evaluating the system in terms of efficiency and security.

The paper is structured as follows. Section 2 provides the overview of our methodology. Details of our methodology are described in section 3 to 5. Section 3 describes the models used in the methodology. Section 4 describes the patterns. Section 5 describes the process. In section 6, we evaluate the methodology by using a example and discusses the methodology. Section 7 describes related work and some final remarks are provided in Section 8.

2 Summary of the Development Process

The process is summarized in Figure 1. The round rectangles denote the sub-processes, the solid rectangles denote the products, and the dotted rectangles denote the patterns presented in this paper. In the process, we use 3 kinds of information: agent structure model for application information, system requirements model for hardware information and access model and confidentiality model for organization information. The method consists of migration decision phase and security decision phase, and in each phase we use patterns: basic patterns and secure patterns respectively.

Mobile Agent Architecture that we use to develop a system is shown in Figure 2. In a system, mobile agents can access applications and databases in other hosts through the agent platform and the wrappers. In addition, an agent consists of some objects or subroutines. In our methodology, we only consider the security for a mobile agent against attacks from others.

3 Models

3.1 Agents Structure Model

This model expresses data flow of agents and the following information.

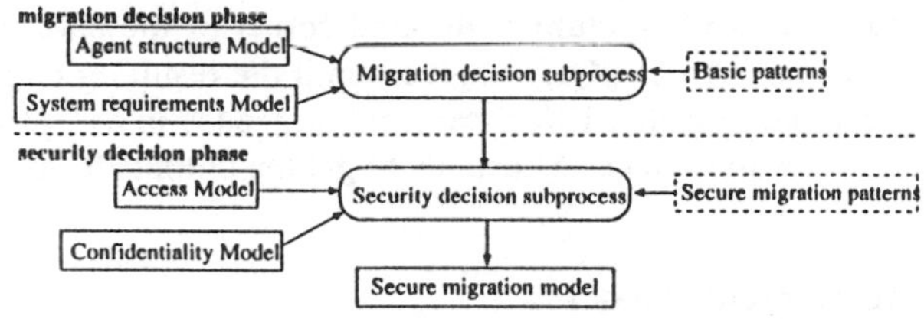

Fig. 1. Summary of process

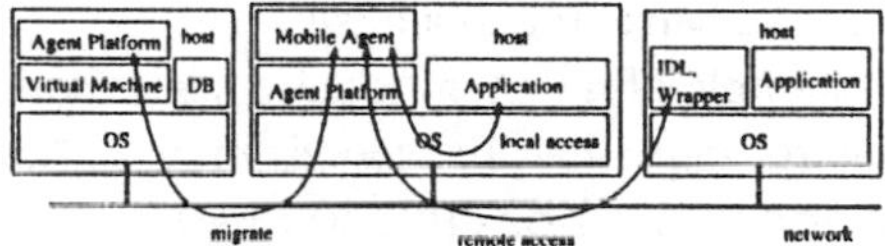

Fig. 2. Mobile Agent Architecture

Amount of data are indicated beside each arrow.

Computing hosts where the computation is performed and the data are stored are indicated at the top left-hand corner of each node.

If any hosts in the system are allowed to perform the computation, "*" is indicated instead of host names.

Initial computation host name : is indicated in the double-lined box and an arrow is drawn from the box to the computation performed first.

Computation time : is indicated in the circle at the bottom left-hand corner of each node.

Code size is indicated after the computation time and "/".

The computation time and the amount of data are set at their average or typical value.

Figure 3 shows an example of an agent structure model. This example represents that `Data store` is a database on `hostA`, and `operation` is performed on `hostA` or `hostB`.

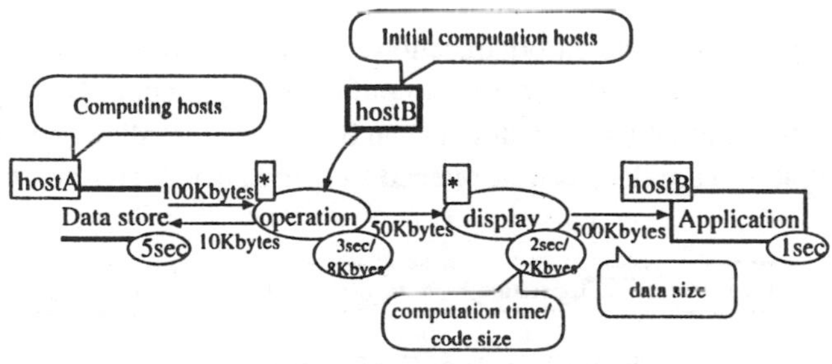

Fig. 3. Agent Structure Model

The times indicated at the bottom right-hand corner of the data stores denote the times from when inputs such as SQL are given until the resulting data are taken. Figure 3, for example, represents that 10K bytes input is needed in order to get 100 Kbytes data from the data store and it takes 5 seconds to get the outputs from the inputs.

3.2 System Requirements Model

This model includes the information on the resource constraint on the hosts and the network: the longest stay time of agent and network transfer speed. The reason we consider stay time is for load balancing of a host.

Figure 4 shows an example of a system requirements model. The figure illustrates that an agent cannot stay for more than 10 seconds in hostA. It also indicates that the transfer speed between hostA and hostB is 30 Kbytes/sec at the worst point.

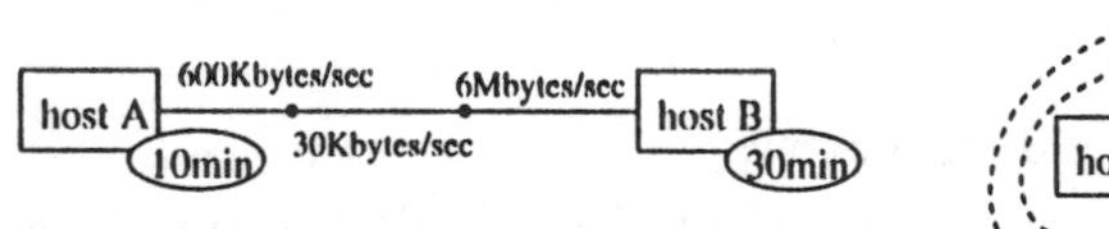

Fig. 4. Example of System Requirements Model

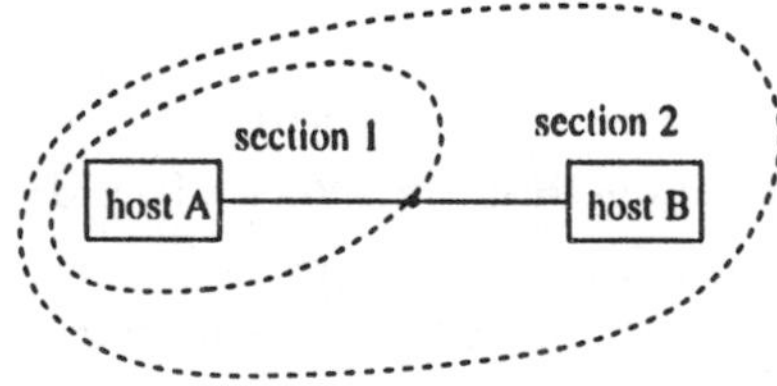

Fig. 5. Control model

3.3 Control Model

This model represents which organization accesses the network and hosts. Figure 5 shows an example of a control model. This example represents that the member of section 1 can access to host A, host B and the network between connected to host A, and the member of section 2 can access to the host B and the network connected to host B.

We assume that person who does not belong to the controlling organizations cannot access to the network and the hosts of the organizations.

3.4 Confidentiality Model

This model represents to which organizations the data handled by the service can be opened. Figure 6 shows an example of a confidentiality model. This figure indicates that the Data store's input and output data can be opened to only section 1 and the input and output of display can be opened to section 1 and section 2.

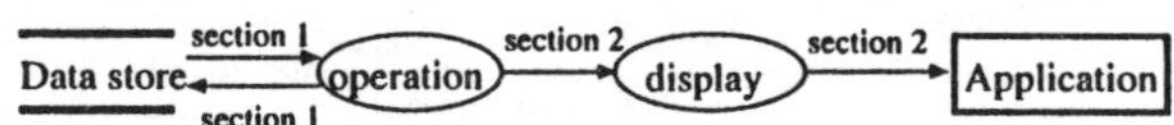

Fig. 6. Example of Confidentiality Model

4 Patterns

4.1 Basic Migration Patterns

Migration patterns that do not consider security are composed of the following basic migration patterns shown in Figure 7. Pb1 and Pb2 are the computation patterns and represent typical situations of computation of mobile agents. Pb3, Pb4 and Pb5 are coupling patterns and represent typical situations of migration of mobile agents between the hosts.

For each computation process, a computation pattern and several coupling patterns are composed and a migration pattern is established.

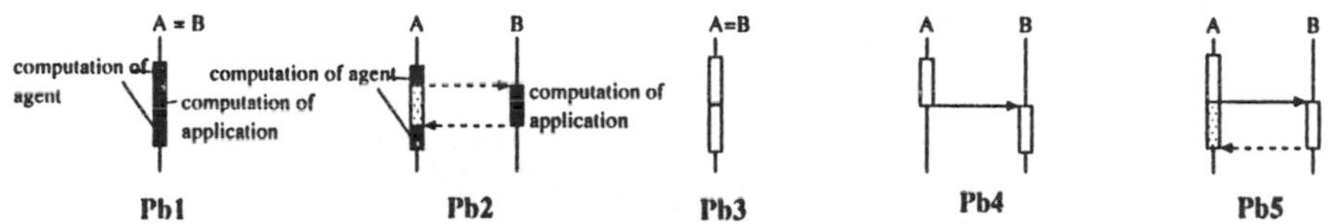

Fig. 7. Basic Migration Patterns

The vertical lines denote hosts and time flows from the top to the bottom. The black rectangles represent that computation is actually performed, and the gray rectangles represent that computation is not performed while the hosts are blocked by computation of some other hosts. The dotted horizontal lines denote communication by the message and the solid lines denote the migrations of mobile agents. The white rectangles denote computation other than the computation in question and are not parts of the patterns.

The following are detail of the patterns.

Pb1 is applied if the host performing the computation and the host that has the actors and the data stores related to the computation coincide.

Pb2 is applied if the host performing the computation interacts by exchanging messages with the host that has the actors and the data stores related to the computation.

Pb3 is applied if the host performing the computation in question and the host performing the next computation coincide. The mobile agent does not migrate.

Pb4 is applied if the host performing the computation in question and the host performing the next computation differ and the mobile agent migrates totally.

Pb5 is applied if the host performing the computation in question and the host performing the next computation differ, the mobile agent migrate partially or totally to the latter host and the original mobile agent is blocked until the remote computation is completed. At least, only the data and the codes necessary to the remote computation migrate and only the results are returned to the original host.

Which pattern of Pb1 or Pb2 is applied can be automatically determined by assignment of the host performing each computation.

4.2 Secure Migration Patterns

The secure migration patterns are the enhanced basic migration patterns considering encryption/decryption time for preventing data leak and signature generation/checking for preventing tampering.

The situations in which security should be considered are classified into 12 categories according to risk of the network on the way to the host for the next computation, risk of the host for the next computation and the basic migration patterns with such dangers.

Figure 8 shows the secure migration patterns. In this figure, Pse1, Pse2, Pse3, and Pse4 are the computation pattern Pb2 enhanced with security techniques, Pse5, Pse6, Pse7, and Pse8 are the migration pattern Pb4 enhanced with security techniques and Pse9, Pse10, Pse11, and Pse12 are the migration pattern Pb5 enhanced with security techniques. The black rectangles in these patterns denote the extra time for increasing the system security.

In general, the countermeasures listed in the following table are used as the ways of increasing the system security.

Insecure part	Kind of attack	Countermeasure
Network	Wiretapping	Encryption
Network	Tampering	Signature
Host	Masquerading	Authenticating

Considering these issues, the patterns here add encryption, signature and authentication costs to the basic migration patterns. In detail, the encryption costs are included in Pse3, Pse4, Pse7, Pse8, Pse11 and Pse12 in which the network is insecure and the authentication costs are included in Pse2, Pse4, Pse6, Pse8, Pse10 and Pse12 in which a host is insecure. In this paper, all the data flowing in the network are given signatures even in Pse1, Pse2, Pse5, Pse6, Pse9 and Pse10 in which the network is secure because we assume that there is the danger of tampering even if the network is secure.

The following patterns are representative ones.

Pse1 is applied to Pb2 if the host A, B and the network between them are secure. In this pattern, the host A sends its data with the signature of the host itself in order to avoid tampering over the network. First, the hosts should exchange their public keys to handle their signatures. Then the hosts sign their data using their secret keys and verify the data using the corresponding public keys. In this pattern, as indicated by the black boxes in the figure, more time is required for the key generation, the key delivery, signing and the signature verification than in the case of Pb2.

Pse7 is applied to Pb4 if the network to the destination host is insecure. In this pattern, the data should be encrypted before the migration so that more time is required for it than in the case of Pb4.

Pse12 is applied to Pb5 if the destination host and the network to it are insecure. In this pattern, it is necessary to authenticate the destination agent platform on the host B, to encrypt the agent before the migration and its result.

As mentioned previously, among the patterns in Figure 8, we have no ways to avoid wiretapping by the destination host in Pse6, Pse8, Pse10 and Pse12 in the case that the destination host is not secure. Therefore, it may be necessary to change the computation assignment or the managers of the hosts so that these patterns are not needed.

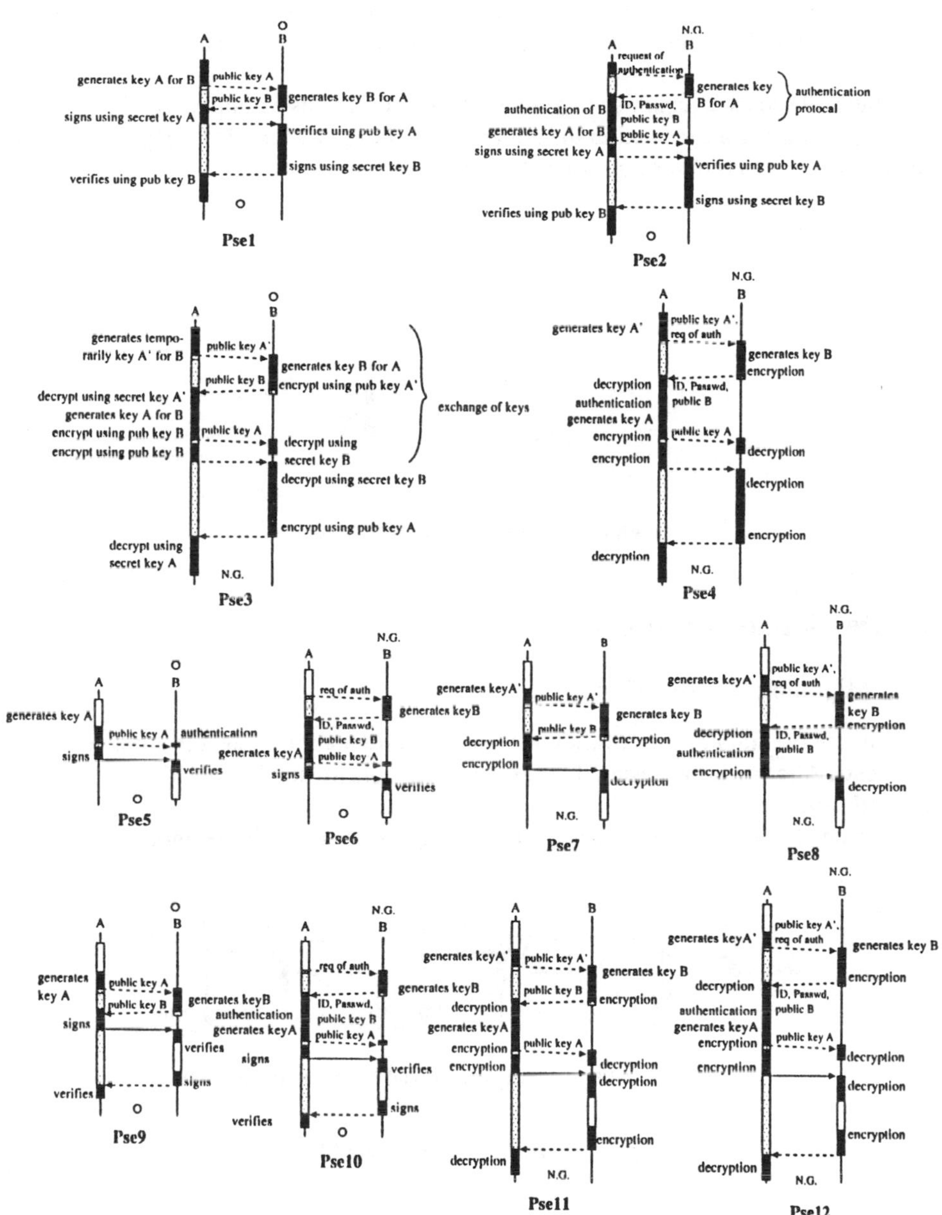

Fig. 8. Secure Migration Patterns

4.3 Migration Model

The migration model consists of combinations of the patterns explained so far. The difference between the patterns and the migration models is that the computation time is the actual one or not, and that the time of the data transfer over the network is considered or not.

Figure 9 shows an example of a migration model. In this example, the four computation processes are executed in the patterns Pb1, Pb2, Pb1 and Pb1, respectively, and the processes are combined by the patterns Pb4, Pb5 and Pb4.

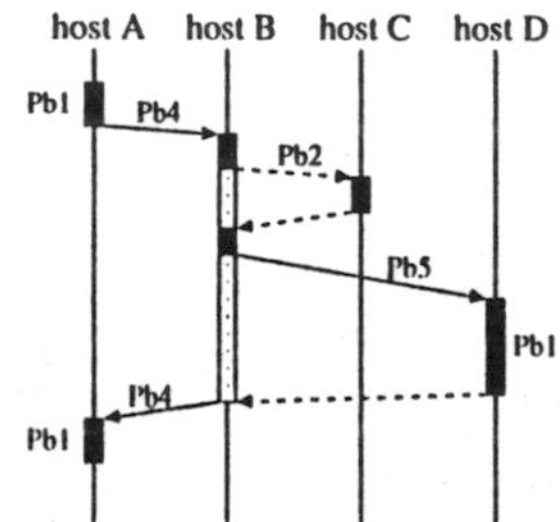

Fig. 9. Example of Migration Model

5 Development Process

5.1 Migration Decision Phase

This phase is summarized as follows. First, the computation in agents are assigned to the hosts. After that, the basic migration model is constructed by selecting appropriate migration patterns.

Figure 10 shows some basic migration models derived for the example.

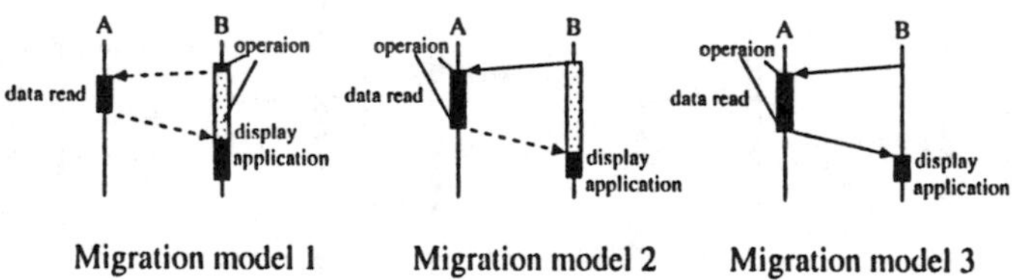

Fig. 10. Derived Basic Migration Model

5.2 Security Decision Phase

In this phase, we apply secure migration patterns to the migration model constructed by previous phase by using an access model and a confidentiality model.

In this paper, we define the security policy as follows. That is network is insecure when data which is sent through network is not open to the organization by which the network can be accessed, and a host is insecure when data which is used in the host is not open to the organization by which the host can be accessed. By this policy, we can apply secure patterns to migration models automatically by using those models.

Finally, we should select a suitable model. For evaluation of migration models, we consider the cost of models. The cost must be including a communication efficiency, insecure communication, and the overhead for security. For example, we can define the overhead for security of each security pattern as follows.

Pattern	Overhead for Security
Pse1	$2key + sign(x) + check(y) + check(x) + sign(y)$
Pse2	$auth + 2key + sign(x) + check(y) + check(x) + sign(y)$
Pse3	$3key + 2decode(d) + 2encode(d) + encode(x) + decode(y) + decode(x) + encode(y)$
Pse4	$3key + decode(id + d) + auth + encode(d) + encode(x) + decode(y) + encode(id + d) + decode(d) + decode(x) + encode(y)$
Pse5	$key + sign(x + code) + check(x + code)$
Pse6	$auth + 2key + sign(x + code) + check(x + code)$
Pse7	$2key + decode(d) + encode(x + code) + encode(d) + decode(x + code)$
Pse8	$2key + decode(id + d) + auth + encode(x + code) + encode(id + d) + decode(x + code)$
Pse9	$2key + sign(x + code) + check(y) + check(x + code) + sign(y)$
Pse10	$auth + 2key + sign(x + code) + check(y) + check(x + code) + sign(y)$
Pse11	$3key + 2decode(d) + 2encode(d) + encode(x + code) + check(y) + decode(x + code) + sign(y)$
Pse12	$3key + decode(id + d) + auth + encode(d) + encode(x + code) + check(y) + encode(id + d) + decode(d) + decode(x + code) + sign(y)$

Where x and y are the amount of the input/output data of computation, d and id are public key size and ID and password size, respectively, and key, $sign$, $check$, $auth$, $encode$ and $decode$ are functions of public key generation time, signing time, signature confirmation time, authentication time and encryption/decryption time, respectively.

The total cost of migration model is defined as follows by using these overheads.

$$\alpha\frac{TC}{TS} + \beta\frac{TTC}{TC} + \gamma\frac{DC}{TS} + \sigma\frac{DT}{TSC} + \epsilon\frac{SO}{TC}$$

where TSC, TTC, TS, TC, DC, DT and SO are total communication size/time, total data size, total computation time, size/time of insecure communication, and overhead for security, respectively.

Figure 11 shows the secure migration models. In this case, we can select model 3 from the cost point of view.

6 Discussion

6.1 Availability of the method

We compared the model derived by our method with the model constructed without method.

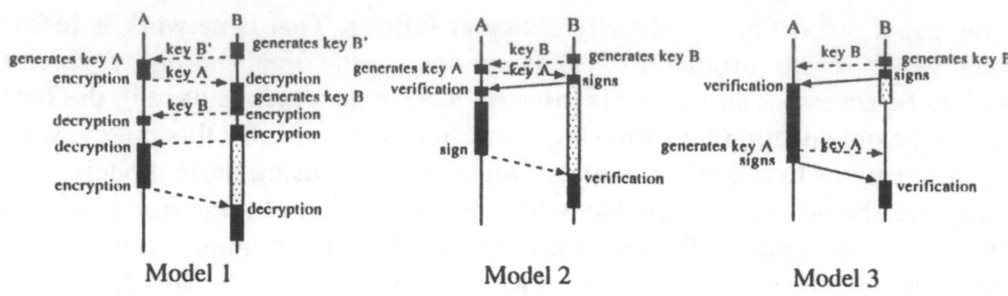

Fig. 11. Derived Secure Migration Model

We constructed the agent which read DB in host A then calculate using simulator on host C to save the results in host B. Figure 12 to 15 are input models. Figure 16 is the migration model finally selected by using our method. Figure 17 is the migration model constructed with ad hoc method.

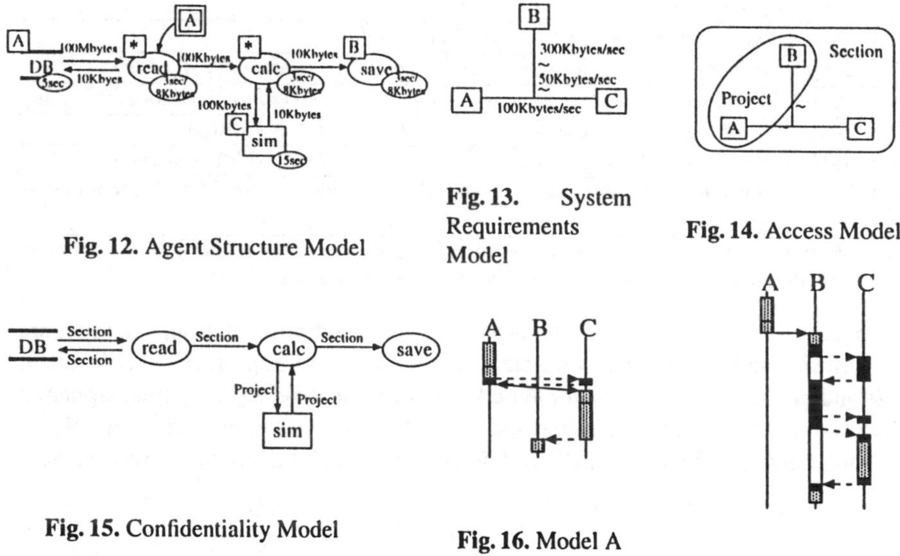

Fig. 12. Agent Structure Model

Fig. 13. System Requirements Model

Fig. 14. Access Model

Fig. 15. Confidentiality Model

Fig. 16. Model A

Fig. 17. Model B

Table 1 illustrate the cost of these migration models, when parameters α to ϵ is 0.1, 0.1, 0.6, 0.1 and 0.1, respectively. It implies that we can construct a migration model that is more suitable than others by using our method.

6.2 Completeness of models and process

Our model and process are simple and we can find more information and patterns for security. But the important factor is to establish the process for constructing a mobile agent system using patterns and its costs.

Table 1. Total Cost

Model	Com. Size	Insecure Com. Size	Insecure Com. Time	Overhead	Total Cost
A	134 bytes	0 bytes	0 sec	2 sec	0.01149
B	226 bytes	110 bytes	2.2 sec	29 sec	0.41353

Parallel computation aims at safety and efficiency. For the computation using the multi-agent framework, It is necessary to consider clones of an agent and communication between the agents. Patterns should be modified.

We can think of additional information for the model, although the information depends on the target system domain. For example, we can consider a message size/time limit over network for resource constraints.

7 Related Work

More and more researchers have been working on patterns for mobile agents since the design patterns of the Gang of Four [10] were shown to be useful for object-oriented system development. Aridor and Lange [9] classify some design patterns into three kinds, that is, the Traveling Patterns, the Task Patterns and the Interaction Patterns, and present some individual patterns. In addition, they apply the patterns to some examples. Kendall et al. [11] examine design patterns for agents with a layered architecture. They illustrate patterns applicable to each layer constructing the agents. Silva et al. [12] propose patterns that are centered on one agent and composed by using collaboration diagrams and class diagrams. Tolksdorf [16] proposes patterns for "Mobile Object Space (MOS)", a mobile agent model based on the coordination model Linda. He includes four patterns, that is, Pull, Push, Index and Traveller.

However, these works only propose some isolated patterns and in most cases there is only one pattern suitable for mobile agents. Therefore, it is difficult for inexperienced developers to decide which patterns they should use in their actual development tasks. On the other hand, since we specified the cost model for our patterns, even inexperienced developers can easily use the patterns on the basis of their costs.

8 Conclusion and Future Work

We have presented the methodology for development of a mobile agent system using patterns and their cost. In this method we introduce the patterns for construction of the migration model. The patterns are considered from the viewpoint security issue. We also introduce the cost which is a numeral guildline for selecting suitable model.

In future work we intend to to the following: (1) to create bigger and useful domain specific patterns, (2) to investigate their ability and scalability, (3) to accumulate more practical know-how to construct a suitable model, and (4) to make CASE and development tools based on our methodology.

Acknowledgements

We wish to thank Dr. Yoshio Masubuchi, general manager of Computer & Network Systems Laboratory, who gave us the opportunity to pursue this research.

References

1. Shimshon Berkovits, Joshua D. Guttman, and Vipin Swarup, Authentication for mobile agents, in Vigna [8], pp. 114–136.
2. David M. Chess, Security issues in mobile code systems, in Vigna [8], pp. 1–14.
3. Fritz Hohl, Time limited blackbox security; protecting mobile agents from malicious hosts, in Vigna [8], pp. 92–113.
4. George C. Necula and Peter Lee, Safe, untrusted agents using proof-carrying code, in Vigna [8], pp. 61–91.
5. John K. Ousterhout, Jacob Y. Levy, and Brent B. Welch, The Safe-Tcl security model, in Vigna [8], pp. 217–234.
6. Tomas Sander and Christian F. Tschudin, Protecting mobile agents against malicious hosts, in Vigna [8], pp. 44–60.
7. Giovanni Vigna, Cryptographic traces for mobile agents, in *Moblie Agents and Security* [8], pp. 137–153.
8. Giovanni Vigna, editor, *Moblie Agents and Security*, LNCS 1419, Springer Verlag, 1998.
9. Yariv Aridor and Danny B. Lange, Agent design patterns: Elements of agent application design, in *Proceedings of Agents'98*, 1998.
10. Erich Gamma, Richard Helm, Ralph Johnson, and John Vlissides, *Design Patterns*, Addison-Wesley, 1995.
11. Elizabeth A. Kendall, Chirag V. Pathak, P. V. Murali Krishna, and C. B. Suresh, The layered agent pattern language, in *Proceedings of PLoP'97*, 1997.
12. Alberto Silva and José Delgado, The agent pattern: A design pattern for dynamic and distributed applications, in *Third European Conference on Pattern Languages of Programming and Computing*, 1998.
13. Tahara,Y., Ohsuga,A. and Honiden,S., Agent System Development Method Based on Agent Patterns, in *Proceedings of the 21st International Conference on Software Engineering*, acm PRESS, pp.356-367, 1999.
14. Amund Aarsten, Davide Brugali, and Giuseppe Menga, Patterns for cooperation, in *Proceedings of PLOP'96*, 1996.
15. Steven Y. Goldsmith, Shanon V. Spires, and Laurence R. Phillips, Object framework for agent system development, in *Proceedings of AAAI-98 Workshop on Software Tools for Developing Agents*, 1998.
16. Robert Tolksdorf, Coordination patterns of mobile information agents, in Matthias Klusch and Gerhard Weiß, editors, *Cooperative Information Agents II*, pp. 246–261, 1998.

Organizational Abstractions for the Analysis and Design of Multi-agent Systems

Franco Zambonelli* Nicholas R. Jennings† Michael Wooldridge‡

* Dipartimento di Scienze dell'Ingegneria
Università di Modena e Reggio Emilia
Via Campi 213-b – 41100 Modena, Italy
franco.zambonelli@unimo.it

† Department of Electronics and Computer Science
University of Southampton, Southampton SO17 1BJ, United Kingdom
nrj@ecs.soton.ac.uk

‡ Department of Computer Science, University of Liverpool
Liverpool L69 7ZF, United Kingdom
M.J.Wooldridge@csc.liv.ac.uk

Abstract. The architecture of a multi-agent system can naturally be viewed as a computational organisation. For this reason, we believe organisational abstractions should play a central role in the analysis and design of such systems. To this end, the concepts of agent roles and role models are increasingly being used to specify and design multi-agent systems. However, this is not the full picture. In this paper we introduce three additional organisational concepts — organisational rules, organisational structures, and organisational patterns — that we believe are necessary for the complete specification of computational organisations. We view the introduction of these concepts as a step towards a comprehensive methodology for agent-oriented systems.

1 Introduction

Autonomous agents and multi-agent systems (MASs) are rapidly emerging as a powerful paradigm for designing and developing complex software systems. However, as is the case with any new software engineering paradigm, the successful and widespread deployment of MASs requires not only new models and technologies, but also new *methodologies* to support developers engineer such systems in a robust, reliable, and repeatable fashion. In the last few years, there have been several attempts to develop such methodologies. However, most of this work is either tuned to specific systems and agent architectures [9, 4] — thus it lacks generality — or it is defined as an extension of existing object-oriented methodologies [14] — thus it exploits abstractions that are unsuitable for modelling agent-based systems.

Against this background, only a few proposals exist that attempt to define complete and general methodologies, specifically tailored to the analysis and design of MASs. One such methodology is Gaia [32]. Gaia views the process of analysing and designing multi-agent systems as one of constructing computational organisations. Thus, multi-agent systems are viewed as being composed of a multitude of autonomous interacting entities (an *organised society* of individuals) in which each agent plays one (or more) specific *roles*. In particular, Gaia, like a few other agent-oriented methodologies [9, 7, 16], suggests defining the structure of a MAS in terms of a *role model*. This model identifies the roles that agents have to play within the MAS and the interaction protocols in which the different roles are involved.

The adoption of a role model as the main organisational abstraction makes the above mentioned methodology mostly targetted at MASs in which the agents are cooperative and in which the system is closed. However, in order to deal with systems that involve self-interested agents operating in an open environment, we believe that additional organisational abstractions have to be introduced in a methodology [33]. In particular, we believe that *organisational rules*, *organisational structures*, and *organisational patterns* must also play a primary role in the analysis and design of MASs. Organisational rules express general, global (supra-role) requirements for the proper instantiation and execution of a MAS. An organisational structure defines the specific class (among the many possibilities) of organisation and control regime to which the agents/roles have to conform in order for the whole MAS to work efficiently and according to its specified requirements. Organisational patterns express pre-defined and widely used organisational structures that can be re-used from system to system (in a manner similar to the way catalogues of patterns are widely exploited in the design of object-oriented systems) [11].

In this paper, we show, with the aid of two application examples, that adoption of the above organisational abstractions can lead to a methodology that is applicable to a wide spectrum of agent systems. We also believe that the introduction of high-level organisational abstractions can lead to more clean, manageable, and re-usable MAS designs. Specifically, the paper is organised as follows. Section 2 introduces the basic concepts underlying agents and multi-agent systems. Section 3 introduces the additional organisational abstractions that are needed for a methodology to apply to open systems and motivates their adoption. Section 4 briefly sketches how our organisational abstractions can be exploited during the analysis and design of MASs. Section 5 discusses related work in this area and section 6 concludes by outlining the open issues and the future research directions.

2 Multi-Agent Systems and Organisations

Agents are software entities that exhibit *autonomous* and *proactive* goal-directed behaviour — their activities are not subject to a global flow of control and they can take the initiative where appropriate — and that are *reactive* to changes in the environment in which they are situated [31, 19]. These characteristics make agents useful as stand-alone entities that are delegated to accomplish a given task on behalf of a user (e.g., personal digital assistants, e-mail filters, or simple robots). However, in the majority of cases, agents exist in the context of *multi-agent software systems*, whose global behaviour derives from the interaction among the constituent agents [13]. In these cases, agents also exhibit *social* behaviour; they interact with one another: either to cooperate to achieve a common objective or because this helps each of the interacting agents to achieve their own objectives.

Here, we distinguish between two main classes of multiple agent system: *(i) distributed problem solving systems* in which the component agents are explicitly designed to cooperatively achieve a given goal, and *(ii) open systems* in which agents, not necessarily co-designed to share a common goal, can dynamically leave and enter the system. In the former case, all agents are known a priori, and all agents are supposed to be benevolent to each other and, therefore, they can trust one another during interactions. In the latter case, the dynamic arrival of unknown agents needs to be taken into account, as well as the possibility of self-interested behaviour in the course of the interactions.

2.1 The Organisational Metaphor

The design of parallel and distributed applications, as well as of distributed object systems, usually relies on an architecture that derives from the decomposition of the functionalities and data required by the system to achieve its goal, and on the definition of their inter-dependencies [2]. In MASs, however, the autonomous and proactive behaviour of the constituent agents suggests that applications can be designed by mimicking the behaviour and structure of human organisations. Thus each agent is assigned a specific role in the system. That is, a well-defined task/responsibility in the context of the overall system, that the agent has to accomplish in an autonomous fashion, without any centralised control. In this model, interactions are no longer merely an expression of inter-dependencies, rather they are viewed as a means for an agent to accomplish its role in the organisation. Therefore, interactions are well-identified and localised in the definition of the role itself, and they help characterise the position of the agent in the organisation.

An organisational perspective can also make the design of the system less complex and easier to manage than more traditional metaphors for concurrent systems. Firstly, each agent becomes a separate *locus* of control, in charge of accomplishing its role and being fully responsible for it. Secondly, since agents typically embed most of the functionality they need to accomplish their role, inter-dependencies between the system components are likely to be reduced. When taken together, these points ease the design process because they lead to a cleaner separation between the component-level (i.e., intra-agent) and system-level (i.e., inter-agent) design dimensions.

A final advantage relates to the fact that, in many cases, MASs are intended to support and/or control some real-world organisation. For example, MASs can be adopted to support the workflow management in a team or to help control the activities of an Internet auction. In such cases, an organisation-based MAS design reduces the conceptual distance between the software system and the real-world system it has to support. Consequently, this simplifies the development of the system.

2.2 An Organisational Characterisation of Multi-Agent Systems

The organisational perspective leads to a general characterisation of a MAS as depicted in figure 1 [7, 15]. Although some simpler systems can be viewed as a single organisation, as soon as the complexity increases, *modularity* and *encapsulation* principles suggest splitting the system into different sub-organisations. Thus, in most cases, a complex multi-agent system can be viewed as several *interacting organisations*. Naturally a given agent can be part of multiple organisations.

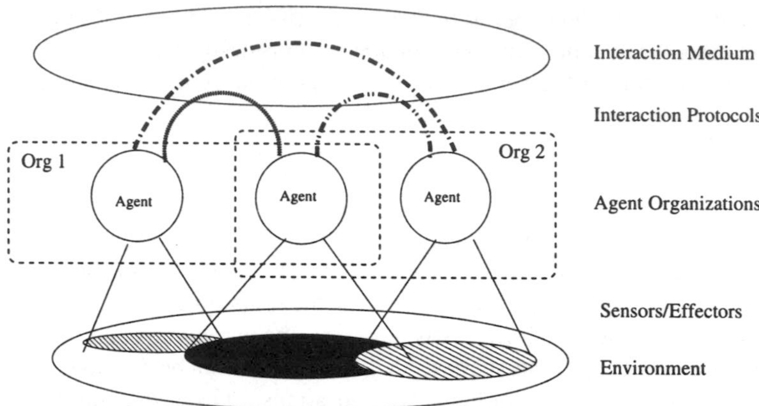

Fig. 1. Characterisation of a Multi-Agent System

In each organisation, an agent can play one or more *roles*. The role is what the agent is expected to do in the organisation: both in cooperation with the other agents and in respect of the organisation itself.

Often, the role of an agent is simply defined in terms of the specific task that the agent has to accomplish in the context of the overall organisation. However, in our work the notion of a role is much more precise, in that it gives an agent a well-defined position in the organisation, with a set of associated expected behaviours.

To accomplish their role in the organisation, agents typically need to *interact* with each other in order to *exchange knowledge* and *coordinate* their activities. Therefore, the concept of inter-agent interactions is strictly related to the role of an agent. It is the role that requires a given form of interaction. Even more precisely, an agent, by the very fact that it plays a given role and has a well-defined position in the organisation, is committed to certain interaction protocols with the other agents in the organisation. Of course, the need to interact according to specific protocols requires the presence of a communication medium between agents. This can be either a traditional network infrastructure, typically enforcing a message-passing interaction model, or another infrastructure possibly enforcing a different interaction model (e.g., a shared dataspace enforcing an indirect, data-oriented interaction model [12]).

Generally speaking, a MAS is immersed in a given *environment* with which the agents may need to interact in order to accomplish their role. This interaction occurs via *sensors* and *effectors*, i.e., mechanisms that enable agents to sense and effect a selected portion of the environment. That portion of the environment that an agent can sense and effect is determined by the agent's specific role, as well as on its current status.

2.3 Exemplar Multi-Agent Systems

To illustrate our points on the need for organisational abstractions, we will consider two sample problems that will act as running examples throughout this paper.

Manufacturing Pipeline: As an example of a MAS that belongs to the class of distributed problem solvers, we will consider a system for the control of a manufacturing process. For example, let us consider the process of assembling, painting and packing metal hardware. Typically, such a control system can be delegated to a multiplicity of agent organisations, each devoted to the control of a well-defined portion of the overall manufacturing process (e.g., the assembling section or the painting section). Within each section, agents can then be associated with the control of a specific tool in the control system or to the control of a specific condition that must be assured to guarantee the correctness of the process.

In this context, we specifically consider a manufacturing pipeline in which items are transformed/augmented (e.g., a pipeline in which metal items are painted). Here, different agents can be devoted to the control of different stages of the pipeline (e.g., an agent is devoted to control the paint spraying, another is devoted to control the heat treatment of the paint, another of controlling the cooling process). Agents interact both indirectly through the environment and directly, through various forms of interaction protocol. In such an organisation, the role of each agent is that of "stage of the pipeline", in charge of ensuring that a specific portion of the pipeline works properly (e.g., that the oven maintains a constant temperature and that the cooling system does not cool items too fast). To this end, agents need to sense and effect that portion of the environment which represents the stage of the pipeline of which they are in charge. In addition, the agents need to interact to achieve a proper global functioning of the pipeline (for instance, by guaranteeing a uniform flux of items throughout the pipeline and by guaranteeing that the global flux of item does not exceed the "processing capabilities" of each of the stages).

Conference Management: As an example of an open system we will consider an agent-based system for supporting the management of an international conference. Setting up and running a conference is a multi-phase process involving several individuals and groups. During the submission phase, authors of submitted papers need to be informed that their papers have been received and they need to be assigned a submission number. Once the submission deadline has passed, the program committee (PC) has to handle the review of the papers; contacting potential referees and asking them to review a number of the papers. After a while, reviews are expected to come in and be used to decide about the acceptance/rejection of the submissions. Authors need to be notified of these decisions and, in case of acceptance, must be asked to produce the camera ready version of their revised papers. Finally, the publisher has to collect the camera ready versions from the authors and print the whole proceedings.

The conference management problem naturally leads to a conception of the whole system as a number of different organisations, one for each phase of the process. In each organisation, the corresponding MAS can be viewed as being made up of agents associated to the persons involved in the process (authors, PC Chair, PC Members,

Reviewers). The roles played by each agent reflect the ones played by the associated person in the conference organisation. They may require agents to interact both directly with each other and indirectly, via an environment composed of papers and review forms. Since an agent is directly associated with a person, and its behaviour can be influenced by that person, opportunistic behaviour can emerge in the application. For example, an author could attempt to review their own paper or a PC Member could try to deal with fewer papers than they should. In addition, as the natural environment for the MAS is the Internet — due to the world-wide nature of the conference organisation — interactions with agents external to the MAS itself are likely to occur. For instance, a reviewer can decide to exploit its own personal agent to interact with the other agents of the organisation.

3 Organisational Abstractions

Organisational role models precisely describe all the roles that constitute the computational organisation; in terms of their functionalities, activities, and responsibilities, as well as in terms of their interaction protocols and patterns, which establish the position of each role in the organisation [32, 9, 7] . However, such role models cannot be considered as the sole organisational abstraction upon which to base the entire development process. Rather, before the design process actually defines the role model and, consequently, the whole organisation, a number of other steps need to be performed. Firstly, the analysis phase should identify *how* the organisation is expected to work. Secondly, the design phase should define *which* kind of organisation best fits the requirements identified in the analysis phase. Thirdly, it needs to be determined whether any re-use of available components can be exploited in some part of the organisational design. When taken together, this necessitates the introduction of three further organisational abstractions: organisational rules (section 3.1), organisational structures (section 3.2), and organisational patterns (section 3.3).

3.1 Organisational Rules

The analysis phase aims to collect all the specifications and requirements for building the MAS. To this end, it is possible to identify the basic skills (functionalities and competences) required by the organisation, as well as the basic interactions that are required for the exploitation of these skills. However, until the design phase has decided *which* organisation is most appropriate for the system, the identified skills and interactions cannot fully define the roles and the interaction protocols that will be played in the system (i.e., at defining a complete *role model*): this would imply an early commitment to a specific form of organisation. Instead, what the analysis phase can further identify — even in the absence of a complete role model — are the constraints that the actual organisation, once defined, will have to respect.

The implementation and/or execution of a computational organisation will have to respect a number of constraints, whose identification can either: *(i)* spread horizontally over all the roles and protocols (or, which is the same in this context, over the identified preliminary roles and protocols), or *(ii)* express relations and/or constraints between roles, protocols, or between roles and protocols. For example, in the case of human organisations: *(i)* social conventions define a set of implicit rules that moderate the interactions between all members (e.g., a clerk cannot contradict or ignore the commands of his manager), *(ii)* company specific conventions might impose constraints on how different roles have to be played in each of its organisations (e.g., a clerk cannot assume a role that would imply a member of the managing staff to be somehow subordinated to his clerk).

In both cases, such global constraints cannot easily be expressed in terms of individual roles or individual interaction protocols. Nevertheless, their identification is important for the correct development of the system and, therefore, they must be taken into account by the designer when actually defining the organisation of the system. To capture this type of information we use the concept of *organisational rules*.

The explicit identification of organisational rules is of particular importance in the context of open agent systems. With the arrival of new, previously unknown, and possibly self-interested agents, the overall organisation must somehow enforce its internal coherency despite the dynamic and untrustworthy environment. The identification of global organisational rules allows the system designer to explicitly define: *(i)* whether and when to allow newly arrived — possibly unknown — agents to enter the organisation, and, once accepted, what their position in the organisation should be; and *(ii)* which behaviours should be considered as an expression of self-interest, and which among them must be prevented by the organisation. In this context, organisational rules may also drive the designer towards the definition of the specific organisation that most eases the enforcement of the organisational rules and, for instance, can facilitate preventing undesirable behaviours of unknown and self-interested agents.

In the manufacturing pipeline example, all the different stages have to maintain the same speed of flow of items in the pipeline. This requirement can be more easily expressed in terms of a global organisational rule, rather than replicating it as a requirement for each and every role in the organisation. In the conference management system, there are a number of rules that drive the proper implementation of the organisation. As notable examples: an agent should be prevented from playing both the role of author and reviewer of the same paper and PC Members should not be in charge of collecting the reviews for their own papers. Neither of these constraints can easily be expressed in terms of properties/responsibilities associated to single roles and protocols. Instead, they represent global organisational rules.

3.2 Organisational Structures

A role model describes all the roles of an organisation and their positions in that organisation. Therefore, a role model also implicitly defines the *topology* of the interaction patterns and the *control regime* of the organisation's activities. That is, it defines the overall *organisational structure*. For example, a role model describing an organisation in terms of a "master role" and "slave roles" — where the former is in charge of assigning work to the latter and of load balancing their activities — implicitly defines an organisational structure based a hierarchical topology and on a load partitioning control regime. Other exemplar organisational structures include collectives of peers, multi-level and multi-divisional hierarchies [10], and they can all be modelled in term of a role model.

However, it is conceptually wrong to think of a role model as something that actually defines the organisational structure. Instead, in the design of a MAS, as well as in the design of any organisation, the role model should derive from the organisational structure that is explicitly chosen. Thus organisational structures should be viewed as first-class abstractions in the design of MASs.

The definition of the system's overall organisational structure can derive from the specifications collected during the analysis phase, as well as from other factors, related to efficiency, simplicity of application design, and organisational theory [10]. In any case, a methodology cannot start the analysis phase by attempting to define a complete role model that implicitly sets the organisational structure. Rather, the definition of the organisational structure is a design choice that should not be anticipated during the analysis phase. In fact:

- starting from the organisational structure — by pretending to know in advance what it should be or by committing a priori to a given organisational structure — may prevent subsequent optimization and change;
- although, in several cases, the organisational structure of a MAS is directly driven by its counterpart in the real-world system that the MAS is supposed to support, automate or monitor, this should not automatically imply that the organisation of the software system should mimic that of the real counterpart. Instead, the MAS may be better adopting a different organisational choice. There are several reasons why this could happen:
  - the real world organisation may not be well structured and the analysis phase could highlight several shortcomings;
  - the software, in itself, may change the way of working. Thus, the mere presence of the software introduces changes in the real organisation and these changes need to be reflected in the MAS;
  - the efficiency issues that may have driven a human organisation towards the adoption of a particular organisational structure may not necessarily apply to the agent organisation.
- the organisation, once defined, has to respect the organisational rules. Starting from a pre-defined organisational structure can make it difficult to have the organisational rules respected and enforced by the organisation. Instead, the choice of the organisation has to follow the identification of the organisational rules and have to be possibly driven by them.

In the manufacturing pipeline example, the most natural choice is to have an organisational structure in which all of the stages in the pipeline are peers, and in which they directly interact with their neighbours as needed. For instance, with reference to Figure 2, the stages Stage1, Stage2, Stage3, and Stage4 are controlled by agents R1, R2, R3 and R4, respectively, and each of these agents directly interacts with its neighbours. This closely mimics the structure of the real-world pipeline. However, this is not the only possible choice. Moreover, it may not necessarily be the best one. For instance, due to the real-time nature of the pipeline control problem, it may happen that

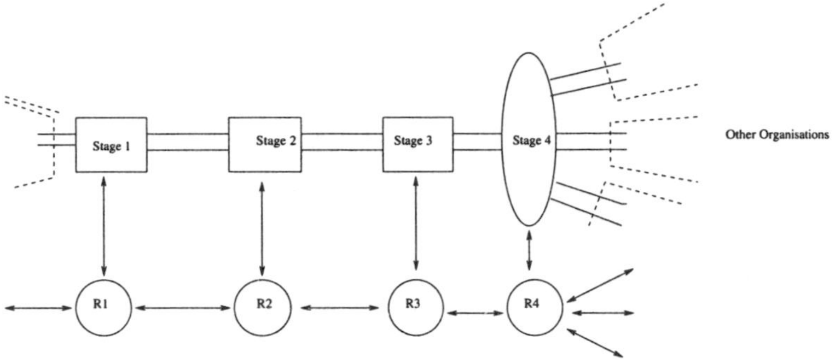

Fig. 2. A Manifacturing pipeline: pipeline organisation

a problem that requires global coordination between all the agents cannot be solved in due time, because of the high coordination costs associated with peer-based systems. In such cases, the designer can adopt a different organisational structure: for example, as sketched in Figure 3, it can introduce a global coordinator agent RC in charge of controlling and mediating the interactions for all the other agents, thus leading to a hierarchical organisation.

In the conference management example, the overall structure of the organisation can generally be derived from the structure the conference organisers have decided to adopt. However, it is often the case that the same conference varies its organisational structure from year to year, depending on both the size of the conference and the organisers' attitudes. For example, a small conference usually relies solely on the PC Members for the review process, and the PC Chair acts as a global coordinator, in a single-level hierarchy, for the work of the PC Member (see Figure 4). In contrast, a big conference usually has to involve external reviewers. This may require the PC Chair to partition the papers among the PC Members, and the PC Members to be in charge of seeking the appropriate number of reviews for their assigned partition. In other words, the organizational structure is a multi-level hierarchy based on a work partitioning control regime at the highest level (the one of the PC Chair) and on a global coordination control regime at the PC Member level (see Figure 5).

If the analysis phase commits the system to a specific organisational structure, the designer of the associated MAS will find it difficult to adapt the system, year after year, to the changing needs. For instance, it is very likely that a conference changes its dimensions in different editions and, consequently, its organizational structure. Thus, if the analysis phase simply describes the system's requirements, abstracting away from any specific organisational structure, the designer can reuse it to produce a new design according to the conference's new organisational structure.

Organisational Relationships The obvious means by which to specify an organisation is by the inter-agent relationships that exist within it. We emphasise that there is no universally accepted ontology of organisational relationships: different types of organisations make use of entirely different organisational concepts. For example, notions such as "command and control", which may be widely accepted in military organisa-

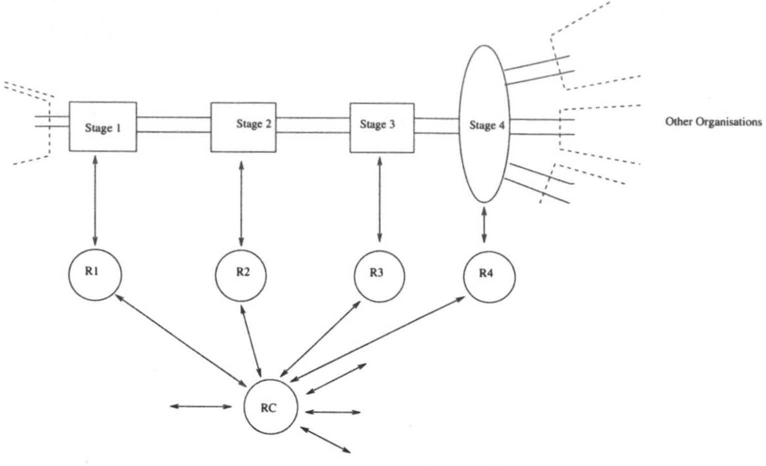

Fig. 3. A Manifacturing pipeline: hierarchical organisation

tions, tend not to be used in (most) academic organisations. Nevertheless, as a first pass towards more complete characterisations and formalisations, we can identify certain types of relationships that frequently occur in human and other organisations:

- *control* — which identify the authority structures within a system;
- *peer* — which identify agents of equal status;
- *benevolence* — which identify agents with shared interests;
- *dependency* — which identify the ways in which one agent may rely on another;
- *ownership* — which delimit organisational boundaries.

Note that these (binary) relationships exist between *roles* within a system — let $\mathcal{R}$ be the set of all such roles. In what follows, we give the intuition behind each type of relation. We then go on to give a precise formal definition of the semantics of these relationships.

Perhaps the paradigm example of an organisational relationship is that of one agent *controlling* another. Intuitively, if a role r controls another role r', then r' will perform any service demanded of it by r. If r controls r', then as far as r is concerned, the role r' is a resource to be used as desired. Any control relationship $\mathcal{C} \subseteq \mathcal{R} \times \mathcal{R}$, must satisfy the following properties:

- (Reflexive): $(r, r) \in \mathcal{C}$, for all $r \in \mathcal{R}$.
  Any role controls itself.
- (Transitive): if $(r, r') \in \mathcal{C}$ and $(r', r'') \in \mathcal{C}$ then $(r, r'') \in \mathcal{C}$.
  If Ann controls Bob, and Bob controls Charles, then Ann controls Charles.
- (Anti-symmetric): if $(r, r') \in \mathcal{C}$, then $(r', r) \notin \mathcal{C}$.
  If Ann controls Bob, then Bob does not control Ann.

Peer relationships capture the notion of "equal status" within organisations. For example, consider two professors in the same university, but in different departments.

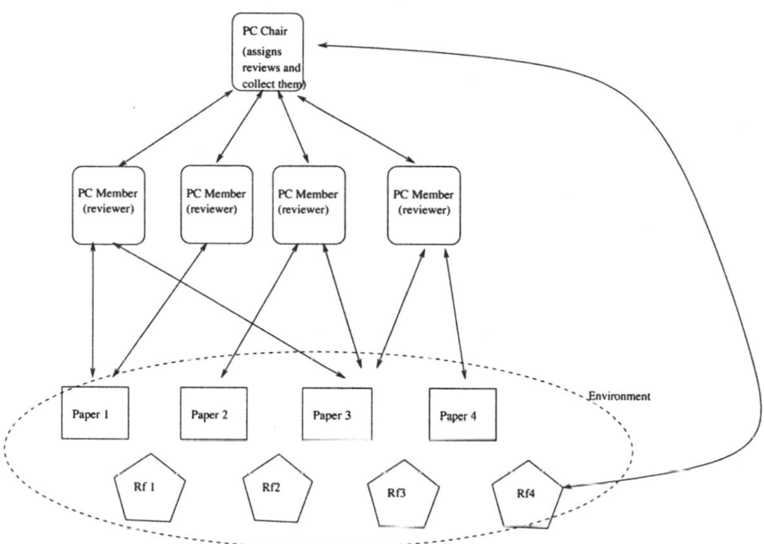

Fig. 4. Conference management: in a small conference, the PC Chair and assigns the reviews directly to PC Members and, possibly, to itself

These professors have equal status, even though they may not interact with one-another in the normal course of events. Status relationships have implications for how agents should interact with one-another. Any peer relationship $\mathcal{P} \subseteq \mathcal{R} \times \mathcal{R}$ must be an equivalence relation: it must be reflexive, symmetric, and transitive.

Benevolence is the classic assumption made in research on distributed problem solving (DPS) [8]. Put simply, an agent i is said to be benevolent to another agent j if i will offer its services to j whenever it is able to do so. Note that this is not the same as control. If Ann is benevolent to Bob, then Ann is inclined to help Bob wherever possible, *except* where helping Bob would prevent one of her own goals being satisfied. Formally, a benevolence relation $\mathcal{B} \subseteq \mathcal{R} \times \mathcal{R}$ must be reflexive and symmetric. Note that a benevolence relation is not (necessarily) transitive. Thus it is entirely possible for r to be benevolent to r', and for r' to be benevolent to r'', without r being benevolent to r''. To see why this is the case, consider for example benevolence relations between countries: it is entirely possible for the USA to be benevolent to (for example) Switzerland, and for Switzerland to be benevolent to Ruritania, without the USA being benevolent to Ruritania. (Situations like this are common in international relations!)

Dependency Relationships exist between agents primarily because of resource restrictions. For example, Ann controls some resource, (for example a piece of information), and Bob requires this information to satisfy one of his goals, then Bob is dependent on Ann. There are in fact many sub-classes of dependence relation that may exist between agents (see, e.g., [27]). For example, Ann and Bob may be mutually dependent on one-another; Bob may be dependent on Ann but Ann does not know it, or he may be dependent on Ann but he does not know it, and so on. Dependency relations are reflexive and transitive, but need not be symmetric.

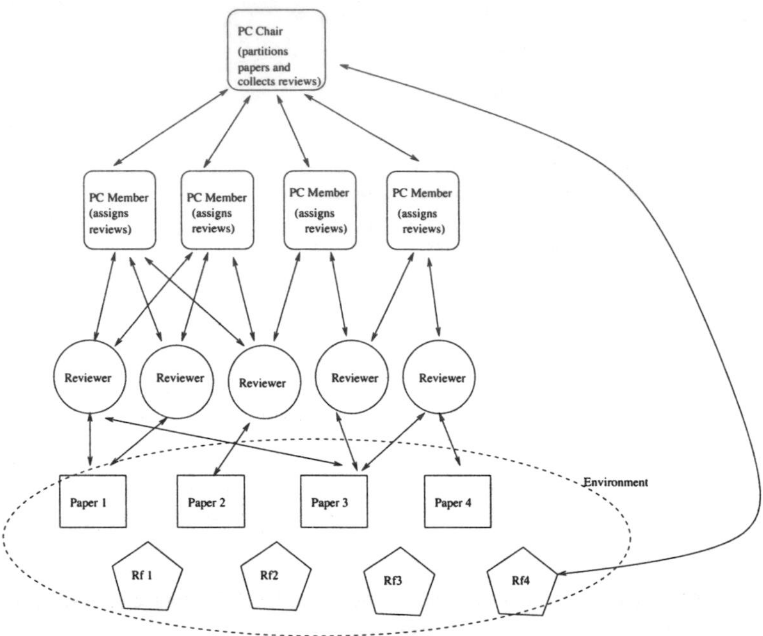

Fig. 5. Conference management: in a big conference, the PC Chair partitions the papers among the PC Members that, in their turns, are in charge of finding the appropriate referees for their assigned papers and of collecting the reviews

Finally, turning to ownership relations, the idea is to delimit boundaries of common ownership — thus all the agents belonging to organisation o are grouped together, as are all the agents belonging to o', and so on. Every agent is required to be the member of at least one ownership group, which may of course be a singleton set. Formally, any ownership relation $\mathcal{O} \subseteq \mathcal{R} \times \mathcal{R}$ must be an equivalence relation.

3.3 Organisational Patterns

There are numerous potential organisational structures, both in terms of topology of the interactions and control regimes [10]. However, we believe that a (comparatively) small subset of these structures are likely to be used most of the time. Thus, only rarely will peculiar structures be adopted (typically when the organisation has a very specific and unusual set of requirements).

Any methodology that encourages re-use of pre-defined components and architectures will ease and speed-up the work of both designers and developers. Object-oriented technology has recognised this need and increased the potential for re-use via design-patterns [11]. In this case, the most widely-used patterns of composition and interaction of object-oriented systems have been catalogued, and precisely described in terms of extent of applicability, sample implementation, and use cases. A software designer can then rely on these catalogues, and build applications by composing and re-using not only single objects, but whole pieces of the software architecture.

In the area of agent-based systems, we envisage something similar with respect to the most widely used organisational structures. Thus with the availability of catalogues of *organisational patterns*, designers can recognise in their MASs the presence of known patterns, and re-use definitions from the catalogue. In addition, designers can also be guided by the catalogue in the choice of the most appropriate organisational patterns for their MAS. Of course, for patterns to be properly exploited, the organisational structure must have been explicitly identified in the design phase.

In the pipeline example, the pipeline organisation between agents expresses an organisational pattern that is likely to re-appear in many applications (and which is already widely exploited as an architectural patterns in traditional software systems). The same can also be said of the hierarchical pipeline structure. In both cases, if a catalogue of patterns was available, the designer could rely on it to help define the system structure.

In the conference management example, the various organisational structures that conferences of different sizes tend to adopt are all fairly typical: from single hierarchies, to multi-level and divisional ones. Therefore, also in this case, it is expected that a methodology that makes explicit use of organisational patterns would ease the application design.

It is worth mentioning that several attempts to analyse and catalogue organisational agent patterns currently exist [28, 16, 17]. However, in most cases, this work abstracts away from any specific methodology for MAS analysis and design which should encourage and facilitate the re-use of these patterns. This, in turn, makes re-use more difficult.

4 Towards an Organisation-Oriented Methodology

The exploitation of the organisational abstractions we have introduced naturally promotes an organisation-oriented methodology for the analysis and design of MASs.

The analysis phase is tasked with collecting all the specifications from which the design of the computational organisation can start. This includes the identification of:

- the overall goals of the organisation and its expected global behaviour;
- the basic skills required by the organisation and the basic interactions required for the exploitation of these skills (that is, a preliminary role model);
- the rules that the organisation should respect and/or enforce in its global behaviour.

The output of the analysis phase should therefore be a triple: $\langle PR, PP, OL \rangle$, where *PR* are the preliminary roles of the system (derived from the identification of the basic skills), *PP* are the preliminary protocols (which have already been discovered to be necessary for the preliminary roles), and *OL* are the organisational rules. It is worth noting that the analysis phase should not committ to any specific organisational structure. Instead, its output should be (and be expressed in terms) independent of any specific organisational structure.

The design phase builds on the output of the analysis phase and produces a complete specification of the MAS. To this end, design can be decomposed into the following phases:

- definition of the organisational structure; by choosing the topology and the control regime. This involves considering: *(i)* the overall organisational efficiency, *(ii)* the need to respect and enforce the organisational rules, and *(iii)* the corresponding (if any) real-world organisation;
- completion of the preliminary role model; based upon the adopted organisational structure, and by keeping the organisational-independent aspects (detected from the analysis phase) and the organisational-dependent ones (deriving from the adoption of a specific organisational structure and from the insertion of roles and protocols in it) as separate as possible;
- exploitation of well-known organisational patterns on the basis of the system's identified organisational structure.

As in the Gaia methodology, we view the output of the design phase as a specification that can be picked up by using a traditional method (such as object orientation or component-ware) or that could be implemented using an appropriate agent-programming framework should one be available.

5 Related Work

Traditional analysis and design methodologies, such as object-oriented ones [2], are poorly suited to MASs because of the fundamental mismatch between the abstractions they provide [32]. Consequently, we believe that those efforts that attempt to simply extend object-oriented methodologies to MAS [18, 16] will inevitably fall short. Moreover, traditional compositional methods for object-oriented software architectures [24, 3] also have limited applicability in the definition of organisations for MASs. On the one hand, the defined interaction models are too static when compared to the dynamic interaction model defined by agents. On the other hand, the functionality-oriented modelling of the interactions between the system components clashes with the role-oriented perspective of MASs.

A number of agent-specific modelling techniques and development methodologies have been proposed in recent years (see [14] for a survey), several of which attempt to exploit the idea of a MAS as a computational organisation. In most of the cases, organisation-oriented systems and modelling techniques define an organisation as a collection of roles (i.e., a role model), without introducing any higher-level organisational abstractions. This is precisely what happens, for example, in the ALAADDIN system [9] where "the group structure" is simply the collection of roles that compose the organisation. Analogously, in the ToolKit approach [7], an organisation is defined simply by the set of roles that compose it and by the interaction protocols that have to occur between roles. Neither of these approaches incorporate the notions of organisational rules or organisational structures and, for the reasons we have outlined, will be limited in the range of agent systems they can deal with. In addition, these proposals do not attempt to define a complete and clear methodology for the development of agent system organisations.

Gaia starts from the organisational metaphor and defines a complete methodology [32] for the development of multi-agent systems. It also provides a clean separation between the analysis and design phases. However, it suffers from several limitations that are caused by the incompleteness of its organisational abstractions. The objective of Gaia's analysis phase is to define a fully elaborated role model, derived from the system specification, together with an accurate description of the protocols in which the roles will be involved. This implicitly assumes that the overall organisational structure is known a priori. However, as already stated, this is not always the case. In addition, by focusing exclusively on the role model, the analysis phase fails to identify any global organisational rules (making Gaia unsuitable for modeling open systems and for controling the behaviour of self-interested agents).

Similar shortcomings also effect most of the recently proposed organisation-oriented methodologies. For example, the MASE (Multi-Agent Systems Engineering) methodology [30] provides clean guidelines for developing multi-agent systems, based on a well-defined six-step process. This process drives developers from analysis to implementation. However, once again, the design process fails to identify any organisational abstraction other than the role model.

From a different perspective, some work in the area of coordination models and languages [12, 5] does explicitly address the problem of defining global rules ("coordination laws") to specify the behaviour and the interaction of agent ensembles. In this work, all interactions have to occur via specific "coordination media", whose internal behaviour can be programmed so as to implement specific policies for governing agent interactions. However, only recently have coordination models been recognised as useful abstractions upon which to define methodologies for the analysis and design of those systems. To achieve this, the coordination media are exploited as both the conceptual and physical repository of the organisational rules [6, 26, 25]. A somewhat similar approach has driven the implementation of the Fishmarket system for agent-mediated auctions [23]. In Fishmarket, the need to force agents to act in accordance with the "social conventions" that rule the organisation of an auction is recognised. To enact social conventions, the system dynamically associates a "controller agent" with each agent in the auction. Controller agents act as a coordination media, in charge of mediating all the interactions and of making agents respect the auction's conventions.

6 Conclusions and Future Work

This paper has discussed a number of issues related to the analysis and design of multi-agent systems. Specifically, we have considered the view of developing multi-agent systems as a process of constructing computational organisations. To date, the organisational concepts of agent roles and role models have become an important research area in the field of agent-based systems. However in this paper we have introduced three further organisational abstractions: organisational rules, organisational structures, and organisational patterns. These concepts, although neglected by the current methodologies for agent-oriented software engineering, are nevertheless of fundamental importance in multi-agent systems, and we therefore believe they should play a central role in any methodology. Having introduced and motivated these organisational abstractions, we sketched some general guidelines for a new methodology for the analysis and design of multi-agent systems that is centered around organisational abstractions.

Further work is needed to detail the proposed methodology, by:

- fully formalising the concepts of organisation rules and organisational structures. This can possibly be achieved by refining the formalism that we have already introduced in Subsection 3.2 with respect to the organizational structures.
- providing suitable notations for expressing the expected outputs of the analysis and design phases. We expect standard notations, such as UML, to be rapidly adapted to the needs of agent-based software engineering [1], as well as new agent-specific methodologies to emerge;
- identifying guidelines that assist the designer in the identification of suitable organisational structures for the system. Here analytical methods, experimental results, and case study experiences are likely to be helpful in supporting the choice.

For all of the above topics, we expect significant cross-fertilisation of models, formalisms and experiences from a number of different research areas. Among others, the research area of requirements engineering [22] can provide useful guidelines towards the identification and the modelling of organisational rules; the research results of both coordination, organizational and management sciences [20, 29, 21], which have widely studied the structures of human organisations and their most common patterns, are also expected to play a significant role.

References

1. B. Bauer, J. P. Muller, and J. Odell. Agent uml: A formalism for specifying multiagent software systems, 2000. In this volume.
2. G. Booch. *Object-oriented Analysis and Design (second edition)*. Addison Wesley, Reading (MA), 1994.
3. F.M.T. Brazier, B.M. Dunin-Keplicz, N.R. Jennings, and J. Treur. Desire: Modelling multi-agent systems in a compositional formal framework. *Journal of Cooperative Information Systems*, 6(1):67–94, 1997.
4. S. Bussmann. Agent-oriented programming of manifacturing control tasks. In *Proceeding of the 3rd International Conference on Multi-Agent Systems (ICMAS 98)*, pages 57–63. IEEE CS Press, June 1998.
5. P. Ciancarini. Coordination models and languages as software integrators. *ACM Computing Surveys*, 28(2), June 1996.
6. P. Ciancarini, A. Omicini, and F. Zambonelli. Multiagent systems engineering: the coordination viewpoint. In *Intelligents Agents VI (ATAL99)*, volume 1767 of *LNAI*, pages 250–259. Springer-Verlag, 2000.
7. Y. Demazeau and A. C. Rocha Costa. Populations and organizations in open multi-agent systems. In *1st National Symposium on Parallel and Distributed AI (PDAI'96)*. 1996.
8. E. H. Durfee. *Coordination of Distributed Problem Solvers*. Kluwer, 1988.
9. J. Ferber and O. Gutknecht. A meta-model for the analysis and design of organizations in multi-agent systems. In *Proceeding of the 3rd International Conference on Multi-Agent Systems (ICMAS 98)*. IEEE CS Press, June 1998.
10. M. S. Fox. An organizational view of distributed systems. *IEEE Transactions on Systems, Man, and Cybernetics*, 11(1):70–80, January 1981.
11. E. Gamma, R. Helm, R. Johnson, and J. Vlissides. *Design Patterns*. Addison Wesley, Reading (MA), 1995.

12. D. Gelernter and N. Carriero. Coordination languages and their significance. *Communications of the ACM*, 35(2):97–107, February 1992.
13. M. H. Huhns. Interaction-oriented programming, 2000. In this volume.
14. C. Iglesias, M. Garijo, and J. Gonzales. A survey of agent-oriented methodologies. In A. S. Rao J.P. Muller, M. P. Singh, editor, *Intelligents Agents IV (ATAL98)*, LNAI. Springer-Verlag, 1999.
15. N. R. Jennings. Agent-based computing: Promises and perils. In *International Joint Conference on Artificial Intelligence (IJCAI 99)*, pages 1429–1436, 1999.
16. E. A. Kendall. Role modelling for agent system analysis, design, and implementation. In *1st International Symposium on Agent Systems and Applications*. IEEE CS Press, October 1999.
17. E. A. Kendall. Agent software engineering with role modelling, 2000. In this volume.
18. D. Kinny and M. Georgeff. A methodology and modelling technique for systems of bdi agents. In *Workshop on Modelling Autonomous Agents in a Multi-Agent World, LNAI 1038*, pages 56–71. Springer-Verlag, 1996.
19. J. Lind. Issues in agent-oriented software engineering, 2000. In this volume.
20. T. W. Malone and K. Crowston. The interdisciplinary study of coordination. *ACM Computing Surveys*, 26(1):87–119, March 1994.
21. H. Mintzberg. *The Structuring of Organizations: A Synthesis of the Research*. Prentice Hall, Englewood Cliffs, N.J., 1979.
22. J. Mylopoulos, L. Chung, and B. Nixon. Representing and using nonfunctional requirements: A process-oriented approach. *IEEE Transactions on Software Engineering*, 18(6):483–497, June 1992.
23. P. Noriega. *Agent-mediated Auctions: The Fishmarket Metaphor*. Ph.D Thesis, Universitat Autonoma de Barcelona, Barcelona (E), 1997.
24. J. Odell, H. Van Dyke Parunak, and C. Bock. Representing agent interaction protocols in uml. In *OMG Document ad/99-12-01*. Intellicorp Inc., December 1999.
25. A. Omicini. Soda: Societies and infrastructures in the analysis and design of agent-based systems, 2000. In this volume.
26. A. Omicini and F. Zambonelli. Coordination for Internet application development. *Journal of Autonomous Agents and Multi-Agent Systems*, 2(3):251–269, 1999.
27. J. S. Sichman, R. Conte, C. Castelfranchi, and Y. Demazeau. A social reasoning mechanism based on dependence networks. In *Proceedings of ECAI94*, pages 188–192, Amsterdam, 1994.
28. Y. Tahara, A. Ohsuga, and S. Honiden. Agent system development based on agent patterns. In *International Conference on Software Engineering*, pages 356–367. ACM, 1999.
29. James D. Thompson. *Organizations in Action*. McGraw-Hill, New York, 1967.
30. M. Wood and S. A. DeLoach. An overview of the multiagent systems engineering methodology, 2000. In this volume.
31. M. Wooldridge and N. R. Jennings. Intelligent agents: Theory and practice. *The Knowledge Engineering Review*, 10(2):115–152, 1995.
32. M. Wooldridge, N. R. Jennings, and D. Kinny. The Gaia methodology for agent-oriented analysis and design. *Journal of Autonomous Agents and Multi-Agent Systems*, 3(3):285–312, 2000.
33. F. Zambonelli, N. Jennings, A. Omicini, and M. Wooldridge. Agent-oriented software engineering for internet applications. In A. Omicini, F. Zambonelli, M. Klusch, and R. Tolksdorf, editors, *Coordination of Internet Agents: Models, Technologies and Applications*. Springer-Verlag, 2000.

Reuse and Abstraction in Verification: Agents Acting in Dynamic Environments

Catholijn M. Jonker* Jan Treur* Wieke de Vries‡

* Department of Artificial Intelligence, Vrije Universiteit Amsterdam, De Boelelaan1081a, 1081 HV Amsterdam, The Netherlands
{jonker, treur}@cs.vu.nl

‡ Institute of Information and Computing Sciences, Universiteit Utrecht, PO Box 80.089, 3508 TB Utrecht, The Netherlands
wieke@cs.uu.nl

Abstract. To make verification a manageable part of the system development process, comprehensibility and reusability of properties and proofs is essential. The work reported in this paper contributes formally founded methods that support proof structuring and reuse. Often occurring patterns in agent behaviour can be exploited to establish a library containing properties and proofs. This is illustrated here by verifying the class of single agents acting in dynamic environments. First, a notion of abstraction for properties and proofs is introduced that provides means to structure and clarify verification. Also, the paper contributes to establishing the library by proposing a reusable system of generic co-ordination properties for applications of agents acting in dynamic environments.

1 Introduction

Verification is an important part of agent-oriented software engineering, because it is the only way to guarantee that demands made on aspects of the system behaviour are satisfied. The high degree of complexity of agent system behaviour is as much the reason as the problem here: by simply checking the code of the agent system or by testing, proper behaviour can never be sufficiently established. Proper functioning is often crucial, because agent systems are increasingly employed in circumstances where mistakes have important consequences, for example in electronic commerce. But verification of agent systems is generally not an easy task. As agents may operate in a world that is constantly changing, and agent systems can consist of a number of interacting but independent agents, expressing behavioural requirements may lead to complex formulae. Therefore verification of agent systems is hardly ever done in practice.

So, means are needed to make verification of agent systems manageable. Developers of agent systems should be enabled to verify the system they are building, assisted by tools, even if they are not specialists in formal theory. Properties and proofs have to be intuitively clear to the verifier and even, at least to some degree, to the stakeholder(s) of the system, as verification results are part of the design rationale of the system. Also, time complexity of the verification process has to be controlled.

This paper discusses some principles that contribute to the support of verification of agent systems. These principles can be used for all agent systems, but here, they are applied in the context of single agents that performs actions in dynamic environments.

In [6] a compositional verification method was introduced. Verifying in a compositional manner supports reuse of verification results and limits the complexity of the process, by making proofs more local. In [1] it was shown how this method can be applied to prove properties of a system of negotiating agents.

However, this does not solve all problems. To manage the complexity of the proofs, and to make their structure more transparent, additional structuring means and reuse facilities are necessary, extending the method of compositional verification. This paper contributes two manners to support proof structuring and reuse.

On the one hand a *notion of abstraction* is introduced that facilitates structuring of properties and proofs. To this end, the language to describe properties of agent systems is extended with new, more abstract, constructs. Parts of formulas can be given an intuitively enlightening name. This leads to a more informal look and feel for properties and proofs, without losing any formal rigour. The abstract notions form a higher-level language to describe system behaviour. The terminology of this language abstracts away from details of the system design, and is closer to the way human verifiers conceptualise agent system behaviour. There are a number of benefits:

- Properties and proofs are more readable and easier to understand.
- Coming up with properties and proofs becomes easier, as the words chosen for the abstracted formulas guide and focus the cognitive verification process of the verification engineer, providing clean-cut agent concepts.
- Verification becomes explainable, as part of the design rationale documentation of a system.

On the other hand, common characteristics of agent systems can be exploited to support reuse. With the paradigm of agents, a range of agent concepts is associated. For example, most agents receive observations and communicated information from their environment and perform actions to manipulate their environment. For this to yield desired results, proper co-ordination with the environment is essential. Properties regarding this apply to many agent systems and thus are highly reusable. Support of reuse requires that a library of predefined templates of properties and proofs is available. By identifying generic elements in the structure of proofs and properties, *reusable systems of properties and proofs* can be constructed. To illustrate this, this paper proposes a system of co-ordination property properties for applications of agents acting in dynamic environments. The properties and proofs of this system are an example of the contents of the verification library. Some advantages of reuse are:

- Verification becomes faster. Often, the verification engineer only has to look up suitable properties and proofs from the verification library and customise these by instantiation.

- Verification becomes easier. The contents of the library are usually phrased using abstraction, so properties and proofs are more intuitively clear, making them more easy to use.

In the following section, the generic system consisting of an agent acting in a dynamic environment is sketched. For this application, a system of co-ordination properties is given in Section 4. But first, Section 3 presents the two languages to describe system behaviour, the detailed language and the abstract language, and the connection between them. In Section 5, the abstraction mechanism is applied; abstract predicates are introduced for parts of properties, yielding an abstract language. In Section 6, proofs are briefly discussed. Finally, Section 7 concludes.

2 The Domain of Agents Acting in a Dynamic Environment

In this section the characteristics of the application class of an agent in interaction with a dynamic environment are briefly discussed. A reusable system of properties for this class will be presented later on, describing correct co-ordination of the agent with its environment.

Agents that can perceive and act in a dynamic environment are quite common. An example is an agent for process control (e.g. in a chemical factory). For this class of single agent systems, an important property is *successfulness of actions*. This means that all actions the agent initiates in its environment yield their expected effects. Because this property is to be proven for a class of systems, it is needed to abstract from domain-dependent details of systems and give a generic architecture that defines the class.

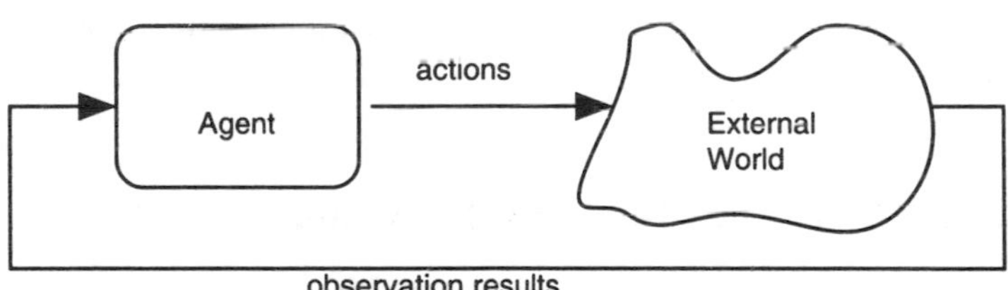

Fig. 1. Agent and external world in interaction

The specification of a generic architecture for a single agent in a dynamic world depicted in Figure 1 consists of two components in interaction: an agent (Ag) and the external world (EW). Only a few aspects of the functioning of the system are specified by the architecture. The agent generates actions that are transferred from its output interface to the external world, and the external world generates observation results that are transferred to the input interface of the agent. Based on the observation results the agent is to decide which actions are to be performed.

The system employs a formal language internally. This language is an order-sorted predicate logic. The *input interface* of the agent is defined by the formal ontology observation results containing a binary relation observation_result. Formulae that can be expressed using the information type observation results are, for example, observation_result(at_position(self, p0), pos), or observation_result(at_position(self, p1), neg).

The *output interface* of the agent is defined by the formal ontology actions to be performed based on the sort ACTION and the unary relation to_be_performed. For example the statement to_be_performed(goto(p)) can be expressed in this ontology. For the external world the input and output interfaces are the opposite of the agent's interfaces.

Realistic characteristics of the agent systems in the class defined above are:

- perceptions take time
- the generation of actions takes time
- execution of actions in the world takes time
- unexpected events can occur in the environment

Proving successfulness of actions under these circumstances is intricate because an action can only succeed when its execution is not disturbed too much. If two executions of actions overlap or evens happen during executions, actions could fail. Also, while an agent is observing and reasoning, the situation in the world might change. A system of co-ordination properties will be proposed that takes all these influences into account.

In the literature, varying attitudes towards these disturbances can be found. In one part of the literature (e.g., standard situation calculus, as described in [9; 11]), these disturbances are excluded in a global manner, e.g., action generation and execution have no duration at all and no events occur at all. The problem with these global assumptions is that they violate the characteristics of most of the application domains. Some literature takes into account duration of action execution (e.g., [13]). Literature that also takes into account the reasoning and decision processes in action generation is very rare. Another lack in the literature is that most authors don't try to verify implemented systems; they only state theories regarding actions, without relating them to practical system engineering.

3 Temporal Models and Temporal Languages

For phrasing properties, a language is needed. Behaviour is described by properties of the execution traces of the system. In this section, the language used for this is introduced. Also, this section introduces the language abstraction formalism.

3.1 Basic Concepts

By adding a formalisation of time to the language internally used in the generic system, a formal language is obtained to formulate behavioural properties. This language is still semantical in nature; properties of traces are described in a direct manner. A formal logic could be added, but this is not essential for our purposes.

The state language SL(D) of a system component D is the (order-sorted) predicate logic language based on the interface ontologies of D. The formulae of this language are called *state formulae*. An *information state* M of a component D is an assignment of truth-values {true, false, unknown} to the set of ground atoms in SL(D). The set of all possible information states of D is denoted by IS(D).

The time frames are assumed *linear with initial time point* 0. Time frames must be discrete; using dense time frames is also possible, as long as some constraints are obeyed. A *trace* $\mathcal{M}$ of a component D over a time frame T is a sequence of information states $(M^t)_{t \in T}$ in IS(D). Given a trace $\mathcal{M}$ of component D, the information state of the input interface of component C at time point t is denoted by state($\mathcal{M}$, t, input(C)), where C is either D or a component within D. Analogously, state($\mathcal{M}$, t, output(C)) denotes the information state of the output interface of component C at time point t.

These information states can be related to formulae via the satisfaction relation $\models$. If φ is a state formula expressed in the input ontology for component C, then

$$\text{state}(\mathcal{M}, t, \text{input}(C)) \models \varphi$$

denotes that φ is true in this state at time point $t \in T$

These statements can be compared to *holds*-statements in situation calculus [9]. A difference, however, apart from notational differences, is that we refer to a trace and time point, and that we explicitly focus on part of the system. Based on these statements, which only use predicate symbol $\models$, behavioural properties can be formulated in a formal manner in a sorted predicate logic with sorts T for time points, Traces(C) for traces of component C and F for state formulae. The usual logical connectives such as $\neg, \wedge, \Rightarrow, \forall, \exists$ are employed to construct formulae, as well as < and = (to compare moments in time). The language defined in this manner is denoted by TL(D) (Temporal Language of D). An example of a formula of TL(S), where S refers to the whole system, is:

$$\begin{aligned} &\forall \mathcal{M} \in \text{Traces}(S): \\ &\qquad \forall\ t1 : \text{state}(\mathcal{M}, t1, \text{output}(Ag)) \models \text{to\_be\_performed}(A) \quad \Rightarrow \\ &\qquad \exists\ t2 > t1 : \text{state}(\mathcal{M}, t2, \text{output}(Ag)) \models \text{to\_be\_performed}(B) \end{aligned}$$

This expresses that every decision of Ag to do action A is always followed by a later decision to do B.

The languages TL(D) are built around constructs that enable the verifier to express properties in a detailed manner, staying in direct relation to the semantics of the design specification of the system. For example, the state formulae are directly related to information states of system components. But the detailed nature of the language also has disadvantages; properties tend to get long and complex. The formalism of abstraction, described in Section 3.2, alleviates this considerably.

3.2 The Language Abstraction Formalism

Experience in nontrivial verification examples has taught us that the temporal expressions needed in proofs can become quite complex and unreadable. Also, details of the formalisation blur the generic agent concepts in properties. As a remedy, new language elements are added as abbreviations of complex temporal formulae. These new language elements are defined within a language AL(D) (meaning Abstract Language of component D). As a simple example, for the property that there is action execution starting in the world at t a new predicate `ActionExStarting` can be introduced. Then the property can be expressed in the abstracted language:

`ActionExStarting`(A, t, EW, $\mathcal{M}$)

which is interpreted as:

state($\mathcal{M}$, t, input(EW)) $\models$ to_be_performed(A)

Semantics of these new language elements is defined as the semantics of the detailed formulae they abstract from. In logic the notion of *interpretation mapping* has been introduced to describe the interpretation of one logical language in another logical language, for example geometry in algebra (cf. Chapter 5 in [5]). The languages AL(D) and TL(D) can be related to each other by a fixed interpretation mapping from the formulae in AL(D) onto formulae in TL(D).

The language AL(D) abstracts from details of the system design and enables the verifier to concentrate on higher level (agent) concepts. Proofs can be expressed either at the detailed or at the abstract level, and the results can be translated to the other level. Because formulae in the abstract level logic can be kept much simpler than the detailed level logic, the proof relations expressed on that level are much more transparent.

4 Properties for Proving Successfulness of Actions

In Section 4.1, an informal introduction to the system of co-ordination properties is given. The system itself appears in Section 4.2.

4.1 Approaching the Problem of Co-ordination of Actions

For the application class described in Section 2, the aim is to prove that under the specified assumptions all actions executed in the agent system are successful, that is, yield all of their effects. To arrive at a reusable and intuitively pleasing proof, it was necessary and illuminating to separate the different aspects into a number of properties. These will constitute the *system of co-ordination properties*. In this section, some important aspects are described informally.

An action succeeds when its execution renders the appropriate effects. This effect has to happen during the execution of the action to be recognisable as an effect of that particular action. We assume there is some means to detect the end of an action execution. Just like the start of an execution of A is indicated by a to_be_performed(A)-atom, the end is indicated by an ended(A)-atom.

Action executions can fail because of three reasons. The first reason is overlapping of action executions. So, to guarantee success, overlapping should not happen. Property COORD0 formalises this. This property is proved from other properties of the agent and the world using induction, but the proof is left out. Figure 2 illustrates COORD0.

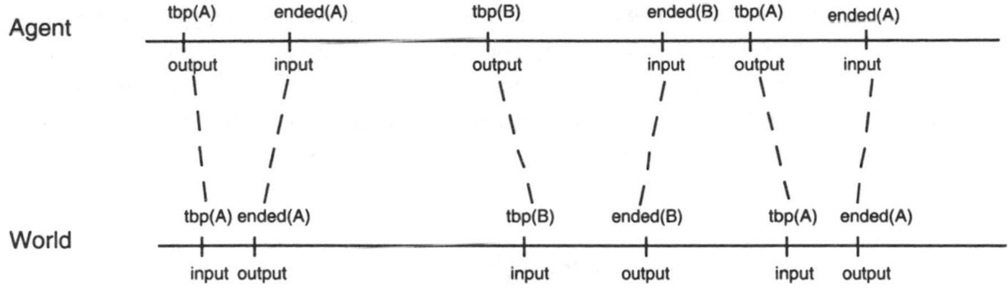

Fig. 2. No overlapping of executions

Note that COORD0 also enables identification of action execution.

But action executions can also fail due to events. In our view, events are changes to the world state that aren't controlled by the agent. These can be due to the dynamics of the world itself (natural events). But changes due to the aftermath of a failed action also are events. So, each change to the world state either is the effect of a successful action or it is an event. In some other approaches, events designate all causes of state changes, including agent-initiated actions. This might be confusing, but is just a matter of definitions.

Property COORD3 is a property of the world, stating that no events happen during action execution. This is quite a strong demand, as not every event might interfere with the action. The demand can be relieved by only forbidding interfering events, which is a minor extension.

A third reason for action failure is that the world can change prior to an action execution starting in the world. Between the moment the world situation arises that gives the agent reason to decide to do an action and the start of the execution of this action, events or other action effects could occur, disrupting the applicability of the action. Property COORD5 states that all actions are still applicable the moment their execution starts in the world.

In the following, it is shown that under the assumptions associated with the class of systems considered here, absence of these three causes for failure is sufficient to prove successfulness of actions.

4.2 The System of Co-ordination Properties

One of the main objectives of this paper is to establish a set of properties that enable the verifier to prove that all actions executed will succeed. The system of co-ordination properties presented here provides a clear separation of all aspects involved. The properties are phrased in the abstract languages AL, although the interpretation of this language in the detailed language is presented later, to show the intuitive power of the abstract languages.

The system is structured in the following way: COORD1 is the target property, formalising action successfulness, COORD0 is the foundational property, parts of which are frequently used as condition in other co-ordination properties, COORD2, -3, -4 and -5 are used to prove COORD1.

COORD0 is the foundation of the system of co-ordination properties. It enables the verifier to identify action executions, by formalising Figure 2. The property states that action executions don't overlap, not in the world and neither in the agent. The agent- and the world-part will be part of the conditions of many properties to come, to enable identification of action executions. This is the abstract formula:

COORD0:
∀ $\mathcal{M}$ ∈ Traces(S)
NoOverlappingInWorld($\mathcal{M}$) ∧
NoOverlappingInAgent($\mathcal{M}$)

COORD1 formalises action successfulness, stating that all action executions of the system are applicable and yield all expected effects. Informally:

> "When an action execution in the world begins at t1 and ends at t2,
> then
> the action is applicable at t1 in the world
> and
> all expected effects of the action in that world situation will be realised during the execution."

This is the abstract formalisation:

COORD1:
∀ $\mathcal{M}$ ∈ Traces(S) ∀ A ∈ ACTION ∀ t1 ∀ t2 > t1 :
(ActionEx(A, t1, t2, EW, $\mathcal{M}$) ⇒
Appl(A, t1, $\mathcal{M}$) ∧
ExpEffectsHappen(A, t1, t2, EW, $\mathcal{M}$))

It is essential that all action executions are applicable at the moment they start in the world. When actions are applicable at the moment the execution starts, the expected effects of the action are the desired effects. When an action is not applicable, there might be no effects at all, or unwanted ones.

COORD2 is an auxiliary property stating that all action executions started at times that the action is applicable will be successful. Informally:

> "When an action execution in the world begins at t1 and ends at t2,
> and
> when the action is applicable at t1 in the world
> then
> all expected effects of the action in that world situation will be realised during the execution."

And this is its abstract formalisation:

COORD2:
∀ $\mathcal{M}$ ∈ Traces(S) ∀ A ∈ ACTION ∀ t1 ∀ t2 > t1 :
ActionEx(A, t1, t2, EW, $\mathcal{M}$) ∧
Appl(A, t1, $\mathcal{M}$) ⇒
ExpEffectsHappen(A, t1, t2, EW, $\mathcal{M}$)

COORD3 is a demand on the world that states that there are no events happening during action executions. Informally:

> "If there is an action execution in the world
> and
> action executions do not overlap
> then
> no events happen during the execution."

And this is the formalisation in the abstract language:

COORD3:
$\forall \mathcal{M} \in$ Traces(EW) $\forall$ A $\in$ ACTION $\forall$ t1 $\forall$ t2 > t1 :
  ActionEx(A, t1, t2, EW, $\mathcal{M}$) $\wedge$
  NoOverlappingInWorld($\mathcal{M}$) $\Rightarrow$
  NoEventsDuring([t1, t2], EW, $\mathcal{M}$)

COORD4 is a demand on the world that says that an action execution in the world will be successful when the action is applicable and there are no disturbances caused by overlapping executions or events. These are all conditions for action success, as long as the world satisfies COORD4. Informally:

> "If an action execution in the world begins at t1 and ends at t2
> and
> action executions do not overlap
> and
> no events happen during the execution
> and
> the action is applicable at t1
> then
> all effects of the action will be realised during the execution."

This is the formalisation:

COORD4:
$\forall \mathcal{M} \in$ Traces(EW) $\forall$ A $\in$ ACTION $\forall$ t1 $\forall$ t2 > t1 :
  ActionEx(A, t1, t2, EW, $\mathcal{M}$) $\wedge$
  NoOverlappingInWorld($\mathcal{M}$) $\wedge$
  NoEventsDuring([t1, t2], EW, $\mathcal{M}$) $\wedge$
  Appl(A, t1, $\mathcal{M}$) $\Rightarrow$
  ExpEffectsHappen(A, t1, t2, EW, $\mathcal{M}$)

COORD5 simply states that an action is applicable at the moment its execution starts. This is a necessary condition for success of this action. This is its formalisation:

COORD5:
$\forall \mathcal{M} \in$ Traces(S) $\forall$ A $\in$ ACTION $\forall$ t1 $\forall$ t2 > t1 :
  ActionEx(A, t1, t2, EW, $\mathcal{M}$) $\Rightarrow$
  Appl(A, t1, $\mathcal{M}$)

Because the abstraction formalism is exploited, these properties are relatively easy to read and understand, even without knowing the formal meaning of abstract terms, which is provided in the next section. Technical details are hidden beneath intuitively clear notions. The clarity and brevity of the formulas make the verification process more manageable, as the abstract concepts yield a natural view of the system's behaviour and prevent getting lost in symbolic clutter while constructing proofs.

The system of co-ordination properties is applicable for many systems with a single agent that performs actions in a changing world. By simple instantiation of the system specific details, such as the set of actions, the conditions of applicability and the effects of these actions, the system can be customised.

5 Abstract Formulations

In this section, a number of predicates of the abstract language are defined. The abstract language enables the verifier to express temporal properties of system behaviour using a vocabulary of clean-cut concepts. To be able to distinguish elements of the abstract language, a `different font` is used to denote them.

But first, some auxiliary abbreviations are introduced. All relate to *changes* in the system state. The ⊕-notation, pronounced as *just*, is used to denote a change to a certain information state. The symbol ≡ means "is defined as".

$$\oplus \text{state}(\mathcal{M}, t1, \textit{interface}) \models \varphi \;\equiv\; \text{state}(\mathcal{M}, t1, \textit{interface}) \models \varphi \;\wedge\; \exists\, t2 < t1\; \forall t: (t2 \leq t < t1 \;\Rightarrow\; \text{state}(\mathcal{M}, t1, \textit{interface}) \not\models \varphi)$$

The definition of $\oplus \text{state}(\mathcal{M}, t1, \textit{interface}) \not\models \varphi$ is analogous. Closely related is the $\otimes t1, t2 \oplus$-notation, defined as follows:

$$\otimes t1, t2 \oplus \text{state}(\mathcal{M}, t2, \textit{interface}) \models \varphi \;\equiv\; \oplus \text{state}(\mathcal{M}, t2, \textit{interface}) \models \varphi \;\wedge\; \forall t: (t1 < t < t2 \;\Rightarrow\; \neg \oplus \text{state}(\mathcal{M}, t, \textit{interface}) \models \varphi)$$

Again, an analogous definition can be given for the variant with $\not\models$ instead of $\models$. This notation can be used to say that the information state has just changed in some way at t2, for the first time since t1.

All further definitions concern elements of the languages AL. Some notions are formally defined; others are only informally sketched.

Concerning action executions

The notion of an *action execution* is central to the system of co-ordination properties, so formalisation is desired. Both for the world and the agent, an action execution is defined to happen between t1 and t2 when a tbp-atom appears at t1 and the first matching ended-atom appears at t2. These definitions only yield the right intuitions when property COORD0 holds. If not, then it is not reasonable to take on the first matching ended-atom as belonging to the tbp-atom, as it could be the end of an earlier executed instance of the same action.

Action executions are defined for the world as well as for the agent. First, new predicates are introduced and explained in informal terms. Next, formal interpretations in terms of the detailed language are given.

Let A ∈ ACTION and t1, t2 > t1 be moments in time. Then, the abstract formula

ActionEx(A, t1, t2, EW, 𝒪𝒞) denotes that there is an execution of A in the world starting at t1 and ending at t2.

Interpretation in terms of the detailed language:

ActionEx(A, t1, t2, EW, 𝒪𝒞) ≡ ⊕state(𝒪𝒞, t1, input(EW)) ⊨ to_be_performed(A) ∧
⊗t1,t2⊕state(𝒪𝒞, t2, output(EW)) ⊨ ended(A)

The predicate ActionEx(A, t1, t2, Ag, 𝒪𝒞) is the corresponding agent notion.

Concerning applicability

Actions can only be successfully executed in certain world states. There must be nothing obstructing the execution of the action. For each action A, the existence of a formula appl(A) is assumed, describing exactly the world situations in which the action can be fruitfully executed. It is not excluded that the effects of the action are already present in these world situations. Now, applicability can be defined straightforwardly:

Let A ∈ ACTION and t1 be a moment in time. Then, the abstract formula

Appl(A, t1, 𝒪𝒞) denotes that action A is applicable in the world at t1.

Interpretation in terms of the detailed language:

Appl(A, t1, 𝒪𝒞) ≡ state(𝒪𝒞, t1, output(EW)) ⊨ appl(A)

Concerning expected effects

When an execution of an action A starts at t1 in the world, the effects expected depend on the factual world situation at t1. So, the following notion takes into account the output information state of EW, at the time the execution starts.

Let A ∈ ACTION, l ∈ groundliterals(world info) and t be a moment in time. Then, the abstract formula

ExpEffect(l, A,t1, EW, 𝒪𝒞) denotes that l is expected to become true as a result of executing A in the world at t1.

Concerning effects of actions and events

A literal is defined to be an *effect of an action* when the literal is an expected outcome that becomes true during execution of the action. Note that this doesn't mean that the literal becomes true as a result of the action, though this will be usually the case. But when during an action execution an event happens, which causes changes that are also expected effects of the action being executed, these changes will be seen as effects of the action. This choice is made because there is no means by which an external observer can distinguish changes caused by actions from changes caused by events. A literal is defined to be an *effect of an event* when it is not an effect of any action.

Let A ∈ ACTION, I ∈ groundliterals(world info) and t be a moment in time. Then, the abstract formula

ActionEff(A, I, t, EW, $\mathcal{M}$) denotes that at t, I becomes true as a result of executing A.

Interpretation in terms of the detailed language:

ActionEff(A, I, t, EW, $\mathcal{M}$) ≡ ∃ t1 < t ∃ t2 ≥ t:
⊕state($\mathcal{M}$, t, output(EW)) ⊨ I ∧
ActionEx(A, t1, t2, EW, $\mathcal{M}$) ∧
ExpEffects(I, A,t1, EW, $\mathcal{M}$)

Let I ∈ groundliterals(world info) and t be a moment in time. Then, the abstract formula

EventEff(I, t, EW, $\mathcal{M}$) denotes that at t, I becomes true as a result of some event.

Interpretation:

EventEff(I, t, EW, $\mathcal{M}$) ≡ ⊕state($\mathcal{M}$, t, output(EW)) ⊨ I ∧
¬ ∃ A ∈ ACTION: ActionEff(A, I, t, EW, $\mathcal{M}$)

The next abstract formula is used to state that during an interval in time there are no effects of events.

Let *int* be an interval in time. Then, the abstract formula

NoEventsDuring(*int*, EW, $\mathcal{M}$) denotes that there are no events taking place in the world during *int*.

Definition within the abstract language:

NoEventsDuring(*int*, EW, $\mathcal{M}$) ≡ ∀ I ∈ groundliterals(world info) ∀ t ∈ *int*:
¬ EventEff(I, t, EW, $\mathcal{M}$)

Concerning successful actions

The following formula of the abstract language states that an execution of A is successful, meaning that all expected effects are achieved during the execution:

Let A ∈ ACTION and t1, t2 > t1 be moments in time. Then, the abstract formula

ExpEffectsHappen (A, t1, t2, EW, $\mathcal{M}$) denotes that all expected effects of doing A between t1 and t2 are achieved.

Definition within the abstract language:

ExpEffectsHappen (A, t1, t2, EW, $\mathcal{M}$) ≡ ActionEx(A, t1, t2, EW, $\mathcal{M}$) ∧
∀ I ∈ world info ∃ t3 ∈ ⟨t1, t2]:
ExpEffect(I, A,t1, EW, $\mathcal{M}$) ⇒
ActionEff(A, E, t3, EW, $\mathcal{M}$)

Concerning overlapping executions

The notions NoOverlappingInWorld($\mathcal{M}$) and NoOverlappingInWorld($\mathcal{M}$) denote that action executions don't overlap, neither in the world nor in the agent. No formal definitions are given.

6 Proofs

In this section, a complete proof tree of COORD1 is given. In order to prove COORD1, it is possible to stay entirely within the abstract language; no abstractions need to be expanded into the detailed language. This makes the proof very easy.

To prove COORD1, all that is needed is performing simple modus ponens on a subset of the system of co-ordination properties. Figure 3 shows the proof tree:

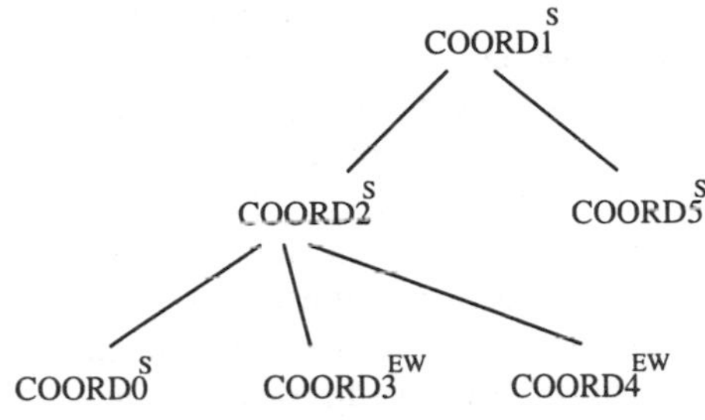

Fig. 3. The proof tree

The proofs of COORD0 and COORD5 are left out. These are more complex, but the really difficult parts of the proof can be done once and for all.

7 Discussion

One of the challenges to improve development methods for agent systems is to provide appropriate support for verification of agent systems being built in practice. The current state is that from the theoretical side formal techniques are proposed, such as temporal logics, but that developers in practice do not consider them useful. Three main reasons for this gap are that

- behavioural properties relevant for agent systems in practice usually have such a high complexity that both fully automated verification and verification by hand are difficult,
- the formal techniques offered have no well-defined relation to design or software specifications of the real systems used in practice, and
- the formal techniques offered require a much higher level of formal skills than the average developer in practice possesses.

This paper addresses these issues in the following manner. Two languages are proposed: a detailed language, with a direct relation to the system design specification, and an abstract language in which properties can be formulated in a more conceptual manner. Both languages have been defined formally; moreover, well-defined relationships exist between the two languages, and between the detailed language and the system design specification. Proof structures can be made visible within the abstract language; by this abstraction, complexity of the property and proof structures are reduced considerably. More detailed parts of proofs and properties can be hidden in the detailed language, and show up in the abstract language only in the form of, more abstractly formulated, reusable lemmas.

Two roles are distinguished within the verification engineering process: the verification support developer, who defines libraries of reusable properties in the abstract language, and their related properties in the detailed language, and the verification engineer, who uses these libraries to actually perform verification for a system being developed in practice.

The approach has been illustrated by addressing the case of co-ordination of actions. Under realistic assumptions, such as action generation and action execution with duration, it is a complex problem to guarantee the successfulness of action executions. A set of reusable co-ordination properties has been defined both in the detailed language and in the abstract language. Indeed, the abstract formulations are much more accessible and explainable than their detailed counterparts. It has been shown that the abstractly formulated relationships between these properties can be expressed within the abstract languages. The co-ordination properties found have become part of a library of reusable properties that is being developed.

When we try to relate our work to the other contributions to the AOSE workshop, our approach of formally verifying requirements of agent systems seems to be unique. Many papers describe methodologies for designing and analysing multi-agent systems. These methodologies enable system developers to build a well-structured agent system, but they don't offer support to verify whether the behaviour of the resulting system obeys the requirements of the prospective user. For example, in [14], a methodology is proposed that supports the developer "through an entire software development lifecycle from problem description through implementation". From the requirements of the user, which may be informal or formal, goals are distilled which guide the development process. These goals are the essence of the set of requirements, but they don't seem to be formal in nature. So, it's not possible to proof whether the resulting multi-agent system reaches its goals.

Many approaches are based on UML. The work of Odell et al. [10] extends UML with agent concepts. Though UML is graphical in nature, UML models do represent requirements, as is also explicated by Depke et al. in [2]. A UML model semantics is represented by a formal metamodel. According to the authors of [10], logical specifications like we use them could be expressed using features of the metamodel. Also, this paper mentions templates as being behaviours common to different problem domains. A template is a behaviour pattern that can be instantiated and customised to fit a specific domain. In our paper, we developed a set of generic properties that describe an often-occurring pattern in agent behaviour, namely performing actions in a dynamic environment. This is similar in spirit.

A very prominent concept in the AOSE workshop was the concept of roles. In [8], Kendall represents patterns of interaction using role models. These role models abstract from application details, just as we do in our system of co-ordination properties. In a recent paper by Ferber et al. [4], the relation between formal requirements on dynamic agent system and the dynamics of abstract organisational concepts like roles and groups is explored.

The languages used in this paper are similar to the approach in situation calculus [9]. A difference is that explicit references are made to temporal traces and time points. In [12], Reiter addresses proving properties in situation calculus. A difference with our approach is that we incorporate arbitrary durations in the decision process of the agent, and in the interaction with the world. Also, we focus on capturing agent concepts in the abstract language, which makes our approach specifically suitable for verifying agent applications.

References

[1] Brazier, F.M.T., Cornelissen, F., Gustavsson, R., Jonker, C.M., Lindeberg, O., Polak, B., and Treur, J., Compositional Design and Verification of a Multi-Agent System for One-to-Many Negotiation, in: *Proceedings of the Third International Conference on Multi-Agent Systems, ICMAS'98*, IEEE Computer Society Press, 1998, pp. 49-56.

[2] Depke, R., Heckel, R., and Küster, J.M., Requirement Specification and Design of Agent-Based Systems with Graph Transformation, Roles and UML, in: *this volume.*

[3] Engelfriet, J., Jonker, C.M., and Treur, J., Compositional Verification of Multi-Agent Systems in Temporal Multi-Epistemic Logic, in: *Pre-proceedings of the Fifth International Workshop on Agent Theories, Architectures and Languages, ATAL'98* (J.P. Mueller, M.P. Singh, and A.S. Rao, eds.), 1998, pp. 91-106. To appear in: *Intelligent Agents V* (J.P. Mueller, M.P. Singh and A.S. Rao eds.), Lecture Notes in AI, Springer Verlag, in press, 1999.

[4] Ferber, J., Gutknecht, O., Jonker, C.M., Müller, J.P., and Treur, J., Organization Models and Behavioural Requirements Specification for Multi-Agent Systems, in: *Proceedings of the Fourth International Conference on Multi-Agent Systems, ICMAS 2000*, IEEE Computer Society Press, in press. Extended version in: *Proceedings of the ECAI 2000 Workshop on Modelling Artificial Societies and Hybrid Organizations*, in press, 2000.

[5] Hodges, W., *Model theory*, Cambridge University Press, 1993.

[6] Jonker, C.M., and Treur, J., Compositional Verification of Multi-Agent Systems: a Formal Analysis of Pro-activeness and Reactiveness, in: *Proceedings of the International Workshop on Compositionality, COMPOS'97* (W.P. de Roever, H. Langmaack, A. Pnueli eds.), Lecture Notes in Computer Science, vol. 1536, Springer Verlag, 1998, pp. 350-380.

[7] Jonker, C.M., Treur, J., and Vries, W. de, Compositional Verification of Agents in Dynamic Environments: a Case Study, in: *Proceedings of the KR98 Workshop on Verification and Validation of KBS* (F. van Harmelen ed.), 1998.

[8] Kendall, E.A., Agent Software Engineering with Role Modelling, in: *this volume.*

[9] McCarthy, J., and Hayes, P.J., Some Philosophical Problems from the Standpoint of Artificial Intelligence, *Machine Intelligence*, vol. 4, 1969, pp. 463-502.

[10] Odell, J., Van Dyke Parunak, H., and Bauer, B., Representing Agent Interaction Protocols in UML, in: *this volume.*

[11] Reiter, R., The Frame Problem in the Situation Calculus: a Simple Solution (Sometimes) and a Completeness Result for Goal Regression, in: *Artificial Intelligence and Mathematical Theory of Computation: Papers in Honor of John McCarthy* (V. Lifschitz ed.), Academic Press, 1991, pp. 359-380.

[12] Reiter, R., Proving Properties of States in the Situation Calculus, *Artificial Intelligence*, vol. 64, 1993, pp. 337-351.

[13] Sandewall, E., *Features and Fluents. The Representation of Knowledge about Dynamical Systems, Volume I*, Oxford University Press, 1994.

[14] Wood, M., and DeLoach, S.A., An Overview of the Multiagent Systems Engineering Methodology, in: *this volume.*

Strategy Selection-Based Meta-level Reasoning for Multi-agent Problem-Solving

K. Suzanne Barber, David C. Han, Tse-Hsin Liu

The University of Texas at Austin
Department of Electrical and Computer Engineering
24th and Speedway, ACES 5.436
barber@mail.utexas.edu

Researchers have developed various techniques to address MAS problem-solving activities, i.e., agent organization construction, plan generation, task allocation, plan integration, and plan execution. An agent's respective problem solving and coordination techniques must be properly understood before they can be included into any other software system. 'Strategies' describe the techniques by which agents perform their individual decision-making processes and coordinate those processes with other agents. This chapter describes current work in characterizing agent operations, specifically, the representation of strategies in terms of roles and interactions as well as a trade-off evaluation mechanism for deciding which strategy is most appropriate for a given situation. On-line evaluation and selection of strategies will allow agents to tailor their behavior to given environment situations and thus, offer increase flexibility and adaptability of response.

1. Introduction

Multi-agent systems (MAS) may be regarded as a group of intelligent entities called agents, interacting with one another to collectively achieve their goals. A generic agent has a set of goals (or intentions), certain capabilities to perform actions, and some knowledge (or beliefs) about its environment. An agent's responsibilities are often specified a priori by assigning domain-specific goals to the agent.

To fulfill its responsibilities, an agent must reason about its environment (as well as behaviors of other agents), to generate a plan of action and execute that plan. By taking actions, agents attempt to fulfill the functionality for which they are responsible. Researchers have developed several process models (or action theories) to represent and reason about actions, including sequencing, selection, non-determinism, iteration, and concurrency [9]. By actions, we mean agents' behaviors including those that are not externally observable. Internal agent activities are as important as external ones and should be considered in the design of an agent. Such activities include reasoning about behaviors, planning, resolving conflicts, and decision making, which cannot be observed directly as explicit actions.

A strategy is a decision-making mechanism that provides long-term consideration for selecting actions toward specific goals [8]. MAS researchers have developed various strategies for agent reasoning and operation, including inter-agent coordination, with impressive results, offering agents the capabilities necessary to operate in many types of problem domains. Each strategy "attacks" a solution space in a different manner. Usually the MAS designers select the strategies an agent will use to execute certain behaviors in an effort to solve specific problems. Strategic decision-making [10] helps to select the appropriate strategy. The selected strategy may not be appropriate if the problems change or are assigned dynamically. In such cases, it is possible to equip the agent with the ability to perform strategic decision-making. In this manner, an appropriate strategy will be applied to each problem faced by the agents, whether selected a priori by the system designer or during runtime by the agent.

Researchers often propose the use of "roles" and "interactions" to abstract agent behaviors [5;14;17-19;24]. This is due to the differences between MAS and traditional centralized AI problem solving approaches; there exist certain interactions among agents. In order to solve problems that require the action of multiple agents, coordination mechanisms are needed to coordinate the agents' planning processes and integrate the resulting individual plans. The role that an agent plays corresponds to the responsibilities assigned to the agent. These roles are determined in relation to the requirements imposed by the problem being addressed as well as the requirements imposed by the strategy used to attack the problem. Interactions specify the relationships between these responsibilities and the coordination mechanism through which these responsibilities are fulfilled.

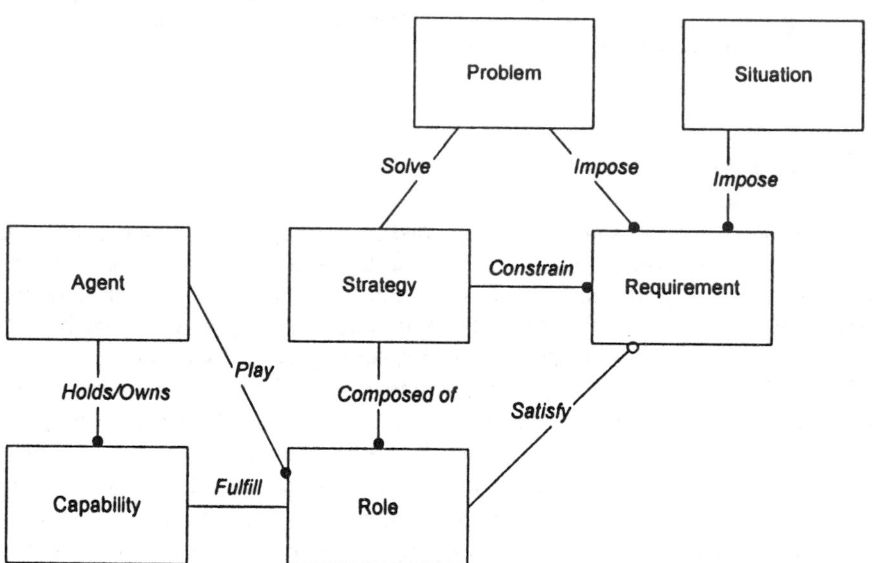

Fig. 1. Relationships among concepts describing how agents solve problems through the use of strategies.

Strategies describe the combination of the roles that agents play and the manner in which the agents interact in solving a given problem. Each agent is equipped with a set of capabilities, meaning a set of strategies that the agent can use as well as resources that the agent controls. The ability of agents to dynamically select a particular strategy can enhance a MAS's flexibility and adaptability to dynamic and uncertain environments through the ability to provide the best match of strategy to the problem to be solved, and the best match of agent capabilities to the responsibilities that need to be fulfilled in implementing that strategy. To achieve this objective, there are several issues to be addressed, including: (1) a uniform representation of various strategies to assist the comparison and evaluation process, (2) a meta-level reasoning mechanism for strategic decision making, (3) and a set of characteristics (including domain dependent requirements) that agents use to evaluate alternative strategies.

This chapter documents the author's progress towards equipping the agents with this strategy selection ability, specifically, the representation of strategy (based on roles) and a comparison of basic strategies. New strategies are being developed at a rapid pace, adding to an existing body of work. The authors do not intend to cover every strategy. Instead, our objective is to provide a uniform and domain independent platform to assist strategic decision-making. Therefore, in this paper, we present four basic (and simplified) generic strategies (i.e. voting, negotiation, arbitration, and self-modification) and their constituent roles. Additionally, different application domains have different needs and concerns, including the distribution of the problem space among the agents, the number of agents in the system resulting from that distribution, the extent of resources including communication and time constraints, and expectations for solution quality. For the purpose of illustration, four characteristics are employed to evaluate strategies, namely, the number of agents, the number of messages required, execution time, and the expected average satisfaction.

This chapter is organized as follows. Some background information about problem solving activities is provided in Section 2. Section 3 describes the representation of strategies based on roles. Section 4 discusses meta-level reasoning for strategy selection, followed by an illustrative application for conflict resolution in Section 5. Section 6 concludes the chapter.

2. Separation of Problem Solving Activities

Prior research has proposed some basic categories of problem-solving activities [2], including:

1. Agent Organization Construction (AOC) specifies how the agents should interact with one another.
2. Plan Generation (PG) works in the organization decided by AOC, selecting the actions or sub goals that the agents must execute to accomplish their goal.
3. Task Allocation (TA) deals with the assignment of actions or goals to specific agents for execution or further planning.
4. Plan Integration (PI) joins the sub-plans and schedules from PG and TA to coordinate agent actions.
5. Plan Execution (PE) deals with monitoring the execution of each agent's schedules to insure that actions are performed as expected from PI.

Example strategies for Agent Organizational Construction for MAS include Self-organization Design [12], Dynamic Adaptive Autonomy [16], teamwork models [21], and so on. Example Plan Generation strategies include hierarchical planning [6], blackboard systems [11], and Partial Global Planning (PGP) [7]. Example strategies developed for Task Allocation include the Contract Net protocols [20] and Group Self Design [15]. Plan Integration strategies include Partial Global Planning and multi-agent planning. To handle unexpected events during Plan Execution, strategies like Jennings's commitment and convention model [13] can be applied.

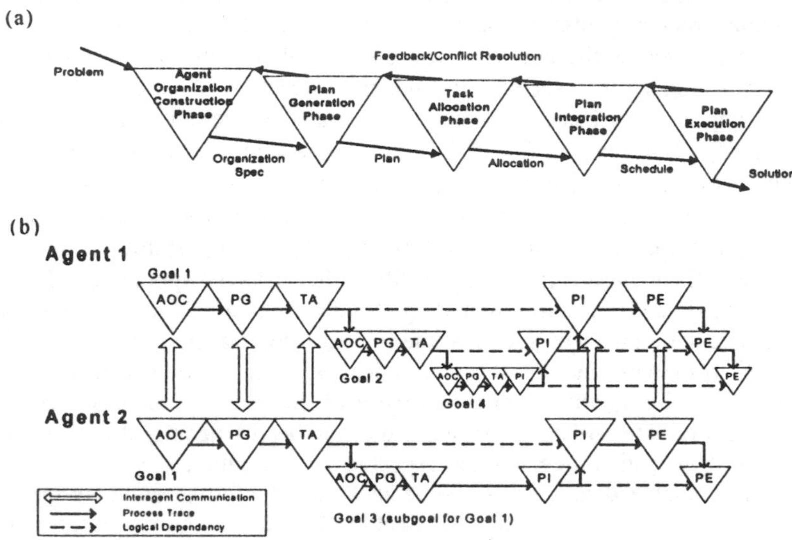

Fig. 2. **(a)** A decomposition of MAS coordinated problem-solving activities. **(b)** Recursive problem-solving activities based hierarchical planning as used by Sensible Agents. [2],

Fig. 2(a) shows the basic flow among these five activities. One example, shown in Fig. 2(b), demonstrates the interactions among these activities for hierarchical planning with dynamic agent organization construction. The agents will decide the organization structure under which they will operate for each of their goals. They then generate plans (with associated sub-goals) and allocate sub-goals, which will trigger another level of agent organizational design. When plans were fully developed, the agents integrate and execute their plans.

This separation of problem solving activities allows for the assignment of different strategies to each respective activity. Rather than selecting the strategy used for each activity statically at design time, the authors propose that agents can be equipped to dynamically select the strategy used for each activity during runtime through a meta-level reasoning process.

For example, conflicts may arise between agents during any of these activities. In order to address these conflicts, the agents may change the manner in which they are performing that activity. The strategy by which conflicts are resolved may be significantly different from the strategy by which the agent first approached solving the problem. This may involve conditional execution, de-clobbering of plans, replanning, or even reconstruction of the organization. Strategies that may be used for conflict resolution include various styles of negotiation, arbitration, voting, self-modification, social law, and so on. These strategies need to be represented in a common manner to allow the agent to compare respective strategies and reason about which is appropriate for any given situation. The strategy representation, presented in the following section, is provided for this purpose.

3. Role-Based Strategy Representation

A role-based strategy representation is offered to generalize the coordination mechanism between agents away from the infrastructure details, such as the selected communication languages. The purpose of a role is to define the actions that the agent is responsible for when interacting with other agents. The strategy indicates how specific roles interact, representing the whole of the coordination process. A description of the role construct is given below, followed by a description of the strategy construct.

3.1. Role Construct

The behavior of agents can be defined by the role the agent plays [23]. Roles represent the responsibilities, services, and tasks [14]. For the purposes of this research, these responsibilities, tasks, and services to be assigned are the result of selecting a particular strategy. The

The role an agent assumes in the execution of a strategy is directly correlated to the agent's responsibilities, and thus dictates agent behavior in the context of that particular strategy. Roles also simplify encapsulation of the behavior of each agent. Roles do not require intimate knowledge of the internal workings of external agents. Roles should be defined in relation to (1) scope of influence, and (2) other roles. The first of these restrictions defines the situation in which the role operates. The second of these restrictions defines the boundaries between roles within that situation. It makes little sense to state the role of an agent in a single agent system. In such a system the agent encapsulates all functionality required of the application. Roles should only be used to describe agents as compared to other agents, for example, the distinction between advisor and student or parent and offspring. A description of roles includes:

- Interface Specifications: The interface is the set of input and output events that the agent should recognize while playing this role. The output events correspond to actions that the agent may execute to change the state of the world (including speech acts). Input events correspond to sensor inputs, including speech acts or other detectable changes of world state. This provides a syntax that the agent must follow to play out this role.

- Reasoning Process Specifications: The interface specifies only the externally detectable events that occur among agents. The specifications for the internal processes the agent executes must also be defined in order to preserve the semantics of the role. Each step of the reasoning process is represented as a task or function that the agent must execute.
- Internal Agent Event Specification: When playing a role, events may be generated to deal with situations of importance internal to the agent. These events inform the agent of important situations, and are important for the interactions between the roles a single agent plays.
- Task Flow: The order in which the reasoning processes are executed as well as the trigger events that start and end such reasoning processes must be defined. The task flow also defines when the internal events are triggered. The Task Flow provides direction for the role, leading the behavior of the agent to the goals associated with this role.

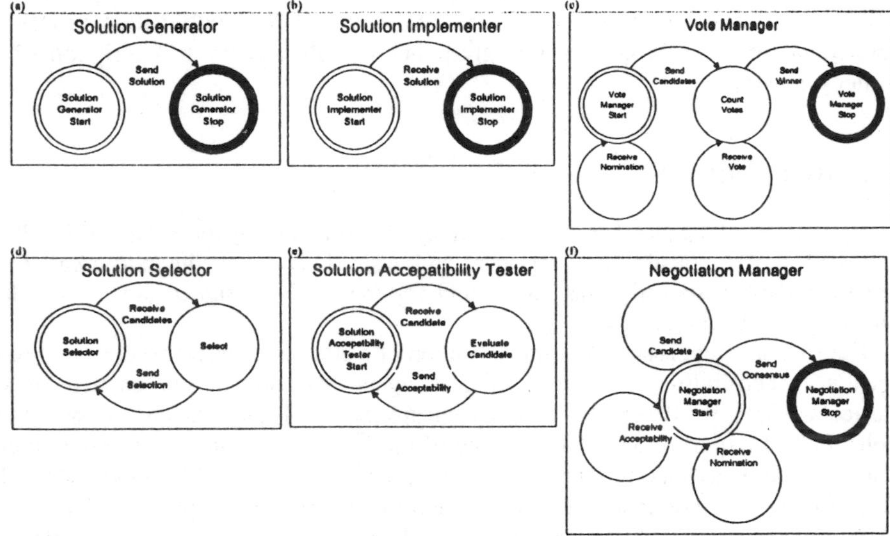

Fig. 3. A basic set of generic roles that can be used to build strategies.

The purpose of a role is to define the actions that the agent is responsible for when interacting with other agents. These actions are defined by the input and output events. Because the role deals with generic events, the role interactions are independent from the implemented language or transport. The coordination process among agents is decomposed into sections, providing a blueprint for each agent to follow. Each role handles a section of the complete protocol. The task flow is used as a state chart to representing the local view of the protocol with which the agents coordinate, similar to the conversation representations used by COOL [4].

Example task flows for some elementary roles an agent can fulfill for problem solving are shown in Fig. 3. These are represented in a format similar to state charts, but each state corresponds to some reasoning process as specified by the role. Fig. 3(a) shows the Solution Generator role. In the start state, the Solution Generator produces a proposed solution to the domain problem (goal or conflict) the agent is addressing. The role is finished when it produces the Send Solution event. When evaluating the prospective solutions to the domain problem, the agent may use either the Solution Selector role (Fig. 3(d)) or the Solution Acceptability Tester role (Fig. 3(e)). The Solution Selector receives a set of candidate solutions and selects the one it deems the best by whatever criteria it chooses. The Solution Acceptability Tester receives a single candidate and decides whether it passes some set of minimum standards. Fig. 3(c) shows the Vote Manager role. The Vote Manager collects candidate solutions, and sends out the set of candidates as a whole. Its next duty is to collect votes, and when a quorum is reached, to send out the results. Fig. 3(f) shows the Negotiation Manager role. This role controls the data flowing through the negotiation process, receiving and forwarding nominations, and receiving acceptance for each nomination. Once there is a single candidate solution that is acceptable to all agents, the Negotiation Manager announces the results. Finally, the Solution Implementer role, shown in Fig. 3(b), waits until a solution for the domain problem is created and agreed upon by all involved agents, then triggers execution of the particular agent's portion of the solution.

3.2. Strategy Construct

A strategy is an abstraction that the agent can use to encapsulate the agent interactions for any of the core problem-solving activities (see Fig. 2(a)). For coordination, each agent must recognize the roles it plays and the interactions it should expect from other roles. The purpose of the strategy construct is to provide a formal description of the interactions among roles. The strategy construct binds roles together, ensuring that the inputs to one role are provided as outputs from another. The strategy is also the vehicle through which the agent evaluates its situation and decides which roles to play in the organization. A strategy consists of:

- Role Input/Output Event Mapping: The strategy must be able to receive events and route them to the appropriate roles. To do this it must maintain a mapping, showing which input event corresponds to which output event.
- Role Interaction Mapping: When using a strategy composed of roles, the agent must decide which roles to play in the given interaction. Decisions on which role to play may sometimes involve coordination with other agents. These decisions will be reflected as an event coming from a role the agent is currently playing. Some examples of these may include a default starting role and processing requirements as well as usage of internal events from the roles. One usage for the internal events is to control the addition of new roles and the deletion of old roles.

Execution in the strategy proceeds as long as there is an active role being played by the agent. Agents may concurrently play more than one role in a given strategy. In many cases the input and output mapping of roles may pass information between roles being played by a single agent. Even in these cases, the roles are still useful in conceptually dividing the tasks that need to occur in each strategy.

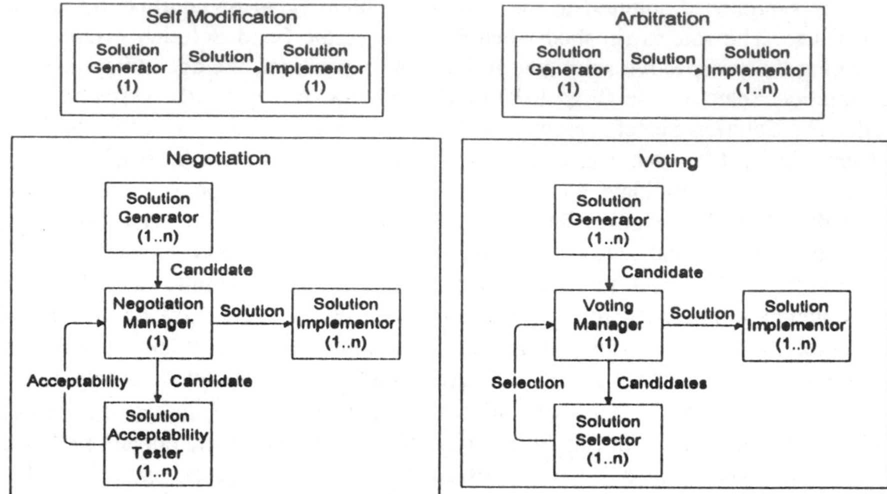

Fig. 4. Four basic strategies composed of generic roles.

Examples of four common coordination mechanisms, including Arbitration, Self Modification, Voting, and Negotiation, have been formulated in terms of the generic roles described above. Fig. 4 consists of data flow diagrams showing the interactions among the roles. Also included are the cardinalities describing the number of instances of each role are required for operation of the strategy. Examining Arbitration and Self Modification first, we notice that Self Modification can be viewed as a special case of Arbitration where there is only one Solution Implementer, which is played by the same agent as the Solution Generator. This strategy represents a centralized planning scheme, where there is one decision maker giving orders to multiple actors. Following a distributed planning paradigm, the Voting and Negotiation strategies represent cases where decision-making power is spread across multiple agents. The Voting Manager controls the Voting process. The solutions created by the Solution Generators match with the candidates the manager receive. The candidates input to and the selection output from the Solution Selector role match with the candidates output from and the votes input to the Vote Manager role. The winning solution is then passed on the Solution Implementer role. The inputs and outputs for the roles in Negotiation match up in a similar manner. Various styles of negotiation may be created depending on when the agents act as Solution Generators. All agents may act in this role in parallel, or they may assume this role in a sequential manner.

4. Meta-level Strategic Reasoning

For any given problem solving activity (Fig. 2(a)) and any given situational context, various strategies may be available. The purpose of dynamic strategy selection is to provide agents with the ability to find the best fit between the problem to be solved and the strategy by which to solve it. Since a given strategy is comprised of roles that must be played to execute the strategy, the agents must also determine the best fit between the capabilities of the involved agents and the responsibilities mandated by the problem and the selected strategy.

For meta-level reasoning, a strategy refers to not only the representation presented in the previous section, but also to the reasoning processes that can be used to fulfill the services and tasks assigned to an agent through the roles that the agent plays.

Although a strategy may help to achieve success, it does not guarantee success. Therefore meta-level reasoning, or strategic decision-making, is needed for strategy selection. The purpose of this meta-level reasoning is to select the strategy that matches best with the resources and capabilities of the involved agents and provides for the best chance for an acceptable solution to the given problem. At this level, various styles have been developed to evaluate strategies, such as utility calculations, priority, or heuristic rules [1].

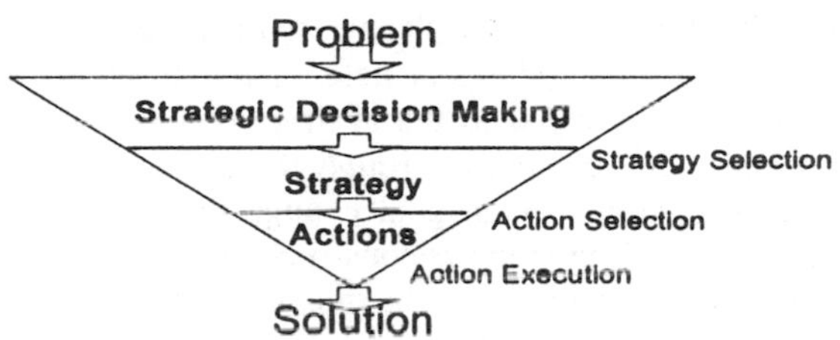

Fig. 5. Relationships between Actions, Strategies, and Strategic Decision Making.

Strategic decision-making [10] helps to select the appropriate strategy. Whether performed on-line or off-line by the MAS designer, decisions must be made with regard to which strategies are most appropriate for each of the problem-solving activities: AOC, PG, TA, PI, and PE (see Fig. 2(a)). The selected strategy serves as a long-term guideline to assist in selecting feasible and appropriate actions to take. By executing actions, agents can provide the solutions to the problems that triggered the decision making process. Figure 4 shows the relations among actions, strategies, and strategic decision-making.

For meta-level reasoning, the characteristics to be considered include both domain dependent and independent characteristics.

1. Requirements imposed by the strategy. Negotiation requires that all agents have communication abilities and individual decision-making ability, while arbitration only requires a single agent to have decision-making ability.
2. Cost of strategy execution. Execution of each strategy consumes a portion of the agent's resources. For example, some strategies may require a larger number of

messages or a longer time. It is important to consider this factor when dealing with deadlines or limited agent resources.

3. Solution quality. Usage of different strategies may produce solutions of differing quality. Longer deliberation may produce a better solution. The agent may have time to perform trade-off reasoning concerning the expected quality of the solution and the cost of strategy execution.
4. Domain requirements. Strategies may or may not be able to satisfy requirements imposed by the application domain itself, which may overlap the above characteristics.

MAS system designers can select from multiple approaches concerning how agents make decisions. There is generally no action which is better than all the others for all criteria considered simultaneously' [22]. For example, a ranking problem will result in an objective solution only if all the separate criteria considered each yield the same ranking. Therefore, it is different from classic optimization problems (which search for some kind of hidden truth or objective best solution). Such trade-off reasoning usually results in compromised solutions, which are highly dependent on the circumstances, methods, and preferences of decision-makers.

For the planning process, the Action Planner module as implemented in the Sensible Agent Testbed [3] makes use of both the strategy abstraction as described above and a planner abstraction [2]. A planner requires as input the current state of the world, the actions available, and a goal state. These three items are maintained by the agent and dynamically provided to the abstract planner each time it is invoked. The world state is constantly changing through the actions of other agents, and the actions available to achieve any given goal change based upon the agents who are helping to achieve the goal. The strategy constructs as described above represent the static interactions among the roles. During run-time, the agent also needs to record the current roles that it plays, as well as the roles that are satisfied by other agents. This information is used when routing events among the roles, possibly requiring conversion of the events into inter-agent messages. For Example, the Action Planner module can select strategies for the purpose of conflict resolution using utility theory.

Agents may use utility to evaluate both potential solutions and also conflict resolution strategies. In order to select an appropriate strategy, the agent must conduct some trade-off reasoning between solutions and strategies. The selecting of proper conflict resolution strategies considers: (1) the nature of conflicts (e.g. goal conflicts that may happen during agent organization construction phase and plan generation phases, plan conflicts that may occur during plan generation phase and plan integration phase, or belief conflicts that may exist at any phases), (2) the agent organization in conjunction with the agent's roles in that organization, and (3) the agent's solution preferences. The following simplified formula shows how an agent can estimate alternative combinations of specific solutions and strategies:

$$TotalValue^i = U_{weight} \times Utility^i - M_{weight} \times Cost^i_{\text{modify}} - CR_{weight} \times Cost^i_{\text{CR strategy}} \quad (1)$$

Equation 1 shows agent i's total value for evaluating both solutions and conflict resolution strategies. U_{weight} is the weight factor for agents' utilities. M_{weight} is the weight factor for the cost of modifying existing plans. CR_{weight} is the weight of executing conflict resolution strategies.

$$\text{Messages}_{\text{Voting}} = \#\text{SolutionGenerators} + (2 \times \#\text{SolutionSelectors}) + \#\text{SolutionImplementers} \quad (3)$$

$$\text{Messages}_{\text{Negotiation}} = \#\text{Proposals} \times (1 + 2 \times \#\text{SolutionAcceptabilityTesters}) + \#\text{SolutionImplementers} \quad (4)$$

From examination, we can see Self Modification is just a special case of Arbitration where a single agent plays both the Solution Generator and Solution Implementer roles. Because the same agent plays both roles, this is the only strategy that does not require inter-agent communication. An unknown number of proposals and counter proposals may occur in Negotiation. Even though, in the best case where the first proposal is accepted, it starts with a lower message bandwidth requirement than Voting, Negotiation quickly begins to require many more messages than any of the other strategies. If message bandwidth is a high cost resource, then Negotiation will be less likely to be selected using utility theory, and arbitration is more likely to be selected.

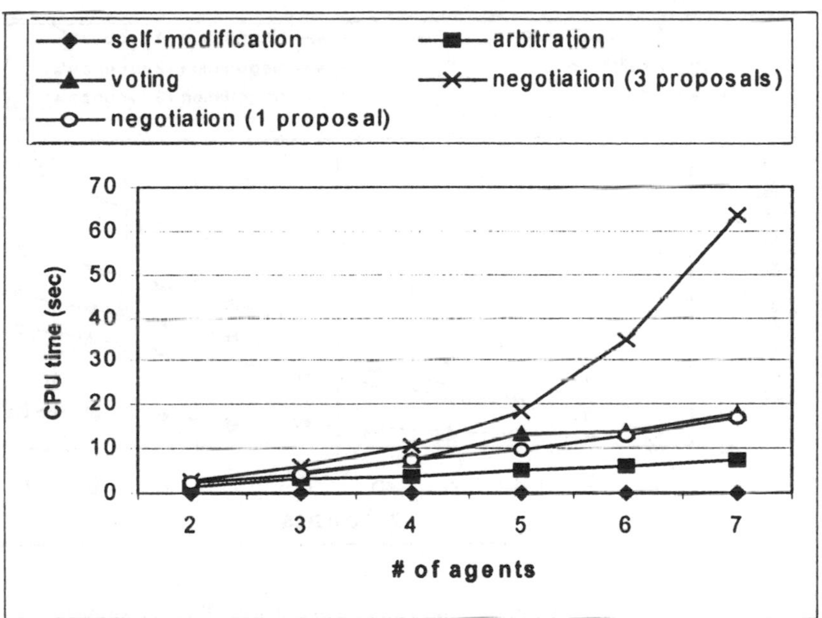

Fig. 7. Comparison of CPU time consumption.

Fig. 7 shows the CPU time consumption for each strategy. The CPU time shown in the figure is the accumulated CPU time for the agent to process the messages and execute the strategies, not including delivery time. The number of messages can serve as the index for time to deliver messages (Fig. 6). In Fig. 7, we can observe that the curves associated with negotiations involving one proposal is close to the curve of voting as expected. Negotiation with three proposals grows very fast, especially when four or more agents are involved.

The characteristics used to evaluate CR strategies include: (1) effectiveness, the complexity and uncertainty involved, (2) performance, the time/messages needed and the desired quality of solution, (3) agent properties, agents' preferences for CR strategies as well as capabilities/resources required to execute a CR strategy, (4) system properties, measure of the extent to which the system provides coordination mechanisms (e.g. available mediator/arbitrator, design convention, and priorities.) for helping agents to resolve conflicts.

5. Strategy Characteristics

In order to apply meta-level reasoning to some problem, over a set of strategies, the strategies need to be analyzed in terms of the characteristics described above. This section provides this type of comparison analysis for the four example strategies described earlier.

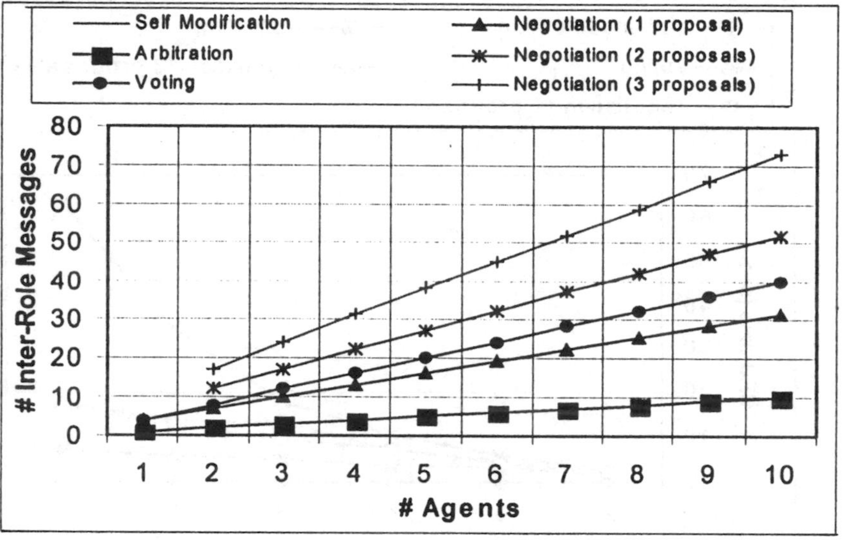

Fig. 6. Relationship between the # of messages and the # of agents for each strategy.

The number of inter-role messages for each strategy is shown in Fig. 6. Inter-role messages refer to each output/input event binding that is executed. The strategies represent the interactions between roles. From this description, it is possible to calculate the number of inter-role messages in terms of the number of agents playing each role and following the data flow necessary to reach a solution through each strategy. The numbers of inter-role messages were calculated from the strategy representations using the following formulas:

$$\text{Messages}_{\text{Arbitration}} = \#\text{SolutionImplementers} \quad (2)$$

As we have analyzed time requirements for different strategies, we have investigated the following issues: (1) the number of messages required, and (2) the actual CPU time required for processing messages and executing strategies as measured through experiments.

Now that some requirement and cost concerns have been addressed, the next step is to analyze the solution quality. Solution quality is highly dependent upon the actual (possibly domain dependent) decision-making capabilities possessed by each agent. If all agents possess the same capabilities, then the quality of the solution candidates produced by each agent is dependent only on their respective knowledge bases. If the agents are heterogeneous, then the quality of solution candidates may vary widely across the agents. Quality is best measured in terms of domain-specific criteria. One domain-independent measure of quality is the number of agents whose input can impact the final solution. The assumption behind this measure is that a solution is deemed 'better' if a larger percentage of the involved agents are required by the strategy to approve the solution.

Negotiation will not terminate until all involved agents have approved of the final solution. Voting requires only a majority, greater than 50%, of the agents to approve of the final solution. The minority has given their commitment to abide by the communal decision, but may have to sacrifice their local priorities for the communal good. Arbitration requires only a single agent to approve of the final solution. As the number of involved agents increases, the percentage involved in the approval process decreases. This quality measure does not capture all the possible concerns about solution quality. It only serves as an illustrative example of the type of analysis that can be performed in terms of quality. In practice, solutions may range from unacceptable, to acceptable, to very favorable to each agent. Other metrics may be generated that incorporate these features.

Each strategy is different enough in some aspect that it can be recommended for certain situations. Self-Modification lends itself well to when there are no communication channels available between agents. Arbitration requires only a single agent to have planning ability. Also, it requires few messages and can be completed in a comparatively short time. The solution generated by Voting allows the input of more agents than in Arbitration. It also scales well to larger groups, although it is not guaranteed to produce a solution at all. Negotiation will always produce a solution that is acceptable to all involved agents. However, the communication and time usage does not scale well with the number of agents. Using these competing characteristics, utility theory allows the agent to trade off the strategies depending on its priorities.

6. Conclusion

This paper presents current progress to equip agents with the ability to operate using a variety of coordination mechanisms and problem solving techniques, applied to all problem-solving phases, namely, agent organization construction, plan generation, task allocation, plan integration, and plan execution as well as conflict resolution. A representation of strategy based on roles and interactions described in this paper has been implemented, providing a uniform representation to assist agents in evaluating alternative strategies. Using competing characteristics, utility theory allows the agent to trade off the strategies depending on its priorities or preferences. Four strategies (negotiation, arbitration, voting, and self-modification) implemented by the authors are different enough that each can be recommended in certain situations. The four strategies can be differentiated using a small number of characteristics (computational time, communication requirements, and expected satisfaction) in a manner that can be used during runtime by the agent to select from among the strategies. Although the authors describe four strategies in the example, other strategies can be represented by using the same approach.

Since a strategy is a decision-making mechanism that provides long-term consideration for selecting actions toward specific goals, agents capable of making strategic decisions can perform this meta-level reasoning to decide the approaches to selection actions. The ultimate objective is to let agents dynamically select strategies during their problem-solving activities, which increase the flexibility of the whole system for dynamic environments and the adaptability for uncertainty. The application of strategy selection could be furthered by incorporating domain-specific requirements into the criteria for evaluating and selecting strategies. Future work includes deeper trade-off reasoning research to handle the difficulty of 'no best objective' choices. Such 'best compromised' choices may highly depend on domain characteristics.

7. Acknowledgements

This research is sponsored in part by the Texas Higher Education Coordinating Board #003658-415.

8. References

1. Barber, K. S., Liu, T. H., Goel, A., and Ramaswamy, S.: Flexible Reasoning Using Sensible Agent-based Systems: A Case Study in Job Flow Scheduling. Production Planning and Control, 10, 7 (1999) 606-615.
2. Barber, K. S., Liu, T. H., and Han, D. C. Agent-Oriented Design. In Multi-Agent System Engineering: Proceedings of the 9th European Workshop on Modelling Autonomous Agents in a Multi-Agent World, MAAMAW'99, Valencia, Spain, June 30 - July 2, 1999. Lecture Notes in Computer Science: Lecture Notes in Artificial Intelligence, Garijo, F. J. and Boman, M., (eds.). Springer, Berlin, (1999) 28-40.
3. Barber, K. S., McKay, R. M., Martin, C. E., Liu, T. H., Kim, J., Han, D., and Goel, A.: Sensible Agents in Supply Chain Management: An Example Highlighting Procurement and Production Decisions. In Proceedings of 19th ASME Computers and Information in Engineering Conference, Internet-Aided Design, Manufacturing, and Commerce Technical Committee (Las Vegas, NV, 1999) CIE-9078.
4. Barbuceanu, M. and Fox, M. S.: COOL: A Language for Describing Coordination in Multi-Agent Systems. In Proceedings of First International Conference on Multi-Agent Systems (San Francisco, CA, 1995) AAAI Press/ The MIT Press, 17-24.
5. Bauer, B., Muller, J. P., and Odell, J. Agent UML: A Formalism for Specifying Multiagent Software Systems. This book.

6. Corkill, D. D.: Hierarchical Planning in a Distributed Environment. In Proceedings of Sixth International Joint Conference on Artificial Intelligence (1979) 168-175.
7. Durfee, E. H. and Lesser, V. R.: Using Partial Global Plans to Coordinate Distributed Problem Solvers. In Proceedings of Tenth International Joint Conference on Artificial Intelligence (Milan, Italy, 1987) Morgan Kaufmann, 875-883.
8. Findler, N. V. Contributions to a Computer-Based Theory of Strategies. Springer-Verlag, New York, NY, 1990.
9. Georgeff, M. P.: A Theory of Action for Multi-Agents Planning. In Proceedings of Proceedings of 1984 Conference of the American Association for Artificial Intelligence (1984) 121-125.
10. Grant, R. M. Contemporary Strategy Analysis. Blackwell Publishers Inc, Oxford, UK, 1995.
11. Hayes-Roth, B. A.: Blackboard Architecture for Control. Artificial Intelligence, 26, 3 (1985) 251-321.
12. Ishida, T., Gasser, L., and Yokoo, M.: Organization Self-Design of Distributed Production Systems. IEEE Transactions on Knowledge and Data Engineering, 4, 2 (1992) 123-134.
13. Jennings, N. R. Coordination Techniques for Distributed Artificial Intelligence. In Foundations of Distributed Artificial Intelligence. Sixth-Generation Computer Technology Series, O'Hare, G. M. P. and Jennings, N. R., (eds.). John Wiley & Sons, Inc., New York, (1996) 187-210.
14. Kendall, E. A. Agent Software Engineering with Role Modelling. This book.
15. Malville, E. and Bourdon, F.: Task Allocation: a Group Self-Design Approach. In Proceedings of Third International Conference on Multi-Agent Systems (Paris, France, 1998) 166-173.
16. Martin, C. E., Macfadzean, R. H., and Barber, K. S.: Supporting Dynamic Adaptive Autonomy for Agent-based Systems. In Proceedings of 1996 Artificial Intelligence and Manufacturing Research Planning Workshop (Albuquerque, NM, 1996) AAAI Press, 112-120.
17. Miles, S., Joy, M., and Luck, M. Designing Agent-Oriented Systems by Analysing Agent Interactions. This book.
18. Odell, J., Parunak, H. V. D., and Bauer, B. Representing Agent Interaction Protocols in UML. In AOSE title to be determined, Ciancarini, P. and Wooldridge, M., (eds.). (2000) .
19. Omicini, A. SODA: Societies and Infrastructures in the Analysis and Design of Agent Societies. This book.
20. Smith, R. G.: The Contract Net Protocol: High-level Communication and Control in a Distributed Problem-Solver. IEEE Transactions on Computers, 29, 12 (1980) 1104-1113.
21. Tambe, M.: Towards Flexible Teamwork. Journal of Artificial Intelligence Research, 7 (1997) 83-124.
22. Vincke, P., Gassner, M., and Roy, B. Multicriteria Decision-aid. John Wiley & Sons., Chichester, 1989.
23. Werner, E. Cooperating Agents: a Unified Theory of Communication and Social Structure. In Distributed Artificial Intelligence II, vol. 2, Gasser, L. and Huhns, M. N., (eds.). Pitman Publishing, London, (1989) 3-36.
24. Zambonelli, F., Jennings, N. R., and Wooldridge, M. Organisational Abstractions for the Analysis and Design of Multi-Agent Systems. This book.

Introducing the Adaptive Agent Oriented Software Architecture and Its Application in Natural Language User Interfaces

Babak Hodjat*　　Makoto Amamiya†

*Dejima Inc.
160 W Santa Clara St. #102
San Jose, CA 95113
Babak@dejima.com

†Kyushu University
Department of Intelligent Systems
Graduate School of Information Science and Electrical Engineering
6-1 Kasugakoen, Kasuga-shi, Fukuoka 816, Japan
amamiya@is.kyushu-u.ac.jp

Abstract. Adaptive Agent Oriented Software Architecture (AAOSA) is a new approach to software design based on an agent-oriented architecture. In this approach, agents are considered adaptively communicating modules divided into a "white box" module, which is responsible for communications and learning and a "black box" which, is responsible for the independent specialized processes. An AAOSA parser can parse context sensitive languages. The use of this methodology in designing user interfaces helps overcome many human-machine interface problems by limiting the domain of language processing to the functional domain of the application.

1 Introduction

Agent abstraction is a natural extension of object-oriented technology, encapsulating the agent's knowledge within an active process and providing a standard interface for communication. The concept of large ensembles of semi-autonomous intelligent agents working together is emerging as an important model for building the next generation of sophisticated software applications (see chapter on Interaction Oriented Programming, and [1]).

An important difference between agents in an agent-oriented system and objects is that agents contain predefined structures and functionality that gives them the ability to communicate. In many cases, this commonality is extended to include such processes as learning and planning. Thus, although the environment and responsibilities of different agents in an agent-oriented system may be different they can still have much in common.

In the Adaptive Agent Oriented Software Architecture (AAOSA) paradigm we encourage the exploitation of this feature as much as possible so that the designer of an AAOSA based system is faced with as simple a task as possible.

AAOSA is a software methodology that proposes the break-up of complex software into a community of simpler, independent, collaborating, adaptive, message-driven components (AAOSA Agents). The goal of AAOSA is to provide software designers with the necessary coordination amongst AAOSA agents representing sub-domains of the software being developed in order to better meet the needs of the entire application. This coordination is provided through pre-defined messaging schemes between AAOSA agents.

We divide an agent into a *white box*, which contains standard data structures and methods for communications, interpretations, and learning provided by AAOSA, and a *black box*, which is defined by the designer and contains the agent roles (see chapter on Agent Software Engineering with Role Modeling), or the agent specific communications, interpretations, and processes (Figure 1). AAOSA, being object oriented in design, allows the black box to override, inherit from, or change any module in the white box (*i.e.,* the data structures and methods in the white box are inherited within the black box, which can therefore access and modify them). In [2] and [3], Baas shows that a problem is covered by a *hyper-structure* of computing elements (Figure 2). We propose the representation of each level of a given hyper-structure by AAOSA agents.

The designer of an AAOSA application will:

1. Break down the software to its manageable sub-domain elements (*i.e.,* AAOSA Agents),
2. Define which agents will be in direct communication with each other. These direct links are important because they concretize the designer's view of the different hyper-structure levels. The higher the level, the higher priority an agent will have in interpreting and processing input.
3. Devise interpretation policies for each agent by considering the input to the application from each agent's point of view to decide if this agent is responsible for processing all or parts of this input. An agent claims a particular input if it, or one or a number of agents

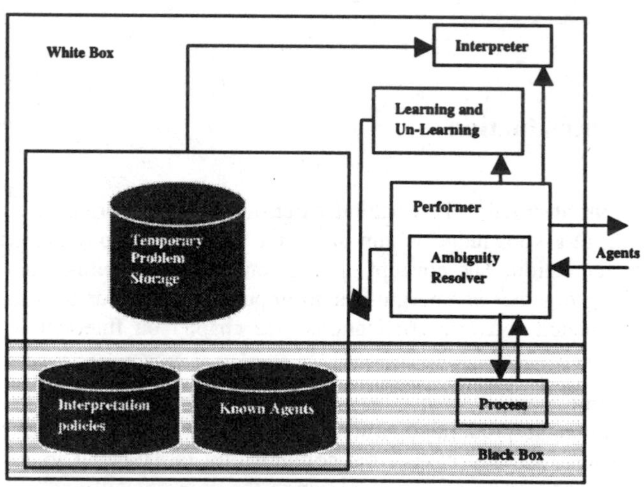

Fig. 1. Each agent is comprised of a black box section (specialties) and a white box section (communications).

down-chain to it are responsible for processing that input. In other words an agent claiming an input would, upon delegation, either process that input, or delegate it down-chain to one or a number of agents that had in turn claimed that input, or both.

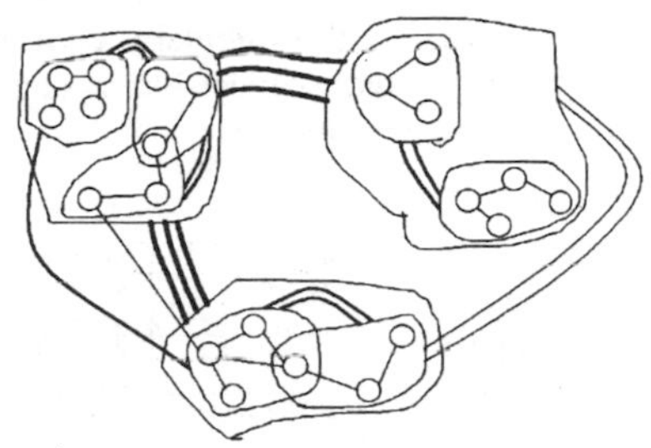

Fig. 2. Example of third-order interaction graph of a hyper-structure allowing cumulative interactions and overlapping aggregates. Circles represent first order hyper-structures or computing modules of the lowest complexity in the given domain.

AAOSA, through predefined communication schemes, should pin point the agent or agents in this hyper-structure that are responsible for processing a certain input, and provide the necessary coordination between them in order to achieve desired output. Our hope is that in this way the designer will have to deal mostly with the breaking up and design of the software elements themselves rather than the complexities of how to coordinate them. Therefore another important difference between AAOSA agents and objects in the Object Oriented methodology is that an agent does not have to know which agents are responsible for a certain process or data structure, or that process' invocation details ([4]).

Unique Query ID
Sender Agent
Message content (input to AAOSA Agent)
Performative
Priority or sender agent's hyperstructure degree
Claim made by agent about the content
Depth of search or allowable distance from initiator of query
Depth so far, or distance query has been propagated down-chain
History of agents that have processed this input before

Table 1. AAOSA standard Inter-agent message fields.

By taking each software module to be an agent we can take advantage of a number of desirable features which we will impose on the designer as definitions of AAOSA agents: Each agent should be independent of the others and the only means of communication is messaging, handled by the white-box. This will provide for the possibility of parallel, distributed, and even mobile modules. Agents can be processing several requests at the same time.

No centralized control is enforced over the resulting network of AAOSA agents covering the scope of a software application. In this architecture, agents introduce themselves and their abilities to one another at the beginning or during execution. Agents can therefore be added to or removed from the application at runtime. This is one of the major differences between AAOSA and its precursor the Open Agent Architecture (OAA, [5]).

Another close relative of AAOSA is ARCHON (architecture for cooperative heterogeneous on-line systems, [6]). Unlike ARCHON though, the predefined portion of each agent (i.e., the white box) does not have to maintain a model for the designer defined portion (i.e., the black box) or any other agent it communicates with.

By now it may be apparent to the reader that the kind of agents we are characterizing in this paper, having taken a bottom-up view of *multi*-agent technology, can be quite fine grained. Unlike the AI sense of multi-*agency* ([7], [8]), AAOSA agents are not centralized human-like agents with potentially conflicting intentions working together. Rather they are distributed software-object-like agents designed to work together cooperatively to implement complex applications.

In this paper, we will introduce the AAOSA architecture and some of its applications. An AAOSA system is actually parsing input in its interpretation phase. By examining the capabilities of an AAOSA parser, we will be able to give concrete evidence of the power of the AAOSA methodology. We have shown that the AAOSA based parser can parse context-sensitive grammars with reasonable complexity. The main application of AAOSA has so far been in natural language user interfaces. We will discuss the differences between natural language processing and grammatical processing of languages and discuss the application of a more robust design for natural language user interfaces. The paper ends with an outline of what has been done and what lies ahead in this area.

Register	**Agents make each other aware of their existence.**
Advertise	**An agent declares it can handle certain input.**
Un-Advertise	**An agent requests not to receive input from another agent.**
This-Is-Yours	**An agent announces another agent as responsible for handling certain input.**
Is-This-Yours?	**An agent that can not interpret a particular input requests interpretation from down-chain agents.**
Restore	**Agent requests another agent to backtrack to a state before processing took place on certain input.**
Not-Mine	**Down-chain agent has failed to interpret input sent down with an Is-This-Yours? Performative.**
Maybe-Mine	**Down-chain agent has encountered an ambiguity in interpreting input sent down with an Is-This-Yours? Performative.**
It-Is-Mine	**Down-chain agent has been successful in interpreting input sent down with an Is-This-Yours? Performative.**
Commit	**Agent requests immediate response, be it incomplete, to input sent down with an Is-This-Yours? Performative.**
Learn	**A new interpretation policy is suggested to an agent that will result in the sender agent being interpreted as responsible for certain input.**
Un-Learn	**An interpretation policy that results in the sender agent being interpreted as responsible for certain input is revoked.**
Dissatisfied	**Alternative process or interpretation is requested for input that has already been processed.**
Forget-Problem	**A previous request is canceled and the receiving agent will remove any temporary storage of interpretation results.**

Table 2. Some AAOSA predefined inter-agent message performatives.

2 AAOSA agents and coordination

Processing of the input is done in two main phases. The interpretation phase, in which the agent, or agents responsible for actuating an input are located, and a delegation phase in which the processes that have been located are called.

Each AAOSA agent must be able to interpret input sent to it as the content field of messages from other agents if so requested in the performative field of that message (Table 1). The result of this interpretation may cause the agent to claim that input as its own and/or to declare certain other agent/s responsible for processing it. Agents may consult other agents in order to complete their claims. These latter agents we will call down-chain agents relative to the requesting agent. This is a relative term and depending on the direction of the flow of requests, an agent may be *down-chain* (receiving) or *up-chain* (requesting) with respect to another agent.

Agents that are first to receive input to the AAOSA system are called *input agents.* These agents initiate the interpretation phase for that input and are the entry points to the system, generating unique query IDs for new input. This does not mean that other agents do not query input agents. Cycles are prevented by preventing the agents from repeating processes already executed over the same query. Input agents are also responsible for announcing the end of the processing of a specific query to all down-chain agents.

Input may also have been generated inside the system and therefore any agent could potentially be an input agent. In the simplest form, a claim means all of input belongs to the agent making the claim. In many cases, as we shall see in the examples, a claim should contain other information as well (e.g., confidence in claim, name of claiming agent or symbol representing various claims one agent can make, the level of the claiming agent relative to the input agent of this query, parts of input that is being claimed).

The software designer is responsible for providing each agent with its interpretation policy. An *interpretation policy* is comprised of a set of rules used to decide to return a claim that a piece of the input belongs to that particular agent. The interpretation criterion may be the message content but is not limited to it. Process history, probabilities and outside information (e.g., interaction with other agents) are examples of some of the other parameters that may be used by the interpretation policy. Note that interpretations do not determine whether a particular input does not belong to the agent. Determining whether an input does not fall into the scope of responsibilities of an agent, as well as whether it does, amounts to modeling the world (W=P∪~P) and undermines the distributed nature of AAOSA agents. Therefore, the application of interpretation policies to input either result in a successful interpretation or a "don't-know" state.

The performer module in the white box actuates other modules in the agent based on the message performatives received from other agents. Each message is comprised of a message content, and a performative that specifies what should be done with that content ([9]). No overall standard data representation is

Priorities		**Claims from agents representing higher degrees in the hyperstructure may have priority over the rest.**
Context	***Recency***	**Agent that has claimed input most recently is more likely to be responsible for processing disputed input.**
	Status	**Current status of a data-structure an agent is responsible for may make it more eligible for claiming disputed input.**
Focus and Focal point		**Agents basing their claims upon a larger portion of the input (i.e., focus), or parts of the input closer to the requesting agent's focus (Focal Point) are more likely to be responsible for disputed input. Agents claiming mutually exclusive input may all be responsible at the same time.**
Statistics and Probabilities		**More successful agents are chosen to process disputed input based on their prior performance history.**
Interaction		**A dispute is settled by referring to another agent.**

Table 3. Ambiguity resolution methods.

needed for the message content. Agent specific data can be transferred in messages in whatever format the sender and receiver agree upon. The designer can add agent-specific performatives in sub-domains to facilitate special communications between agents. AAOSA provides a set of predefined general performatives by which the coordination of agents is managed (Table 2).

In the interpretation phase, each agent, upon receiving input with an "*Is-This-Yours?*" performative, attempts to interpret the input by itself. If interpretation is successful, the agent will report claims using the "*It-Is-Mine*" performative. As we shall see, this does not always mean that this agent will be assigned to do its processing of the input.

On the other hand, if an agent can not interpret the input as its own, before reporting failure, it must check with other down-chain agents. If all down-chain agents report "*Not-Mine*", this agent will also report "*Not-Mine*" to its requesting agent. If at least one down-chain agent is able to interpret the input successfully and reports back with "*It-Is-Mine*", our agent will also report success. It follows that agents that have no down-chain agents to query may report *"Not-Mine"* upon failure to find an interpretation policy that applies to the contents of the query message they have received. To prevent agents from repeatedly processing the same queries in a cycle, each agent keeps track of queries it has processed and will reply *"Not-Mine"* to any query it has already responded to and has no new claims for.

After a path of down-chain links from a top-level agent to some agent or agents responsible for processing input is found (using the "*Is-This-Yours?*" performative), the delegation phase can start. In this phase, the "*This-Is-Yours*" performative is used to call agents on these paths to do the actual processing. Agents receiving a "*This-Is-Yours*" request may reinterpret the delegated input, or they may use pre-stored interpretation or down-chain query results to, in turn, process or delegate (or both) the input or parts of it.

Ambiguities of which agent owns a particular piece of input, and methods for resolving them, are central to the proper operation of AAOSA. Ambiguities occur when an agent that a job has been delegated to (i.e., has received a message with the *This-Is-Yours* performative) has not been able to interpret the message content as belonging to it based on it's interpretation policies, and

- Either more than one down-chain agent that was consulted with claim it, or,
- None of the agents consulted with claim it.

An ambiguity can be resolved by explicit interaction with another agent (e.g., an agent representing the human user). This is not always desirable or possible and therefore implicit resolution methods must be used. Table 3 describes methods that can be used to resolve ambiguities in AAOSA. The choice of ambiguity resolution methods and the way they are combined to achieve best results depend on the application in which they will be used.

Ambiguity and its resolution is particularly important in AAOSA because it provides a means by which agents can change their behavior (i.e., learn) and react to unexpected input.

As said before, an agent that does not have a suitable interpretation for input contents of

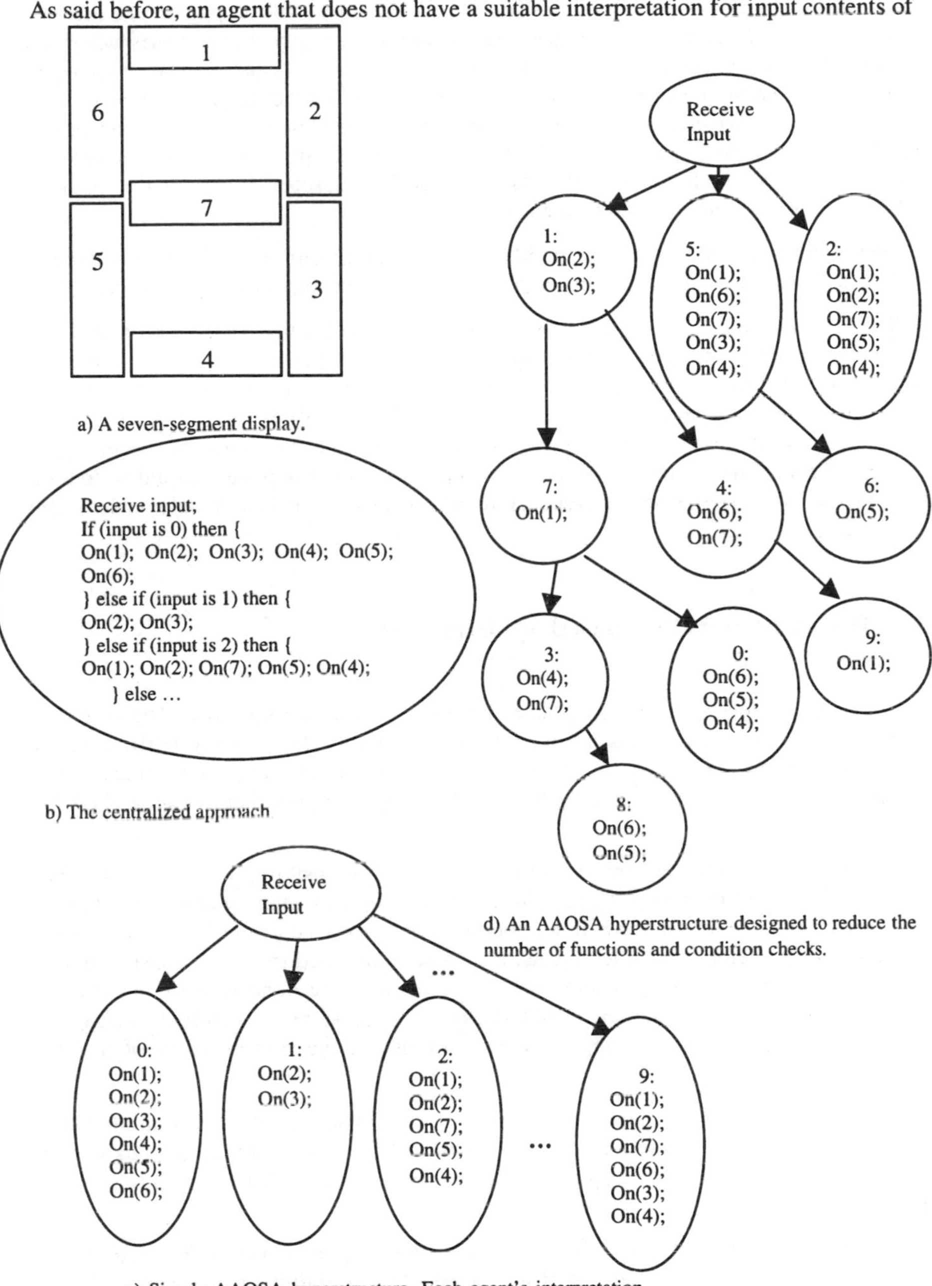

Fig. 3. Designing a seven-segment system using AAOSA. Arrows depict the direction of querying.

a message sent to it with the *"Is-This-Yours?"* performative will propagate this message to it's down-chain agents. By suitable interpretation, we imply that in cases where the interpretation policy uses a small part of the whole input as its decision making focus, the agent may decide to query down-chain agents on the remainder of the input anyway, so as to make more accurate claims. In other words, agents complete their claims after receiving the results of their queries to their respective down-chain agents. Hence, there may even be cases in which an agent that has successfully interpreted parts of the input decides to query its own down-chain agents.

Even if this was not allowed, the problem of query propagation should be addressed by AAOSA: When do we decide to abandon a query or stop propagating it down-chain?

This depends very much on the application. In cases where the depth of propagation is not that much there may be no need for stopping it. In other cases, such as interactive applications, in which response time is important, time elapsed since first agent received input from user may be used to issue a message with the *"Commit"* performative. This performative will cause receiving agents to abandon any query response not received and act upon the information they have, be it incomplete. Another approach would be to time-stamp requests at origin so each agent can reject requests older than the allowable overall response time.

3 Designing AAOSA-based applications

The AAOSA design methodology is essentially a bottom-up approach: The tasks necessary to achieve overall goals are identified and suitably decomposed ([6]). Then the data-flow between these tasks is determined. This way, pre-existing code can also be incorporated in the design as non-decomposable tasks by wrapping them into the black-box of AAOSA agents.

The break up of software into sub-domains is the responsibility of the designer who should also define the interpretation policies. This is done by looking at the system input from each agent's point of view. It is important not to over-generalize to avoid claiming input that really belongs to other agents. But there is no need to be too conservative either. Designers should keep in mind that interpretations are done in the context of the communication path by which the input has arrived to the agent and resolving ambiguities that arise as a result of overlapping interpretations are the responsibility of up-chain agents.

It is advisable that each agent be kept simple in its responsibilities and be limited in the decisions it needs to make to reap the benefits of distribution and to enhance its learning abilities. The overhead of the required units (the white box) should be taken into consideration.

Agents can be replaced at run-time with other more complete agents. The replacement can even be a hierarchy or network of new agents breaking down the responsibilities of their predecessor. This feature provides for the incremental design and evaluation of software.

In AAOSA, the emphasis is on the distribution of capabilities. Therefore if a capability is general enough to be coded into the White-box and distributed over all agents it is much more desirable than assigning a specific agent to be responsible for it (e.g., Using the learning module in the white-box rather than creating a separate learning meta-agent).

In the following example we shall see that the manner by which a system is agentified depends on the various objectives the designer has in mind.

3.1 The seven-segment example

Let us follow the design of a simple application to observe the various advantages AAOSA may bring. The system to be designed takes a number between 0 and 9 and switches on the appropriate LEDs in a seven-segment display (Figure 3.a). There are, of course, tried and tested algorithms for designing this system that give us optimal results. This is mainly because the problem is a limited one, and all possible input and desired output is known.

The first step in the design of this system would be to identify the range of possible input to the system and the set of output functions available. In this case, there are 10 possible inputs namely the numbers 0 to 9. There are 7 functions which should be used to produce the overall desired output: Switch LED 1 on (or On(1) for short), On(2), On(3)... On(7) on. A non-modular centralized solution (Figure 3.b) would involve 48 functions and 5.5 condition checks on average assuming each number is inputted with equal probability (1/10).

An alternative to this approach would be to have an agent represent each function and an input agent to receive the input and distribute it (Figure 3.c). If this agent (i.e., the Input-agent) were to have any interpretations of its own, they would be of the transitive kind, declaring an input to belong to one of the down-chain agents. However, in this example, transitive interpretations are not necessary because the fact that input has been handed down through the Input-agent does not effect the route or process it may be taking later. It is always preferable not to use transitive interpretations as this prevents the agents from being self-sufficient (Figure 4).

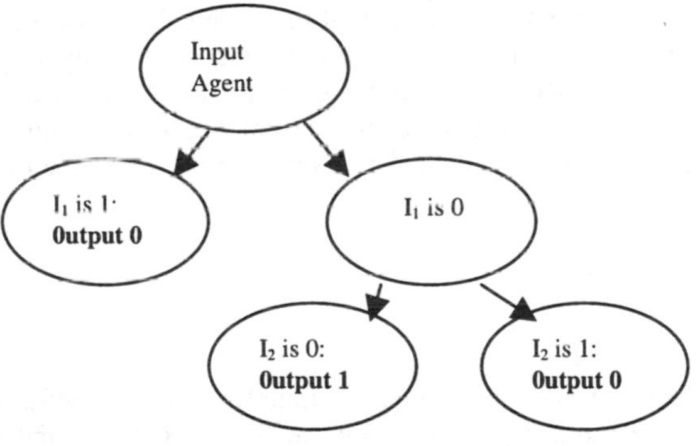

Fig. 4. The NOR function using AAOSA. The Input Agent receives I_1I_2 as input. This proves that there exists an AAOSA hyperstructure with no transitive interpretations for any computable function.

Therefore, in the case of the hyperstructure in figure 3.c, each agent will have its own interpretation policy, namely checking its input against the number it represents.

Although the number of functions in this system is the same as the centralized one in 3.b, certain useful features have come about because of the way we have modularized. Each agent is reusable in other systems, and, in the case of using a parallel platform, the number of conditions that may be checked on average would be much less (in a fully parallel system it would be 1 condition on average).

As we stated before, a system can be modeled using many different hyperstructures and the choice of the hyperstructure to be used depends on the requirements of the application. Let us consider the hyperstructure in figure 3.d. This system is modularized based on the optimization of the number of functions, while maintaining a relatively low number of average condition checks. The total number of functions implemented here is 24 (half that of the last two designs). The average condition check, if the system is taken as a running on a fully parallel platform, can be calculated as follows.

Each possible input between 0 to 9 would occur 1/10 of the time,

If input were 1, 2, or 3, we would be checking 1 condition,

For inputs 4, 6 and 7, 2 conditions would have been checked,

For inputs 0, 3 and 9, the number of conditions checked would be 3, and

For input 8, 4 conditions would have to be checked.

Thus, the average conditions checked would be 2.2. Of course, in calculating this number we disregarded the conditions checked in the white-box of the agents during the query and delegation phase. However in general, unlike this example, the complexity of the interpretation process for each agent, usually outweighs the complexity of the processes involved in these two phases. In comparison to the hyperstructure in 2.c, we have reduced the reusability and increased the average condition checks, in order to minimize the number of functions.

3.2 Learning in AAOSA

The combination of machine learning and multi-agent systems can have benefits for both. Multi-agent systems having learning capabilities will reduce cost, time, and resources and increase quality in a number of ways ([10]):

- Ease of programming
- Ease of maintenance
- Widened scope of application
- Efficiency
- Coordination of activity

On the other hand, machine learning in a multi-agent setup becomes faster and more robust.

Learning can improve performance in AAOSA software by improving speed and accuracy, reducing interactions, providing generalizations, and helping the system to tune in to different user preferences.

Learning can be applied to AAOSA in a number of ways depending on the objectives and application of the software:

- Inside the agents: In large and complex software, distributing the learning over a hyperstructure of more simple sub-domains is less complex than centralized learning. Learning can be used to improve the agent's own specialized performance and also to improve it's interpretation policy to reduce ambiguities. This latter form of learning is driven by the ambiguities themselves. There are various machine learning algorithms that can be used in the learning module of the white box, sometimes in combination. For instance, Reinforcement Learning can be used to fine-tune the choice of relevant interpretation rules, while rule learning algorithms add or update them. The former being more gradual and statistic based while the latter changes the agent behavior in quantum leaps and is based on a comparison of the actual interpretation with the desired one.
- Over the architecture (Dynamic AAOSA): Evolutionary and statistical learning can be used to split agents that are more complex into hyper-structures of simpler ones, or join redundant agents to form more efficient ones. This brings about the possibility of hyper-structures self-organizing themselves to achieve a balance between the degree of distribution and the efficiency of the overall software.

  AAOSA should guarantee:

  - The agents each stay responsible for the limited domain they were originally assigned to, while:
  - Containing the distribution of responsibilities, thus:
  - Containing the simplicity of each component through adaptive change or developmental upgrades.

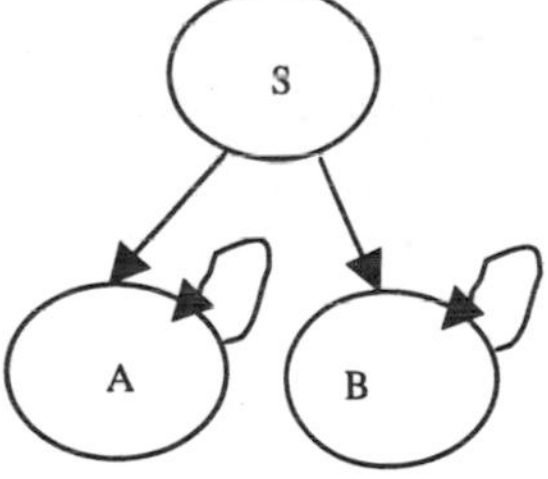

Fig. 5. An AAOSA hyper-structure for example 1.

Therefore learning should guarantee the balance of distribution and learning methods should not impede each other. For instance when a new interpretation rule is learned by a down-chain agent, "A", it may have to send Un-Learn messages to all up-chain agents requesting them to remove any identical rule that results in delegation of input to agent "A".

Learning can be deployed to automate disambiguation, and/or resolve conflicts between interpretation rules in a single agent. The latter case occurs when a single agent has rules that may result in conflicting interpretations based on similar decision criteria. In these cases, weighting the rules based on past experience is a form of learning.

The learning used in the current version of AAOSA, on the other hand, is a very simple rote-learning algorithm that records interpretation results for ambiguities explicitly disambiguated for the agent by the user. As we shall see in the next section, this learning algorithm is sufficient in the interactive natural language interface application. In other cases where implicit statistical (history-based) disambiguation is used more often, the learning algorithm will also have to be more complex. In these cases reinforcement learning methods could be used.

4 An AAOSA Parser

The examples of the previous section are relatively simple because:

- All possible input is known and manageable at design time,
- Only one agent is delegated to at each one time,
- No ambiguities can occur because the interpretation policies of each agent are mutually exclusive over the input.

We will now discuss examples in which some or all of the conditions above are not met.

AAOSA can be used to parse input given in the form of strings of characters. We show that the AAOSA parser can parse any context-sensitive grammar and discuss the time-complexity of this parser in [12]. A parser only interprets input and so an interpretation phase similar to that discussed in section 2 is enough. We will also not need any learning therefore a subset of the performatives in the previous section are needed here. The AAOSA parser is of importance to us because it shows the power of the interpretation phase of the AAOSA methodology.

In a parser, input is not predictable at the time of design and so each agent will have to consider parts of the whole input when interpreting it. Therefore, the claims made by different agents will have to include the portions of the input being claimed.

Example 1. Consider the context-free grammar $G = (\{S, A\}, \{a, b\}, P, S)$, where P consists of:

$S \rightarrow AB$

$A \rightarrow aAb \mid ab$

$B \rightarrow cBd \mid cd$

The string *aabbccdd* does belong to the language this grammar represents because:

$$S \Rightarrow AB \Rightarrow aAbcBd \Rightarrow aabbcBd \Rightarrow aabbccdd$$

4.1 The Algorithm

To parse a language using AAOSA we first need to build a hyperstructure based on the grammar to be parsed:

I. We create an AAOSA agent for each production rule. We are assuming that each production rule in the grammar has a unique left-hand side. We will denote the production rule represented by agent A with R_A.

II. Agent B should be down-chain with respect to agent A, if in the right-hand side of R_A, there is a reference to a variable that exists in the left-hand side of R_B.

III. The agent representing S is the input-agent to this hyperstructure.

IV. The right-hand side of the production rule an agent is representing is that agent's interpretation policy.

As an example, the hyperstructure for parsing the grammar of example 1 is shown in figure 5.

In an agent new claims can only be made based on existing claims C_n, ..., C_m, $(m \geq n)$

Figure 5 shows the AAOSA hyperstructure for example 1. Note that agents may be down-chain with respect to themselves. There is no need, in this case, for agents to query themselves and they may simply reapply their interpretation policies on the claims they have made so far every time they make a new claim. Let us see how this system can parse the input *aabbccdd* to see if it belongs to the language represented by the grammar in example 1:

1) Agent S receives input. No new claims apart from the input claims can be made by S at this point,

2) Agent S queries agents A and B (*Is-This-Yours?*),

3) Agent A makes the following claims and sends them up to agent S:

   (A, {[1..2]}) (A, {[0..3]})

4) Agent S cannot make any new claims based on Agent A's response,

5) Agent B makes the following claims and sends them up to agent S:

   (B, {[5..6]}) (B, {[4..7]})

6) Agent S is able to make the following new claim

   (S, [0..7])

   and we conclude that *aabbccdd* is valid in this language:

Note that the order of the sending and receipt of queries and responses does not have any effect on the overall outcome.

The grammar in example 1 is that of a context-free grammar. A less restricted form of grammar is the context-sensitive grammar. In this grammar for every production $\alpha \rightarrow \beta$ in P, we may have $|\beta| \geq |\alpha|$ (we use $|x|$ to stand the number of symbols in the string x).

Example 2. The following grammar is context-sensitive:

$$S \rightarrow aSBC \mid aBC$$

$$CB \rightarrow BC$$

$$aB \rightarrow ab$$

$$bB \rightarrow bb$$

$$bC \rightarrow bc$$

$$cC \rightarrow cc$$

The language $L(G)$ contains the word $a^n b^n c^n$ for each $n \geq 1$.

The AAOSA hyperstructure for this grammar is shown in figure 6. Let us see how this system can parse the input *aabbcc* to see if it belongs to the language represented by the grammar in example 1:

1) Agent *S* queries all at *Depth of Search* 1,
2) Agent "*aB*" makes claim ({[2..2]}, *B*) in reply to agent *S*'s query,
3) Agent "*bB*" makes claim ({[3..3]}, *B*) in reply to agent *S*'s query,
4) Agent "*bC*" makes claim ({[4..4]}, *C*) in reply to agent *S*'s query,
5) Agent "*cC*" makes claim ({[5..5]}, *C*) in reply to agent *S*'s query,
6) (*S* cannot make any new claims and increments *Depth of search* to 2)
7) Agent "*CB*" receives first responses from down-chains and claims ({[3..3]}, *C*) and ({[4..4]}, *B*),
8) S, having received this latest claim from "*CB*" can claim ({[1..3]}, *S*) based on ({[1..1]}, a), ({[2..2]}, B), and ({[3..3]}, *C*),
9) The checking loop for *S* will not break because the resulting claim from step 8 makes the agent be able to make a new claim, namely ({[0..5], *S*) based on ({[0..0]}, *a*), ({[1..3]}, *S*), ({[4..4]}, *B*), and ({[5..5]}, *C*). The parsing thus ends successfully at a depth of 2.

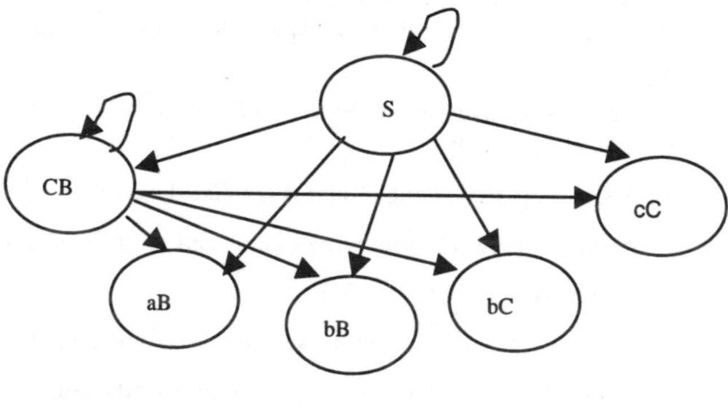

Fig. 6. An AAOSA hyperstructure for example 2.

5 AAOSA and Natural Language User Interfaces

Most human-computer interfaces being used today are complicated and difficult to use. This is due mostly to the growing number of features the interface should provide easy access to.

Users usually have the following problems with current interface [11]:

- Prior to selecting an action. They have to consider if the application provides an appropriate action at all. This hints on a need for some sort of feedback from the application.
- It is hard to access the actions they already know about. This implies that the user should be able to freely express his or her needs without being bound to the limited conventions preset by the application.
- They have to imagine what would be an appropriate action to proceed with in order to perform a certain task of the application domain. The application, therefore, should be able to guide the users through the many options they may at any stage of the interaction.

Thus, some of the desirable features in a user interface may be as follows:

Natural expression: The user should be able to express his or her intentions as freely and naturally as possible.

Optimum interaction: Interaction should be limited to the following:

- The user is in doubt as to what she can do next or how she can do it.
- The system is in doubt as to what the user intends to do next.

Adaptability: Adaptability could be about the changing context of interaction or application, but most importantly, the system should be able to adapt to the user's way of expressing her intentions. Two main issues that will have to be taken into account in this regard are generalization and contradiction recovery:

- Generalization: An adaptable system in its simplest form will only learn the instance that it has been taught (implicitly or explicitly). Generalization occurs when the system uses what it has learned to resolve problems it deems similar. The success and degree of generalization, therefore, depend directly on the precision of the similarity function and the threshold the system uses to distinguish between similar and dissimilar situations.
- Contradiction: A system that generalizes may well over-generalize. The moment the system's reaction based on a generalization is in a manner the user does not anticipate, the system has run into a contradiction. The resolution of this contradiction is an integral part of the learning and adaptability process.

Ease of change and upgrade: The application designer should easily be able to upgrade or change the system with minimum compromise to the adaptation the system has made to users. This change should be done at run-time (i.e., on the fly).

5.1 Extending the AAOSA parser

Although, as shown in section 4, a grammatical parser can be implemented using AAOSA, practical problems force us to make some improvements to it. Creating a grammar, be it context-sensitive, is a complicated task. Changing grammars based on learning (section 5) is also difficult. Grammars alone are not enough to fulfill the requirements noted above.

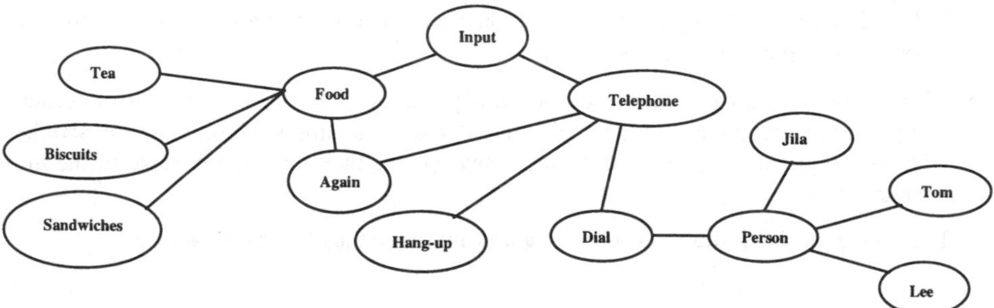

Fig. 7. An example hyperstructure covering the semantic domain for the servant robot. Lines show communication paths.

Furthermore parsing alone is not sufficient either. A parser, after all, tells us if the input string belong to a language or not. Our objective though, is to find the best match for any given input. This means the AAOSA system:

- Should be able to accept non-grammatical input (e.g., "Tea for Jila bring!"),
- Should be able to handle previously unencountered input (e.g., "Yabadabadee some milk for me!").

On the other hand, AAOSA should also be able to pinpoint the semantic sub-domains responsible for responding to input. Therefore, we propose a semantic approach to the problem of grammar definition. The designer of a natural language interface application should design a semantic hyperstructure of agents. The input agent at the top would be responsible for receiving input and initiating the query and delegation phase, and the agents representing the functionality of the system would be lowest order nodes of the hyperstructure.

The interpretation policies should be much fuzzier than that of the parser. For instance, rather than requiring the claims on which a new claim is based to be in sequence (step V in section 4), we can require them only to be exclusive. Two claims C_1 and C_2 are *exclusive* ($C_1 \otimes C_2$) if:

$$\forall\, i,\ 0 \le i < length(focus(C_1)),\ \neg\exists\, j,\ 0 \le j < length(focus(C_2))\ |$$

$s(focus(C_1[i]) \leq s(focus(C_2)[j]) \leq e(focus(C_1[i]) \vee$

$s(focus(C_1[i]) \leq e(focus(C_2)[j]) \leq e(focus(C_1[i])$

It can be shown that:

$$C_1 \otimes C_2 \Leftrightarrow C_2 \otimes C_1$$

The interpretation policies will determine what the best reduction condition is and each agent will compute a confidence factor for its claims based on the extent the reduced claims differ from the desired ones. Using a threshold, claims of higher confidence are used as query responses. For instance, take the grammatical rule $A \rightarrow BC$ as an interpretation policy. The desired relative position of B and C, according to the definition of grammatical production rules, is that $B \ll C$. But in our proposed system it would be enough for B and C to be exclusive. A number of heuristics may be used to approximate the extent of difference from the desired status (e.g., differences in order or proximity of the foci). Confidence in the claims themselves will also have to be taken into account when basing a new claim on them.

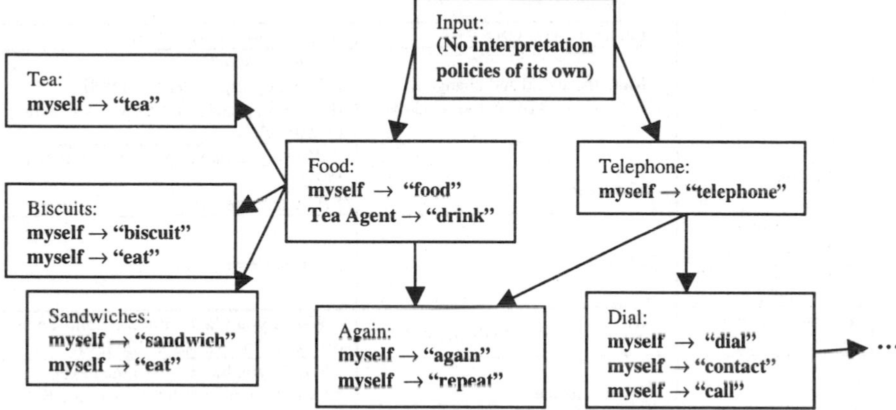

Fig. 8. Simple keyword interpretation policies for the robot servant example.

Another main difference between the parser and our proposed natural language system is that the context considered in the reductions of a context-sensitive grammar is limited to the input. In the real world, though, the decision to make a claim may be made based on context information that is not necessarily present in the input. For instance, an AAOSA agent may decide to make a claim based on the history of successful claims made, or the status of the semantic domain it is representing, or even based on interactions with the user.

5.2 The robot Servant Example

We will explain our implementation on a toy problem: A robot is to run certain errands around the house using a natural language interface. We will start with a limited set of functions and show that this set is extendible:

- Serve tea, biscuits or sandwiches,
- Make telephone calls.

The idea is to distribute the natural language processing over nodes that represent different levels of a hyperstructure covering the functionality space. One example of such an hyperstructure is given in figure 7.

Notes	User	System
1. Flexibility	-"Show me ESPN"	[Channel jumps to 206 on DSS]
	-"Put on freakin' CNN"	[Channel jumps to 202 on DSS]
	-"Mute the sound and change to HBO and put ABC in the window."	[Sound is muted] [Channel jumps to 910 on DSS] [Picture in picture is put on and switched to channel 7]
2. Ambiguity	-"play" -"The VCR!"	-"Would you like to play, the VCR or the DVD?" [VCR starts playing]
3. Context-based ambiguity resolution (DVD and VCR can both "stop")	-"Stop it!"	[VCR stops playing]
4. Ambiguity based Query handling	-"What can I do with the lights?"	-"Would you like to turn the lights on or off, or set them at a specific level?"
5. Learning	-"Sports channel" -"I mean ESPN"	-"Would you like to go to the next or previous channel or jump to a specific one?" [Channel jumps to 206 on DSS]
6. Complex operations	-"Record the Sports channel in half an hour"	[Okay]
7. Limited scope	-"What! You can do that?"	-"Would you like to use the TV, the VCR, the DVD, or the lights?"

Table 5. Examples from the AAOSA based home A/V interface (Scotty). A total of 42 agents are involved in interpreting user responses.

The natural language interpretation is done through a series of claims and delegations carried out by the agents. Agents claim an input string as belonging to them (*internal interpretation*), or decide that it belongs to some other agent or agents based on their interpretation policies (*transitive interpretation*). Agents that are not able to find appropriate policies that interpret certain input will consult down-chain agents. In our example the sandwich agent claims input such as "I want a sandwich" because of the presence of "sandwich" (Figure 8). In this case, the presence of the keyword "Sandwich" is the interpretation policy. An example of transitive interpretation would be in the case of the input,

"I want to drink"; in which case the processing is delegated to the tea agent by the food agent based on the presence of the keyword "drink" which is a clue as to what kind of food the user is referring to.

As mentioned before processing of input is done in two phases: interpretation and delegation. For example, let us say the input agent takes "Give me biscuits!". This agent itself can not claim the input without consulting other down-chain agents. These agents (Food and Telephone agents), in turn are not capable of interpreting and therefore ask their respective down-chain agents. The Biscuit agent claims this input based on the presence of the keyword "biscuits" and answers the Food agent's question positively, causing the Food agent to send a similar affirmative response to the Input agent.

So far, no processing has been done. It is now up to the initiator agent (i.e., the Input agent) to decide whether this input should be actuated. Upon actuation, agents use temporarily stored interpretation results to send the actuation request down to the responsible agents and have them execute the necessary processes without having to reinterpret the input. In our example, "Give me biscuits!", the Biscuit agent will be sent down the actuation command and it will issue the necessary commands needed for the robot to get some biscuits.

Ambiguities occur when the interpretation of input is not possible because of there not being any agents to claim it, or more than one agent claiming it. In the first case something unknown to the system has been inputted and should be clarified and possibly learned by the agents. Take for example the input: "I'm thirsty!". Let's say none of the agents claims this input. In this case, the input agent can ask the user whether "I'm thirsty!" has something to do with telephones or food (i.e., its immediate down-chain agents). The result of this interaction may be learned by the Input agent (e.g., Input agent learns that the input "I'm thirsty!" should be delegated to the Food agent). The Food agent, in turn not being able to interpret, will ask the user whether "I'm thirsty!" has anything to do with tea, biscuits, or sandwiches. Eventually it is up to the Tea agent to learn that "I'm thirsty!" belongs to it. To keep the responsibilities from drifting up-chain or down-chain in the hyperstructure of agents, the Tea agent should at this point declare to it's up-chain agents (in this case the Food agent) to remove any interpretations of "I'm thirsty!" that result in the delegation of the input to the tea agent (i.e., uses the *Un-learn* performative). The Food agent, having received an *Un-learn* performative and processed it, should in turn propagate it further up-chain.

Another example of ambiguity is when the natural language input is vague. For example, "I want to eat!" would cause the Biscuit agent and the Sandwich agent both to claim it.

By adding agents to the system, we can extend its capabilities. An example would be adding fax capability to the system in which Fax agent will be added at the same level as the Telephone agent connecting to the same down-chain agents as the telephone agent. Note that by doing so we have also added ambiguity to the system. For instance, "Contact Jila" may result in both the Fax and Telephone agents claiming it.

Some of the interesting attributes of our interface are as follows:

- It is modeless, in that the user does not have to follow preset menus in order to achieve her intentions; (e.g., "Tea!" is a valid input).
- It supports context-based interaction (e.g., If you have just ordered it to "Get some tea!" and follow that order up with "Again!" it can resolve the ambiguity between the Telephone and Food agents based on this context information, namely recency of invocation.)
- It can be upgraded easily to be able to handle Multi-lingual input because each agent's interpretation policy is relatively simple and the grammar and semantics are mostly handled over the architecture.
- When mistakes are made by the system graceful error recovery can be achieved by backtracking to the furthest down-chain point of ambiguity resolved implicitly and interact with the user to resolve it. For instance in the "Again!" example if the user really means a re-dial should be attempted, she can express her dissatisfaction by, say, pressing the escape key, and the system will respond with: "Should I re-dial the phone or bring you tea again?"
- Handles incomplete, unpredictable, and grammatically incorrect input. This is possible due to the simple interpretation policies in each agent and the fact that agents can extend their interpretation policies by learning.
- Relatively small memory/processor requirements with respect to similar interfaces based on classical Natural Language Processing methods.

6 Conclusions and future plans

AAOSA is currently being used as a natural language interface to home theater systems (Table 5) and electronic messenger systems, and it is being investigated as a web-browsing interface. Dynamic AAOSA (DAAOSA) is also being investigated as a means to adaptively index large amounts of information. In DAAOSA, agents are created or removed based on the complexity requirements of the system and thus the hyperstructure of agents is created by the agents themselves.

The current version of AAOSA has been implemented in Java because if it's unique portability and multi-platform execution capabilities and multi-threading features. We have used simple rote learning as the learning module in the white-box and other, more robust machine learning methods are being investigated.

In this paper we introduced AAOSA as a new software architecture and gave an example of its implementation in the form of a natural language interactive interface. AAOSA is flexible, primarily because there is no rigid predetermination of valid input. It is modular providing for easier revision, extension and development. AAOSA agents can be re-used inside an application or in other software. The independent nature of AAOSA agents provides for an inherently parallel architecture. Agents can run and communicate over a network of heterogeneous hosts. Run-time addition of new AAOSA agents is possible and therefore incremental development and evaluation is possible. Following guidelines set by the original designer; other designers can also contribute to a system making it commercially attractive. The built-in learning and ambiguity resolution features make AAOSA a more intelligent software architecture.

As in most other distributed designs, AAOSA's unpredictable nature makes it hard to guarantee the correctness or stability of applications. More work needs to be done in this regard to provide sound evaluation and testing methods. AAOSA is highly reliant on messages and the high message traffic between AAOSA agents may create bottlenecks and network load problems.

References

[1] V. R. Lesser. Reflections on the Nature of Multi-Agent Coordination and its implications for an Agent Architecture, *Autonomous Agents and Multi-Agent Systems.* pp. 89-111, Kluwer Academic Publisers, 1, 1998.

[2] N. A. Baas. Emergence, Hierarchies, and Hyper-structures. *C.G. Langton ed., Artificial Life III.* Addison Wesley, 1994.

[3] N. A. Baas. Hyper-structures as Tools in Nanotechnology and Nanobiology. *S. Rasmussen, S. R. Hameroff, J. Tuzinki, P. A. Hansson ed.'s, Towards a Nanobiology: Coherent and Emergent Phenomena in Bimolecular Systems.* MIT Press, 1995.

[4] M. R. Genesereth and S. P. Ketchpel. Software Agents. *Communications of the ACM.* Vol. 37, No. 7, July 1994.

[5] D. Martin and D. Moran. Building distributed software systems with the open agent architecture. Proc. of the Third International Conference on the Practical Application of Intelligent Agents and Multi-Agent Technology. The Practical Application Company Ltd., Blackpool, Lancashire, UK, March 1998.

[6] D. Cockburn and N. R. Jennings. ARCHON: A Distributed Artificial Intelligence System for Industrial Applications. *G. M. P. O'Hare, N. R. Jennings, ed.'s, Foundations of Distributed Artificial Intelligence.* pp. 319-344. John Wiley & Sons, 1996.

[7] B. Hayes-Roth, K. Pfleger, P. Lalanda, P. Morignot and M. Balabanovic. A domain-specific Software Architecture for adaptive intelligent systems. *IEEE Transactions on Software Engineering.* April 1995.

[8] S. Franklin, and A. Graesser. Is it an Agent or just a Program? A Taxonomy for Autonomous Agents. *Proceedings of the Third International Workshop on Agents Theories, Architectures, and Languages.* Springer-Verlag, 1996.

[9] J. M. Bradshaw. KaoS: An Open Agent Architecture Supporting Reuse, Interoperability, and Extensibility. *Proceedings of Tenth Knowledge Acquisition for Knowledge-Based Systems Workshop.* http:// ksi.cpsc.ucalgary.ca/KAW/KAW96/KAW96Proc.html, 1996.

[10] P. Brazdil, M. Gams, S. Sian, L. Torgo, and W. Van de Velde. Learning in Distributed Systems and Multi-Agent Environments. *Machine Learning: EWSL-91 (European Working Session on Learning), Y. Kodratoff (Ed.), Lecture Notes in Artificial Intelligence*, Springer-Verlag, 1991.

[11] T. Kuhme. Adaptive Action Prompting – A complementary aid to support task-oriented interaction in explorative user interfaces. *Technical Report #GIT-GVU-93-19*. Georgia Institute of Technology, Dept. of Computer Science, Graphics, Visualization, and Usability Center, 1993.

[12] B. Hodjat, M. Amamiya, Applying the Adaptive Agent Oriented Software Architecture to the Parsing of Context Sensitive Grammars, IEICE Trans. Vol.E83-D, No.5, pp.1142-1152, May 2000.

Adding Extensible Synchronization Capabilities to the Agent Model of a FIPA Compliant Agent Platform

Agostino Poggi Giovanni Rimassa

Dipartimento di Ingegneria dell'Informazione, University of Parma
Parco Area delle Scienze, 181A, 43100, Parma, Italy
{poggi,rimassa}@ce.unipr.it

Abstract. In this paper, we present an agent platform, called JADE (Java Agent Development Environment), that tries to ease development applications in compliance with the FIPA specifications. Moreover, we describe an extension to JADE original agent model that allows expressing agent synchronisation constraints better and provides wider foundations to build higher-level agent architecture on. JADE agent model is more "primitive" than the agent models offered by other systems, and mainly deals with message handling and plan scheduling. Exploiting research results about concurrent OO languages, JADE agent model has been extended in a way that solves the inheritance anomaly problem and will be useful to JADE users when they will create more complex agents.

1 Introduction

Agent-based technologies represent one of the most promising technological paradigms, however, they cannot realise their full potential, and will not become widespread, until standards to support agent interoperability are available and used by agent developers and adequate environments for the development of agent systems are available.

A lot of organisations are working towards the standardisation of agent technologies starting from the work done by the Knowledge Sharing Effort [20] In this respect, FIPA (Foundation for Intelligent Physical Agents) represents one of the most interesting answers to the need for standards [5].

The standardisation work of FIPA is in the direction to allow an easy interoperability between agent systems, because FIPA, beyond an agent communication language, specifies the key agents necessary for the management of an agent system and the ontology necessary for the interaction between two systems.

The output documents of FIPA specify the normative rules that allow a society of agents to inter-operate, that is effectively exist, operate and be managed. First of all they describe the reference model of an agent platform identifying the roles of some key agents necessary for the management of the platform, that is, the Agent Management System (AMS), the Agent Communication Channel (ACC) and the Directory Facilitator (DF).

A lot of people is involved in the realisation of development environments to build agent systems (see, for example, AgentBuilder [24], Bee-gent [32], dMARS [22], MaSE [30], MOLE [26], the Open Agent Architecture [16], RETSINA [28] and Zeus [18]). Such development environments provide predefined agent models and tools to ease systems development. Moreover, some of them try to allow interoperability with other agent systems through the use of a well-known agent communication language, that is, KQML [4] or following a standard as, for example, FIPA. However, none of them can be used to realise efficient and reusable agent software because they offer some specific agent architectures that must be used to realise all the agents of the system even if some of them must perform simple, primitive tasks which do not justify the complexity of the architecture used and because other agents execute tasks for which some other agent architectures are more suitable.

In this paper, we present an agent platform we implemented to realise efficient and reusable agent software, that is called JADE [9]. JADE (Java Agent Development Environment) is a software framework to make easy the development of agent applications in compliance with the FIPA specifications for interoperable intelligent multi-agent systems. JADE uses an agent model and a Java implementation that offer a good runtime efficiency and solve inheritance anomaly. Such an agent model is more "primitive" than the agent models offered by other systems, but they can be implemented on the top of our " primitive" agents model. JADE communication architecture tries to offer flexible and efficient messaging, transparently choosing the best transport available and leveraging state-of-the-art distributed object technology embedded within Java runtime environment.

In the next section, we introduce related work on agent construction tools. Section three presents the JADE agent platform. Section four, five and six describe the problems faced in designing and implementing agents, JADE agent model and implementation, and how the behaviours of JADE agents can be reused through inheritance and composition. Section seven shows an example of building JADE agents. Finally, Section eight concludes with a brief discussion about the relationships between the JADE agent models and the other agent software frameworks introduced in the paper, and about the current use of JADE to develop applications and to test the interoperability with other agent platforms.

2 Related Work

A lot of research and commercial organisations are involved in the realisation of agent applications and a considerable number of agent construction tools has been realized [23]. Some of the most interesting are AgentBuilder [24], MOLE [26], the Open Agent Architecture [16], RETSINA [28] and Zeus [18].

AgentBuilder [24] is a tool for building Java agent systems based on two components: the Toolkit and the Run-Time System. The Toolkit includes tools for managing the agent software development process, analysing the domain of agent operations, defining, implementing and testing agent software. The Run-Time System provides an agent engine, that is, an interpreter, used as execution environment of agent software. AgentBuilder agents are based on a model derived by the Agent-0

[25] and PLACA [29] agent models. Agents usually communicate through KQML messages; however, the developer has the possibility to define new communication commands to cope with her/his particular needs.

dMARS [22] is an agent-oriented development and implementation environment for building distributed system based on the BDI agent model offering support for system configuration, design, maintenance and re-engineering. Such a development environment has been successfully used to realise application in the fields of air traffic control and of telecommunication and business process management.

MOLE [26] is an agent system developed in Java whose agents do not have a sufficient set of features to be considered truly agent systems [8; 30]. However, MOLE is important because it offers one of the best solution to support agent mobility. Agents interact through two types of communication through RMI in the case of client/server interactions and message exchange in the case of peer-to-peer interactions.

The Open Agent Architecture [16] is a truly open architecture to realise distributed agent systems in a number of languages, namely C, Java, Prolog, Lisp, Visual Basic and Delphi. Its main feature is its powerful facilitator that can receive tasks from agents and decompose them to award them to other agents. However, all the agents must communicate via the facilitator that can become application bottleneck.

RETSINA [28] offers reusable agents to build applications. Each agent has four reusable modules for communicating, planning, scheduling and monitoring the execution of tasks and requests from other agents. However, agents developed by others and non-agent software can inter-operate with RETSINA agents by building some specialised gateway agents (one for each non-RETSINA agent or non-agent software system). RETSINA provides three kinds of agent: interface agents managing user interaction; task agents helping users in the execution of tasks; and information agents providing access to heterogeneous collections of information sources.

Zeus [18] allows the rapid development of Java agent systems by providing a library of agent components, supporting a visual environment for capturing user specifications, an agent building environment that includes an automatic agent code generator and a collection of classes that form the building blocks of individual agents. Agents are composed of five layers: API layer, definition layer, organisational layer, co-ordination layer and communication layer. The API layer allows the interaction with non-agent world. The definition layer manages the task the agent must perform. The organisational layer manages the knowledge about the other agents. The co-ordination layer manages co-ordination and negotiation with other agents. Finally, the communication layer allows the communication with the other agents.

3 JADE Agent Platform

The JADE agent platform complies with FIPA specifications and includes all the mandatory agents that manage the platform, that is the AMS, and the default DF. Agent communication is performed through message passing, where FIPA ACL is the language to represent messages.

JADE communication architecture tries to offer flexible and efficient messaging, transparently choosing the best transport available and leveraging state-of-the-art distributed object technology embedded within Java runtime environment. While appearing as a single entity to the outside world, a JADE agent platform can be split over several hosts with one among them acting as a front end for inter-platform IIOP communication. A JADE system is made by one or more *Agent Container*, each one living in a separate Java Virtual Machine and delivering runtime support to JADE agents. Java RMI is used to communicate among the containers and each one of them can also act as an IIOP client to forward outgoing messages to foreign agent platforms. A special, *Front End* container is also an IIOP server, listening at the official agent platform ACC address for incoming messages from other platforms. The two mandatory system agents, that is the AMS and the default DF, run within the front-end container. Figure 1 shows a representation of a JADE agent platform.

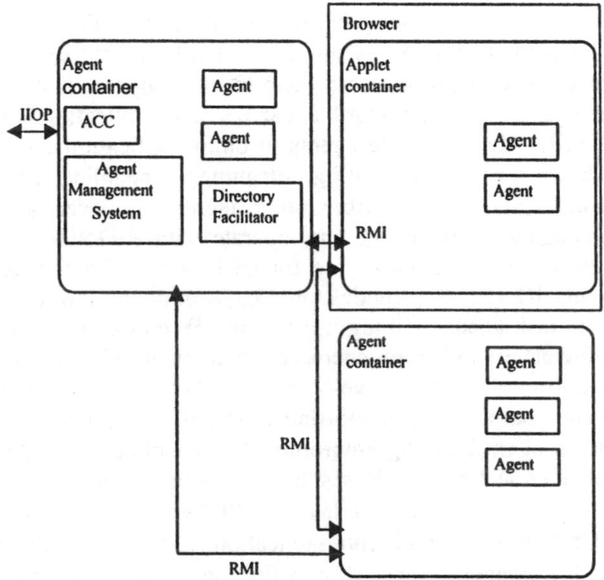

Fig. 1. Software architecture of a JADE agent platform.

A software agent, in compliance to FIPA agent model, has a *globally-unique identifier* (*GUID*), that can be used by every other agent or software entity to address it with ACL messages. Likewise, an agent will put its GUID into the *:sender* slot of ACL messages it sends around. So, JADE must figure out receiver location by simply looking at *:receiver* message slot; since a FIPA GUID resembles an email address, it is fairly easy to recover the agent name and the platform address from it, as they are separated by an "@" character. JADE then compares the receiver address with its own platform address: if they differ, the receiver resides on some other platform, possibly a non-JADE one, and standard IIOP messaging is to be used.

Otherwise, if the receiver and the sender reside on the same agent platform, JADE uses event dispatching when the two agents are within the same container and Java RMI when they are on different containers of the same agent platform.

Therefore, when an ACL message is sent to a software agent, three possibilities are given:

? *Receiver on the same container of the same platform:* Java events are used, the cost is a cloning of the *ACLMessage* object and a local method call.

? *Receiver on a different container of the same platform:* Java RMI is used, the cost is a message serialisation at sender side, a remote method call and a message unserialisation on receiver side.

? *Receiver on a different platform:* CORBA IIOP is used, the cost is the conversion of the *ACLMessage* object into a *String* object and an IIOP marshalling at sender side, a remote method call and an IIOP unmarshalling followed by ACL parsing at receiver side.

JADE uses a form of address caching that is transparent and completely orthogonal to message transport, so local, RMI and IIOP addresses are all cached the same way and on cache hits the agent container does not even need to know the specific kind of address it is using. This is meant to support agent mobility: an address referring to a mobile agent can change its kind (e.g., from local to RMI) over time; transparent caching means that messaging subsystem will not be affected when agent mobility will be introduced into JADE. Moreover, if new remote protocols will be needed in JADE (e.g., a wireless protocol for nomadic applications), they will be seamlessly integrated inside the messaging and address caching mechanisms. JADE cache replacement policy is a standard LRU one, and a stale cached address is not invalidated until it is used, according to an optimistic attitude; when a container tries to use a stale address, local or remote, it gets back a exception and refreshes the cache item.

4 Agents Design and Implementation Problems

A distinguishing property of a software agent is its *autonomy* [31]; an agent is not limited to react to external stimuli, but it is also able to start new communicative acts of its own. Besides, actions performed by an agent do not just depend on received messages but also on mental state and attitudes of the agent. The first property requires each software agent to be an *active object*, while the other one suggests to use a *pull consumer* messaging model [19].

A software agent, besides being autonomous, is said to be *social* [31], because it can interact with other agents in order to pursue its goals and can even develop an overall strategy together with its peers. The abstract need for sociality has the practical outcome of allowing an agent to engage in multiple conversations simultaneously; so implementing a software agent requires a significant amount of concurrency.

The above considerations show that an agent must perform different tasks in parallel and help in deciding how many threads of control are needed in an agent implementation; the autonomy requirement forces each agent to have at least a thread, and the sociality requirement pushes towards many threads per agent, maybe even a thread for every conversation the agent gets involved with, and more threads to carry on agent reasoning.

To achieve runtime efficiency, the various costs associated with multithreading must be evaluated. In decreasing cost order, they are:

1. Thread creation and deletion.
2. Synchronization between threads.
3. Thread scheduling.

Moreover, the execution of different tasks in parallel might raise a software engineering problem if we implement agents through an object-oriented programming language. The problem is *inheritance anomaly*, that is, the conflict between inheritance and concurrency that often causes the need to redefine the inherited methods in order to maintain the integrity of objects with a loss of software reuse [17; 2]. Such conflicts between inheritance and concurrency occur for three main reasons:

1. *Partitioning of Acceptable States*. A subclass partitions the sets of states where the different methods of the superclass can be executed. Therefore, the superclass methods must be redefined in the subclass to cope with such new sets of states.
2. *History-only Sensitiveness of Acceptable Methods*. A subclass adds a method that can be executed only after a particular sequence of events. Therefore, the superclass methods must be redefined in the subclass to track the required events.
3. *Modification of Acceptable States*. A subclass adds a method that modifies the state where the inherited methods can be executed. Therefore, the superclass methods must be redefined in the subclass to cope with such a modification.

5 JADE Agents Design and Implementation

JADE uses an agent design and a Java implementation that offer a good runtime efficiency and solve inheritance anomaly.

Each JADE agent holds a collection of behaviours which are scheduled and executed to carry on agent duties. Behaviours represent logical threads of a software agent implementation. JADE uses delegation to associate an agent with its tasks, in order to achieve flexible agent composition: an agent can aggregate several behaviours and a behaviour can be reused across agents and applications. If a role modelling approach is used [11], agent roles can be mapped to JADE behaviours, blending nicely the middleware infrastructure into the chosen agent development methodology.

According to *Active Object* design pattern [13], every JADE agent runs in its own Java thread, thereby satisfying autonomy property; instead, in order to keep small the number of threads required to run an agent platform, all agent behaviours are executed co-operatively within a single Java thread. So, JADE uses a *thread-per-agent* execution model with co-operative behaviour scheduling.

The main advantage of using a single Java thread for all agent behaviours lies in greatly reduced multithreading overhead. Recalling the three major costs paid to enjoy multithreading benefits, one can see that with JADE model thread creation and deletion happens rarely, because agents are rather long lived software objects. Besides, synchronisation between different threads is not even needed, since different agents share no common environment. Thus, only the third cost, i.e., thread scheduling, remains; this is the least among the three and could only be avoided by making the whole agent platform single-threaded.

Adopting a *thread-per-behaviour* execution model would incur in significant synchronisation costs (a Java *synchronized* method is about 100 times slower than an ordinary method) because all behaviours share a common representation of agent mental state. Moreover, it is often the case that an agent creates new behaviours on demand. For that kind of agents, *thread-per-behaviour* would also have significant thread creation overhead.

Sometimes real intra-agent multithreading may seem unavoidable: for example, an agent acting as a wrapper onto a DBMS could issue multiple queries in parallel, or an agent might want to block on a stream or socket while still being able to engage in ordinary conversations. Really, this kind of problems occur only when an agent must interact with some non-agent software; FIPA acknowledges that these are boundary conditions for the execution model and deals with them in a separate part of the standard (namely, FIPA part 3). When writing agent wrappers for non-agent software, application developers are free to choose whatever concurrency model they feel is needed.

Using a single Java thread to handle multiple agent behaviours needs some sort of scheduling policy. JADE relies on a *"co-operative scheduling on top of the stack"* , in which all agent behaviours are run from a single stack frame without context saving (*on top of the stack*) and a behaviour continues to run until it returns from its main function and cannot be pre-empted by other behaviours (*co-operative scheduling*); of course ordinary pre-emption is still active between different agent threads and among JADE system threads: co-operative scheduling is strictly an intra-agent policy.

Using co-operative behaviours to model multiple agent conversation is a lightweight approach to concurrency, trying to achieve low latency by working entirely in user space. Similar techniques are customary in modern high performance network protocols and messaging libraries [1; 3]. A likewise, stack based execution model is followed by Illinois Concert runtime system [12]; willing to provide a runtime environment for parallel object oriented languages, Concert can execute concurrent method calls optimistically on the stack, reverting to real thread spawning only when the method is about to block.

Choosing not to save behaviour execution context means that agent behaviours start from the beginning every time they are scheduled for execution; besides, local variables are reset every time. So, behaviour specific state that must be retained across multiple executions is to be stored into behaviour instance variables. Therefore a JADE behaviour is not given by an ordinary Java method, but by a Java class having:

? a method performing the task of the behaviour, and
? a set of instance variables representing behaviour context.

Moreover, such a behaviour model does not take into account the inheritance anomaly problem. To cope with inheritance anomaly we decomposed the code of the behaviour method in three parts (methods) as proposed in [21]. The three parts are:

1. A *guard*, that is a Boolean predicate without side-effect, representing the precondition for the behaviour execution.
2. A *body* that contains the part of code executing the behaviour task.
3. A *transition* that can enable/disable some other agent behaviours.

Therefore, when a behaviour must be executed, the guard is checked; if it is true, the body and the transition are executed in sequence, else another behaviour is executed and this behaviour is blocked until the guard becomes true. The blocking of the behaviour is not the only possible policy when a guard is not true [14]. In fact, we could return immediately (balking policy) or wait up to a specific maximum time (timed-wait policy).

Behaviours are divided in two classes: the writers and the readers, respectively representing the behaviours that modify agent state and the ones that just read it. This separation allows to implement a reader/writer synchronisation policy where readers can be executed in parallel and writers are executed in sequence. This separation has only a formal value with the current implementation where agent behaviours are scheduled in a single thread, but it would be useful in a multi-threaded agent.

6 Behaviour Reuse via Inheritance and Composition

Our behaviour model allows to reuse software via inheritance. In fact, new behaviours can be realised as specialisation of other behaviours.

Such a model allows the reuse of software via composition too. A class hierarchy rooted in the *Behaviour* class support the tasks to be performed. According to the *Composite* design pattern [7], the *ComplexBehaviour* class is itself a *Behaviour,* but can have an arbitrary number of sub-behaviours or *children*.

In the case of a behaviour represented by a *ComplexBehaviour* class, the agent scheduler only considers the top-most tasks for its scheduling policy: during each "time slice" assigned to an agent task only a single subtask is executed. Each time a top-most task returns, the agent scheduler assigns the control to the next task in the ready queue.

JADE recursive aggregation of behaviour objects resembles the technique used for graphical user interfaces, where every interface widget can be a leaf of a tree whose intermediate nodes are special container widgets with both rendering and children management features. An important distinction, however, exists: JADE behaviours are reifications of execution tasks, so task scheduling and suspension are to be considered too.

Thinking in terms of patterns [7], if *Composite* is the main structural pattern used for JADE behaviours, on the behavioural side we have a *Chain of Responsibility*: agent scheduling directly affects only top-level nodes of the behaviour aggregation tree, but every composite behaviour is responsible for its childrenѣ scheduling within its time frame. Likewise, when a behaviour object is blocked or restarted, a notification mechanism built around a bi-directional *Chain of Responsibility* scheme provides all necessary event propagation.

The agent developer can use behaviour classes not only to implement the different tasks of their agents. In fact, he/she can, for example, find behaviours to perform atomic tasks only once (such as in the *OneShotBehaviour* class) or forever (as in the *CyclicBehaviour* class) and can also compose behaviours in a sequential way (using the *SequentialBehaviour* class), or schedule them in a non deterministic fashion (*NonDeterministicBehaviour* class) or in a parallel way (*ParallelBehaviour* class).

7 An Example

As an example of the use of the JADE agent model to implement reusable software agents, we describe a simple yellow pages agent able to manage information about a community of agents and the services its agents offer. After that, we specialise it to support some other services.

Such a yellow pages agents offers four services: the registration and the deregistration of agents and their services, the modification of the agent profiles, and the search for agents on the basis of a requested service. This agent manages different conversation in parallel, notifies the caller if it cannot satisfy the request, and periodically cleans its knowledge base from the died agents that did not deregister themselves.

We can realise such an agent as a JADE agent named *DF*. This agent contains at the beginning five behaviours: *RegisterBh*, *DeregisterBh*, *ModifyBh*, *SearchBh* and *CleanBh*.

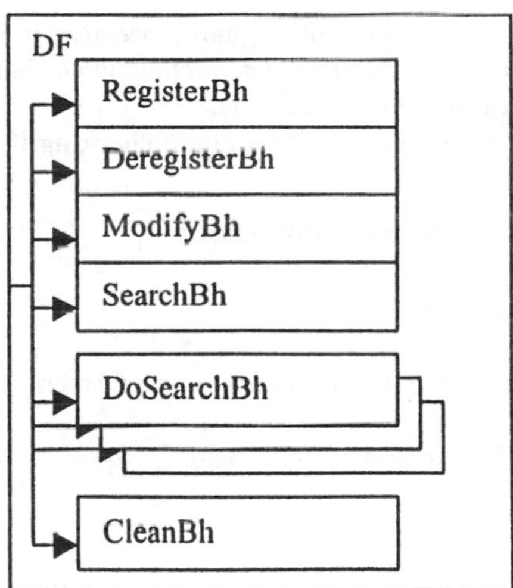

Fig. 2. Diagram of the *DF* agent. The behaviours on the same vertical line are executed concurrently.

When they receive a message, *RegisterBh*, *DeregisterBh*, *ModifyBh* perform in sequence the following actions:

1. Check whether the action can be performed.
2. Send an *agree* or *refuse* message to the caller.

3. Try to perform the requested action.
4. Send an *inform* message or a *failure* message to the caller depending upon whether the action execution succeeds or not.

SearchBh allows to serve different requests in parallel. When it receives a message, it creates a new behaviour, called *DoSearchBh,* that serves a message in the same way of the previous three behaviours, and goes back to wait for a request.

Finally, *CleanBh* cyclically waits for the end of a time interval and then checks its agents table to look for died agents to remove. Figure 2 shows a graphical representation of *DF* behaviours.

The code of *RegisterBh*, *DeregisterBh*, *ModifyBy* and *SearchBh* is composed by the body method and a guard checking the kind of action requested. For example, the *RegisterBh* code has the form:

```
RegisterBh extends CyclicBehaviour {

 boolean guard() {

  return (msg.content.actionName == "Register"); }

 void body() { … register code … }

}
```

The code of *DoSearchBh* has not a guard, because it is directly activated by *SearchB*h, but implements an interface *ReaderBehaviour* indicating that is a reader behaviour (a behaviour is a writer by default).

Finally, the code of *CleanBh* contains a guard checking if it is the time for a new cleaning. It has the form:

```
CleanBh extends CyclicBehaviour {

 boolean guard() {

  return ( timeAfterCleaning > cleaningInterval) }

 void body() { … cleaning code … }

}
```

A more complex yellow pages agent has the capability to give also information about agents that it does not know, but that are known through other yellow pages agents and to stop the services when required by its manager agent.

We can realise such an agent as a specialisation of the *DF* Agent, called *MultiDF,* that adds four new behaviours respectively called *MultiSearchBh*, *MultiDoSearchBh, DisableBh* and *EnableBh*.

MultiSearchBh allows to serve different requests concurrently too. When it receives a message, it creates a new behaviour, called *MultiDoSearchBh*, and goes back to wait for a request. *MultiDoSearchBh* behaviour is a sequential behaviour composed of two behaviours. The first is a parallel behaviour, called *ParallelSearchBh*, that spawns a *LocalSearchBh,* performing the local search, and a *RemoteSearchBh* for each other known yellow pages agents. The second, *CollectBh*, collects the results and informs the caller. In particular, *RemoteSearchBh* first sends a request message to the remote DF and then waits for the response.

Figure 3 shows a graphical representation of *MultiDF* behaviours.

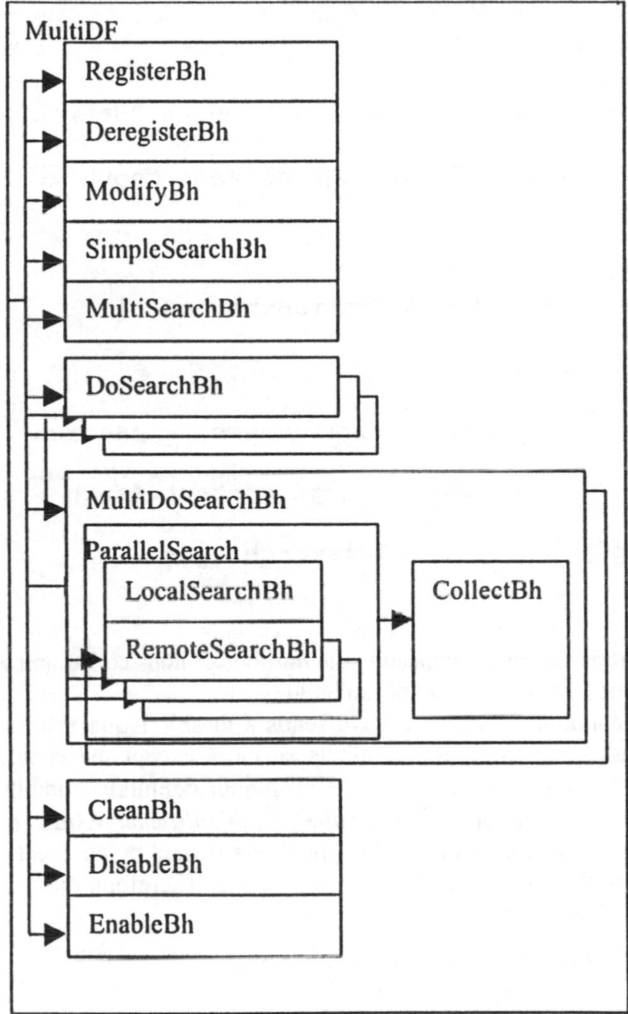

Fig. 3. Diagram of the *MultiDF* agent. The behaviours on the same vertical line are executed in parallel; the behaviours on the same horizontal line are executed in sequence.

MultiSearchBh is activated by a search request, then it conflicts with the activation of *SearchBh*. However, the conflict can be solved stating that *MultiSearchBh* is activated when the depth service parameter (indicating the number of hops constraining the search in the hierarchy of DFs the current DF can build.) is greater than one and *SearchBh* is activated when the depth service parameter is equal to one.

Therefore, we can redefine the *SearchBh*, but separating and isolating its synchronization code in the guard, we must redefine only the guard in a new behaviour *SimpleSearchBh* that is a specialisation of *SearchBh*. Then, the code of *SimpleSearchBh* and *MultiSearchBh* has the form:

```
class SimpleSearchBh extends SearchBh {

 boolean guard() {

  return ((msg.content.actionName == "Search") &&

        ((SearchDFMsg) msg).content.depth == 1)); }

}

MultiSearchBh extends CyclicBehaviour {

 boolean guard() {

  return ((msg.content.actionName == "Search") &&

        (((SearchDFMsg) msg).content.depth > 1)); }

 void body() { /* ... multisearch code ... */ }

}
```

where *depth* is an integer indicating the number of hops constraining the search in the hierarchy of DFs the current DF can build.

When the community manager agent sends a disable request to the yellow pages agent, this last agent must disable all its services except the enable service. The introduction of a transition method in the behaviour definitions, and the introduction of a set of their specific operations (*enable*, *enableAll*, *enableAllExcept*, *disable* and *disableAllExcept*) acting on the list of behaviours owned by an agent, allow to avoid the rewriting of the methods to be enabled/disabled. Therefore, the code of *EnableBh* and *DisableBh* has the form:

```
EnableBh extends CyclicBehaviour {

 void transition() { enableAll(); }

}

disableBh extends CyclicBehaviour {

 void transition() { disableAllExcept("EnableBh"); } }
```

8 Conclusions

In this paper, we presented an agent model and platform we defined and implemented to realise efficient and reusable agent software through a development environment called JADE. JADE (Java Agent Development Environment) is a software framework to make easy the development of agent applications in compliance with the FIPA specifications for interoperable intelligent multi-agent systems.

In comparison to the agent development tools introduced in the Related Work Section, JADE offers a more efficient implementation and a more general and reusable agent model.

The efficient implementation mainly depends both on the use of a communication architecture offering flexible and efficient messaging, transparently choosing the best transport available and leveraging state-of-the-art distributed object technology embedded within Java runtime environment, and on the use of an agent model implementation that allows the realisation of multi-activities agents eliminating Java multi-threading overhead.

The JADE agent model is more "primitive" than the agents models offered, for example, by AgentBuilder, dMARS, RETSINA and Zeus; however, the overhead due to such sophisticated agent models might not be justified for agents that must perform some simple tasks. Starting from FIPA assumption that only the external behaviour of system components should be specified, leaving the implementation details and internal architectures to agent developers, we realise a very general agent model over which programmers can build more specific models, such as reactive or BDI architectures or other sophisticated architectures taking also advantage of the separation between computation and synchronisation code inside agent behaviours through the use of guards and transitions. In particular, we can realise a system composed of agents with different architectures, but able to interact because on the top of the "primitive" JADE agent model. Moreover, the behaviour abstraction of our agent model allows an easy integration of external software. For example, we realised a *JessBehaviour* that allows the use of JESS [6] as agent reasoning engine.

JADE is a trademark registered by CSELT. It has been distributed to some partners of the ACTS AC317 "FACTS" project for evaluation and because some packages are foreground of the project. A mailing list has been set up for the users to discuss requirements, report bugs and, more in general, to discuss programming idioms and exchanging ideas. The feedback received so far is positive as developers can actually concentrate on the realisation on their application specific tasks rather than on the building of the middle-ware for the management of agents.

At the beginning of 1999, during a meeting of FIPA, in Seoul, JADE participated to the interoperability tests with some other FIPA compliant platforms, that is, ASL of Broadcom [12], MECCA of Siemens [15] and the agent platform of Comtec [27]. The results of the tests showed JADE is very near to offer full interoperability with the other platforms passing a large part of the tests [5]. The failure on a few tests depended mainly on the incomplete definition of agent management ontology in the FIPA specifications that caused some differences in its implementation inside the different platforms. The results of Seoul tests were very important because the comparison with other platforms allowed us to correct and improve its implementation.

Acknowledgements

We wish to thank Fabio Bellifemine for his contribution to the realisation of JADE. The present work has been supported by a grant from CSELT, Torino.

References

[1] G. Chiola and G. Ciaccio. Implementing a Low Cost, Low Latency Parallel Platform. Parallel Computing, 22:1703-1717. 1997.
[2] L. Crnogorac and A.S. Rao. Inheritance by extensions and restrictions in agent systems. In Proc. ACSC'97, Sidney, Australia, 1997.
[3] D. Dunning, G. Regnier, G. McAlpine, D. Cameron, B. Shubert, F. Berry, A.M. Merritt, E. Gronke and C. Dodd. The Virtual Interface Architecture. IEEE Micro, 18(2):58-64, 1998.
[4] T. Finin and Y. Labrou. KQML as an agent communication language. In: J.M. Bradshaw (ed.), Software Agents, pp. 291-316. MIT Press, Cambridge, MA, 1997.
[5] FIPA - Foundation for Intelligent Physical Agents. http://www.fipa.org.
[6] E.J. Friedman-Hill. Jess, The Java Expert System Shell. Sandia National Laboratories, Livermore, CA. 1999. http://herzberg1.ca.sandia.gov/jess/.
[7] E. Gamma, R. Helm, R. Johnson and J. Vlissides. Design Patterns: Elements of Reusable Object Oriented Software. Addison Wesley, 1995.
[8] M.R. Genesereth and S.P. Ketchpel. Software Agents. Comm. of ACM, 37(7):48-53.1994.
[9] JADE home page. http://sharon.cselt.it/projects/jade
[10] V. Karamcheti, J. Plevyak and A. Chien. Runtime Mechanisms for Efficient Dynamic Multithreading. Journal of Parallel and Distributed Computing, 37:21-40, 1996.
[11] E. A. Kendall. Agent Oriented Software Engineering with Role Modelling. In this volume.
[12] D. Kerr, D. O'Sullivan, R. Evans, R. Richardson and F. Somers. Experiences using Intelligent Agent Technologies as a Unifying Approach to Network and Service Management. In Proc. of IS&N 98, Antwerp, Belgium. 1998.
[13] G. Lavender and D. Schmidt. Active Object: An object behavioural pattern for concurrent programming. In J.M. Vlissides, J.O. Coplien, and N.L. Kerth, Eds. Pattern Languages of Program Design. Addison-Wesley, Reading, MA, 1996.
[14] D. Lea. Concurrent Programming in Java™: Design Principles and Patterns. Addison Wesley. 1996.
[15] A.D. Lux and D. Steiner. Understanding Cooperation: an Agent's Perspective. In Proc. ICMAS'95. San Francisco, USA. 1995.
[16] D.L. Martin, A.J. Cheyer and D.B. Moran. The Open Agent Architecture: A Framework for Building Distributed Software Systems. Applied Artificial Intelligence. 1998.
[17] S. Matsuoka and A. Yonezawa. Analysis of Inheritance Anomaly in Object-Oriented Concurrent Programming Languages. In G. Agha, P. Wegner and A. Yonezawa, Eds. Research directions in Concurrent Object-Oriented Programming, pp. 107-150. The MIT Press, Cambridge, MA, 1993.
[18] H.S. Nwana, D.T. Ndumu and L.C. Lee. ZEUS: An advanced Tool-Kit for Engineering Distributed Multi-Agent Systems. In: Proc of PAAM98, pp. 377-391, London, U.K., 1998.
[19] Object Management Group. 95-11-03: Common Services. 1997. http://www.omg.org.
[20] R.S. Patil, R.E. Fikes, P.F. Patel-Scheneider, D. McKay, T. Finin, T. Gruber and R. Neches. The DARPA knowledge sharing effort: progress report. In: Proc. Third Conf. on Principles of Knowledge Representation and Reasoning, pp 103-114. Cambridge, MA, 1992.

[21] A. Poggi and G. Rimassa. An efficient and flexible C++ library for concurrent programming. Software Practice & Experience, 28(13):1437-1463, 1998.

[22] A.S. Rao and M. P. Georgeff. BDI agents: from theory to practice. In Proc. of the First Int. Conf. On Multi-Agent Systems, pp. 312-319, San Francisco, CA, 1995.

[23] Reticular Systems. Agent Construction Tools. 1999. http://www.agentbuilder.com.

[24] Reticular Systems. AgentBuilder - An integrated Toolkit for Constructing Intelligence Software Agents. 1999. http://www.agentbuilder.com.

[25] Y. Shoham. Agent-oriented programming. Artificial Intelligence, 60(1):51-92. 1993.

[26] M. Straßer, J. Baumann and F. Hohl (1997): Mole - A Java based Mobile Agent System. In: M. Mühlhäuser: (ed.), Special Issues in Object Oriented Programming. dpunkt Verlag, pp. 301-308, 1997.

[27] H. Suguri. COMTEC Agent Platform. 1998. http://www.fipa.org/glointe.htm.

[28] K. Sycara, A. Pannu, M. Williamson and D. Zeng. Distributed Intelligent Agents. IEEE Expert, 11(6):36-46. 1996.

[29] S.R. Thomas. The PLACA Agent Programming Language. In M.J. Wooldrige & N.R. Jennings (Eds.), Lecture Notes in Artificial Intelligence, pp. 355-370. Springer-Verlag, Berlin. 1994.

[30] M. Wood and Scott A. DeLoach. An Overview of the Multiagents Systems Engineering Methodology. In this volume

[31] M. Wooldrige and N.R. Jennings. Intelligent Agents: Theory and Practice, The Knowledge Engineering Review, 10(2):115-152, 1995.

[32] N. Yoshioka, Y. Tahara, A. Ohsuga, S. Honiden. Safety and Security in Mobile Agents. In this volume.

Author Index

Amamiya, Makoto 285

Barber, K. Suzanne 269

Bauer, Bernhard 91, 121

Bussmann, Stefan 141

Ciancarini, Paolo 1

DeLoach, Scott A. 207

Depke, Ralph 105

Han, David C. 269

Heckel, Reiko 105

Hodjat, Babak 285

Honiden, Shinichi 223

Huhns, Michael N. 29

Jennings, Nicholas R. 141, 235

Jonker, Catholijn M. 253

Joy, Mike 171

Kendall, Elizabeth A. 163

Küster, Jochen Malte 105

Lind, Jürgen 45

Liu, Tse-Hsin 269

Luck, Michael 171

Miles, Simon 171

Müller, Jörg P. 91

Odell, James 91, 121

Ohsuga, Akihiko 223

Omicini, Andrea 185

Parunak, H. Van Dyke 121

Petrie, Charles 59

Poggi, Agostino 307

Rana, Omer F. 195

Rimassa, Giovanni 307

Shehory, Onn 77

Tahara, Yasuyuki 223

Treur, Jan 253

de Vries, Wieke 253

Wood, Mark F. 207

Wooldridge, Michael 1, 141, 235

Yoshioka, Nobukazu 223

Zambonelli, Franco 235

Author index

Lecture Notes in Computer Science

For information about Vols. 1–1910
please contact your bookseller or Springer-Verlag

Vol. 1911: D.G. Feitelson, L. Rudolph (Eds.), Job Scheduling Strategies for Parallel Processing. VII, 209 pages. 2000.

Vol. 1912: Y. Gurevich, P.W. Kutter, M. Odersky, L. Thiele (Eds.), Abstract State Machines. Proceedings, 2000. X, 381 pages. 2000.

Vol. 1913: K. Jansen, S. Khuller (Eds.), Approximation Algorithms for Combinatorial Optimization. Proceedings, 2000. IX, 275 pages. 2000.

Vol. 1914: M. Herlihy (Ed.), Distributed Computing. Proceedings, 2000. VIII, 389 pages. 2000.

Vol. 1915: S. Dwarkadas (Ed.), Languages, Compilers, and Run-Time Systems for Scalable Computers. Proceedings, 2000. VIII, 301 pages. 2000.

Vol. 1916: F. Dignum, M. Greaves (Eds.), Issues in Agent Communication. X, 351 pages. 2000. (Subseries LNAI).

Vol. 1917: M. Schoenauer, K. Deb, G. Rudolph, X. Yao, E. Lutton, J.J. Merelo, H.-P. Schwefel (Eds.), Parallel Problem Solving from Nature – PPSN VI. Proceedings, 2000. XXI, 914 pages. 2000.

Vol. 1918: D. Soudris, P. Pirsch, E. Barke (Eds.), Integrated Circuit Design. Proceedings, 2000. XII, 338 pages. 2000.

Vol. 1919: M. Ojeda-Aciego, I.P. de Guzman, G. Brewka, L. Moniz Pereira (Eds.), Logics in Artificial Intelligence. Proceedings, 2000. XI, 407 pages. 2000. (Subseries LNAI).

Vol. 1920: A.H.F. Laender, S.W. Liddle, V.C. Storey (Eds.), Conceptual Modeling – ER 2000. Proceedings, 2000. XV, 588 pages. 2000.

Vol. 1921: S.W. Liddle, H.C. Mayr, B. Thalheim (Eds.), Conceptual Modeling for E-Business and the Web. Proceedings, 2000. X, 179 pages. 2000.

Vol. 1922: J. Crowcroft, J. Roberts, M.I. Smirnov (Eds.), Quality of Future Internet Services. Proceedings, 2000. XI, 368 pages. 2000.

Vol. 1923: J. Borbinha, T. Baker (Eds.), Research and Advanced Technology for Digital Libraries. Proceedings, 2000. XVII, 513 pages. 2000.

Vol. 1924: W. Taha (Ed.), Semantics, Applications, and Implementation of Program Generation. Proceedings, 2000. VIII, 231 pages. 2000.

Vol. 1925: J. Cussens, S. Džeroski (Eds.), Learning Language in Logic. X, 301 pages 2000. (Subseries LNAI).

Vol. 1926: M. Joseph (Ed.), Formal Techniques in Real-Time and Fault-Tolerant Systems. Proceedings, 2000. X, 305 pages. 2000.

Vol. 1927: P. Thomas, H.W. Gellersen, (Eds.), Handheld and Ubiquitous Computing. Proceedings, 2000. X, 249 pages. 2000.

Vol. 1928: U. Brandes, D. Wagner (Eds.), Graph-Theoretic Concepts in Computer Science. Proceedings, 2000. X, 315 pages. 2000.

Vol. 1929: R. Laurini (Ed.), Advances in Visual Information Systems. Proceedings, 2000. XII, 542 pages. 2000.

Vol. 1931: E. Horlait (Ed.), Mobile Agents for Telecommunication Applications. Proceedings, 2000. IX, 271 pages. 2000.

Vol. 1658: J. Baumann, Mobile Agents: Control Algorithms. XIX, 161 pages. 2000.

Vol. 1756: G. Ruhe, F. Bomarius (Eds.), Learning Software Organization. Proceedings, 1999. VIII, 226 pages. 2000.

Vol. 1766: M. Jazayeri, R.G.K. Loos, D.R. Musser (Eds.), Generic Programming. Proceedings, 1998. X, 269 pages. 2000.

Vol. 1791: D. Fensel, Problem-Solving Methods. XII, 153 pages. 2000. (Subseries LNAI).

Vol. 1799: K. Czarnecki, U.W. Eisenecker, Generative and Component-Based Software Engineering. Proceedings, 1999. VIII, 225 pages. 2000.

Vol. 1812: J. Wyatt, J. Demiris (Eds.), Advances in Robot Learning. Proceedings, 1999. VII, 165 pages. 2000. (Subseries LNAI).

Vol. 1932: Z.W. Raś, S. Ohsuga (Eds.), Foundations of Intelligent Systems. Proceedings, 2000. XII, 646 pages. (Subseries LNAI).

Vol. 1933: R.W. Brause, E. Hanisch (Eds.), Medical Data Analysis. Proceedings, 2000. XI, 316 pages. 2000.

Vol. 1934: J.S. White (Ed.), Envisioning Machine Translation in the Information Future. Proceedings, 2000. XV, 254 pages. 2000. (Subseries LNAI).

Vol. 1935: S.L. Delp, A.M. DiGioia, B. Jaramaz (Eds.), Medical Image Computing and Computer-Assisted Intervention – MICCAI 2000. Proceedings, 2000. XXV, 1250 pages. 2000.

Vol. 1936: P. Robertson, H. Shrobe, R. Laddaga (Eds.), Self-Adaptive Software. Proceedings, 2000. VIII, 249 pages. 2001.

Vol. 1937: R. Dieng, O. Corby (Eds.), Knowledge Engineering and Knowledge Management. Proceedings, 2000. XIII, 457 pages. 2000. (Subseries LNAI).

Vol. 1938: S. Rao, K.I. Sletta (Eds.), Next Generation Networks. Proceedings, 2000. XI, 392 pages. 2000.

Vol. 1939: A. Evans, S. Kent, B. Selic (Eds.), «UML» – The Unified Modeling Language. Proceedings, 2000. XIV, 572 pages. 2000.

Vol. 1940: M. Valero, K. Joe, M. Kitsuregawa, H. Tanaka (Eds.), High Performance Computing. Proceedings, 2000. XV, 595 pages. 2000.

Vol. 1941: A.K. Chhabra, D. Dori (Eds.), Graphics Recognition. Proceedings, 1999. XI, 346 pages. 2000.

Vol. 1942: H. Yasuda (Ed.), Active Networks. Proceedings, 2000. XI, 424 pages. 2000.

Vol. 1943: F. Koornneef, M. van der Meulen (Eds.), Computer Safety, Reliability and Security. Proceedings, 2000. X, 432 pages. 2000.

Vol. 1944: K.R. Dittrich, G. Guerrini, I. Merlo, M. Oliva, M.E. Rodriguez (Eds.), Objects and Databases. Proceedings, 2000. X, 199 pages. 2001.

Vol. 1945: W. Grieskamp, T. Santen, B. Stoddart (Eds.), Integrated Formal Methods. Proceedings, 2000. X, 441 pages. 2000.

Vol. 1946: P. Palanque, F. Paternò (Eds.), Interactive Systems. Proceedings, 2000. X, 251 pages. 2001.

Vol. 1948: T. Tan, Y. Shi, W. Gao (Eds.), Advances in Multimodal Interfaces – ICMI 2000. Proceedings, 2000. XVI, 678 pages. 2000.

Vol. 1949: R. Connor, A. Mendelzon (Eds.), Research Issues in Structured and Semistructured Database Programming. Proceedings, 1999. XII, 325 pages. 2000.

Vol. 1950: D. van Melkebeek, Randomness and Completeness in Computational Complexity. XV, 196 pages. 2000.

Vol. 1951: F. van der Linden (Ed.), Software Architectures for Product Families. Proceedings, 2000. VIII, 255 pages. 2000.

Vol. 1952: M.C. Monard, J. Simão Sichman (Eds.), Advances in Artificial Intelligence. Proceedings, 2000. XV, 498 pages. 2000. (Subseries LNAI).

Vol. 1953: G. Borgefors, I. Nyström, G. Sanniti di Baja (Eds.), Discrete Geometry for Computer Imagery. Proceedings, 2000. XI, 544 pages. 2000.

Vol. 1954: W.A. Hunt, Jr., S.D. Johnson (Eds.), Formal Methods in Computer-Aided Design. Proceedings, 2000. XI, 539 pages. 2000.

Vol. 1955: M. Parigot, A. Voronkov (Eds.), Logic for Programming and Automated Reasoning. Proceedings, 2000. XIII, 487 pages. 2000. (Subseries LNAI).

Vol. 1956: T. Coquand, P. Dybjer, B. Nordström, J. Smith (Eds.), Types for Proofs and Programs. Proceedings, 1999. VII, 195 pages. 2000.

Vol. 1957: P. Ciancarini, M. Wooldridge (Eds.), Agent-Oriented Software Engineering. Proceedings, 2000. X, 323 pages. 2001.

Vol. 1960: A. Ambler, S.B. Calo, G. Kar (Eds.), Services Management in Intelligent Networks. Proceedings, 2000. X, 259 pages. 2000.

Vol. 1961: J. He, M. Sato (Eds.), Advances in Computing Science – ASIAN 2000. Proceedings, 2000. X, 299 pages. 2000.

Vol. 1963: V. Hlaváč, K.G. Jeffery, J. Wiedermann (Eds.), SOFSEM 2000: Theory and Practice of Informatics. Proceedings, 2000. XI, 460 pages. 2000.

Vol. 1964: J. Malenfant, S. Moisan, A. Moreira (Eds.), Object-Oriented Technology. Proceedings, 2000. XI, 309 pages. 2000.

Vol. 1965: Ç. K. Koç, C. Paar (Eds.), Cryptographic Hardware and Embedded Systems – CHES 2000. Proceedings, 2000. XI, 355 pages. 2000.

Vol. 1966: S. Bhalla (Ed.), Databases in Networked Information Systems. Proceedings, 2000. VIII, 247 pages. 2000.

Vol. 1967: S. Arikawa, S. Morishita (Eds.), Discovery Science. Proceedings, 2000. XII, 332 pages. 2000. (Subseries LNAI).

Vol. 1968: H. Arimura, S. Jain, A. Sharma (Eds.), Algorithmic Learning Theory. Proceedings, 2000. XI, 335 pages. 2000. (Subseries LNAI).

Vol. 1969: D.T. Lee, S.-H. Teng (Eds.), Algorithms and Computation. Proceedings, 2000. XIV, 578 pages. 2000.

Vol. 1970: M. Valero, V.K. Prasanna, S. Vajapeyam (Eds.), High Performance Computing – HiPC 2000. Proceedings, 2000. XVIII, 568 pages. 2000.

Vol. 1971: R. Buyya, M. Baker (Eds.), Grid Computing – GRID 2000. Proceedings, 2000. XIV, 229 pages. 2000.

Vol. 1972: A. Omicini, R. Tolksdorf, F. Zambonelli (Eds.), Engineering Societies in the Agents World. Proceedings, 2000. IX, 143 pages. 2000. (Subseries LNAI).

Vol. 1973: J. Van den Bussche, V. Vianu (Eds.), Database Theory – ICDT 2001. Proceedings, 2001. X, 451 pages. 2001.

Vol. 1974: S. Kapoor, S. Prasad (Eds.), FST TCS 2000: Foundations of Software Technology and Theoretical Computer Science. Proceedings, 2000. XIII, 532 pages. 2000.

Vol. 1975: J. Pieprzyk, E. Okamoto, J. Seberry (Eds.), Information Security. Proceedings, 2000. X, 323 pages. 2000.

Vol. 1976: T. Okamoto (Ed.), Advances in Cryptology – ASIACRYPT 2000. Proceedings, 2000. XII, 630 pages. 2000.

Vol. 1977: B. Roy, E. Okamoto (Eds.), Progress in Cryptology – INDOCRYPT 2000. Proceedings, 2000. X, 295 pages. 2000.

Vol. 1979: S. Moss, P. Davidsson (Eds.), Multi-Agent-Based Simulation. Proceedings, 2000. VIII, 267 pages. 2001. (Subseries LNAI).

Vol. 1983: K.S. Leung, L.-W. Chan, H. Meng (Eds.), Intelligent Data Engineering and Automated Learning – IDEAL 2000. Proceedings, 2000. XVI, 573 pages. 2000.

Vol. 1984: J. Marks (Ed.), Graph Drawing. Proceedings, 2001. XII, 419 pages. 2001.

Vol. 1987: K.-L. Tan, M.J. Franklin, J. C.-S. Lui (Eds.), Mobile Data Management. Proceedings, 2001. XIII, 289 pages. 2001.

Vol. 1989: M. Ajmone Marsan, A. Bianco (Eds.), Quality of Service in Multiservice IP Networks. Proceedings, 2001. XII, 440 pages. 2001.

Vol. 1991: F. Dignum, C. Sierra (Eds.), Agent Mediated Electronic Commerce. VIII, 241 pages. 2001. (Subseries LNAI).

Vol. 1992: K. Kim (Ed.), Public Key Cryptography. Proceedings, 2001. XI, 423 pages. 2001.

Vol. 1995: M. Sloman, J. Lobo, E.C. Lupu (Eds.), Policies for Distributed Systems and Networks. Proceedings, 2001. X, 263 pages. 2001.